# The New Testament

## AN INTRODUCTION

# The New Testament

## AN INTRODUCTION

*Proclamation and Parenesis, Myth and History*

**NORMAN PERRIN**
*University of Chicago*

## HARCOURT BRACE JOVANOVICH, INC.
*New York   Chicago   San Francisco   Atlanta*

For Nancy,
in token of my love

© 1974 by Harcourt Brace Jovanovich, Inc.

ISBN:  0–15–565725–9

Library of Congress Catalog Card Number:   73–18623

Printed in the United States of America

## PICTURE CREDITS AND ACKNOWLEDGMENTS

*Cover*   Fragment of a Coptic limestone relief, about A.D. 400. The Brooklyn Museum, Charles Edwin Wilbour Fund.

2 American Bible Society, New York City. 16 Archives Photographiques, Paris. 38 Archie Lieberman. 118 Institute for Antiquity and Christianity, Claremont, California. Photo by Jean Doresse. 142 The Chester Beatty Library, Dublin. 168, 194 Archie Lieberman. 220 The John Rylands University Library of Manchester. 252 André Held. 276 *top left:* Editions Skira, Geneva; *top right:* The National Gallery, London; *bottom left:* The Cleveland Museum of Art, gift of Hanna Fund; *bottom right:* Columbia Pictures Industries, Inc.

# Preface

In recent years the approach to the study of the New Testament at the college level has been changing rapidly, largely because the center of such study has been shifting from seminaries and church-related schools to the "secular" colleges and universities. This focus has led to a greater emphasis on the New Testament as part of the general history of religion and as an important aspect of the religious and cultural history of Western man. These changes are reflected in this introduction to the New Testament. It has been written with the conviction that a book about religion is not necessarily a religious book, that a book about the New Testament must seek to understand what the New Testament is trying to say but not necessarily pass judgment on what it says. The aim is to help the student understand the New Testament, nothing more, and nothing less.

The study of the New Testament at all levels has recently been affected by developments within the discipline of biblical scholarship itself. The discoveries of the Qumran texts (the Dead Sea Scrolls) and the Nag Hammadi codices have added very considerably to our knowledge of the immediate historical environment of earliest Christianity by offering us new materials to work with. At the same time, there have been important developments in *method* in New Testament scholarship. Our understanding of the New Testament has been greatly influenced by the general acceptance of the insights of form criticism and the subsequent development of redaction criticism. Both have affected the scholar's approach to the New Testament, with the result that the scholar's view of the New Testament has changed dramatically in the last decade or so. To mention only one example of this change of view, today the gospel writers Matthew, Mark, and Luke are seen as major theologians in their own right, with viewpoints every bit as distinctive as those of John and Paul. These changes and developments are reflected in the pages that follow; indeed, a major reason for writing a new *Introduction* is to present the New Testament as it now appears to modern scholarship.

There are two further features of this book the reader should note. The first is that the book is designed to introduce the reader to the New Testament, and at any and every stage it is assumed that the New Testament itself will be read. Much of the text will be unintelligible without constant reference to the New Testament. The second of these features is the Further Reading found at the end of every chapter and appendix. Here a deliberate attempt is made to present a cross section of scholarly opinion and yet suggest books the reader might reasonably expect to find in any good reference library. The basic resources are six standard works (described in a note following this preface), although others have been added when they are especially helpful.

There now remains the pleasant task of acknowledging my debt to the many who have helped me directly and indirectly in the writing of this work. The book itself is the product of twenty-five years of studying and teaching the New Testament. At almost every point I am indebted to my teachers and to my colleagues, students, and friends during those years. In particular, I owe much to my colleagues at the Divinity School of the University of Chicago: to Mircea Eliade and his colleagues in the field of the History of Religions; to Nathan Scott and his colleagues in Religion and Literature; to Paul Ricoeur; and to my own colleagues in New Testament, Robert Grant and Allen Wikgren, to whom I have often turned for information on matters beyond my particular competence.

The careful reader will note that at many key points the interpretation of a book or a writer is built upon an observation concerning the Christology involved. I am grateful to the John Simon Guggenheim Memorial Foundation for the means to spend a year working on various aspects of New Testament Christology.

A number of my former students were most helpful to me as the book was being written. They are John Donahue, Vanderbilt University; Dennis Duling, Boston University; Richard Edwards, Virginia Polytechnic Institute; Vernon Faillettaz, St. Olaf College; Werner Kelber, Rice University; James Miller, Reed College; and Vernon Robbins, University of Illinois. Each of them commented on a first draft of the manuscript, Donahue and Kelber in very considerable detail.

The comments of Professor William G. Doty of Douglass College, Rutgers University, and Professor Jonathan Z. Smith of the University of Chicago were extremely helpful to me in the preparation of the final draft.

During the academic year 1971–72, when the text of this book was actually written, my graduate assistants were Joseph Comber and Leon Roose. They both made important contributions to the work as it was in progress, and Mr. Comber, who is writing a dissertation on the gospel of Matthew, provided a complete exegetical survey of that gospel, which became the basis for the presentation in chapter 8. In the summer of 1973 my graduate assistants, Mary Ann Tolbert and Kim Dewey, helped in the final stages of the book, reading proofs and preparing indexes.

I am very grateful to the Divinity School of the University of Chicago and its dean, Joseph M. Kitagawa, who were extraordinarily understanding and provided me with help and support in many ways.

Three members of the publisher's staff contributed a great deal to the final form of the book, sometimes in what I hope was creative tension with the author: Joan Levinson as editor, Andrea Haight as copy editor, and Kate Guttman as art editor.

My thanks are finally due to my family, Nancy, Alison and Sara, who have cheerfully endured the consequences of a man totally absorbed in a project.

**Norman Perrin**

# A NOTE ABOUT THE RESOURCE BOOKS

The following are the six works continually referred to in the Further Reading section at the end of each chapter and appendix.

Feine, P., J. Behm, and W. G. Kümmel, *Introduction to the New Testament*. New York and Nashville: Abingdon Press, 1966. (Since Kümmel is solely responsible for this edition, it is quoted as Kümmel, *Intro*.) An English translation of a standard German reference work deliberately encyclopedic in scope.

Marxsen, W., *Introduction to the New Testament*. Philadelphia: Fortress Press, 1968. (Quoted as Marxsen, *Intro*.) The English translation of a work by a member of the "Bultmann school," and hence representative of the more radical wing of contemporary New Testament scholarship.

Fuller, R. H., *A Critical Introduction to the New Testament*. London: Duckworth, 1966. (Quoted as Fuller, *Intro*.) Representative of the best Anglo-American scholarship.

*Peake's Commentary on the Bible*. Revised Edition. London and New York: Thomas Nelson and Sons, Ltd., 1962. (Quoted as *PCB*.) A one-volume commentary on the Bible, largely a product of British scholarship.

*The Jerome Biblical Commentary*. 2 vols. bound together. Englewood Cliffs, N.J.: Prentice-Hall, 1968. (Quoted as *JBC*.) In effect, a one-volume commentary on the Bible; although there is separate pagination for the volumes on the Old Testament and the New, the two are bound together. It is a product of the growing American Roman Catholic scholarship, and the present writer, a Baptist, found it most exciting to work with throughout the writing of this book. All the references are to the part of the volume that deals with the New Testament.

*The Interpreter's Dictionary of the Bible*. 4 vols. New York and Nashville: Abingdon Press, 1962. (Quoted as *IDB*.) The most comprehensive reference work available in English. The articles vary in quality, but at their best they are very good and always extremely informative.

# ABBREVIATIONS AND EXPLANATIONS

Books of the Bible and the Apocrypha are abbreviated to the first three or four letters of their titles; e.g., Gen = Genesis, Matt = Matthew, 1 Cor = 1 Corinthians. We have followed the example of the Oxford Annotated Bible in using *Sir* for The Wisdom of Jesus the Son of Sirach, a book in the Apocrypha sometimes called Ecclesiasticus. The abbreviation *par.* (for *parallel*) is used to refer to passages in the gospels that are parallel to the one cited; e.g., "Mark 13 par." means "Mark 13 and its parallels in Matthew and Luke."

Qumran materials are abbreviated according to the standard established in the official publication *Discoveries in the Judaean Desert,* edited by J. T. Milik and D. Barthélemy (Oxford: Clarendon Press, 1955–      ).

The following is a list of other abbreviations used.

| | |
|---|---|
| ASV | American Standard Version (of the Bible) = SV |
| AV | Authorized Version (of the Bible) = KJV |
| ERV | English Revised Version (of the Bible) = RV |
| IDB | *Interpreter's Dictionary of the Bible* |
| JBC | *Jerome Biblical Commentary* |
| KJV | King James Version (of the Bible) = AV |
| LXX | Septuagint (the Greek translation of the Jewish scriptures, transmitted as the Old Testament by Christians) |
| NAB | New American Bible |
| NEB | New English Bible |
| OAB | Oxford Annotated Bible |
| PCB | *Peake's Commentary on the Bible* |
| RSV | Revised Standard Version (of the Bible) |
| RV | Revised Version (of the Bible) = ERV |
| SV | Standard Version (of the Bible) = ASV |
| TEV | Today's English Version (of the Bible) |

Unless otherwise identified, quotations from the Bible are from the RSV.

"Matthew," "Mark," "Luke," and "John" are used to refer both to the evangelists (gospel writers) and to the gospels themselves. Further definition ("the evangelist Matthew," or "the gospel of Matthew") is given only for the sake of emphasis or where it is necessary to avoid confusion. This usage is purely a matter of convenience and is not intended to imply anything about the actual names of the evangelists.

Publication details of all books and articles quoted or referred to are given in the bibliography at the end of the book, except that individual articles in the resource books (*PCB, JBC,* and *IDB*) are not further listed there.

# Contents

# 5    Paul and His Letters                                        89

# 6    Deutero-Pauline Christianity                                119

# 7    The Gospel of Mark: The Apocalyptic Drama                   143

## 12  The Presupposition of the New Testament: Jesus                                                                277

# The New Testament

## AN INTRODUCTION

Johns baptime. Then sayde Paul: John verely baptysed with the baptyme of repentaüce/ saying vnto the people that they shulde beleue on hym which shulde come after hym/ that is on Christ Jesus. When they hearde that/they were bapty sed in the name of the Lorde Jesu. And Paul lay de his hondes vpon them/ q the Holye goost ca me on them/q they spake with thonges / q pro phesied/q all the men were about.xii.

And he went into the synagoge/and beganed hym selfe boldely for to space of thre monethes disputinge q geuinge them exhortacions of the kingdome of God.

Whe diuers weyed harde herted q beleued not but spake euyl of the waye/q that before the mul titude/he departed frö them/q seperated the dis ciples. And he disputed dayly in the scole of one called Tirannus. And this continued by the spa ce of two yeares/so that al they which dwelt in Asia/hearde the worde of the Lorde Jesu / both Jewes q Grekes. And God wrought no smal myracles by the hondes of Paul / so that frö his body/were brought vnto the sicke / napkins or **Napkyn** partelettes/ q the diseases departed from them/ **partlet.** q the euyl spretes went out of them.

Then certayne of the vagabounde Jewes exorcistes/toke apon them to call ouer the whi che had euyll spretes/the name of the Lorde Je sus/saying: We adiure you by Jesu whom Paul preached. And ther were seuē sonnes of one Sce ua a Jewe and chefe of the prestes whiche dyd so. And the euyll sprete answered q sayde: Jesus I know/ q Paul I knowe: but who are ye? And the man in whome the euyll sprete was ranne on them q ouercame them q preuayled agaynst
a iii      them

A page of the New Testament translated by William Tyndale, from the 1549 edition, published in Antwerp.

# 1

# Approaching
# the New Testament

This book introduces students and other interested readers to the New Testament so that they may enter into dialogue with it, understanding what it is saying and why it says it the way it does. Our starting point is the New Testament itself, which is clearly both a book and a collection of books. Beyond that, the reader immediately recognizes that the New Testament is trying to convince him that certain things are true and, being true, make a difference to him at the level of the existential reality of his life in the world. In other words, there is a strong element of *proclamation* in the New Testament. It is trying to say, "This is where it's at," or whatever it is that men and women say when they try to get others to listen to them about what they believe really matters and really makes a difference. At the same time the various books of the New Testament were written not only to convince the readers that certain things were true, but also to claim that because these things were true they had consequences both important and practical at the level of living one's life in the world. So the New Testament writers seek to exhort and to instruct, to guide and to comfort, to advise and to encourage, and quite often to reprimand. Scholars tend to use a technical term to cover this whole gamut of verbal activity: they call it *parenesis*.

These considerations account for the first part of the subtitle of this book, and for our approach to the New Testament. The second part of the subtitle derives from the further consideration that the New Testament is a fascinating blend of history and myth. At one level there is concrete factuality: the Romans crucifying a potentially dangerous leader of a rebellion against their authority (they crucified a hundred such men) or a wandering missionary of a new religion or philosophy having trouble with rivals in the city of Corinth (which happened in every city in the Hellenistic world). At another level, however, these concrete, factual, and even commonplace events are presented as unique, as forever changing the possibilities for human existence in the world, as revealing the nature of God's judgment on the wisdom and power of the world. In other words, they become *myths*. We develop this theme in our

3

next chapter, and it will be a constant factor throughout our discussion of the New Testament.

The reader of this book will find, therefore, that it exhibits a particular understanding of the New Testament, based on a particular kind of New Testament scholarship. The techniques and methods of this scholarship are discussed briefly later in this chapter to make the reader aware of how our conclusions were reached and also to prepare the way for the more technical aspects of the discussion.

The New Testament consists of a series of literary texts produced in the actual circumstances of early Christianity. These circumstances were historical in that the Christians lived in the concrete factuality of life in the world and responded to such events as the fall of Jerusalem and the Roman persecution of the Christians. They were historical also in that they were conditioned by the challenges and problems of a developing understanding of the nature and meaning of Christian faith itself. New Testament Christianity went through a series of phases determined by both kinds of historical circumstances, and the books that now make up the New Testament were produced in one or another of these phases in response to the needs, problems, and opportunities of that phase. They can properly be understood historically only if they are placed firmly in the context of the particular circumstances of the phase of New Testament Christianity from which they come. In order to make this possible chapter 3 presents a systematic account of the theological history of New Testament Christianity. The term "theological history" deliberately calls attention to our concern with both these aspects of historical circumstances. The following chapters discuss each part of the New Testament against the background of its place in the spectrum of that theological history.

Chapters 4–11 discuss the various parts of the New Testament in chronological order. We should perhaps point out several features of that discussion, in addition to those already indicated.

*The treatment of apocalyptic Christianity.* The first actual discussion of the literary texts of the New Testament, chapter 4, deals with a group of texts of which only one, the book of Revelation, is a complete work, and that is comparatively late. The subject of the chapter, however, is really *apocalyptic* Christianity; apocalyptic is a major feature of the very earliest days, and we therefore discuss it first. Since it continued to be a strong influence in the Christian movement and constantly exhibits the same features, we bring together in that discussion all the specifically apocalyptic texts to be found in the New Testament.

*Emphasis on literary factors.* Our discussion of the books that make up the New Testament emphasizes literary factors and especially a *literary analysis* of the longer books. Several years of intensive work on the gospels and the Acts of the Apostles have convinced me that the authors of these books signaled their intentions by the literary structure they gave to their work and by various literary devices utilized within that structure.

*The synoptic gospels and the Acts of the Apostles.* A third feature of this book is the considerable space devoted to the evangelists Matthew and Mark and the author of the gospel of Luke-Acts of the Apostles. A major development in recent New Testament scholarship has been the recognition that each of these men is a major theologian in his own right, and that the contribution of each to the development of New Testament Christianity is as distinctive as that of the Apostle Paul.

*Material ascribed to Jesus in the synoptic gospels.*   The synoptic gospels are in the literary form of sayings and teaching of Jesus and of stories about him. All this material, however, reflects the teaching, understanding, and concerns of early Christian communities, and much of it was in fact created by prophets and scribes in those communities.[1] A fourth feature of this book is that this view of the synoptic gospel material is taken seriously both in the discussion of the gospels in chapters 7, 8, and 9, and in the discussion of Jesus in chapter 12.

*Jesus as the presupposition of the New Testament.*   A fifth feature of this book is the place assigned to Jesus. It is normal to begin a survey of the New Testament with Jesus—that is, with the historical Jesus—and then to go on to examine developments in the later church, understanding those developments as moving forward from the mission and message of the historical Jesus. This was the present writer's own understanding until he was confronted by the work of the German New Testament scholar Rudolf Bultmann. Bultmann begins his *Theology of the New Testament* with the sentence, "The message of Jesus is a presupposition for the theology of the New Testament rather than a part of the theology itself," and his book *Primitive Christianity in its Contemporary Setting* discusses Jesus under the rubric of Judaism, *not* primitive Christianity. Over the years I have wrestled with this problem and am finally convinced that Bultmann is right. Hence, in this book the chapter on Jesus is the last chapter and not the first, and the title of that chapter is a deliberate allusion to Bultmann's phrase.

*Hellenism and Judaism as the "background" to the New Testament.*   A sixth feature of this book is that it does not begin with a discussion of the "background" to the New Testament in Hellenism and Judaism. Again, this is the traditional way, but my own experience as a teacher has been that students tend either to skip these chapters or to forget their contents in reading the New Testament where it is most necessary to remember them. So this book begins with the New Testament itself and then discusses relevant aspects of Hellenism and Judaism where they are important to understanding the New Testament. At the end of the book Appendices 1 and 2 present, respectively, general discussions of the Hellenistic world and the history of the Jewish people in the New Testament period.

*The "Exegetical Surveys."*   The seventh general feature of the book is the extensive use of "exegetical surveys." Every major book in the New Testament

---

[1]This is the consensus viewpoint of the scholarship this book represents, and I argued the matter in detail in the first chapter of my *Rediscovering the Teaching of Jesus.*

is surveyed, and when considerations of space make it impossible to treat a book in this way, it is outlined and the contents are briefly discussed. This procedure was chosen deliberately to encourage the reader to read the New Testament itself rather than only a book about the New Testament, and to help him understand what he is reading. I regard these exegetical surveys as the heart of the book. They are designed to be read in conjunction with a good English translation of the Bible. The more important of the available translations are discussed in Appendix 5. Perhaps the best of these for the student is the Revised Standard Version, which is good and which is concerned to stay close to the Greek text. Unless otherwise noted, our own quotations are from the Revised Standard Version.

## TECHNIQUES AND METHODS OF NEW TESTAMENT SCHOLARSHIP

There are three aspects of New Testament scholarship that must now be briefly described since their insights and methods are constantly presupposed in the chapters to follow. These are consideration of authorship and sources, form criticism, and redaction criticism.

### Consideration of Authorship and Sources

In a modern translation of the New Testament such as the Revised Standard Version all the books except one are attributed to an author. We find "The Gospel According to Matthew," "The Letter of Paul to the Romans," "The Revelation of John," and so on. The one exception is "The Letter to the Hebrews," which in most modern translations is not ascribed to any individual, although the King James Version has it as "The Letter of the Apostle Paul to the Hebrews." All the men named as authors are known to us from the New Testament itself. James and Jude were brothers of Jesus (Matt 13:55); Peter, Matthew, and John were among the original group of Jesus' disciples (Mark 3:16–19); Paul is prominent in the Acts of the Apostles; and Luke and Mark are mentioned in 2 Tim 4:11. All were either apostles or closely associated with apostles, and, indeed, the traditional claim of the church has been that they were either "apostles" or "apostolic men." Were this claim substantiated, it would lead to a particular understanding of the New Testament—that it is largely a historical chronicle of the ministry of Jesus and the life of the early church, for the most part written by men who were either relatives of Jesus or closely associated with him, or by the apostle Paul and men who had been associated with him. This would have very important consequences for our understanding of the New Testament. It is obviously important, therefore, to establish as far as we can the authorship of the books of the New Testament. The question is whether the books of the New Testament themselves show evidence of having been written by the men whose names are attached to them, and New Testament scholars have investigated this question very carefully. The position taken in this book is as follows.

The gospels were not written by eyewitnesses of the ministry of Jesus. They were written in the period between A.D. 70 and 100, forty years or more after the crucifixion, and originally they circulated anonymously. We simply do not know who wrote them, though as we shall see, the gospels themselves tell us a great deal about the gospel writers—the evangelists—and their concerns. But they do not tell us their names, and when we speak of "Matthew," "Mark," "Luke," or "John" we do so only for convenience; the actual names of the evangelists are forever lost to us.

Of the thirteen letters traditionally ascribed to Paul, seven were written by him: 1 Thessalonians, Galatians, 1 and 2 Corinthians, Philippians, Philemon, and Romans. Two of these, 2 Corinthians and Philippians, are not single letters but rather collections of several letters and remnants brought together into single letters when Paul's letters were collected and circulated as a group. The other letters are pseudonymous, written by men who used Paul's name, not by Paul himself. These pseudonymous letters fall naturally into two groups. First there is the group comprising 2 Thessalonians, Colossians, and Ephesians. These were written by pupils and followers of the apostle, men who deliberately represented their teacher and who wrote in his name. We call these letters "deutero-Pauline." Then there is the group consisting of 1 and 2 Timothy and Titus. These are a generation or more later, written early in the second century A.D. Because they so obviously reflect the concerns of a Christian pastor for the churches committed to his care, they are usually called the "Pastoral Epistles." They belong together with 1 and 2 Peter, James, and Jude, all of which are pseudonymous, and all of which were written between about A.D. 90 and 140. This whole group of letters represents the interests and concerns of the church on the way to becoming an institution in the Greco-Roman world, and we discuss them as "the literature of emergent Catholicism." The reasons for regarding 2 Thessalonians, Colossians, and Ephesians as "deutero-Pauline" and the Pastorals, 1 and 2 Peter, James, and Jude as "the literature of emergent Catholicism" are given in detail in the relevant chapters later.

We may summarize our conclusions with regard to the authorship of the books of the New Testament as follows, giving approximate dates.

A.D. 50–60   Paul writes 1 Thessalonians; Galatians; 1 Corinthians and [the collection of letters that is now] 2 Corinthians; [the collection of letters that is now] Philippians; Philemon; and Romans—probably in that order, though we cannot be sure of the place in the order of the individual elements in 2 Corinthians and Philippians.

*All the remaining New Testament literature comes after the fall of Jerusalem to the Romans and the destruction of its Temple, in A.D. 70.*

70–90   Pupils and followers of Paul write the deutero-Pauline letters: 2 Thessalonians, Colossians, and Ephesians.

Unknown Christians write what we now know as the gospels of Matthew, Mark, and Luke, and the Acts of the Apostles.

80–100   The gospel and letters of John are produced most probably not by one individual but by men who were members of a tightly-knit group. We do not know their names but for convenience we will call them "the Johannine school."

90–100   A church leader named John writes the book of Revelation while in exile on the island of Patmos.

90–140   Leaders in various churches write the pseudonymous literature of emergent Catholicism: the Pastorals, 1 and 2 Peter, James, and Jude.

The reasons for these conclusions and the evidence that supports them are given at the appropriate places in the chapters that follow.

The gospels of Matthew, Mark, and Luke are usually called the synoptic gospels (from the Greek *synoptikos*, "seeing the whole together") because they tell much the same story in much the same way. They can be set side by side and read together. But if we do set them side by side it becomes evident that there is some kind of literary relationship among them. This relationship is of two kinds. First, in some sections of the gospels it is clear that all three gospels are related to one another; second, there are passages in which it is evident that Matthew and Luke are related to each other but not to the gospel of Mark. We examine each of these phenomena in turn.

The first example of the interrelatedness of all three gospels is the Baptism of Jesus (Matt 3:13–17 = Mark 1:9–11 = Luke 3:21–22):

| **Matt 3:13–17** | **Mark 1:9–11** | **Luke 3:21–22** |
|---|---|---|
| Then Jesus came from Galilee to the Jordan to John, to be baptized by him. John would have prevented him, saying, "I need to be baptized by you, and do you come to me?" But Jesus answered him, "Let it be so now; for thus it is fitting for us to fulfil all right-eousness." Then he consented. | In those days Jesus came from Nazareth of Galilee | Now when all the people were baptized |
| And when Jesus was baptized, he went up immediately from the water, and behold, the heavens were opened | and was baptized by John in the Jordan. And when he came up out of the water, immediately he saw the heavens opened | and when Jesus also had been baptized and was praying, the heaven was opened, |

| and he saw the Spirit of God descending like a dove and alighting on him; and lo, a voice from heaven, saying, "This is my beloved Son, with whom I am well pleased." | and the Spirit descending upon him like a dove; and a voice came from heaven, "Thou are my beloved Son; with thee I am well pleased." | and the Holy Spirit descended upon him in bodily form, as a dove, and a voice came from heaven, "Thou art my beloved Son; with thee I am well pleased." |
|---|---|---|

If we look at these passages closely, we find a distinct pattern to their interrelatedness. The pattern is that Matthew and Mark can agree against Luke, and Mark and Luke can agree against Matthew, but Matthew and Luke do not agree against Mark. In Matthew and Mark Jesus came from Galilee, but this is not mentioned in Luke. The Spirit descends like a dove on Jesus in Mark and Luke; the Spirit descends like a dove *and alights* on Jesus in Matthew. The voice from heaven says, "Thou art my beloved Son; with thee I am well pleased" in Mark and Luke, but "This is my beloved Son, with whom I am well pleased" in Matthew.

This pattern of verbal interrelatedness continues throughout the three gospels with only very minor exceptions, and it is matched by a similar pattern in the order of the events presented: where there is a common order of events, it is always the order of Mark that is being followed. As far as the order of events is concerned, Matthew and Mark can agree against Luke, and Luke and Mark against Matthew, but Matthew and Luke never agree against Mark.

This consistent pattern in the verbal relationship among the three gospels and the order of the events presented shows that the gospel of Mark was written first and that Matthew and Luke have both used it as a source. This conclusion of the *priority of Mark* is presupposed in our subsequent discussions of the synoptic gospels.

A further phenomenon of the verbal relationships among the synoptic gospels is that sections of Matthew and Luke are so close verbally that they must be using a common source, but that source cannot be Mark since he does not have these sections. The first occurrence of this phenomenon is the Preaching of John the Baptist (Matt 3:7–10 = Luke 3:7–9):

| **Matt 3:7–10** | **Luke 3:7–9** |
|---|---|
| But when he saw many of the Pharisees and Sadducees coming for baptism, he said to them, "You brood of vipers! Who warned you to flee from the wrath to come? Bear fruit that befits repentance, and do not presume to say to yourselves, 'We have Abraham as our father'; for I tell you, God is able from these stones to raise up children to Abraham. Even now the ax is laid to the root of the trees; every tree therefore that does not bear good fruit is cut down and thrown into the fire." | He said therefore to the multitudes that came out to be baptized by him, "You brood of vipers! Who warned you to flee from the wrath to come? Bear fruits that befit repentance, and do not begin to say to yourselves, 'We have Abraham as our father'; for I tell you, God is able from these stones to raise up children to Abraham. Even now the ax is laid to the root of the trees; every tree therefore that does not bear good fruit is cut down and thrown into the fire." |

This material common to Matthew and Luke but not to Mark is almost always *teaching material*. The first example is teaching of John the Baptist, but the remainder is teaching of Jesus. Other examples of it are the teaching on anxiety (Matt 6:25–33 = Luke 12:22–31), and on judging (Matt 7:1–5 = Luke 6:37–38). The constant appearance of such parallel passages in the gospels of Matthew and Luke has led to the conclusion that they have a source in common in addition to the gospel of Mark, a source consisting mostly of sayings material. The existence of this source is hypothetical since no copy of it has been found, but the verbal relationships between Matthew and Luke show that it did once exist. For the sake of convenience this source is called Q (for the German *Quelle*, "a source"), and we discuss it in detail in chapter 4.

In addition to the sources they have in common, the gospel of Mark and source Q, both Matthew and Luke present a good deal of special material of their own, e.g., sections of the Sermon on the Mount in Matthew 5–7 (Matt 5:17–20, 21–22, 27–29, 33–37; 6:1–6, 16–18, 34; 7:6, 15) and the parables in Luke 15. We may represent the interrelatedness of the synoptic gospels in diagram form as follows.

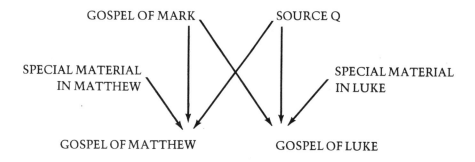

## Form Criticism

An important development in New Testament scholarship took place in Germany after World War I. It came to be called *Formgeschichte*, literally "form history" but more often translated "form criticism." Its point of departure was the realization that the New Testament writers had made extensive use of traditional material. It came to be realized that Paul and other writers of the letters in the New Testament constantly quote hymns, confessions, benedictions, and other elements from the liturgies of the New Testament churches. Similarly, they use lists of virtues and vices and lists of the duties of the various members of a household, which were in constant use for the purpose of ethical instruction not only in the Christian churches, but also in the Jewish synagogues and in the schools of Greek moral philosophy. Perhaps more startling, it came to be realized that much of the material presented by the evangelists in the gospels was also in fixed literary form and that it had functioned in the life and work of the Christian churches before its use by the evangelists in their gospels. Moreover, these forms were by no means unique to the Christian movement but were found in the literary traditions of other religious and philosophical movements in the Hellenistic world.

One such form was the *biographical apothegm,* a story from the life of a wise man that culminates in a pregnant saying, or sayings, or in a brief dialogue. It is the characteristic of these biographical apothegms that when they occur in several versions, the biographical setting is the variant but the saying, sayings, or dialogue remain constant. Such stories were extraordinarily popular in the ancient world, and we find them in every possible cultural context, including the New Testament with its stories about Jesus. Examples of each of the possibilities we have mentioned from the New Testament stories about Jesus would be: Mark 3:19b–22 = Matt 12:22–24 = Luke 11:14–16 (story culminating in a single saying, in this instance to the effect that Jesus casts out demons by the power of the prince of demons); Matt 8:18–22 = Luke 9:57–60 (story culminating in two sayings, one about the homelessness of the Son of Man, and one about the dead burying their dead); Mark 3:31–35 = Matt 12:46–50 = Luke 8:19–21 (story about Jesus' true relatives, culminating in a dialogue). In each of these instances, and in the many others that could be quoted, the relative freedom of the story compared to the relatively fixed nature of the saying, sayings, or dialogue indicates the evangelists' understanding of the essential nature of this category. Even knowing the version in Mark, Matthew and Luke do not consider themselves bound by its biographical element, and either vary it themselves or follow another version known to them.

Another popular form known to us from every culture in the world of the New Testament is the *miracle story,* especially the healing miracle. Typically these stories all emphasize the seriousness of the ailment, the actual process of the cure (special words or gestures) and a demonstration of the fact of the cure to the satisfaction of onlookers. These would all have to be constants in a readily memorizable healing miracle story. A particularly interesting cycle of such stories about Jesus is found in Mark 4:35–5:43: the Gerasene Demoniac; the Woman with the Hemorrhage; Jairus' Daughter. Each of these has all the characteristics of the popular miracle story, and each contributes to the impression of a divine aura surrounding Jesus. His power is such that the Gerasenes beg him to leave their district, the touch of his clothes can effect a cure, and he can raise the dead by strange-sounding words. Two further stories in Mark exhibit exactly the same characteristics of a divine aura: 7:24–30, the Syrophoenician Woman's Daughter (healed from a distance); and 7:31–37, the Deaf Man with a Speech Impediment (the astonishment of the crowd). In these we certainly have the remnants of a popular cycle of stories about Jesus, originally designed as propaganda for him as the founder of the Christian faith in a world in which such stories were commonly told of heroes of faith—Hellenistic Greek, Syrian, Jewish, and Egyptian.

The first concern of form criticism is with distinctive literary forms; the second is with the cultural context in which the form has a definite function. Form critics call this context the *Sitz im Leben*, "setting in life." A striking example of form criticism's concern for a context in which forms *functioned* is Ernst Käsemann's work on what he calls "sentences of holy law."[2]

Here the form is that of a two-part sentence, the first part describing the activity of the person being judged and the second describing the eschatological judgment of God on that person, *with the same verb in each part*. Examples are:

| | |
|---|---|
| 1 Cor 3:17 | If anyone destroys God's temple, God will destroy him. |
| 1 Cor 14:38 | If he does not acknowledge this, God does not acknowledge him (NEB). (Supply: And will not acknowledge him at the Last Judgment.) |
| Mark 8:38 | If anyone is ashamed of me and mine . . . the Son of Man will be ashamed of him, when he comes. . . . (NEB). (Supply: And enacts the final judgment of God.) |
| Matt 6:14f. | For if you forgive others . . . your heavenly Father will also forgive you; but if you do not forgive others, then the wrongs you have done will not be forgiven by your Father (NEB). (Supply: At the Last Judgment.) |

More important perhaps than the form is the function. Käsemann was able to show that this form had a very real function at the early Christian sacred meal where, by the use of this form, dissident members of the local congregation were handed over to the eschatological judgment of God by the charismatic leader of that congregation. This leader was probably known as a prophet, but whether he was called "prophet," "elder," "apostle," or "overseer" (i.e., "bishop") is unimportant. What is important is that this individual functioned as the direct and immediate representative of Jesus in the local congregation of Christians, able to announce in advance the judgmental activity of God that he, and all the members of that congregation, expected imminently.

Form criticism therefore stresses the *form* of traditional material used by the New Testament writers, and it stresses, further, the *context* in which those forms originally functioned (the *Sitz im Leben*). It has, however, a third concern: the *history of the transmission* of this traditional material in earliest Christianity. Form critics have been able to show that the sayings and stories in the synoptic gospels have a long history of transmission in the tradition of the church, during which they have been changed and developed in all kinds of ways. Perhaps the most successful example of this work is J. Jeremias' book *The Parables of Jesus*, where he is able to trace the long and complex process through which the parables reached the form they now have in the gospels.

---

[2]Käsemann, "Sentences of Holy Law in the New Testament," in his collected essays, *New Testament Questions of Today*.

## Redaction Criticism

As important as form criticism is and always will be, it suffers from one handicap. In its concern for the forms and tradition underlying the written texts of the New Testament it tended to do less than justice to the originality and creativity of the writers of those texts, particularly the synoptic evangelists Matthew, Mark, and Luke. This imbalance was corrected immediately after World War II with the rise of the discipline of *Redaktionsgeschichte,* literally "redaction history" but more often translated "redaction criticism." Redaction criticism assumes the work of form criticism on the individual forms and the history of the tradition of the church. It goes on from there to inquire into the use made of this material by the final author of the text, into his redaction of this material (the German word *Redaktor* means primarily "editor") and what it tells us about his theological viewpoint. As developed in Germany the discipline takes its point of departure from an ability to distinguish between tradition and redaction of tradition and to determine the theological view implied by that redaction. But once it was recognized that the final author was in fact an *author* and not merely a transmitter of tradition, it became natural and inevitable to inquire into his total literary activity as revealing his purpose and theology, not only into his redaction of previously existing tradition. In this connection redaction criticism shades over into general literary criticism, especially in the redaction critical work carried on in America, where the influence of general literary criticism is strong on New Testament scholars.

We may illustrate the work of redaction criticism by turning again to the accounts of the baptism of Jesus, which we used above as the basis for a discussion of the interrelatedness of the synoptic gospels. This time, however, we are concerned only with the relationship between Luke 3:21–22 and its source, Mark 1:9–11.

| Mark 1:9–11 | Luke 3:21–22 |
|---|---|
| In those days Jesus came from Nazareth of Galilee and was baptized by John in the Jordan. And when he came up out of the water, immediately he saw the heavens opened and the Spirit descending upon him like a dove; and a voice came from heaven, "Thou art my beloved Son; with thee I am well pleased." | Now when all the people were baptized and when Jesus also had been baptized and was praying, the heaven was opened, and the Holy Spirit descended upon him in bodily form, as a dove, and a voice came from heaven, "Thou art my beloved Son; with thee I am well pleased." |

In Luke's version all the emphasis is on the descent of the Spirit on Jesus. His baptism has become but one of the three circumstances (a general baptism, his baptism, the fact that he was praying) that set the stage for the descent of the Spirit, whereas in Mark the baptism and the descent of the Spirit are equally significant. Incidentally, the introduction of the theme of Jesus at prayer is characteristic of Luke's gospel. He does it in at least six places where it is not to be found in his sources (3:21; 5:16; 6:12; 9:18, 28, 29). The emphasis in

Luke's gospel is on the fact that the ministry of Jesus began not with his baptism but with the descent of the Spirit on him. This becomes important when we recall that in Acts the ministry of the church begins in exactly the same way. In Acts 2 the ministry of the church begins with the descent of the Spirit at Pentecost, which in Acts 1:5 is interpreted in advance as a baptism. The author clearly intends to set these two things—the ministry of Jesus and the ministry of the church—in close and formal parallelism with one another, and this becomes an important clue to his theology, as we shall see when we come to discuss Luke-Acts in detail.

Another important insight into the theology of the author of Luke-Acts involves both redaction criticism and general literary criticism. If we pay careful attention to the order of events in the gospel of Mark, it is immediately evident that the major redaction by Luke of the *order* of Mark is the insertion of a long, rambling travel narrative (Luke 9:51–18:14). This Lukan special section begins with the well-known literary device of a mental resolve on the part of the chief protagonist (Jesus), which indicates the further course of the narrative (Luke 9:51): "As the time approached when he was to be taken up to heaven [Luke uses the technical term for the ascension, *analempsis*], he [Jesus] set his face resolutely towards Jerusalem. . . ." (NEB). This literary device is precisely paralleled in the Acts of the Apostles where in Acts 19:21, "Paul made up his mind to visit Macedonia and Achaia and then go on to Jerusalem; and he said, 'After I have been there, I must see Rome also'" (NEB). The rest of the narrative of Acts is concerned with Paul's journey to Rome, and it ends on the note of Paul preaching in Rome "quite openly and without hindrance" (Acts 28:3, NEB). Again the parallelism between the gospel and Acts is so close that it must be intentional, and from it we can learn a great deal about the theology and purpose of the author of Luke-Acts. We return to this point in our discussion of Luke-Acts.

Redaction criticism is the newest development in the historical criticism of the New Testament, and it has already made possible immense advances in our understanding of the theologies of the synoptic evangelists. Our chapters on the gospels of Matthew and Mark and on Luke-Acts are built on the insights of redaction criticism, as defined in America to include aspects of literary criticism.

## FURTHER READING

A good general history of New Testament scholarship is Kümmel, *The New Testament: The History of the Investigation of its Problems.* Two of our resource books contain useful, although necessarily brief accounts:

> IDB, vol. 1, pp. 407–13, "Biblical Criticism" (K. Grobel); pp. 413–18, "Biblical Criticism, History of" (S. J. De Vries).
> JBC, pp. 7–20, "Modern New Testament Criticism" (J. S. Kselman).

Detailed discussion of the authorship and sources of the books of the New

Testament will be found in the relevant sections of Kümmel's, Marxsen's, and Fuller's *Introductions*.

The classical works on form criticism are Dibelius, *From Tradition to Gospel*, and Bultmann, *The History of the Synoptic Tradition*. There are useful discussions of the matter in *IDB*, vol. 2, pp. 320–21 (K. Grobel); *PCB*, pp. 683–85 (E. Dinkler); and Marxsen, *Intro.*, pp. 120–33, and there is an extended treatment of it in McKnight, *What is Form Criticism?*

The classical works on redaction criticism are: Bornkamm, Barth, Held, *Tradition and Interpretation in Matthew*; Conzelmann, *The Theology of St. Luke*; and Marxsen, *Mark the Evangelist*. Of these, the first is perhaps the best introduction to the process of redaction of tradition by an evangelist, since Matthew's redaction of traditional material is more deliberate and obvious than that of the other evangelists. Marxsen, *Intro.*, has valuable brief discussions of "the editorial process" in connection with Matthew, Mark, and Luke. I discussed and described the movement in Perrin, *What is Redaction Criticism?*

The "Crucifixion" window from the church
of St. Remi, Reims (ca. 1190).

# 2

# The Nature of the
# New Testament

## THE NEW TESTAMENT AS A BOOK
## AND AS A COLLECTION OF BOOKS

The first thing to be said about the New Testament is that it is both a book and a collection of books; it is a text and a collection of texts brought together by the church and declared to be the New Testament. Both descriptions are important. As a book the New Testament represents a single entity of foundational importance to Christians and Christian churches; as a collection of books it is a variety of documents of different literary forms and sometimes of different religious viewpoints.

There is a real tension between the "text" and the "collection of texts." We can proclaim that the New Testament is a unity, but in actual reading differences in literary form and religious viewpoint may make the reader more comfortable in one part than another. The most famous example is Martin Luther, who found himself at home (to put it mildly) in the letter to the Romans with its view of justification by faith, but who dismissed the letter of James as "a right strawy epistle" because it expressed a very different view. In point of fact these two letters show differences in specific theological doctrine and even in general understanding of what it means to be religious in the world. There are similar differences between the gospel of John and the two-volume gospel of Luke and Acts of the Apostles, or for that matter between Paul's letter to the Romans and his letter to the Thessalonians.

The differences are theological in that the concept of justification by faith is present in Romans and absent in James;[1] salvation history is present in Luke-Acts[2] and absent in the gospel of John; "faith" reflects quite different concepts in the genuine letters of Paul and in the pseudonymous Pastoral

[1] On this see chapter 11, p. 255.
[2] On this see chapter 9, pp. 200–05.

**17**

Letters (first and second letters to Timothy, letter to Titus).[3] The religious differences represent different understandings of what it means to be Christian in the world. So, for example, the Thessalonian letters concentrate on the parousia, the (second) coming of Jesus as judge of the world;[4] to be religious is to prepare for that coming by rigorously following the instructions given by and through the Jesus who is to come. In Romans, however, Paul celebrates the benefits of the cross and exults in the present experience of Christians, and the parousia no longer dominates the field of vision. Although the two viewpoints can be reconciled in the theology of Paul—but just barely—the fact remains that the Thessalonian and Roman Christians were religious in very different ways.

Another difference among the various books collected in the New Testament is in their literary forms. In recent years we have become increasingly aware that different literary forms function in different ways. The reader of the realistic (mimetic) narrative of the gospel of Mark is caught up in the story as participant, whereas he is an observer of the sacred drama of the gospel of John. The reader of the letters of Paul, which are real letters, is directly addressed by them, but he has to wrestle with the meaning of the letter to the Hebrews, which is not a letter at all but a theological treatise. Each of these literary forms works differently and so addresses its reader differently, and it is important for the reader to know what kind of text he is reading if he is to understand it correctly.

Paralleling the differences in form are the differences in language. Not all language is alike; there are many kinds of language, and each tends to function differently. In the New Testament itself the direct discourse of the Sermon on the Mount is in form and function unlike the exalted revelatory style of the "I am" discourses in John's gospel, as also are the down-to-earth realism of the parables and the exotic imagery of the book of Revelation.

Though the books in the New Testament differ from one another in their understanding of the nature of Christian faith in the world, they are in common wrestling with the problems of that faith and no other. Their authors are at different stages in the development of New Testament Christianity and so face different problems, and they necessarily develop their understanding of the nature and meaning of Christian faith differently. When they face the same problems they sometimes respond to them in different ways. But there is an overall unity in the New Testament: each writer attempts to relate to and to make sense of life in the world by means of his faith in Jesus Christ.

The diversity of the New Testament is matched by the diversity of Christian churches in subsequent Christian history. Over and over again a particular viewpoint in the New Testament is developed historically by a group of

---

[3]On this see chapter 11, p. 269.

[4]*Parousia* is the Greek term for the visit of an important official to a province or district to regulate its affairs. Early Christian writers used it to denote their expectation of the coming of Jesus from heaven to judge the world (e.g., Matt 24:27): "For as the lightning comes from the east and shines as far as the west, so will be the coming [*parousia*] of the Son of man." Modern scholars follow this practice and use parousia as a technical term to denote the early Christian expectation of the imminent coming of Jesus from heaven as Son of Man to judge the world.

churches. Chapter 4 of this book describes "apocalyptic Christianity," a viewpoint represented by many Christian sects even today. The particular perspective of "justification by faith" found in Paul's letters to the Galatians and to the Romans is the central thrust of the churches that owe allegiance directly or indirectly to Martin Luther. Further, both the gospel of Matthew, which we argue later on is preeminently the "Church's book," and the literature of "emergent Catholicism" are clearly the inspiration of the Catholic church through the centuries. The Luke-Acts understanding and presentation of Jesus as the first Christian, the model and paradigm of Christian faith and practice, is as clearly the foundation of the "liberal" understanding of Christian faith as the literature of the "Johannine school" is the inspiration for centuries of Christian mysticism.

The New Testament represents the whole spectrum of possibilities of what it means to be Christian in the world, and either anticipates or inspires every subsequent development within the Christian churches. The Roman Catholic and the Lutheran, the liberal Protestant and the fundamentalist, the contemplative mystic and the apocalyptic visionary, all find themselves at home in one part or another of this collection from the literature of earliest Christianity.

## THE NEW TESTAMENT AS PROCLAMATION AND PARENESIS

In 1918 Martin Dibelius stated a thesis that has come to dominate the modern understanding of the New Testament: "At the beginning of all early Christian creativity there stands the sermon: missionary and hortatory preaching, narrative and parenesis, prophecy and the interpretation of scripture."[5] In the next year he published a book, *From Tradition to Gospel,* developing his thesis and interpreting the New Testament in its light. There we find, for example, the statement, "In the sermon the elements of the future Christian literature lay side by side as in a mother cell" (page 70). "In the beginning was the sermon" usually summarizes this view, calling attention to the fact that the New Testament texts were the product of preaching, teaching, exhortation, and comforting, and that in turn they preach, teach, exhort, and comfort.

It would be hard to overestimate the element of proclamation in the New Testament. Jesus "proclaimed" the Kingdom of God and in turn the early Christians "proclaimed" Jesus as the one through whom God had acted decisively for the salvation of man. The major form of proclamation in the church is preaching, and the New Testament itself testifies to the centrality of its role. "I must remind you of the gospel that I preached to you," says Paul to the Corinthian Christians (1 Cor. 15:1, NEB); in a crucial passage in Romans he speaks of the word of faith which we "proclaim" (Rom 10:8, NEB).[6] The

---

[5]Quoted from the translation of the sentence in Perrin, *What is Redaction Criticism?* p. 15, n. 19.

[6]There are two Greek verbs involved here. 1 Cor 15:1 uses the verb *evangelizo,* "to announce good news," a verb Christians came to use specifically in the sense of "to

Acts of the Apostles features frequent and extensive sermons and closes with Paul "proclaiming the Kingdom of God and teaching the facts about the Lord Jesus Christ quite openly and without hindrance" (Acts 28:31, NEB). For all that Acts expresses the theological viewpoint of its author, there can be no doubt that it is correct in the emphasis upon the sermon. Moreover, this emphasis is distinctive to early Christianity. The Jewish synagogue featured homilies, and itinerant Greek philosophers taught publicly, yet no other group in the first century preached in houses and on street corners in quite the same way the Christians did. "In the beginning was the sermon" is not only true of, but special to, early Christianity.

Martin Dibelius also called attention to the role of parenesis in the New Testament, using it as a technical term to describe the activities of the church in exhorting, advising, and edifying her members.[7] It is a rare word, but the Greek from which it comes is found in the New Testament—in Acts 27:9 (NEB) where Paul "gives advice" to the ship's crew and in 27:22 (NEB) where he "urges" them not to lose heart. The rarity of the word makes it a suitable technical term, and it is now used as such by New Testament scholars, but there can be no doubt of the prominence of the activity it designates. Paul's letters are fundamentally parenesis or, to use the adjective, parenetical. Even a letter like Romans, which comes near to being a theological treatise, contains four chapters of parenesis, chapters 12–15, and the letter to the Hebrews, which also is a theological treatise, has carefully spaced parenetical sections. In this characteristic the early Christians were not distinctive. Both Jews and Greeks exhorted, advised, composed all kinds of homilies, and constantly attempted to edify one another. But to recognize the twofold emphasis on proclamation and parenesis in the New Testament is to come closer to appreciating its essential nature.

The parenetical material in the New Testament is sometimes specifically Christian exhortation developed from specifically Christian themes. Examples are the parenesis on the basis of interpreting Jesus as the true High Priest in Hebrews and that on the basis of a different Christology in the first letter of John. But at other times the Christian writers simply borrow their material from the moralizing literature of the Hellenistic world, for example, in the

---

preach the gospel." The word gospel is a translation of the Greek noun evangelion, "good news." In Old English this was translated "godspell," and our modern word is a corruption of that. Rom 10:8 uses the verb kēryssō, "to act as a herald," i.e., "to proclaim." The noun from this root is kerygma, "proclamation," and this is used in the N.T., e.g., Rom 16:25 (RSV translates it "preaching"); 1 Cor 1:21 (RSV, "what we preach"); 2:4 (RSV, "message"). Modern scholars use the word kerygma to denote the proclamation of the N.T. or of the church.

[7]In modern English all this would be described loosely as "preaching," but in the N.T. there is a real difference between proclaiming the Good News of what God has done through Jesus Christ on the one hand and exhorting, advising, and attempting to edify on the other. It is because of the loose usage of "preaching" in modern English that I am using the two distinct terms "proclamation" and "parenesis" to describe these two different verbal activities in the N.T. As can be seen from the previous footnote, in N.T. Greek, "preaching" is a form of proclamation.

"household codes" of the deutero-Pauline letters and the literature of emergent Catholicism.[8]

We have characterized the New Testament literature as fundamentally proclamation and parenesis, and we hope to justify this description in our subsequent discussion of the literature. But this is a very broad and general characterization, and there are innumerable subcategories within the literature: various kinds of Jesus material, apocalyptic imagery and instructions, exegesis of the Old Testament in various ways, instructions for missionaries and for the organization of the church, liturgical hymns and confessions, and much else. The New Testament represents much of the literary productivity of the Christian movement over the first century of its existence and contains within itself a great variety of literature and literary forms, but the broad categories of proclamation and parenesis are helpful in approaching the material as a whole.

## THE NEW TESTAMENT AS MYTH

One of the hotly debated questions in New Testament scholarship has been how far and in what ways the word *myth* may be used in connection with the texts of the New Testament, more especially with the texts concerning Jesus, the gospels. The problem came dramatically into focus in the middle of the nineteenth century in Germany, and it has remained with us ever since. The story is worth outlining so that the reader may better understand the current discussion of myth in the New Testament.

The Enlightenment and the rise of the natural and historical sciences created a grave problem for the world of New Testament scholarship, for the New Testament narratives are full of references to things that clearly have no place in the post-Enlightenment world in which the natural sciences are so convincing: angels, demons, miracles, resurrection and ascension, the (second) coming of Jesus on the clouds of heaven, and much more. At the beginning of the nineteenth century in Germany there were two ways of facing this problem. The supernaturalist way was to hold that the narratives were indeed factually true—angels, demons, miracles, and all. The rationalist way was to argue that factual history could and should be reconstructed from the narratives by explaining away the obviously legendary, miraculous, and absurd. Both sides took for granted that factual history was what mattered and that one had either to be able to claim the New Testament narratives as factually historical or to reconstruct factual history from them. Then came D. F. Strauss' two-volume *The Life of Jesus Critically Examined*, published in 1835–36. What Strauss did in effect was to cry "a plague on both your houses" and to introduce the idea of the New Testament narratives as *myth*, an idea that was, to say the least, strenuously resisted.

To understand the impact of Strauss' bombshell and the course of the

[8]See chapter 6, p. 129, and chapter 11, p. 259.

subsequent discussion among New Testament scholars, it is important to recognize that Strauss' work contrasted myth and factual history, and that he had a particular understanding of myth. For Strauss, *myth is fundamentally the narrative expression of an idea.* So the gospel narratives as myth are an unhistorical cycle of sagalike glorification, "a series of sacred narratives through which . . . a whole complex of ideas . . . was given concrete form in a series of single moments in his [Jesus'] life. . . ."[9] As myth a story is not historical; it expresses an idea. As myth the gospel narratives are unhistorical stories expressing a series of religious ideas.

The attempt to counter Strauss' concept of the New Testament narratives tried to establish the factual historicity of the gospel of Mark. The so-called Markan hypothesis[10] states that Mark is the earliest gospel and hence nearest to the events it relates and so is fundamentally historical in character. A century and more of "life-of-Jesus research" was built upon this hypothesis and only recently has it been abandoned. Today New Testament scholarship in general recognizes that the nineteenth-century emphasis on factual historicity is inappropriate to interpreting a first-century text in the twentieth century. At the same time Strauss' understanding of the nature of myth has become very influential among New Testament scholars, who when they talk about myth usually mean the narrative embodiment of an idea. In this context the most important scholar is Rudolph Bultmann, whose "demythologizing program" is the most creative and serious contemporary attempt to understand and interpret myth in the New Testament.[11] Bultmann's ultimate indebtedness to Strauss is open and acknowledged, and when he speaks, as he so often does, of *Jenseits* and *Dieseits,* of the "other side" and "this side," then he is heir to Strauss. Bultmann regards myth as a story about the "other side" told in terms of "'this side,'" that is, a story about gods and religious reality told in terms of men and the world. The story of the resurrection of Jesus is myth, a crassly human story about the resuscitation of a corpse and its eventual elevation to a region above the earth via the clouds as a kind of celestial elevator. But the reality so described is the spiritual presence of Jesus in the kerygma, the proclamation of the church;[12] it is the power of the proclamation to manifest Jesus and his offer of authentic existence to any generation of men in the world. Bultmann boldly asserts that for him Jesus is risen—into the kerygma of the church. In addition, Bultmann is an existentialist, and as such he claims that myths that speak of the "other side" in terms of "this side" are really talking about the historical reality of being human in the world. So he accepts Martin Heidegger's existentialist analysis of the reality of being human in the world and calls attention to the distinction between "authentic" and

[9]From Kee's discussion of Strauss in Kee, *Jesus in History*, p. 8.

[10]On the role of the Markan hypothesis in recent N.T. studies see Perrin, *What is Redaction Criticism?* pp. 3–13.

[11]Bultmann's views on myth and his demythologizing program are to be found in his essays "New Testament and Mythology," "A Reply to the Theses of J. Schniewind," and "Bultmann Replies to His Critics," now in Bartsch (ed.), *Kerygma and Myth*, and in his book *Jesus Christ and Mythology.* See also Perrin, *The Promise of Bultmann*, pp. 74–85, and the Further Reading at the end of this chapter.

[12]See footnote 6 for the explanation of this use of "kerygma."

"inauthentic" human existence. To go back to the resurrection, then, the possiblity of authentic human existence in the world is just that, only a *possibility*, apart from the power and challenge of the kerygma of the church. By responding to the kerygma, and only by responding to the kerygma, can men achieve the reality of authentic existence. For Bultmann to say that the kerygma offers man the genuine possibility of human existence in the world is the same as to say that Jesus is risen into the kerygma: the myth of the resurrection is now being properly understood and interpreted.

To give another example, the parousia, the idea of the return of Jesus as judge of the world, is as dependent on a view of heaven as spatially "above" the earth as is the myth of the resurrection-ascension and features the same celestial elevator moving in the opposite direction. But it is also interpretable as dealing with the futurity of human existence in the world; to speak of the parousia of the Son of Man is to speak of the futurity of human existence in the world, that "openness to the future" of which Bultmann and the existentialists speak so eloquently. The success of this particular view of such central New Testament myths as the resurrection and the parousia guarantees its continuing and legitimate role in the interpretation of the New Testament. But this widely held view of myth is not the only possible one, and in fact does not command outstanding support among historians of religion. An urgent challenge confronting contemporary New Testament scholarship is to approach the New Testament with views of myth other than and in addition to the Strauss-Bultmann view.

A second view of myth with which to approach the New Testament is that of Mircea Eliade, the distinguished Rumanian-born historian of religion. "Myth narrates a sacred history; it relates an event that took place in primordial time, the fabled time of the 'beginning.' . . . Myth tells how, through the deeds of supernatural beings, a reality came into existence. . . . Myth . . . relates how something was produced, began to be."[13] Myth can be "known," "experienced," "lived" by means of recitation and ritual. ". . . In one way or another one lives the myth, in the sense that one is seized by the sacred, exalting power of the events recollected or reenacted."[14] These words are immediately applicable to the Jewish Passover and to the Christian sacred meal (Lord's Supper or Eucharist, 1 Cor 11:23–26; Mark 14:17–25; Matt 26:20–29; Luke 22:14–23). Passover celebrates the events of the Exodus, the deliverance from Egypt, in recitation and ritual, and it is believed that there is renewal in an experience that can certainly be described as being seized "by the sacred, exalting power of the events recollected and reenacted." Similarly, in reciting the account of Jesus' institution of the meal that celebrates and interprets his death, the Christian reenacts that meal. In saying "Every time you eat this bread and drink this cup, you proclaim the death of the Lord" (1 Cor 11:26, NEB), Paul is claiming that the Christian experiences the event of the cross in all its significance.

In a very real sense, therefore, Jews and Christians are constantly involved in

---

[13]From Eliade's article on myth in the 1968 *Encyclopaedia Britannica*, vol. 15, pp. 1132–42, especially p. 1133.

[14]Ibid, p. 1135.

something Eliade would recognize as myth; there is for both renewal by a conscious return to a beginning. At the same time there is also another element present in both the Passover and the Christian meal—an orientation toward the future. The Jewish family looks for the coming of Elijah on a Passover night, and Paul finishes the sentence quoted above, "until he comes." In addition, there are the claims that the Exodus events and the cross of Jesus are historical, occurring in secular as well as sacred time, but the vitality of the celebration comes from their mythic quality rather than from their factuality.

Both the Strauss-Bultmann and the Eliade understanding of myth have to be considered seriously by a student of the New Testament. Certainly there are narratives in the New Testament that should be demythologized and understood as directly addressing the realities of human existence in the world. Bultmann correctly interprets the resurrection as Jesus being risen into the kerygma of the church, i.e., as affecting the potentialities for human existence in the world under the faith found in response to the kerygma. But Easter is also celebrated as a time of renewal by a return to the power of the First Easter in recitation and ritual. These alternatives are not mutually incompatible; rather, they explore the richness of the possibilities inherent in understanding the resurrection of Jesus as myth.

A further view of myth is that of the French philosopher Paul Ricoeur, as presented in his book *The Symbolism of Evil*.[15] His concern is with "primary symbols," which man uses to express his experience of defilement, of sin, of guilt. The force and depth of these primal experiences resist expression in the language of direct discourse, and man must use symbols to express them. To give an instance: a marriage ring or the flag of a country both symbolize experience and commitment so deep that the dramatic act of accepting the ring or rejecting it, of bearing the flag or burning it, are necessarily more meaningful than any verbal expression. The symbols themselves have immense potency precisely because they are symbols, because as symbols they effectively represent an acknowledged aspect of the reality of human experience.

Symbols, however, do not emerge in a vacuum, but in an account of how the symbol came to express what it does. The marriage ring is presented in the narrative context of how marriage came to be an institution and of the meaning and promise of that institution. The flag of a country is presented in the context of how that particular flag came to be chosen and of the meaning and promise it came to represent. This narrative is, technically speaking, a myth, and in this sense a "myth" is a narrative account of the effective origin of a symbol, which is acknowledged as representing a primary aspect of experienced reality.

To return to the New Testament in the light of Ricoeur's symbolism of evil, it is obvious that the New Testament uses the primary symbols of sin and redemption from sin. It accepts the myth of the rebellion of the primal man,

---

[15]I am deliberately contrasting the views of Bultmann, Eliade, and Ricoeur because it seemed necessary to call attention, at an introductory level, to the different nuances in their views. But at a deeper level they are much closer together than this presentation makes them appear, and Ricoeur constantly acknowledges his indebtedness both to Bultmann and to Eliade.

Adam, as a narrative account of the origin of the primary symbol "sin," and it accepts the primary symbol "sin" as corresponding to a fundamental aspect of reality experienced in the world. Paul says that "sin came into the world through one man and death through sin, and so death spread to all men because all men sinned" (Rom 5:12). This is the language of the symbolism of evil, and the myth of the fall of Adam is its original narrative context. But in the New Testament there is also a corresponding primary symbol of "redemption from sin." Paul says: "Then as one man's trespass led to condemnation for all men, so one man's act of righteousness leads to acquittal and life for all men. For as by one man's disobedience many were made sinners, so by one man's obedience many will be made righteous . . . so that, as sin reigned in death, grace also might reign through righteousness to eternal life through Jesus Christ our Lord" (Rom 5:18–21). This is the language of the symbolism of redemption, and its original narrative context is the myth of the redemptive death of Jesus on the cross. The myth has its home in the Christian sacred meal, where the cross of Jesus is interpreted as redemptive by means of symbolic language derived ultimately from the passage concerning the suffering servant of God in Isaiah 53. The servant "was wounded for our transgressions, he was bruised for our iniquities; upon him was the chastisement that made us whole, and with his stripes we are healed. . . . the Lord has laid on him the iniquity of us all" (Isa 53:5–6). The early Christians expressed their understanding of the redemptive death of Jesus in Mark 10:45, "For the Son of Man also came . . . to give his life as a ransom for many," and in Mark 14:24, "This is my blood of the covenant, which is poured out for many," which are deliberate allusions to the language of that chapter.[16] But to use the cross of Jesus as a symbol for redemption requires the narrative myth of the event of the cross itself, and that is provided by the brief pregnant references to the death of Jesus at the Christian meal in Mark 14:17–25 and 1 Cor 11:23–26. These references were no doubt expanded into a longer narrative at the celebration of the meal itself, either in the words of the leader of the celebration or in the thought of the participants who would know the story of the cross. So the use of the symbolism of redemption through the cross of Jesus requires and presupposes the myth narrated in the account of the death of Jesus; to use the technical language of New Testament scholarship, it requires and presupposes a "passion narrative." In practice in the New Testament and subsequent Christian history the cross itself comes to represent the symbolism of redemption, so we may speak quite simply of the symbolism of the cross and its essential narrative context, the myth of the passion narrative. We are therefore dealing with three things: a primary symbol, the symbol of redemption itself; a secondary symbol, the Cross, which represents the particular form of redemption Christians believe in; and the narrative myth of the passion of Jesus, in which the cross has its context and from which Christians first learn of its meaning.

This brief discussion of the element of myth in the New Testament should

---

[16]In the gospel of Mark, as in 1 Corinthians 11, these words are given to Jesus, but they were nonetheless coined in the early church in accordance with a procedure we discuss in detail in connection with the gospel of Mark in chapter 7.

serve to show that the New Testament is particularly rich in myth, which is one reason for its impact on generations of readers. But the New Testament is not only rich in myth; it is also rich in history. The Jesus who is the central figure in the myth is a man who lived and taught, suffered and died in Palestine in the first century. The New Testament is essentially concerned, therefore, with *both* myth *and* history, and this is a matter we must now discuss.

## THE NEW TESTAMENT AS MYTH AND HISTORY

Let us point out again that it is regrettable that the discussion of myth in the New Testament began in an atmosphere of bitter controversy about the reliability of the gospels. In that particular historical context myth was interpreted as false or unreliable narrative, and the battle was joined. "Myth" became a pejorative term concerning the gospels, and the study and interpretation of the gospels labored under a handicap from which it has still not recovered. It must, therefore, be stated once more that myth is a rich, meaningful, and honorable term used in connection with a religious text, including the gospel texts.

One way to make our point is to claim that a myth cannot be true or false; it can only be effective or ineffective. Another way is to state, as Eliade has done orally, that no one can self-consciously create a myth. A myth has to arise out of the consciousness of the people; it has to correspond to reality as they experience it; and it has to make sense for them of that reality, or a significant part of it. If it does these things, then it is "true," or "effective"; if it does not, it is false and ineffective.

Men and women do in fact and in practice live by means of myth. They understand themselves and their place in the world according to the myths of origins they accept, and their behavior is in many ways determined by the myths to which they subscribe, whether recognized as such or not. In England there is the myth of the "British gentleman"; in America that of the "South." Examples could be multiplied indefinitely: the role of "manifest destiny" in American history, the myth of "Aryan supremacy" in Hitler's Germany, or the nineteenth-century myth of the inevitable progress of humanity that shattered on the harsh realities of World War I and its aftermath. Myths operate at the conscious level of verbalization as individuals and groups use them to express their fundamental understanding of themselves and their existence in the world. But they also operate at a more primal level as they are accepted without conscious thought as expressing the way things are, or can be, or should be.[17]

---

[17]A recent discussion of the natural function of myth in the lives of men and women even today is Campbell, *Myths to Live By*. As examples of the power of myths, Campbell cites "the economics of the Pyramids, the cathedrals of the Middle Ages, Hindus starving to death with edible cattle strolling all around them, or the history of Israel, from the time of Saul to right now" (p. 22).

The New Testament is a rich source of myths, and this is not the least of its importance. But it also blends history with these myths and thus introduces a new factor. The Christian myth of origins is built around a historical figure crucified by a Roman official whose name has been found on an inscription. The New Testament interweaves myth and history, which introduces a new element into the discussion. In general, myths do not involve an element of history; they normally take place in a special kind of mythical time, like the seven "days" of God's creation of the world. The history they narrate, like the history of the Flood in Genesis 6–10, is usually not a history that critically-minded historians can investigate. But the myths of the Passover and of the cross as redemptive are different. Both involve events that took place in historical time, the flight of Jews from Egypt and the crucifixion of Jesus. In some way both myths involve an interrelationship between myth and history.

This interrelationship between myth and history may be considered in three ways: (a) the element of correlation between the claims of the myth and the factual data of the history; (b) the use of myth to interpret and give meaning to history; (c) the history itself as remembered and retold becoming the bearer of the myth. In our discussion we find that these three possibilities are necessarily interwoven, but it is convenient to use them as three approaches to the single problem of the interrelationship of myth and history in the New Testament.

## A Preliminary Point:
## The Meanings of "History" in Any Discussion of Myth and History

Before any discussion of myth and history can be meaningful, a further point must be made. There is a range of meanings in the word "history," a range we ought to discuss with some care.

### History as the historical

History means first of all factual history, things "as they actually happened." Here we are concerned with "getting at the facts," with reconstructing the data in a way that would satisfy a court of law. A major concern of New Testament scholarship in modern times has been to investigate the factual data of Jesus and the early church, and the results of such an investigation are the presupposition of any contemporary understanding of the New Testament.

### History as the historic

Historians everywhere have sought to reach historical figures or events important to them or to their culture, to establish the facts about every possible kind of figure or event from the past. It is the natural tendency of modern man to ask for "the facts" and to value them above all else in attempting to understand his own experience of his past. But facts by themselves are not enough for evaluation or understanding. They have to be interpreted; their significance has to be appreciated in the broader context of the totality of human experience. This brings us to a second meaning that can be given to the word *history*, history as the "historic."

As an example outside New Testament studies, there have been many American presidents, and each has made many public speeches: in one sense all are equally "historical." But if we think in terms of their significance for the future, there were few presidents as "historic" and few presidential addresses as "historic" as Abraham Lincoln and his Gettysburg Address. So also the cross of Jesus is as "historical" as that of any other Jew executed by the Romans, but it is also "historic" in the significance it came to have for future generations in a way the others did not.

We are using "historical" to designate history as what actually happened and "historic" to designate the ongoing significance of a person or event for subsequent generations. German has two nouns for history, and German scholars speak of the former as *Historie* (adjective: *historisch*) and of the latter as *Geschichte* (adjective: *geschichtlich*). Though English does not have two nouns, it has two adjectives, and we have used them. Regardless of the words, the distinction is real and important. Every person or event is historical in that there are facts to be established, and every person or event is historic in that there is an ongoing significance for subsequent generations. But even this distinction does not exhaust the significance of the word *history*: there is also history as "historicity."

## History as the historicity of human existence in the world

Every man and woman lives out his or her life in concrete historical circumstances, and the possibilities for that life are in no small measure determined by those circumstances. An Asian peasant has one set of possibilities; a western European, a second; a black American, a third; and so on. Moreover, the possibilities for that life are affected by external historical occurrences: wars, technological advances, natural catastrophes, political decisions. All these and many more can change one's life, sometimes dramatically and drastically. We speak of this as the "historicity" of human existence in the world. But human existence in the world is affected not only by historical circumstances and events, but also by the impact of ideas and the interpretation given to the data present to one's consciousness at all kinds of levels. So, to return to our primary example, we may speak of the historical Jesus as he actually was, or we may speak of the historic Jesus as interpreted in his significance for future generations. But then we must go on to recognize that there is another side to the historic Jesus; that is, there is the historicity of human existence in the world as affected by the historic Jesus and by the response of an individual to the impact of that aspect of Jesus.

Each of these possibilities in the meaning of the word *history* is important in discussing myth and history in the New Testament, and we now turn to that relationship.

## The Relationship Between Myth and History in the New Testament

### *The element of correlation between the claims of the myth and the factual data of the history*

The immediately obvious thing about the New Testament myths is that they are built around historical personages and events. The central characters actually lived, and their lives are subject to historical investigation. The ministry of Jesus, the spread of the church in the Hellenistic world, the fall of Jerusalem, and the persecution of Christians that triggered the writing of the book of Revelation are all events that can be the subject of historical investigation. At the same time, each of these persons and events becomes part of one or more of the myths in which the New Testament is so rich.

Let us take as our example the myth of the cross of Jesus as effecting human redemption, the central feature of the Christian sacred meal. Jesus is a historical person, and his death on the cross is a historical event; both are proper subjects for historical investigation. Our question then becomes, what are the consequences of the results of such historical investigation for the functioning adequacy of the myth? Or to put it another way, does the historical data about Jesus and his cross affect the subsequent influence of the myth at the level of the historicity of human existence in the world?

In one way this question is no sooner asked than answered, because the general study of the history of religions, including Christianity, has shown that there is no discernible correlation between the factual element of history and the functioning adequacy of a myth, and we have already acknowledged that this is the case for Christian myth. Christian myths, like all myths, function precisely because they are myth, and the only kind of history by which they may be judged or validated is that of the history of an individual or people in the concrete circumstances of life in the world. In the final analysis, myths may be judged true or false, valid or invalid, effective or ineffective, only by judging their impact at that level; with most myths that is the end of the matter. So in the myth of the cross of Jesus as redemptive the only criterion of truth or validity is its effectiveness on the historicity of the life in the world of the participants in the Christian sacred meal. Whether the narrative recited at the meal, and indeed the passion narrative itself, is historically factual is simply irrelevant. But another factor is at work in this particular myth, as in some others in the New Testament: it is not only claimed that the central figure in the myth was a historical person, but also that *he exemplified the reality that the myth claims to mediate.*

Historical data with regard to Jesus himself is extraordinarily difficult to reach, as we shall see in chapter 12; the evidence seems to indicate, however, that Jesus did not make any claims for himself, but focused attention entirely upon God and the proclamation of the Kingdom of God. The New Testament writers are a different matter: they make extensive claims for him, one being that he exemplified the myth of redemption. In understanding his cross in terms of Isaiah 53, they necessarily imply that he died with noble dignity and a sure confidence in God, as the righteous servant is in Isaiah 53 described as dying; this claim is made explicitly in 1 Pet 2:21–25 and implicitly in every use of Isaiah 53 in the New Testament. But the manner of Jesus' dying, unlike the significance of his death in the myth, is subject to factual historical investigation. What would happen were it shown that Jesus did not accept his death with the noble dignity claimed in 1 Peter and described in the passion narratives themselves? What if it could be shown that Jesus was carried to the cross railing against God and his fate? It would surely become difficult to accept the myth, because the claim that Jesus exemplified the myth in his own life, which brings an aspect of the myth into the realm of history as the historical, would be in fact false.

Not all aspects of the narrative of a myth where the myth moves into history as the historical are equally important. For example, the narrative of the Christian sacred meal gives details of Jesus arranging the meal, breaking bread, passing wine to the disciples, saying various words, and so on. All this is in the realm of the historical and has been subject to investigation, with almost entirely negative results. Most New Testament scholars would agree that the narrative is a product of the piety of early Christianity, excepting possibly a core of the words spoken over the bread and the wine, and many scholars, including myself, would ascribe even those words to early Christianity. But the effectiveness or validity of the myth is not weakened, since these "historical details" are either the narrative setting of the myth (the arrangements and so on), or the verbal expression of the symbol (the words over the bread and wine). In neither case is it claimed that these "historical" elements *embody* the myth. They provide the narrative setting or express verbally the central symbol, but they are not affected by an element of historical factuality or by the lack of it.

Let us pursue the matter further by taking another example. In the Acts of the Apostles there is the myth of the necessary move of the center of Christian faith and experience from Jerusalem to Rome. As chapter 9 makes clear, it is important to the author of Acts that his readers come to terms with the destruction of Jerusalem and find a new geographical center for their faith. This center is now Rome, and Christians may now understand themselves and their place and responsibility in the world by accepting the divine necessity for the destruction of Jerusalem and the consequent shift of the center of Christian faith and experience. The foundation myth of Christian origins demands that there be an abandonment of Jerusalem and a movement to Rome. The author of Acts is not the author of this myth, which would have developed in the churches he writes for in response to the urgent needs of Christians in the world following the destruction of Jerusalem. But although he has not created it, the author has certainly accepted it and given it a most vivid narrative expression.

One aspect of the narrative expression of this myth is to be found in the three accounts of the conversion of Paul given in Acts 9:1–30; 22:4–21; 26:9–23. In each of these Paul begins his witness as a Christian in Jerusalem immediately after his conversion, and each of them indicates that he will move into the wider world of the Gentiles. Moreover, the narrative of Acts itself deliberately ends with Paul preaching "quite openly and unhindered" in Rome itself (Acts 28:31). The purpose of the myth is admirably served: Paul is the exemplary Christian apostle, and it is important that his witness begin in Jerusalem and end in Rome. But the beginning of his witness in Jerusalem and its ending in Rome are historical facts subject to historical investigation. They have indeed been investigated and have not been substantiated. According to his own account in Galatians 1 and 2, Paul did not go up to Jerusalem until long after his conversion, and he could never have witnessed there until he was well established as a missionary to the Gentile world. Furthermore, all our evidence indicates that he went to Rome as a prisoner about to suffer martyrdom. The two years of preaching "quite openly and unhindered" in Rome serve the needs of the myth very well, but their historical factuality is dubious.

Again, as in the case of the narrative and words of the account of the Last Supper between Jesus and his disciples, the validity of the myth is not affected. A myth can *distort* history, as myth has certainly distorted the history of Jesus' last meal with his disciples and as myth has distorted the accounts of Paul's conversion. Distortion does not matter unless it is claimed that the history *embodies* the myth. The claim that Jesus embodied the myth of the Christian sacred meal (the Last Supper) made the manner of his death significant to the myth, but not the historical details of the meal. Similarly with Paul. Since he is the exemplary Christian witness, it would indeed matter could it be shown that he was not at all interested in the Christian mission to the Gentiles. But the narrative details of his conversion are important only as expressions of the myth, and as such they are not subject to historical verification. A Paul hostile to the Christian mission to the Gentiles would be fatal to the myth of origins of the Christian church, and a Jesus carried to his cross railing against God and his fate would destroy the myth of the cross as redemptive, but the narrative details of the supper or of Paul's conversion do not matter except as expressions of the myth.

The element of correlation between the claims of the myth and the factual data of the history in the New Testament is limited but significant. The significant historical data is what concerns an aspect of the history that is claimed to embody the myth. That the myth can, and indeed does, distort the history is of no significance to the functioning adequacy of the myth as myth.

## Myth as the interpretation of history

A striking element in the New Testament is the fact that it narrates a whole series of events as God's revelation of himself to man and of the working out of man's redemption by God: the coming of Jesus into the world, his life and teaching, his death and resurrection-ascension, the church's possession of his spirit, the experience of Christian witness-martyrs paralleling the passion of Jesus, the certainty of his parousia as judge and redeemer, and so on. The individual variations among the various books are immense, but all can be interpreted as seeing this complex of events as the central aspect of Christian faith.

Contemplating such a list of events held to be central to Christian faith reveals a difference between the first century and the twentieth. For a man of the first century these events hold together because they are all important at the level of his existence in the world and at the level of his existence before God. But in twentieth-century man's distinctions between myth and history, some of these events are historical—the coming of Jesus into the world, his life and teaching and death, the various religious enthusiasms in the early church—whereas others are myth—the resurrection-ascension, the parousia. Even as sophisticated a man of the New Testament as the author of Luke-Acts could write about all these things in exactly the same way. On the one hand, he has "gone over the whole course of these events in detail" and "written a connected narrative" to give "authentic knowledge" about these matters (Luke 1:3–4, NEB), and then he firmly establishes the birth of Jesus as a factual event in the context of a census taken for taxation purposes (Luke 2:1–7). On the other hand, he is personally responsible for introducing into the New Testament narratives of the myth of the ascension as separate from the resurrection, and hence for the ascension narrative of Acts 1:9–11. But today we have to distinguish between the factual history of Roman officials ordering a census for taxation purposes and the myth of Jesus ascending to heaven and disappearing from the disciples' sight on a cloud. That they are held together by the author of Luke-Acts means they are related events so far as the New Testament is concerned. The question is, are they related "events" so far as we are concerned?

The answer surely lies in the myth that interprets the history. The "events" are related at the level of the historicity of human existence in the world. The one interprets the other at the level of its meaning for human life in the world, and hence they can be spoken of in the same breath. The birth of Jesus did change forever the possibilities for a man living in the world; his ascension is a way of saying that there is now a futurity for human existence in the world that was not there before. The myth is a vividly pictorial way of interpreting the history.

Consider also how the New Testament writers use narrative to interpret events. In the crucifixion, for example, Mark has narrative details taken from Psalms 69 and 22, which are concerned with the righteous sufferer and God's vindication of him: Mark 15:23, the offering of the wine mingled with myrrh (= Psa 69:21); 15:24, the dividing of the clothes (= Psa 22:18); and 15:29, the mocking (= Psa 22:7). In his turn Matthew adds another, Matt 27:43, where the words of the taunting are from Psa 22:8. These narrative details are not "true" at the level of factual history but are included because the crucifixion of Jesus is being interpreted as the death of a righteous sufferer whom God vindicated, and hence as the fulfillment of Psalms 22 and 69. In that sense (the only sense that interests the evangelists Mark and Matthew), they are true, and we may therefore say that the narrative interprets the event. Another striking example is Luke's use of Mark's reference to the false witnesses at the trial of Jesus, Mark 14:57–58. Luke is following and using the gospel of Mark at this point, but when he edits the Markan trial scene for his own use he omits this reference (Luke 22:71), only to use it in his account of the trial of Stephen (Acts 6:11). He does this to make the point that the passion of Stephen, the first martyr-witness, is an echo and imitation of the passion of Jesus. That the suffering of early Christians echoes and imitates the passion of Jesus is, of course, a well-known feature of early Christian martyrologies and martyrological thinking. The New Testament expresses it by using features of the passion of Jesus in the account of Stephen's martyrdom; the narrative is interpreting the event. In the New Testament, therefore, the myth interprets the history.

### History itself functioning as myth

If the myth interprets the history, or to put it another way, if the narrative interprets the event, we can now claim that the history narrated in the New Testament is history as the historic (*Geschichte*), and, furthermore, that history as the historic necessarily involves history as the historical and the historical as interpreted by myth. Finally, history as the historic itself comes to function as myth. To speak of history as the historic is to speak of the narration of events that brings out the significance of those events for future generations. The passion narratives in the gospels deliberately narrate the story of the death of Jesus in order to interpret it and to express what the gospel writers, the evangelists, understand to be its significance for them and their readers. The events are, as we have seen, of different orders: some are historical, some are mythical, and some no doubt are simply legendary. But the total configuration is historic; it is history narrated to bring out its significance for the writer and his readers.

Narration of history is almost always concerned with the historic. Factual history belongs in the scholar's study and the law court, and even there it is difficult to attain. The natural tendency is always to narrate in such a way as to express what one holds to be significant in the events, and this is expressly stated in the New Testament. In Mark 1:1 the use of "the gospel of Jesus Christ" indicates that what is to follow is in some sense a sermon, designed to elicit the response of faith; in Luke 1:4 what is to follow is designed to instruct Theophilus in "the truth concerning the things of which you have been informed"; and John 20:31 sums up the purpose of the preceding narratives as having been written so that the reader "may believe that Jesus is the Christ, the Son of God." In our words, the events are narrated to bring out their significance for faith; the history in them is history in the sense of the historic.

But history in the sense of the historic necessarily shades over into myth, since the story of Jesus is told as the focal point of God's revelation of himself to men, the story of the cross of Jesus is told as the means of man's redemption, the story of the movement of the church from Jerusalem to Rome is told as the story of an essential aspect of the founding of the church, and so on. The time concerned has become a sacred time; the events narrated make possible the reality of Christian existence in the world: the history itself has become myth.

## THE NEW TESTAMENT AS TRADITION AND AS INTERPRETATION OF TRADITION

The texts of the New Testament are to a large extent the result of a long period in which a tradition was established and in which that tradition was instantly interpreted, added to, and further reinterpreted. The parables of Jesus were remembered and handed on as tradition within the Christian communities, but as they were handed on they were reinterpreted both by changes within the texts of the parables themselves and also by the addition of new conclusions or explanations to them.[18] Then, when the evangelists incorporated them into their gospels, they introduced further changes to make them express the meaning they saw in them.[19] Further examples of this process are the apocalyptic discourse in Mark 13 and the hymn Paul quotes in Phil 2:6–11. The discourse in Mark 13 was developed and interpreted in the Christian community before the gospel of Mark was written and then the evangelist himself reinterpreted what he received: giving it a setting, adding a section in which the sufferings of Christians exactly parallel what happened to Jesus in his passion (Mark 13:9), and so on. In Phil 2:6–11, Paul quotes a hymn from the tradition of the church, but he reinterprets as he quotes, for example, by referring specifically to the cross by adding "even death on a cross," a phrase not found in the original hymn. A fundamental aspect of the New Testament texts is that they are in no small part the end product of a long and constant process of interpretation and reinterpretation. At the same time, their authors were by no means content simply to hand on what they had themselves received, but further reinterpreted the tradition they received. The process does not necessarily end with the production of a given text; Matthew and Luke freely reinterpret a text they themselves received, the gospel of Mark.

Recognizing this fact about the texts of the New Testament not only adds great complexity to New Testament scholarship, but is critical to understanding the nature of the New Testament itself. The New Testament is on one hand the product of the vision of reality of individual authors, but it is also the deposit of a long period of Christian experience and Christian tradition. Both these elements are important in understanding the texts themselves, and they enable us not only to focus our attention on the faith and understanding of the authors, but also to reach behind them into earlier stages of primitive

---

[18]This process is carefully described by Jeremias in his book *The Parables of Jesus*, especially chapter 2, "The Return to Jesus from the Primitive Church."
[19]A very good example of this is to be found in Kingsbury, *The Parables of Jesus in Matthew 13*.

Christianity. Furthermore, this constant process of interpretation and reinterpretation of traditional material indicates the dynamic nature of early Christianity. These Christians did not simply depend on their traditions for guidance, but rather interpreted those traditions to give them new meaning in light of their experience as Christians in the world and the expectations they were developing.

Let us examine how the men and women of the New Testament use their own sacred scriptures—what we would call the Old Testament and the Apocrypha, together with several other texts that didn't make it into either the Jewish or Christian version of the canon, such as the book of Enoch. In the speech of Peter at Pentecost in Acts 2:14–36 there is a lengthy quotation from the prophet Joel (Acts 2:17–21 = Joel 2:28–32). But the fact that the text of the book of Joel has been reinterpreted in the speech is shown by significant additions and changes. In Acts 2:17 "in the last days" and "God declares" have been added to Joel 2:28. In Acts 2:18 "they shall prophesy" has been added to Joel 2:29. In Acts 2:19 there are two small but very significant additions to the text of Joel 2:30—"above" and "beneath." The text of Joel has only one set of portents or signs, the cosmic indications of the coming of "the day of the Lord." But in Acts there are two such sets of signs, those in the sky *above* and those on the earth *beneath*. The significance of this change is apparent when in Acts 2:22 (NEB) Jesus of Nazareth is "a man singled out by God and made known to you through miracles, portents, and signs, which God worked among you through him, as you well know." The signs in the sky above remain outstanding, to be fulfilled at some point in the future, but those on the earth below have been given in the coming of Jesus, the first act of the great divine drama. The text is reinterpreted in the light of immediate experience and imminent expectation. The same is true of the two earlier additions. "In the last days" expresses the Christians' conviction that the text applies to them and that they are the community of the End Time; they are experiencing the first act of the divine drama that will shortly reach its climax in the (second) coming of Jesus to judge the world, the parousia. "And they shall prophesy" emphasizes a matter very important to early Christianity, the possession of the spirit of prophecy, the sure sign that they were indeed the community of the End Time.

# FURTHER READING

For the formation of the canon of the N.T. (i.e., the process by which the collection of books that make up the N.T. came to be the one book of the N.T.), see Appendix 3 at the end of the book.

In this volume the word *text* is used in the literary critical sense of a written (or orally fixed) text, and so we speak of the N.T. as a "text" and a collection of "texts." Another use of the word, more common in N.T. scholarship, is to refer to the original written text of the N.T. as we know it or can reconstruct it from our various sources in manuscripts and versions (early translations). This matter is briefly discussed in Appendix 4 at the end of the book.

For the work on the N.T. as proclamation and parenesis, there is no need to go beyond Martin Dibelius' classic, *From Tradition to Gospel*.

The dilemma of the nineteenth century with regard to the gospels as factual history, the introduction of the idea of the gospels as myth, the subsequent reaction of an ever more sophisticated attempt to derive history from the gospels, and the final counter reaction in Bultmann's return to the kerygma of the church have all been reviewed in Kee, *Jesus in History*, pp. 1–25. Kee, however, does not go into the question of myth in its present form nor into Bultmann's demythologizing program.

Bultmann's view of myth is presented in two works already mentioned:

Bartsch, ed., *Kerygma and Myth*.
Bultmann, *Jesus Christ and Mythology*.

For a more detailed discussion of Bultmann, his view of myth, and his demythologizing program, see Perrin, *The Promise of Bultmann*, especially pp. 74–84, "Demythologizing and the Existential Interpretation of the Documents of Faith."

Discussions of Bultmann, his view of myth and his demythologizing program, are of course legion. Among the more readily available are:

Althaus, *The So-Called Kerygma and the Historical Jesus*. Althaus is a German scholar more conservative than Bultmann.
Cairns, *A Gospel Without Myth? Bultmann's Challenge to the Preacher*.
Gogarten, *Demythologizing and History*. Gogarten is a German scholar sympathetic to Bultmann.
Henderson, *Myth in the New Testament*.
Jaspers and Bultmann, *Myth and Christianity: An Inquiry into the Possibility of Religion without Myth*. A most important debate between Bultmann and a leading existentialist philosopher more radical than he.
Jones, *Christology and Myth in the New Testament*.
Macquarrie, *The Scope of Demythologizing: Bultmann and His Critics*. A perceptive discussion of the issues by a philosophical theologian.
Ogden, *Christ Without Myth*. The most important English language discussion of Bultmann's theology and program.

Eliade's view of myth is to be found in his *Encyclopaedia Britannica* article, quoted in the text, and in the following books:

Eliade, *The Quest; History and Meaning in Religion*; especially pp. 72–87, "Cosmogonic Myth and 'Sacred History.'"
———, *Cosmos and History: The Myth of the Eternal Return*.
———, *Myth and Reality*.

The present writer knows of no other systematic discussion of "the New Testament as Myth and History."

The section on the "New Testament as Tradition and as Interpretation of Tradition" is built on insights gained through the historical critical disciplines of form criticism and redaction criticism. On these see Perrin, *What is Redaction Criticism?* and the literature given there.

The process of constant reinterpretation that lies behind the apocalyptic discourse in Mark 13 is discussed in Hartmann, *Prophecy Interpreted.*

The reinterpretation of Old Testament texts as they are used in the N.T. texts is particularly discussed in Lindars, *New Testament Apologetic.*

The "Wailing Wall," a remnant of the
Jerusalem Temple destroyed by the Romans.

# 3

# A Theological History of New Testament Christianity

To understand the works that constitute the New Testament it is necessary to know something of the history, especially the theological history, of the churches in and for which they were produced. Historical information about the Christian movement down to A.D. 140, the approximate date of the writing of 2 Peter, the last work to come into the New Testament canon, is hard to come by. Early Christians lived in expectation of the imminent end of the world and so were uninterested in chronicling the events of their own history. In that state one chronicles the events of contemporary history, if at all, only in the form of apocalyptic symbolism, as in the book of Daniel, in Mark 13, or in the book of Revelation. Significantly the author of Luke-Acts does not share this imminent expectation of the end, and he is the first to write anything approaching a chronicle of the early church.

Furthermore, the narratives in the New Testament are didactic, that is, they are intended to instruct and exhort rather than record. The story they tell is history dramatized to give it meaning, to involve the reader in the necessity for decision, and to inspire him with a desire to emulate. It is easy to understand how factual accuracy became an early victim of these circumstances. Wherever the Acts of the Apostles covers the same ground as some autobiographical information given in the letters of Paul, the two accounts are difficult to reconcile. Acts is not intended to give biographical information about the apostle Paul but to present him in his significance for Christian faith and to present him as a challenge for emulation.

The New Testament itself is our only source, and it is difficult to reconstruct historical information from its narratives. But winning such information is not impossible.[1] Once we have learned to read them critically, we can learn a good deal from the narratives, usually indirectly. In Acts 8:1 the author reports a

---

[1] Progress in the reconstruction of the history of New Testament Christianity concerning Paul is now conveniently represented in English by Bornkamm's *Paul*, of which we shall make unhesitating use in what follows.

violent persecution of the church in Jerusalem and says that "they were all scattered . . . except the apostles." That the Jewish authorities would distinguish between the apostles and other members of the Jerusalem church is unlikely, but "except the apostles" does indicate some kind of distinction. Now in Acts 6:1–6 the author reports a dispute between "the Hebrews" (i.e., Jews speaking a Semitic language) and "the Hellenists" (i.e. Greek-speaking Jews) over the distribution of the property held by the community in common. Seven are appointed to take care of the matter, all with Greek names and hence presumably "Hellenists." But these seven are never reported as serving the function for which they were allegedly selected. They appear only as evangelists, and their leader, Stephen, is martyred for a speech criticizing his fellow Jews; this martyrdom is the beginning of a violent persecution of the church. Modern scholars have concluded that there was a real distinction in earliest Jerusalem Christianity between aggressive Hellenistic Jewish Christians, who tended to be critical of Judaism as such, and more conservative Jerusalem Christians, who differed from their fellow Jews only in holding Jesus to have been the Messiah. The aggressive Hellenistic Jewish Christians were persecuted and driven out of Jerusalem; the conservative Jewish Christians were allowed to remain. The former would have been driven out of Jerusalem, not because they claimed that Jesus was the Messiah, but because they developed a criticism of Judaism and of its Law.

Another help in reconstructing a theological history of earliest Christianity is that form criticism can isolate units of tradition and inquire into their *Sitz* (setting, functional context) in the tradition of the church before the writing of Paul's letters or the gospels. To this we may now add the ability of the redaction critic to establish the theology of the evangelists and of the source Q, which gives us a firm hold at various points in the theological history of New Testament Christianity. We owe to form criticism such ability as we have to distinguish the various stages through which the Christian movement must have gone before Paul wrote I Thessalonians or Mark his gospel, and we owe to redaction criticism our ability to speak with a fair degree of certainty about the periods represented by Q and the synoptic evangelists.

A major source for our knowledge of the earlier period is, of course, the various allusions in the letters of Paul. Once we stopped the vain and misleading attempt to harmonize Paul's letters with Acts and to interpret one in the light of the other, then the way opened for real progress to be made.


# THE FALL OF JERUSALEM
# AND THE DELAY OF THE PAROUSIA

An important factor in New Testament Christianity to which sufficient attention has not been paid is the significance of the fall of Jerusalem to the Romans and the destruction of the Temple in A.D. 70. Jerusalem and its Temple were holy to Christians (many of whom were Jews) as well as to Jews, and the Pauline letters attest to the special status of the church at Jerusalem and its emissaries. The destruction of Jerusalem and the Temple by the

Gentiles sent a shock wave through the Jewish-Christian world whose importance it is impossible to exaggerate. Indeed, much of the subsequent literature both of Judaism and Christianity took the form it did precisely in an attempt to come to terms with the catastrophe of A.D. 70. Deprived of the Holy City and the Temple, the Jews turned to the synagogue and the Law, and the result was the Mishnah and eventually the Talmuds. Deprived of the Sacred Place they shared with the Jews through Jesus and the Jerusalem church, the Christians turned to the time of Jesus as a Sacred Time and produced the gospels. Nothing was ever to be the same again for either Jews or Christians.

Another important factor in the historical situation of New Testament Christianity is the negative one of what is technically known as the "delay of the parousia." The first Christians were dominated by the expectation of the End, of the coming of Jesus as Son of Man or Lord to judge and to redeem, to destroy and to remake. They expected this to happen imminently, in a matter of months at most, and with this event their world would end and another, different and more perfect, would be created. The evangelist Matthew uses the Greek term _parousia,_ a technical term for the visit of a high official, for this expected and anticipated event, and it has passed into New Testament scholarship as a technical term. But the months and years passed by, and the parousia simply did not take place. It became necessary, therefore, for the New Testament Christians to come to terms with this delay of the parousia, and the attempts to do so have left a deep impression on the New Testament texts. Broadly speaking, there were three ways that were taken. In the first place the expectation was simply reiterated even more firmly, as if doubts could be overcome by using a louder voice. This is essentially the procedure of 2 Peter. A second way was to push the parousia into the more distant future, though still maintaining the expectation, and then to make theological sense of the extended interim period. This is essentially the procedure followed by the evangelists Matthew and, especially, Luke. The third way was to claim that the parousia had in effect already taken place, that the cross and resurrection of Jesus were in fact the "final" (the technical term would be "eschatological") events and that the "new" life was in fact and in practice to be known by Christians now. This is the main thrust of the gospel of John.

# THE RAPID SPREAD OF CHRISTIANITY
# INTO THE HELLENISTIC WORLD

New Testament Christianity spread very rapidly from Palestine into the Hellenistic world and from Jerusalem to Rome. Jesus proclaimed the Kingdom of God in Palestine in Aramaic and died in Jerusalem, according to Mark 15:34, with an Aramaic version of Psalm 22:1 on his lips. Within twenty years Paul writes in Greek to the Christians in Thessalonica and can assume that they await expectantly the appearance from heaven of God's Son, "Jesus our deliverer from the terrors of judgment to come" (1 Thess 1:10, NEB). In twenty years we have moved from Aramaic to Greek, from Palestine to Europe, from the Jewish world to the Hellenistic, and from the proclamation by Jesus of the

Kingdom of God as God's eschatological event to the proclamation of Jesus by the church as God's eschatological event. This is no small shift; we describe it in what follows.

Jesus proclaimed the Kingdom of God; i.e., he proclaimed the imminence of the irruption of God into history to judge and to renew, to destroy and to remake. The whole emphasis of his message was on God and his activity, and not on himself or his person. The Romans crucified him as a potentially dangerous revolutionary who might lead the Jewish people to war against Rome, promising that if they would begin the war, God himself would end it in their favor. This kind of thinking is now amply attested to in the War Scroll (1 QM) from Qumran, as well as by the fact that in A.D. 66 and 132 such revolts did break out against Rome: in 66 the Jewish War, which led to the fall of Jerusalem and the destruction of its Temple in 70; and in 132 the revolt led by an acknowledged Messiah, Simon bar Cochba (Simeon ben Kosebah), which was put down by the Romans in 135.

Earliest Christianity was born of the conviction that God had vindicated Jesus out of his death, that he had raised him from the dead and taken him into heaven. Moreover, the expectations associated with the coming of the Kingdom of God—the judgment of evil, the reward of the good, the destruction and remaking of the world—were now associated with the expectation of a return of Jesus from heaven as God's envoy, as Lord, as Son of Man. This conviction and this expectation shaped Palestinian Jewish Christianity, to a description of which we now turn.

## THE PHASES OF NEW TESTAMENT CHRISTIANITY

### Palestinian Jewish Christianity

The Christian church began as a sect within ancient Judaism, a group of Jews differing from their fellow Jews only in that they believed the crucified Jesus had been the Messiah and that God had vindicated him by raising him from death into heaven, from whence he would shortly come as judge and redeemer. In the early chapters of Acts and in the references to the Jerusalem church and its leaders in Paul's letters, expecially Galatians 2, we can sense the existence of a group of devout Jewish Christians in Jerusalem, practicing the religion of their fathers—attending the Temple regularly and obeying the Jewish Law in all its rigor with regard to circumcision, food taboos, the Sabbath rest, and all else that the interpreters of the Law held to be well pleasing to God.

We must recognize that the Jews of Palestine thought of themselves as living in an occupied land. Theirs was the Holy Land, and the Holy of Holies in their Jerusalem Temple was the truly Sacred Place. Their God was creator and ruler of the world and all within it, and he had given them his Law, the Torah, the five books of Moses, Genesis through Deuteronomy, in order that they might know how to live in his world rightly and so be blessed in that living. But they were not in fact blessed in that living. Wicked, lawless Gentiles, the Romans, occupied the Holy Land and controlled the Sacred Place. Their own rulers, Herod the Great and his sons, were Idumeans and therefore at best half-breeds;

moreover, they ruled only at Roman pleasure and by virtue of their own rigorous support of Rome. By the time of Jesus and the early church, even this situation had worsened, for Herod's son, Archelaus, to whom the rule of Jerusalem and Judea was entrusted, proved unfit and was deposed in favor of direct Roman rule through a prefect or procurator in A.D. 6. So Jerusalem and the Temple were directly under Roman control, and the High Priests, the direct representatives of the people before God and of God to the people, held their office by Roman fiat.

This intolerable state of affairs could be brought to an end only by God, and, God being God, it could only be that he would bring it to an end speedily. The Jews believed this; they believed that God would shortly intervene directly in the affairs of world history.[2] They looked especially for an anointed one, a "Messiah" (i.e., anointed as God's chosen one), a "Son of David" (i.e., in the succession of David), a "prophet like Moses," through whom God would act. Waiting for such a leader, they were anxious to follow anyone who proclaimed himself to be such in taking up arms against Rome, believing that this would be the sign to begin a war that God would end. In the meantime they prepared themselves for these eschatological events by adhering to the Law of God ever more strictly. Thus, they not only prepared themselves for the coming of the End and assured themselves a favorable verdict at the judgment, but they believed they were helping to hasten the End, for they were convinced that God would act the more speedily in response to the anguish of his people if his people proved themselves especially worthy by obeying his Law.

The earliest Jewish Christians in Jerusalem shared all these convictions, with two differences. In the first place, they believed that Jesus of Nazareth was the Messiah, the anointed one of God, and that he had, therefore, perfected the interpretation of the Law of God. They were eager to fulfill the will of God as revealed in his Law as that Law had been interpreted by Jesus. To this end they collected stories of Jesus' interpretations of the Law as their model and pattern, and since they believed that Jesus was risen from the dead and his spirit was at work in their midst, they also created such stories. The Jesus who had interpreted the Law for them was still doing so, and the guidance of his spirit could be cast in the form of a story about Jesus instructing his disciples, a fact that had momentous consequences for the future shape of Christian literature.

We have no direct literary remains of the church at Jerusalem, and the most we can do is suggest what might, and indeed we can almost say, what must have happened. In Mark 10:2–12 we read the following:

> And Pharisees came up and in order to test him asked, "Is it lawful for a man to divorce his wife?" He answered them, "What did Moses command you?" They said, "Moses allowed a man to write a certificate of divorce, and to put her away." But Jesus said to them, "For your hardness of heart he wrote you this commandment. But from the beginning of creation, 'God made them male and female.' 'For this reason a man shall leave his father and mother

---

[2]This is the "apocalyptic hope" of ancient Judaism discussed in more detail in the next chapter.

and be joined to his wife, and the two shall become one flesh.' So they are no longer two but one flesh. What therefore God has joined together, let not man put asunder."

And in the house the disciples asked him again about this matter. And he said to them, "Whoever divorces his wife and marries another, commits adultery against her; and if she divorces her husband and marries another, she commits adultery."

This is an extraordinarily interesting passage. The idea represented in verses 10–12 of Jesus teaching his disciples privately is a characteristic literary device of the evangelist Mark and very probably of the tradition before him, whereby the teaching of Jesus was reinterpreted in the church. The device was legitimate: the spirit of Jesus was leading the church to a new understanding of the truth he had taught. So we have to think of verses 2–9 as the original narrative, and then of verses 10, 11, and 12 as additional reinterpretations.

Verses 2–9 radically reinterpret Jewish teaching about divorce and make it much more rigorous. The Jewish teaching was based on Deut 24:1.

"When a man takes a wife and marries her, if then she finds no favor in his eyes because he has found some indecency in her, and he writes her a bill of divorce and puts it in her hand and sends her out of his house, and she departs out of his house . . ."

There were three interpretations of this verse current in the Judaism of New Testament times. One, associated with Rabbi Shammai, emphasized the "indecency" and claimed that divorce was permissible only for sexual misbehavior, a view the evangelist Matthew (Matt 19:9 with its addition "except for unchastity") agrees with completely. A more liberal view, associated with Rabbi Hillel, claimed that "indecency" could refer to anything that gave the husband serious offense, even (deliberately) burning his meal! A third view, connected with Rabbi Aqiba, emphasized "finds no favor in his eyes" and argued that divorce was permissible on the grounds that the wife no longer pleased her husband.[3] Mark 10:2–9 argues against these views by claiming that Deut 24:1 should be regarded as canceled out by Gen 1:27 (Mark 10:6) and 2:24 (Mark 10:7–8) so that divorce is not permissible at all. This conservative view would certainly have been characteristic of the church in Jerusalem and may well go back to that church. (It may also go back to Jesus himself, but a discussion of that possibility, itself actually very real, would take us too far afield.)

Verses 10–12 are also extremely interesting. Verses 10–11 draw out the implications of verses 2–9 and make a specific application; they could have been added either in Palestinian Jewish Christian tradition or in Hellenistic Jewish Mission Christianity (which is described on page 49). But verse 12 could only have been added in the Hellenistic world, because only in the Greco-Roman world, and not in the Jewish, was a woman free to divorce her husband and remarry. So verse 12 has certainly been added by Hellenistic Jewish Mission Christianity (purely Gentile Christianity was not that

---

[3]Manson, *Teaching of Jesus*, pp. 292–95, with reference to the Mishnah tractate Gittim 9:10.

interested in reinterpretation of the Jewish Law). In all this we have, therefore, an example of the growth of Christian tradition. Verses 2–9 represent the conservative and rigorous interpretation of the Jewish Law characteristic of the Jerusalem Christian church. Verses 10–12 represent successive adaptations and reinterpretations as the church and its tradition move out into the Hellenistic, Greco-Roman world, and Matthew's version (Matt 19:9) represents assimilation to the strictest of the characteristically Jewish views. An important point is that in all this the *form* of a story about Jesus and his opponents is strictly maintained.

The conservative, legalistic aspects of the Jerusalem church are well attested to by the Pauline letters and by the fact that major representatives of that church were left unmolested when other Christians were driven out of Jerusalem by persecution. Lacking direct literary remains of this church, anything we say is necessarily speculative, but a further and very real possibility is that this church is responsible for the first connected narrative of the arrest, trial, and death of Jesus, a "passion narrative," and also for the interpretation of the Christian sacred meal, the "Lord's Supper," which Paul struggles to establish in Corinth (I Corinthians 11). It would be the Jerusalem Christians who would be constantly brought face to face with the physical circumstances of the passion of Jesus and consequently with the need to explain to their fellow Jews how it came about that Jesus, whom they claimed to be the Messiah of God, had suffered an ignominious death at the hands of the Romans. The latter they did by arguing that God had himself prophesied it beforehand in the sacred scriptures, especially in the Psalms concerned with a righteous sufferer, and the narrative of the crucifixion is practically a mosaic of such references, especially from Psalms 22 and 69.[4] In interpreting the "Lord's Supper" (1 Cor 11:23–26), with its parallels in the synoptic gospels, one can say only that the whole is so obviously Semitic in linguistic cast, so full of allusions to the Passover (celebrated mostly in Jerusalem), and comes to Paul with such authority, that it is hard to see where it could have originated except in the church in Jerusalem.

But this is at best speculative, and we have to admit that in the last analysis all we know of earliest Jerusalem Christianity is that it shared the common Christian conviction that Jesus was the Messiah and would shortly come again as judge and redeemer; it was conservative, legalistic, and possessed a certain amount of authority. The case is rather different with regard to Palestinian Christianity at large, if we deliberately leave aside the question of whether some particular thing was or was not characteristic of Jerusalem Christianity itself. For Palestinian Christianity at large we have concrete literary remains in that we can reconstruct the sayings source Q used by the evangelists Matthew and Luke, which certainly stems from early Palestinian Christianity, and that on form critical grounds we can isolate elements in the New Testament texts that certainly go back to the early days of Christianity in Palestine. We will begin with the sayings source Q.

[4]See chapter 2, pp. 32–33, for the explicit allusions to Psalm 22 in Mark 15:23, 24 and Matt 27:43. The offering of "wine mingled with myrrh," Mark 15:23, is from Psa 69:21, as is the similar act in Mark 15:36. The cry of Jesus in Mark 15:34 is from Psa 22:1, and the cry in Luke 23:46 is from Psa 31:5.

As we pointed out in our first chapter, there is a literary relationship between the three synoptic gospels, and the generally accepted explanation of this relationship is that Mark has been used as a source by Matthew and Luke and that, in addition, Matthew and Luke used a common source consisting mostly of sayings material, a source designated "Q." This source will be discussed in some detail in our next chapter; for the moment it is sufficient to point out that it is dominated by a particular form of eschatology, by the expectation of Jesus returning from heaven as Son of Man. The community that created the source Q proclaimed the imminent coming of Jesus from heaven as Son of Man and prepared themselves for that coming, challenging others to do the same.

A most important point about the Q source is its *form*: it is in the form of sayings of Jesus and stories about him. Jerusalem Christianity developed its interpretation of the Jewish Law in the form of stories of Jesus interpreting that Law, in part because Jesus had in fact done so and they had such stories in their tradition, and in part because they believed the risen Jesus was in their midst, guiding them in their interpretation. In its turn the Q community began its proclamation by repeating Jesus' proclamation of the Kingdom of God. This they could do because Jesus' proclamation of the Kingdom was in fact the proclamation of the eschatological activity of God,[5] and the eschatological activity of God was what they too were proclaiming. So they repeated the proclamation of Jesus in the form of sayings of Jesus. When they came to give a specific form and content to this expectation of the eschatological activity of God, namely that of the coming of Jesus as Son of Man, they were led to this by what they believed to be the spirit of Jesus inspiring prophets in their midst, and so they continued to use the same sayings form.[6] The eschatological teaching that came to them in the name of Jesus through their prophets was cast in the form of sayings of Jesus, and eventually their whole teaching came to take this form. In this way the particular form of Christian tradition in Jerusalem and Palestine took the shape of sayings of Jesus and stories about him, even when the content echoed the concerns of the church and the material was created by the church. Thus the seed was sown that reached fruition in the one distinctive Christian literary form, the gospel.

A prominent feature of Palestinian Christianity, and indeed of New Testament Christianity altogether, was *prophecy*. The Christians were particularly conscious that the spirit of prophecy had returned to them as a community, which they claimed as evidence that they were indeed God's elect and chosen community. The importance they attached to prophecy is evident in the speech attributed to Peter at Pentecost, Acts 2:14–36, which is based on Joel 2:28–32, a passage understood as a prophecy concerning the End Time now

---

[5]This statement about the proclamation of Jesus will be justified in chapter 12.

[6]In anticipation of matters to be discussed in chapters 4 and 12, we may perhaps say that the crux of the matter with regard to both Jesus and early Palestinian Christianity was that they were both concerned to proclaim the eschatological activity of God, i.e., God's final, decisive intervention in the history of the world whereby the wicked would be punished, the righteous rewarded, and the world itself transformed, indeed re-created. Jesus used the symbol "Kingdom of God," which expresses the idea of God acting directly; early Christianity used the symbol "Jesus coming as Son of Man," which expresses the idea of God acting through an intermediary figure.

being fulfilled among the Christians. It contains two references to prophecy, Acts 2:17 and 2:18, the second having been added to the original text of Joel by the Christian exegete in order to emphasize the role of the gift of prophecy in the End Time and to emphasize further the fact that the Christian community possessed this gift. A further example of the prominence of prophecy in earliest Christianity is that, as Ernst Käsemann has shown,[7] we can trace prophetic sayings that reflect the conditions of primitive Christianity in Palestine in the text of Matthew's gospel: 7:22–23, the warning against false prophets and exorcists; 23:8–10, the warning not to acknowledge any leadership save that of Christ; 5:17–20, with its core in verse 19 and its emphasis on the imminence of eschatological judgment (being called least or great in the Kingdom); 10:41 and 13:16–17, with their reference to "prophets" and "righteous men"; 19:28–29, the sitting on the thrones with the Son of Man; 10:23, the command to urgency in the mission to Israel in light of the imminence of the coming of the Son of Man; and others. Käsemann argues, correctly, that these sayings go back to earliest Palestinian Christianity and show that that movement was dominated by the apocalyptic hope for the coming of the Son of Man in judgment and that prophets were among its charismatic leaders. Käsemann isolates these sayings on form critical grounds as being pre-Matthean and primitive, and his observations bear out what we have claimed on the basis of the sayings source Q. Earliest Palestinian Christianity was a charismatic movement, dominated by the expectation of the coming of Jesus as Son of Man and prominently featuring prophecy among its characteristics.

## Hellenistic Jewish Mission Christianity

Though earliest Christianity was an apocalyptic sect within Palestinian Judaism and though Jesus himself was a Palestinian Jew, Palestinian Judaism is not really the world of the New Testament. Hellenism, the civilization created by the conquests of Alexander the Great from the Isthmus of Corinth to the Indus Valley, from the Black Sea to the Red Sea, is the world of the New Testament. Politically his conquests did not survive his death, but the stamp of Greek civilization did. Greek cities sprang up in every land, everywhere Greek culture was imitated, and every people spoke Greek and felt the impact of Greek life and thought. Greek was the common language, and the sheer existence of such a lingua franca understood everywhere facilitated the interaction of ideas. In stamping itself on the known world as a common language, Greek was itself transformed from classical or Attic Greek into *koinē* (common) or Hellenistic Greek, the Greek of the New Testament, simplified in syntax and structure but bursting with the vitality created by the interaction of words and ideas from other languages. Similarly, the classical civilization of Athens of the fifth century B.C. developed into what we know as Hellenism, also a product of the interaction of the cultures on which it was superimposed by Alexander and his successors. The Roman conquests culminating in the establishment of the *Pax Augusta* (Augustan peace) by

---

[7]In the essays referred to in the Further Reading at the end of this chapter, especially "The Beginnings of Christian Theology."

Caesar Augustus in 27 B.C. did not change the cultural situation significantly. Rome derived her culture from Hellenism rather than imposing her own on it. Only at the close of the New Testament period did Latin begin to spread from the West, ultimately to split the world of the New Testament into a Latin world centering on Rome and a Greek world centering on Byzantium. The world of the New Testament was still one, that of Hellenism, speaking *koine* Greek.

The Hellenistic culture was, however, a culture of conflicting faiths and philosophies; moreover, any faith, any philosophy, was subtly influenced and changed as it spread within that culture. This was as true of Judaism as of any other faith. There were large settlements of Jews in Babylonia and in the city of Alexandria, and, indeed, Jews were scattered throughout the Hellenistic world. In part they were the scattered remnants of past catastrophes such as the Babylonian conquest of Jerusalem and the subsequent Exile of the Jewish people; in part they were the dynamic movement of venturesome people into a world that offered them more scope and opportunity than was to be found in a chronically depressed Palestine. These Jews thought and spoke in Greek, so much so that maintaining the language of the "old country" within the family was a matter of pride, as it was for Paul (Phil 3:5). They translated the sacred scriptures of their people into Greek, the Septuagint version of the Old Testament, so called because of the tradition that it was translated by seventy [two] scribes. More than that, they created a new religious literature of their own strongly influenced by the culture of the Hellenistic world. Much of what is now known as the Apocrypha of the Old Testament is in fact a product of Hellenistic Judaism.

Hellenistic Judaism was not confined to the Diaspora (the communities of Jews living outside the homeland, Palestine), but was also to be found in Palestine itself, where Greek culture spread despite the efforts to contain it. An example of the direct influence of Hellenistic Judaism in Palestine was that there were synagogues in Palestine, and indeed in Jerusalem itself (Luke 4:16; Acts 6:9). The synagogue was a place of worship and prayer, a place set aside for the study and teaching of scripture. It was developed in Hellenistic Judaism to meet the needs of Jews who had no regular opportunity to go to the Temple in Jerusalem. When it was not possible to build a synagogue, the local Jews would settle for a "place of prayer," as in the Roman colony of Philippi (Acts 16:16).

Palestinian Jews, however, tended to be suspicious of Hellenistic Jews as not having truly kept the faith, which no doubt exacerbated the tension between Hellenistic and Palestinian Jews ("Hellenists" and "Hebrews") in the primitive Christian church in Jerusalem (Acts 6:1–6). This factor made it possible for the Hellenistic Jewish Christians to be expelled from Jerusalem while the Palestinian Jewish Christians were allowed to remain (the historical reality behind Acts 8:1–2). At the same time, Judaism made its own impact on the Hellenistic world. Its monotheism and moral code attracted many Hellenistic Gentiles, and Hellenistic Judaism was itself an aggressive and successful proselytizing movement. Its success was limited, however, because a male proselyte had to accept circumcision, and also because the dietary laws of Judaism were not especially attractive to Hellenes. The functional result was that around a local Jewish community there would be a fringe of non-Jewish Hellenists sharing a good deal of Judaic life and worship while resisting full proselytization. They were sufficiently numerous and their presence sufficiently constant in Hellenistic Judaism for a technical term to be devised to describe them: they were "God-fearers" (Acts 10:2, 22; 13:16, 26).

From the very beginning of its days in Jerusalem the Christian church numbered among its members active Hellenistic (Greek-speaking) Jews, the "Hellenists" of Acts 6, who were the spearhead of the movement of Christianity into the Hellenistic world. They understood the Greek world; they were missionary-minded and theologically venturesome. Even without the persecution that drove them out of Jerusalem they would certainly have become Christian missionaries among their fellow Greek-speaking Jews, among the "God-fearers," and to the Hellenistic world at large. Persecution hastened the process. It is permissible, therefore, to speak of Hellenistic Jewish Mission Christianity, the Greek-speaking Jewish Christianity that carried the gospel into the Hellenistic world.

The literary monument to this movement is the Acts of the Apostles. The author of Acts is himself a product of the movement, and in his work he has given us a dramatic and dramatized account of it. The speeches he reports are particularly important, for they represent typical samples of Hellenistic Jewish Christian preaching in synagogues, to "God-fearers," and on the street corners of the Greek cities.

Theologically, Hellenistic Jewish Mission Christianity was such that it was almost explosively creative. In it Jewish, Hellenistic, and developing Christian traditions met and interacted with dynamic results that are today the backbone of New Testament theology. An illustration is the developments in Christology. In Palestinian Jewish Christianity Jesus was characteristically "Messiah," i.e., the one anointed (chosen) by God, or "Son of Man," i.e., eschatological judge and redeemer. He was also "Lord" in the Aramaic form *Mar*[8] and *Mar* is an Aramaic honorific designation used especially of persons with authority to judge. In Hellenistic Jewish Mission Christianity, the Hebrew "Messiah" became the Greek "Christ," but it lost its force so that "Jesus Christ" became practically a proper name rather than meaning "Jesus, the anointed one of God." "Son of Man" was abandoned because in Greek it had no meaning, being replaced by either "Son of God" or "Lord." In Hellenism, Son of God indicated "possessing divine qualities," "exhibiting a divine aura," or the like, and how Jesus came to be regarded as Son of God can be seen in the cycle of miracle stories now found in Mark 5 and 7: the Gerasene Demoniac (5:1–20: the reference to the Decapolis in verse 20 indicates that this is Greek territory); Jairus' Daughter and the Woman with the Hemorrhage (5:21–43); the Syrophoenician Woman (7:24–30); the Man with a Speech Impediment (again in the Decapolis, 7:31–37). In all these, Jesus exhibits an aura of divine power—he heals by fiat, at a distance, or by the touch of his garments, and so on—and there are enough explicit references to Greek places and non-Jewish people and still enough contacts with Judaism, to show that these stories developed in Hellenistic Jewish Christianity. That these stories are designed to exhibit why Jesus is Son of God is seen from the occurrence of the title in the introduction to the whole section (3:11) and in the first story

---

[8]*Maranatha*, 1 Cor 16:21, is an Aramaic eucharistic prayer, "Our Lord, come"; compare Rev 22:20.

(5:7). "Son of God" was also used in apocalyptic contexts where Palestinian Christianity would have used "Son of Man" (e.g., I Thess 1:10, "to wait for his [God's] Son from heaven"). But the major christological development concerned the use of the title "Lord" (Greek *kyrios*). In Hellenism it was the most common honorific title, used for gods, emperors, and kings, as well as for men of power and authority everywhere. Hellenistic Jewish Christianity developed this title extensively, so that the confession "Jesus [Christ] is Lord" became the characteristic Christian confession, and the coming of Jesus as judge was now his coming as Lord rather than as Son of Man (e.g., I Thess 4:15).

Hellenistic Jewish Christianity was equally creative in other respects. It made extensive and imaginative use of the Septuagint, as the speeches in Acts show. It adapted and developed the liturgy of the Jewish synagogue for its own use, devising confessions and liturgical formulas of all kinds. It laid great stress on the resurrection, both in liturgy (the formula-like references to "God who raised Jesus from the dead" in Paul's letters are from the Hellenistic Jewish Christian liturgy, as is his christological confessional formula in Rom 1:3–4) and in preaching (the speeches in Acts). When in Rom 10:9 Paul says, "If you confess with your lips that Jesus is Lord and believe in your heart that God raised him from the dead, you will be saved," he is breathing the very spirit of Hellenistic Jewish Mission Christianity.

## Gentile Christianity (Apart from Paul)

Christianity began as an apocalyptic sect within ancient Palestinian Judaism and moved into the Gentile world through the Hellenistic Jewish Christian mission. But once established in the Gentile world it tended to take on emphases of its own, no longer necessarily dependent on the Palestinian Judaism that spawned it, nor on the Hellenistic Judaism that propelled it into the wider world. It interpreted itself in new ways in response to the challenges of the new environment, and it reached new understandings of itself and its Lord by using the categories available in the Hellenistic Gentile culture. An apocalyptic Jewish sect begun in Palestine and continued as a missionary movement within Hellenistic Judaism now became a cult in the world of Hellenistic religiosity and began to exhibit many of the characteristics of that religiosity. We deal with the details when we discuss Paul and his relations with the church at Corinth in chapter 5; for the moment we will simply draw a general picture of Hellenistic Gentile Christianity as Paul found it.

Hellenism was a world of contrasts. Greek culture offered a conception of a good, harmonious life in a world in which the reality experienced daily tended to be neither good nor harmonious. Until the Augustan peace in 27 B.C. warfare was constant, and as a result, a family would be living prosperously in a city one year and its members would be dead or sold into slavery the next. The growth of cities and the emphasis on urban living created the need to feed the inhabitants of those cities, a problem never satisfactorily solved, and so famine became an ever present and all too frequent possibility. Further, the "closure of the Eurasian ecumene,"[9] the establishment of one Eurasian world,

[9]The phrase is from McNeill, *The Rise of the West.*

led not only to a dramatic cultural interchange, but also to the spread of diseases against which the inhabitants of one part or other of that world had no natural immunity. All this led to a focus on "fate" and to a longing for salvation from the vicissitudes of life and the ever present fear of death. There spread through the Hellenistic world a series of "mystery cults," religions promising their initiates security and immortality. The hero, or heroine, of a mystery cult was characteristically a divine figure who had conquered life in the world and achieved immortality and who could promise a share in that conquest and that immortality to the believer who would accept initiation into the rites of the cult. The rites were "mysteries" kept rigidly secret from all but the initiates. They generally consisted of some kind of recital or reenactment of the deeds of the hero or heroine, an act of initiation, and the eating of a sacred meal, by which the initiate came to share the divine power and immortality of the deity.

That Christianity could be interpreted as a cult within Hellenism is obvious at first glance. It too had its myth of the hero, the gospel story of Jesus; its initiation rite, baptism; its sacred meal. The Christians did not borrow directly from the mystery cults; it was rather that the Christian faith came to expression most naturally in a way responsive to the particular needs of the environment of which it became a part. Were it not capable of doing so, it could never have been established in that environment. But Christianity did establish itself and in so doing developed different emphases from what had gone before. For one thing, it was difficult to maintain the traditional Jewish-Christian apocalyptic hope with its expectation of the coming of Jesus as Son of Man, and judgment and transformation of the earth. The Greeks thought more naturally in terms of redemption from the world to a higher level of existence than of the transformation of the world itself, and with the spread of Greek culture in the Hellenistic world, this style of thinking became generally accepted. Significantly, the deeper Paul gets into the Hellenistic world, the less we hear about the characteristic apocalyptic hope of Jewish Christianity. Then a real problem was posed by the characteristic Christian emphasis on the resurrection of Jesus and the hope of the future resurrection of the believer. The Greek world thought more naturally in terms of the immortality of the soul than of the resurrection of the body, and that created the problems for the Christian belief dramatized by the author of the Acts of the Apostles (Acts 17, especially verse 32) and amply evident in Paul's first letter to the Corinthians. On the other hand, religious enthusiasm was very much a part of the Hellenistic world in general, and so the Christian emphasis on the possession of the Spirit and its gifts found both ready acceptance and rapid development there. Paul spends no small part of I Corinthians attempting to restrain his Corinthian converts in this regard.

But perhaps the most important contribution of Gentile Christianity to the developing Christian movement lay in the sphere of Christology. There are in the New Testament a series of christological hymns that betray a quite remarkably uniform pattern of thought:[10]

---

[10]We are now following in the main Jack T. Sanders, *New Testament Christological Hymns.*©1971, Cambridge University Press. Used by permission.

**Phil 2:6–11**

Who, being in the form of God,
 Did not think it robbery to be equal with God.
 But emptied himself,
 Taking the form of a slave.

Becoming in the likeness of men
 And being found in fashion like a man,
 He humbled himself,
 Becoming obedient unto death.

Wherefore God highly exalted him
 and bestowed upon him the name above
 every name,

That in the name of Jesus every knee may bow
 in the heavens and on earth,
 And every tongue confess,
 "Jesus Christ is Lord."

**Col 1:15–20**

Who is the image of
 the invisible God,
 first born of all
 creation

For in him was
 created everything
 in heavens and on
 earth

Everything was created
 through him and
 unto him.

Who is the beginning,
 the first born of
 the dead.

For in him all the
 fullness was
 pleased to dwell,

And through him to
 reconcile everything
 unto himself.

And he is before everything
And everything is united in him
And he is the head of the body (the church).

**I Pet 3:18–19, 22**

Having been put to
 death in the flesh,
Having been made alive
 in the spirit,
Having gone to the spirits
 in prison,
He preached.

Who is at the right
 hand of God,
Having gone into heaven,
Angels and authorities
 and powers having been
 made subject to him.

**I Tim 3:16**

Was manifested in
 the flesh,
Was vindicated by
 the spirit,
Was seen by angels,

Was proclaimed among
 the nations,
Was believed on in the
 world,

Was taken up into glory.

**Eph 2:14–16**

He is our peace,
Who has made both one
And has broken down the dividing wall
    of the fence,
In order to make the two into one new
    man in him
And to reconcile both in one body to God.


**Heb 1:3**

Who, being the reflection of his glory and
    the stamp of his essence,
Bearing everything by the word of his power,
Having made purification for sins,
Sat down on the right hand of the
    majesty on high.



In all these hymns we can see the pattern of a redeemer figure who descends to the earth from a higher sphere, achieves his redemptive purpose on earth, and ascends again to the higher, heavenly sphere. This pattern of thought appears to have influenced both Hellenistic Judaism and Christianity. It is found in the New Testament with quite remarkable consistency wherever there is strong contact with the Hellenistic Gentile world, not only in these hymns, but also in the gospel of John. The understanding of Jesus as a descending-ascending redeemer is one of Gentile Christianity's great contributions to the developing Christian theology.

A special problem for early Christianity was the Hellenistic Gentile tendency to think in terms of "divine men," that is, of men who particularly represented the power of a god, of men who had about them the aura of divinity.[11] We noted above that Hellenistic Jewish Christianity responded to this aspect of its environment by interpreting Jesus in this way, for example in the miracle stories now found in Mark 5 and 7. (Incidentally, Philo of Alexandria, the greatest Hellenistic Jew, responded to the same Hellenistic emphasis by interpreting Moses in a similar way in his *On the Life of Moses.*) In Christianity this emphasis led not only to a particular understanding of Jesus, a "divine man Christology," but also to a particular understanding of the nature of Christian discipleship, namely that Christians now share the glory of their Lord and can confidently expect to overcome in their lives what Jesus overcame in his life and death. In these traditions the death of Jesus would not have been represented as a sacrificial suffering but as a translation to an even more glorious existence. The evangelist Mark is at war with this understanding of Christology, Christian discipleship, and Christ's passion, as we shall see in a later chapter. The Hellenistic Jewish Christian church understood its

[11] In all that I say here and elsewhere about the Hellenistic "divine man" I am consciously indebted to my friends Hans Dieter Betz and Dieter Georgi, who opened my eyes to this aspect of the impact of Hellenism on New Testament Christianity.

heroes as "divine men," as we can see from the portrayal of Peter and Philip in the early chapters of Acts and from such things as the note about Paul's garments possessing miraculous powers (Acts 19:12). In Corinth Paul ran into a related problem in that his opponents there, especially those he argues against in 2 Corinthians, understood a Christian apostle as one who exhibited the aura and power of a "divine man," and they claimed it of themselves and wanted Paul to demonstrate it of himself.

A most interesting aspect of Gentile Christianity, and a sharp contrast with Palestinian Christianity, is the *form* of its traditional material. We pointed out earlier that Palestinian Christianity traditionally used the form of sayings of Jesus and stories about him, even though the content reflected the concerns of the church and came from the church. As far as we can tell, this form was not preserved in Gentile Christianity. In I Thessalonians, for example, we are theologically very close to the Q community; the Thessalonian community, like the Q community, awaits the coming of Jesus from heaven as eschatological judge and redeemer and prepares itself for that coming. But Jesus is now expected as Lord and Son of God, not Son of Man, and the instruction is given in the form of general Christian instruction, not sayings of Jesus. True, there is enough left of the Palestinian emphasis for Paul to say that "we beseech and instruct you in the Lord Jesus," but even when the instruction is from Q material (I Thess 5:2 = Luke 12:39–40 par.) it no longer has the form of a saying of Jesus. Nor is there anywhere in the Pauline letters the slightest hint that the churches he represents and to which he writes used sayings of Jesus or stories about him as did Palestinian Christianity. When Paul quotes a "word of the Lord" (I Cor 7:10; 9:14; 11:23; 14:37) he is quoting established Christian tradition, but not in the *form* of a saying of Jesus. Moreover, neither his letters nor the tradition they represent show any interest in a story of Jesus other than the founding of the Lord's Supper (I Cor 11:23–26) or accounts of the passion (necessarily implied by the frequent references to the cross) and resurrection (I Cor 15:3–6). Where Hellenistic Jewish Christianity stood on this matter we can only guess—probably somewhere in between—but between Palestinian and Gentile Christianity the form of Christian tradition as sayings of Jesus and stories about him is simply lost.

## The Apostle Paul

The apostle Paul is discussed in some detail in chapter 5, but he is so important a figure in the development of New Testament Christianity that some brief indication of his place in it must be given here. A man of the Hellenistic Jewish Christian mission, he became its outstanding representative and natural leader. Among his letters, 1 Thessalonians may be regarded as representing the typical emphases, concerns, and problems of the movement. Paul's mission took him ever deeper into the Hellenistic Gentile world, and his Corinthian correspondence must be held to represent not only the particular problems he faced in Corinth, but also the characteristic problems Christianity faced everywhere it established itself in a predominantly non-Jewish environment:

the impact of Hellenistic forms of religious enthusiasm on the Christian understanding of the possession of the Spirit; difficulties with the doctrines of the resurrection of Jesus and the future resurrection of the believer; the tendency to think of Jesus and his most immediate representatives, the apostles, as "divine men"; and so on.

A major historical event in earliest Christianity in which Paul played a leading part was the "Jerusalem Council," of which we have two accounts, one from Paul himself in Gal 2:1–10 and one in Acts 15:1–29. The problem for the historian of New Testament Christianity is that both these accounts are tendentious. Paul is fighting for his view of the faith and for the very existence of his mission in the Gentile world, and no doubt he is interpreting the event he describes. The author of the Acts of the Apostles is writing a generation later, when the issues confronting the Council were dead and a whole new set of issues had arisen in the churches. Moreover, Acts is in a tradition of historical writing that consciously put speeches on the lips of protagonists in historical events, interpreting their significance for the present reader rather than recording what had been said. The assumption has to be that Acts 15 represents a reinterpretation of the Council for a later generation and that it is addressed to the issues confronting that generation, rather than being what the modern world would recognize as a historical report.

In the light of these factors and of our general knowledge of this period of Christian history, the most probable hypothesis is that the Jerusalem Council grew out of the success of the Hellenistic Jewish Christian mission in the Gentile world. It should be emphasized that this success took everyone by surprise. Earliest Christians in general devoted their missionary activity toward their fellow Jews and expected that the Gentiles would be brought into the divine plan by a direct act of God at the End itself. But the Christian mission to the Jews was largely a failure, whereas that to the Gentiles developed into an astonishing movement of vitality and power no one could have anticipated. This created a major problem, namely, how far the new Gentile Christians should also become Jews: should it be demanded of them that they accept circumcision and Jewish dietary laws?

This crucial question was loaded with every possible kind of emotional overtone and practical consequence. Jewish Christians were no less proud of their Jewish heritage than were their fellow Jews, and even Paul himself on one occasion went so far as to circumcise one of his Gentile converts, Timothy, with his own hands (Acts 16:3). This tradition has to be historical if only because of the syntax of Gal 2:1–3, which reads as if Paul is struggling not to mention it and hoping that no one else will do so! On the other hand, the Christian mission to the Gentiles found its most fruitful field among the "God-fearers," and was there successful precisely because it did not demand acceptance of circumcision and food taboos as did Judaism, while offering all and more than Judaism itself offered. The question required the most careful handling and was in fact the occasion for a Christian "summit conference," held in Jerusalem and attended by Paul and some of his fellow workers among the Gentiles and also by the leaders of the conservatively minded church in Jerusalem. The result of this, the "Jerusalem Council," was not the decree given in Acts 15:22–29, for the subsequent history of Paul's work and correspondence shows that he knew of no such decree; moreover, the decree reads like the kind of compromise reached in a later period when the question was not the legitimacy of the Gentile mission, but the relationship between Jews and Gentiles in well-established Christian churches. For the results of this Council we have to interpret Gal 2:7–10.

The most reasonable interpretation of this passage is that the agreement reached was that the Council was discussing the work of God in the world and no preconceived limits should be set to the nature of that work. In itself this was a major achievement and a magnificent testimony to the caliber of earliest Christianity. So Paul and his colleagues were to be free to go on working in their way in the Gentile world, and Peter and his in their way in the Jewish world. The distinction was not so much geographical as ideological, i.e., between predominantly Gentile and predominantly Jewish communities wherever they might be located. The one thing asked of Paul and his colleagues was that they should "remember the poor [in Jerusalem]." This was a request for charity—Jerusalem was an economically depressed area compared with Antioch, Ephesus, or Corinth—but more than that it was a challenge to recognition of the particular status of Jerusalem, the Holy City, and of Jerusalem Christians, these nearest to Jesus himself in birth and physical circumstances. "Poor" in the Jewish world was a synonym for "particularly pious." Paul himself took this responsibility to Jerusalem very seriously, as can be seen from his subsequent correspondence (1 Cor 16; 2 Cor 8 and 9; Rom 15:25–29).

The Jerusalem agreement left unresolved the question of table fellowship (the practice of eating together) between Jewish Christians who accepted the Jewish dietary laws and Gentile Christians who did not. Paul's account of the situation between himself and Peter in Antioch (Gal 2:11–21) indicates the problems that could and did arise. They were probably not resolved until the Jewish War of A.D. 66–70 effectively removed Palestinian Jerusalem Christianity from the scene, and the compromise now represented by Acts 15:22–29 became possible. Another problem was that not all members of either side lived up to the spirit of the agreement—by no means a unique phenomenon in human history—and so incidents arose such as the one that called forth Paul's letter to the Galatians. But generally speaking, agreement was a major achievement and made possible the subsequent advances of the Christian movement in the two decades that separated the Jerusalem Council (most probably A.D. 48) from the catastrophe of the Jewish War and destruction of Jerusalem (A.D. 66–70), which changed forever the circumstances of New Testament Christianity.

## The Impact of the Fall of Jerusalem

We have attempted to sketch some aspects of the phases through which the Christian movement must have gone before the mission and achievement of the apostle Paul. It should be emphasized that these phases were neither mutually exclusive nor chronologically successive. Any given Christian community could share to a greater or lesser extent the conservatism of the

Jerusalem church, the apocalypticism of Palestinian Christianity, the concerns of the Hellenistic Jewish mission, or the emphases of the Gentile Christian churches. Moreover, all these phases coexisted with and influenced each other until everything was changed by the destruction of Jerusalem and the Jerusalem Temple. But it is helpful to recognize the variety of stages through which the Christian movement passed, so to speak, on its way from Jerusalem to Rome, and hence to appreciate something of the variety as well as of the unity of the New Testament.

The Jews revolted against Rome in A.D. 66, beginning the war they expected God to end in their favor. But the war went the way of the Roman legions, and Jerusalem fell in A.D. 70. The war deeply affected the Christian communities. Jerusalem and Palestinian Christians were caught in the midst of the conflict. To the Romans they were Jews, but to the Jews they were suspect as Christians; so they fled Jerusalem and Palestine, going to Pella and other places in Trans Jordania, to their Christian brethren in the cities and towns of Syria and Asia Minor, and no doubt also to Alexandria and Egypt. They took with them their Jesus traditions—their traditional material in the form of sayings of Jesus or stories about him. This material must have made a tremendous impact on Christianity outside Palestine. It must have been known in part before, but the dynamism of its interaction with the developing theologies of Hellenistic Jewish Christianity and of the Gentile Christian churches was certainly in no small part responsible for the writing of the synoptic gospels, as was also the fall of Jerusalem itself.

We shall return to these points when we discuss the gospels in detail; for the moment we wish to emphasize the importance to early Christianity in general of the Jewish War and the fall of Jerusalem. Practically speaking, it meant that the Christians in the Hellenistic world no longer had to reckon with the influence of the conservatively minded church in Jerusalem. After A.D. 70 there were no influences like those that Paul wrestled with in his letter to the Galatians and no occasion for an altercation like the one he had with Peter in Antioch (Gal 2:11–21). Also, with the effective disappearance of Jerusalem Christianity, and indeed of Palestinian Christianity generally, together with the effects of the sheer passage of time, the three phases of the Christian movement we have been distinguishing thus far simply ceased to exist. After A.D. 70 there was in effect only a Hellenistic Gentile Christianity, which in any one place might have a greater or lesser concern for or with the Judaism from which it was ultimately descended.

## The Middle Period of New Testament Christianity

The New Testament texts relate themselves only indirectly or theologically to the events of their historical world, mostly because New Testament Christians awaited the imminent end of that world. But there is enough indirect and theological relationship in the texts for us to be able to say something about what may be described as the middle period of New Testament history, the twenty-five years or so that followed the fall of Jerusalem.

Theologically speaking, the period was characterized in the main by the necessity for coming to terms with the catastrophe of A.D. 70 and the delay of the parousia, by the continuing influence of the apostle Paul, and by the development of Johannine Christianity, associated now with the gospel and letters of John, the "Johannine corpus." Furthermore, in this period the church became more conscious of being a distinct entity with a history in the world and hence with a need to normalize her relations with both Hellenism and Judaism. But before going further we should note that the period began and ended with a resurgence of Christian apocalyptic.

## The resurgence of Christian apocalyptic

We have said that Christianity began as an apocalyptic sect within Judaism. The earliest Christians awaited the imminent end of the world, which would take the form of the return of Jesus as eschatological judge and redeemer. With the movement into the Gentile world and with the sheer passage of time and the failure of the expected events to occur, other emphases developed. But apocalyptic thinking, thinking of a world about to end and be replaced by a different world, always tended to flare up in response to a crisis, a tendency that has continued throughout Christian history. In the New Testament period one such crisis was the Jewish War. To Christians as well as to Jews it seemed to be the beginning of the End, the beginning of the war that God would terminate by direct intervention in human history. There was a resurgence of apocalyptic expectation among Christians and Jews, and its literary monument in the New Testament is the gospel of Mark. In our later discussion we shall argue that in many respects this gospel is an apocalypse, and it is certainly a product of the resurgence of apocalyptic expectation occasioned by the Jewish War.

The persecution of the church could also have strengthened apocalyptic expectations. It could have led to the belief that the end of history as known was at hand and that God was about to change everything; it was simply a question of hanging on. One such persecution in the New Testament period was under the Roman emperor Domitian (A.D. 81–96), which was most probably the occasion for writing the one completely apocalyptic work in the New Testament, the book of Revelation.

## Coming to terms with the fall of Jerusalem and the delay of the parousia

As we have said, two major factors in the development of New Testament Christianity were the fall of Jerusalem and destruction of its Temple (which should not have happened but did) and the delay of the parousia, the coming of Jesus from heaven as eschatological judge and redeemer (which should have happened but did not). Much of the literature now in the New Testament attempts directly to come to terms with these elements in early Christian history. In what we are describing as the "middle period" of New Testament history, there came the gospel of Matthew, the two-volume gospel of Luke and Acts of the Apostles, and the letter to the Hebrews. The gospel of Matthew sees the ministry of Jesus as the new Sacred Time, the fulfillment of the hopes of Judaism, so that Jerusalem is no longer necessary to the Christian. The parousia is still to be expected, but in the meantime there is work to be done in the world. Luke-Acts sees Jerusalem as the place that rejected Jesus and so has been itself rejected. The time of Jesus is the new Sacred Time, and while Christians are still to expect the parousia, they have also to settle down to the long haul of history wherein they must witness. Hebrews sees all that was good in Judaism and the Jerusalem Temple having been superseded by Jesus.

### The continuing influence of the apostle Paul

An important aspect of Paul's work was that he trained men to work with and after him in the Gentile Christian churches. Though we have no direct reference to this training in the New Testament itself, it would have been a natural thing to do (Jewish rabbis regularly trained disciples, as tradition has it that Paul himself was trained by Gamaliel, Acts 22:3), and his letters and the narrative of Acts are studded with references to "fellow workers" or "helpers." But the real evidence for the existence of a Pauline "school" are the deutero-Pauline letters, written in the name of Paul and close to his thinking yet sufficiently different from the genuine letters to allow us to conclude they were not written by the apostle himself. These letters—2 Thessalonians, Colossians, Ephesians—all come from what we are calling the "middle period" of New Testament Christianity. Whereas 2 Thessalonians attempts to maintain the earlier hope for the parousia, Colossians and Ephesians represent the church developing her doctrines and settling down to the problems and opportunities of her ongoing life in the Gentile world. They also represent the continuing influence of the apostle a generation after his death in a world where Jerusalem and the Jerusalem church were no longer to be reckoned with but in which what was later to be called Gnosticism was developing as a major problem.

### The development of Johannine Christianity

The gospel and letters of John represent a distinct and distinctive understanding of Christian faith. To move from the synoptic gospels to John's gospel is to move from one world to another, as it is to move from Paul's letters to these letters. Here the Christian faith comes to terms with the Hellenistic world as thoroughly and successfully as did the apostle Paul (but in a different way), and "Christianity according to St. John" became a major influence on the Christian piety of subsequent centuries. The famous Anglican archbishop William Temple confessed that he felt at home in the Johannine corpus as he did nowhere else in the New Testament, and in this he is representative of countless Christians. This understanding of the faith was hammered out somewhere in Syria during the middle period of the New Testament, most probably by a strong leader with a group of close followers—a Johannine school to which we owe the Johannine corpus, as we owe the Pauline corpus to a Pauline school. Whether the leader's name was John does not matter; what matters is that the "Johannine" understanding of the Christian faith is a major achievement of the New Testament period.

## The Final Period: The New Testament Church on the Way to Becoming an Institution

The New Testament church began as an apocalyptic sect within Judaism, expecting the imminent end of the world. But by the end of the New Testament period it was on the way to becoming an institution with a credal basis, a distinctive literature, and a fixed organizational structure. The full establishment of these things—a creed, a canon, and an episcopate—did not come until later, but the movement toward them is evident in the final stages of the New Testament history and literature, especially in the Pastoral Epistles (1 and 2 Timothy and Titus). In these letters we have a third-generation Paulinist writing in the name of the illustrious apostle, but the language and thought are those of the church at the beginning of the second century. Sayings are worthy of acceptance if they are "faithful" (1 Tim 1:15; RSV says, "sure"); we are on the way to a creed. The "office of a bishop" is "a noble task" (1 Tim 3:1); we are on the way to the episcopate. The church is "the pillar and the bulwark of the truth" (1 Tim 3:15); we are on the way to the church as an institution. An equally pseudonymous letter written in the name of an illustrious apostle, 2 Peter, speaks of the letters of Paul as a collection and equates them with "the other scriptures" (2 Pet 3:16); and we are on the way to the New Testament canon.

The remainder of the literature in the New Testament belongs to this last period. First Peter, again pseudonymous, is most probably a developed baptismal homily from the end of the first or the beginning of the second century, reflecting the situation of the church under persecution. James' letter, also pseudonymous, is a Christian moral homily in a style familiar to Hellenism and Hellenistic Judaism, and its view of faith as the acceptance of a doctrinal proposition (Jas 2:18–19) is characteristic of the developing institutionalization of Christianity. The letter of Jude polemicizes against heretics not by setting out a positive theological standpoint in opposition to the heresy, but simply by appealing to the authority of tradition.

All these texts represent, therefore, the church on the way to becoming an institution with a creed, a canon, and an episcopate: needing and using baptismal and moral homilies, viewing faith as the acceptance of doctrinal propositions, and appealing to an authoritative tradition against what is considered heresy. After the dynamism of Paul, John, or the synoptic evangelists, it is something of an anticlimax, but the Christian faith could not have survived through the centuries except as the depository of an institutionalized organization, and the preservation of the New Testament as a set of texts meant that the potential influence of the more dynamic moments was always there. That dynamism has been frequently active, sometimes to the embarrassment of the institution, as when Martin Luther began to read the letters of Paul. This period of New Testament Christianity is the period of "emergent Catholicism," and its literature is the "literature of emergent Catholicism." We use *emergent* and *Catholicism* because the features characteristic of the Catholic church down into the Middle Ages began to emerge in this period.

## FURTHER READING

As far as the present writer is aware, this chapter represents the first attempt at a systematic presentation of a theological history of earliest Christianity as it appears in the light of form and redaction criticism. Much of it is built on the author's own researches and those of his students, so there can be no "further reading" for the chapter as a whole. However, there is good material available for various parts of it.

The idea of distinguishing various phases in pre-Pauline Christianity goes back essentially to W. Bousset, who in his *Kyrios Christos* (1970; German original 1913) distinguished between early Palestinian and early Gentile Christianity. It was taken up by Bultmann, who in his *Theology of the New Testament* distinguished between "the earliest church" and "the Hellenistic church aside from Paul," and Conzelmann, in his *History of Primitive Christianity*, follows Bultmann in this regard. It has been a particular feature of recent work on New Testament Christology and is exemplified in Fuller's *The Foundation of New Testament Christology* as a distinction between "the earliest church," "the Hellenistic Jewish mission," and "the Hellenistic Gentile mission." The distinctions made in our chapter are a deliberate modification of these.

Bruce, *New Testament History*, is a full-scale treatment and a mine of information on the historical background of New Testament Christianity; it is the best source for such information that is presently available. But the author has a view of the historical trustworthiness of the New Testament narrative and of early Christian tradition that most New Testament scholars would not share.

Information on Palestinian Judaism itself is readily available:

> PCB, pp. 693–98, "The Development of Judaism in the Greek and Roman Periods" (M. Black).
> JBC, pp. 535–60, "Apocrypha, Dead Sea Scrolls, Other Jewish Literature" (R. E. Brown).
> JBC, pp. 692–702, "A History of Israel: From Pompey to Bar Cochba" (J. A. Fitzmeyer).
> Foerster, *From the Exile to Christ.*

Simon, *Jewish Sects at the Time of Jesus.*

See also the relevant articles in *IDB.*

Bultmann, *Theology of the New Testament,* vol. 1, pp. 33–62, discusses "The Kerygma of the Earliest Church," by which he means what we are calling Palestinian Jewish Christianity. Käsemann, *New Testament Questions of Today,* pp. 82–107, "The Beginnings of Christian Theology," and pp. 108–37, "On the Subject of Primitive Christian Apocalyptic," discusses the apocalyptic element in Palestinian Jewish Christianity. Fuller, *Foundations of New Testament Christology,* pp. 142–74, discusses the Christology of Palestinian Jewish Christianity (the attentive reader will note differences of opinion between Fuller and the present writer, especially in the matter of the origin of the Son of Man in the New Testament).

Information on Hellenistic Judaism is readily available:

> *PCB,* pp. 686–92, "The Jewish State in the Hellenistic World" (W. D. Davies).
> Tarn and Griffith, *Hellenistic Civilization,* pp. 210–38.

The present writer knows of no systematic discussion of Hellenistic Jewish Mission Christianity apart from the discussion of its Christology by Fuller, *Foundations of New Testament Christology,* pp. 182–202, "The Hellenistic Jewish Mission." Bultmann, *Theology of the New Testament,* does not distinguish it as a separate phase.

On Hellenism itself, see:

> *PCB,* pp. 712–17, "Pagan Religion at the Coming of Christianity" (M. Wilson).
> Bultmann, *Primitive Christianity in its Contemporary Setting,* pp. 135–74.
> Tarn and Griffith, *Hellenistic Civilization.*
> Grant, *Hellenistic Religions.* Texts in translation with an introduction.

On Gentile Christianity, see:

> Bultmann, *Theology of the New Testament,* vol. 1, pp. 63–184, "The Kerygma of the Hellenistic Church Aside from Paul."
> Fuller, *Foundations of New Testament Christology,* pp. 203–42.
> Nock, *Early Gentile Christianity and Its Gentile Background.*

On the christological hymns, see Sanders, *The New Testament Christological Hymns: Their Historical Religious Background,* which has full references to earlier literature.

Other treatments of New Testament Christianity after the fall of Jerusalem are Brandon, *The Fall of Jerusalem and the Christian Church,* and Gaston, *No*

*Stone upon Another.* The discussion we have offered of this subject is independent of both of these.

We have spoken of "the New Testament church on the way to becoming an institution." This is the present writer's way of talking about what Käsemann calls *Frühkatholizismus*, "early (or "emergent") Catholicism." See especially:

Käsemann, *Essays on New Testament Themes*, pp. 63–107, "Ministry and Community in the New Testament."

_____, *New Testament Questions of Today*, pp. 236–51, "Paul and Early Catholicism."

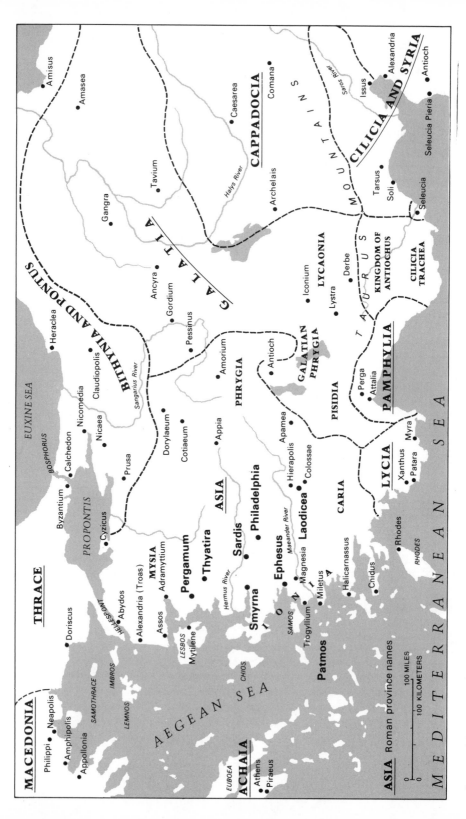

*The world of John of Patmos and the churches to which he wrote.*

# 4

# Apocalyptic Christianity

**The Synoptic Gospel Source "Q," the Apocalyptic Discourses, and the Book of Revelation**

We claimed in our last chapter that Christianity began as an apocalyptic sect within ancient Judaism and that apocalypticism was a constant element of much of New Testament Christianity, resurging especially at times of catastrophe or persecution. We must now go into greater detail, but first an explanation of the terms *apocalyptic* and *eschatology* is in order. *Apocalyptic* is from the Greek *apocalypsis,* "an uncovering," and it describes a movement in Judaism and Christianity that characteristically claimed that God had revealed to the writer the secrets of the imminent end of the world and so had given him a message for his people. It features a distinctive view of the end of the world, described in the next section of this chapter. Though this kind of thinking was not confined to Jews and Christians in the Hellenistic world, being found for example also in Babylonia, we are concerned only with its Jewish-Christian manifestation. *Eschatology* is from the Greek *eschatos,* "furthest," and *logos,* "word" or "teaching," and it therefore means "teaching concerning the end of things." This teaching can take any form, and the end can be conceived in any manner. Some modern scholars tend to use the term for a decisive transformation of life, thinking in existentialist terms, but this is a metaphorical usage. In considering the world of the New Testament, *apocalyptic* is a particular form of *eschatology.*

## CHARACTERISTICS OF JEWISH-CHRISTIAN APOCALYPTIC

In ancient Judaism and early Christianity, apocalyptic was a child of hope and despair: hope in the invincible power of God in the world he created, despair of the present course of human history in that world. God was the creator of the world and the ruler of all within it: that was the primary tenet of Jewish faith. At the same time the actual experience of the people of God in the world was

**65**

catastrophic: the Babylonians conquered them; they returned to the Holy Land at the pleasure of Persian kings; the brief period of independence under the Maccabeans was followed by Roman conquest, by the establishment of the half-breed Idumean rule over them, and by direct Roman control of the Holy City and the Temple with its Holy of Holies. This situation was intolerable, and it could mean only that human history was a descent into hell. But God was the ruler of all things and, therefore, the tragic events of human history must have been foreordained by him. Thus, there was some divine plan through which the horrors of history would reach a climax and everything would then change. In the meantime the people of God must prepare themselves for the change and watch for the signs of its coming.

These are the characteristics of apocalyptic: a sense of despair about history that bred the belief that it was rushing to a foreordained tragic climax; a hope in God that fostered the conviction that he would act in that climactic moment to change things utterly and forever; and a conviction that it would be possible to recognize the signs of the coming of that climactic moment.

> "And when you hear of wars and rumors of wars, do not be alarmed; this must take place, but the end is not yet. For nation will rise against nation, and kingdom against kingdom; there will be earthquakes in various places, there will be famines; this is but the beginning of the birth-pangs. . . .
> But in those days, after that tribulation, the sun will be darkened, and the moon will not give its light, and the stars will be falling from heaven, and the powers in the heavens will be shaken."
>
> MARK 13:7–8, 24–25

This is the language of Jewish apocalyptic looking for the signs of the coming of the End.

Ideas about the form of the End varied tremendously. The passage from Mark 13 continues:

> "And then they will see the Son of man coming in clouds with great power and glory. And then he will send out the angels, and gather his elect from the four winds, from the ends of the earth to the ends of heaven."
>
> MARK 13:26–27

This is the characteristic Christian form of the apocalyptic hope, derived ultimately from Dan 7:13–14:

> I saw in the night visions,
>     and behold, with the clouds of heaven
>         there came one like a son of man,
>     and he came to the Ancient of Days
>         and was presented before him.
>     And to him was given dominion
>         and glory and kingdom,
>     that all peoples, nations, and languages
>         should serve him;
>     his dominion is an everlasting dominion,

which shall not pass away,
and his kingdom one
      that shall not be destroyed.

The literature of a Jewish apocalyptic sect that reached a similar form of the hope is preserved in a work known as 1 Enoch (sometimes called Ethiopic Enoch). This group focused their hope on the figure of Enoch who, according to Gen 5:24, "walked with God; and he was not, for God took him." They interpreted these words to mean that Enoch had been transported to heaven whence he would come as Son of Man to judge the world. Whether this sect influenced the Christians or the Christians influenced this sect is a matter of dispute. Our opinion is that both reached a similar position independently, and that the similarity is explained by three factors the Christians and the sect that produced 1 Enoch have in common: they are Jewish apocalyptic sects, they have a hero translated to heaven, and they use Dan 7:13.

There are many other forms of the apocalyptic hope. The Assumption of Moses, a work contemporary with the New Testament, is particularly interesting because of its use of "Kingdom of God," a key concept in the teaching of Jesus.

And then his [God's] kingdom shall appear
throughout all his creation,
And then Satan shall be no more.
And sorrow shall depart with him.
Then the hands of the angel shall be filled
Who has been appointed chief,
And he shall forthwith avenge them of their
enemies.
For the Heavenly One will arise from his
royal throne,
And he will go forth from his holy habitation
With indignation and wrath on account of his sons.
And the earth shall tremble: to its confines
shall it be shaken:
And the high mountains shall be made low
And the hills shall be shaken and fall.
And the horns of the sun shall be broken and he
shall be turned into darkness;
And the moon shall not give her light, and be
turned wholly into blood.
And the circle of the stars shall be disturbed.
And the sea shall retire into the abyss,
And the fountains of waters shall fail,
And the rivers shall dry up.
For the Most High will arise, the Eternal God
alone,
And he will appear to punish the Gentiles,
And he will destroy all their idols.
Then thou, O Israel, shalt be happy,
And thou shalt mount upon the necks and wings

of the eagle,
And they shall be ended.
And God will exalt thee,
And he will cause thee to approach to the heaven
of the stars,
In the place of their habitation.
And thou shalt look from on high and shalt see
thy enemies in Gehenna,
And thou shalt recognize them and rejoice,
And thou shalt give thanks and confess thy Creator.

ASSUMPTION OF MOSES 10

Another form of the hope is associated with the coming of a Son of David, here expressed in the Psalms of Solomon, a work slightly earlier than the New Testament.

Behold, O Lord, and raise up unto them their
king, the son of David,
At the time in the which thou seest, O God, that
he may reign over Israel thy servant.
And gird him with strength, that he may shatter
unrighteous rulers,
And that he may purge Jerusalem from nations that
trample her down to destruction.
Wisely, righteously he shall thrust out sinners
from the inheritance,
He shall destroy the godless nations with the word
of his mouth;
At his rebuke nations shall flee before him,
And he shall reprove sinners for the thoughts
of their heart.
And he shall gather together a holy people, whom
he shall lead in righteousness,
And he shall judge the tribes of the people
that has been sanctified by the Lord his God.
And he shall not suffer unrighteousness to lodge
any more in their midst,
Nor shall there dwell with them any man that
knoweth wickedness,
For he shall know them, that they are all sons
of their God.
And he shall divide them according to their tribes
upon the land,
And neither sojourner nor alien shall sojourn
with them any more.
He shall judge peoples and nations in the wisdom
of his righteousness.
And he shall have the heathen nations to serve him
under his yoke;
And he shall glorify the Lord in a place to be
seen of all the earth;

And he shall purge Jerusalem, making it holy as of
   old:
So that nations shall come from the ends of the
   earth to see his glory,
   Bringing as gifts her sons who had fainted,
   And to see the glory of the Lord, wherewith
   God hath glorified her.

PSALMS OF SOLOMON 17

Despite the variety of the forms of expression, the hope itself is constant for
a climactic series of events that will lead to the final, eschatological
intervention of God into human history, directly or through intermediary
figures. Through these events the world would be forever changed,
transformed into a perfect world in which the people of God would be forever
blessed for their fidelity, and their enemies and God's forever punished.

This hope is called the "apocalyptic" hope because the characteristic claim
of the literature that expresses it is that God has uncovered or revealed to the
writer or seer his plan for the further course of history and the coming of the
End. This revelation frequently takes the form of dreams or visions, which are
then interpreted by a heavenly figure. The dreams or visions generally use
symbols to recount the history of the Jewish (or Christian) people and to
express the hope for the immediate future. So, for example, Daniel 7 tells in
symbols the history of the Near Eastern world from the Babylonian Empire
through the Persian Empire to the conquests of Alexander the Great and his
ten successors as kings of the Macedonian Seleucid Kingdom of Syria. The
final symbol used to represent a king is the "little horn" (Dan 7:8), which
represents Antiochus IV Epiphanes, who began persecuting the Jews in 168 B.C.
in an attempt to consolidate his empire. The result was the Jewish revolt
against Syrian overlordship, led first by Judas Maccabeus (i.e., Judas the
"hammerer" of his enemies), which achieved religious and ultimately political
independence for the Jews—an independence that lasted almost exactly a
hundred years, until the coming of the Romans in the person of Pompey in 63
B.C. The author of Daniel 7 is living at the time of the Maccabean revolt,
writing to inspire his people with confidence that the war is the beginning of
the End, that it will shortly be ended by the coming of the Son of Man as judge
and ruler of the world.

## Literary Features of Apocalyptic

From the standpoint of literary form the apocalyptic movement has a number
of interesting features. In the first place its writers make extensive use of
symbols, necessary in attempting to depict the final, eschatological intervention of God in human history and the subsequent judging of nations and
transformation of the world. How else could one depict these events except in
symbols? But symbols were not only used in depicting the End, they were also
used in giving an account of the events of past and present history that
preceded, in the apocalyptic view, the coming of the End. So though in Daniel

11 the history of the Jewish people is sketched in direct language—the "Kings of Persia," the "King of the South" (the Egyptian king), the "King of the North" (the Syrian king), the "ships of the Kittim" (the Romans)—in Daniel 7 the same story is told in terms of beasts and horns.

A second literary characteristic of the movement is pseudonymity. Apocalyptic writers regularly wrote under the pseudonym of a distinguished figure of the past. The unknown author of the book of Daniel, for example, writing at the time of the Maccabean revolt, wrote in the name of Daniel, a legendary hero of the Jews from an earlier age. Others wrote in the guise of other Jewish heroic figures: the Enoch group wrote in the name of their hero, Enoch; the Christians in the name of theirs, Jesus. The book of Revelation is a remarkable exception to this tendency in that the author used his own name: "The revelation of Jesus Christ . . . to his servant John" (Rev 1:1).

A third literary characteristic of apocalyptic is the extensive quotation of previously existing texts. The apocalyptic writers constantly used and reused, interpreted and reinterpreted, the sacred texts of their tradition, especially earlier apocalyptic texts. We illustrate this facet of apocalyptic later in our analysis of Mark 13.

## The Influence of Apocalyptic

Apocalyptic passages appear in earlier prophetic works (e.g., Isaiah 24–27), but the first major apocalyptic text known to us is the book of Daniel, a product of the Maccabean revolt. Apocalyptic texts can be dated according to the last historical event detectable in their review of history. Daniel 8–12 bewails the desecration of the Jerusalem Temple by Antiochus IV Epiphanes in 168 B.C. but does not mention its cleansing and rededication by the Maccabees in 165 B.C., so the work is normally dated between those years. From this first full flowering, apocalyptic came to be a major influence in Judaism and later in Christianity, producing a flood of works, many now lost to us. The period of its major influence lasted approximately three centuries. The reason for the decline of apocalyptic is largely that it tended to foster a spirit of revolt against Rome, a passion to begin the war that God would end. After the failure of the bar Cochba rising in A.D. 135, it fell into disrepute in what was becoming mainstream Judaism, and of the many Jewish apocalyptic works, only the book of Daniel found its way into the Jewish canon. Among the Christians its influence also dwindled. The delay of the parousia (the particularly Christian form of the apocalyptic hope), the necessity of coming to terms with the Roman world rather than constantly hoping for its total destruction, the fact that apocalyptic visionaries were free spirits essentially resistant to the growing institutionalization of the church—all this combined to bring about a decline of Christian apocalyptic, and only one of the many Christian apocalyptic works is in the Christian canon, the book of Revelation. But during the three centuries or so of its flowering, apocalyptic was a profound influence in both Judaism and Christianity.

After the return from their exile in Babylonia the Jews experienced a decline of prophecy, and apocalyptic replaced it as the means whereby God still spoke directly to his people. It was the claim of early Christianity that prophecy had returned to them as an eschatological gift, but that prophecy largely took the form of apocalyptic. A major contribution of apocalyptic was that in Judaism it provided the successor to prophecy and in Christianity the vehicle for the return of prophecy. Strange as the characteristic visions of the apocalyptic seers may appear to us today, they were the means whereby the Jews after their return from the Exile in Babylonia were convinced that God was still revealing his will and purpose directly to his people. With the decline of apocalyptic, the rabbi interpreting the Law revealed God's will, a process already begun during the period of the ascendancy of apocalyptic. But between the decline of prophecy and the coming of rabbinic Judaism it was apocalyptic, itself a child of prophecy, that fulfilled this essential function and convinced the people that God was still addressing them directly.

Another contribution was apocalyptic's intensive concern for the sacred texts of its tradition and its conviction that these texts could and should be reinterpreted according to changing circumstances. Later the rabbis were to see the scriptures as essentially deposits of God's eternal truth, which could and should be distilled and applied to the current situation by the proper interpretative method, the proper hermeneutics, and the Jewish scribes of the New Testament period were well on their way to this view of the text as fixed and immutable. Apocalyptic, however, envisaged a more dynamic interaction between the past text and the present situation, whereby the text interpreted the situation and the situation interpreted the text, so that the text itself could be modified and rewritten. Ultimately, of course, both these ways of looking at a sacred text are important, and it is not the least contribution of apocalyptic to the future of Judaism, as well as of Christianity, that it developed one of them as extensively as it did.

Apocalyptic contributed to the field of theology and doctrine. It was the vehicle for bringing into Judaism a developed *dualism*, a concept of reality divided into two antithetical forces—good and evil, darkness and light, angels and demons—and of the arena of human history and experience as a battleground where these forces were at war with one another. Further, apocalyptic brought into Judaism the concept of a resurrection, in the form of an expectation of the general resurrection of the dead: "And many of those who sleep in the dust of the earth shall awake, some to everlasting life, and some to shame and everlasting contempt" (Dan 12:2). It also developed within Judaism the concept of a redeemer figure who would act as God's intermediary and whose coming would be the central act of the apocalyptic dramas: Messiah, Son of David, Son of Man, Elect One, the archangel Michael, a prophet like Moses, a Restorer—the possibilities were endless. Sometimes God was conceived of as acting directly rather than through a redeemer figure, as in Assumption of Moses 10 where "And then his (God's) kingdom shall appear throughout all his creation" and "For the Heavenly One will arise from his royal throne" are two different ways of saying the same thing. The Kingdom of God is God acting as King; to use the expression is a way of talking about the direct and unmediated eschatological activity of God.

It is obvious even from this short list, which could be considerably extended, that apocalyptic had much influence on ancient Judaism and still more on the movement that began as an apocalyptic sect within ancient Judaism—earliest Christianity.

## THE QUMRAN COMMUNITY

It is not our purpose here to present still another brief account of the community whose writings were discovered in 1947 in some caves near the Dead Sea (and hence were called the "Dead Sea Scrolls") and whose headquarters were in what the Arabs call Wadi Qumran, which empties into the northwest corner of the Dead Sea. To be of any value, such an account would have to go beyond the confines permissible in an introductory book, and excellent accounts are readily available in our resource materials, especially the *Interpreter's Dictionary of the Bible* and the *Jerome Biblical Commentary*. But we do want to call attention to the existence of this community and to how being aware of it has increased our understanding of New Testament Christianity.

To begin with the obvious point, both the Qumran community and earliest Christianity were apocalyptic sects within ancient Judaism. The last days of the Qumran community and the first of the Christian coincided, for Qumran perished in the Jewish War of A.D. 66–70. There were many differences between the two communities, the chief being that Qumran was a monastic community that waited for the world to come to it, whereas Christianity went out into the world as a missionary community—but then Qumran numbered no "Hellenists" in its midst. But both communities shared the apocalyptic hope: the men at Qumran expected two Messiahs—a Messiah of Aaron, a priest who would sanctify them, and the Messiah of Israel, a warrior who would lead them in the battle against the Gentiles that would mark the beginning of the End. Indeed one of their texts, 1QM, the War Scroll ("War of the Son of Light and the Son of Darkness") is a battle plan for this war, which they would begin and God would end. The Christians expected the Messiah Jesus to come as eschatological judge and redeemer, but they seem to have abandoned the concept of a Holy War, perhaps under the influence of Jesus himself. The Qumran community ate their communal meals in anticipation of the day when they would eat with the Messiahs, as the Christians ate theirs in anticipation of the Kingdom of God (Mark 14:25). Qumran had an initiatory baptism and subsequent ceremonial lustrations, and great pains were taken to ensure an adequate water supply for these rites. Christianity had an initiatory baptism, but no subsequent ceremonial lustrations. The reason for this difference lay in the fact that the Christians were mostly laymen, but Qumran was essentially a community of priests. Both communities reached the point of sharing their goods in common, Qumran rigidly so, Christianity at the beginning according to the tradition of the "voluntary communism" in Acts 2:43–47. Both communities came to be headed by an individual whose office was described by the same term, the Christian Greek *episkopos* ("bishop," literally "overseer"), an equivalent for the Qumran Hebrew *paqid* or *mebaqqer*. Moreover, the "overseers" in both communities had the same responsibilities: the instruction of initiates and the control of the material resources.

But the most important commonality was their method of interpreting scripture—the common hermeneutics. At Qumran the scribes of the community developed a special form of the method of interpretation whereby the text and the circumstances of the interpreter were brought into a dynamic relationship with one another and the one interpreted in light of the other. This is the *pesher* method, so called because the form is that of a quotation of the passage of scripture followed by the word *pishro* ("its interpretation is" from *pesher*, "interpretation") and then the interpretation itself. It was based on an understanding of the relationship among God, scripture, and community that is indicated in one of the texts, the *pesher* on Habakkuk (1QpHab) 2:8–10 (Vermes' translation):

> They, the men of violence and breakers of the Covenant, will not believe when they hear all that [is to happen to] the final generation from the Priest [in whose heart] God set [understanding] that he might interpret all the words of His servants the Prophets, through whom he foretold all that would happen to His people [and His land].

This method of interpretation exercised great freedom in regard to the text of the scripture concerned. Let us take an example from the *pesher* on Psalm 37 (4QpPs37). Psalm 37:20 reads in part, "the enemies of the Lord are like the glory of the pastures," where the Hebrew represented by "the glory of the pastures" is very difficult and can also be translated "the fat of lambs" (ERV). Clearly, however, either the pastures or the lambs is a good thing to be, and the puzzle has always been why it is that "the enemies of the Lord" should be likened to something good. The New English Bible conjectures a reading, "like fuel in a furnace." The rabbis interpreted the passage, "like the fat of lambs being fattened for a sacrifice." The priests of Qumran read the passage as referring to themselves, not as "the enemies of the Lord" but as "those who love the Lord," a change involving the substitution of one letter for another in the Hebrew, and then interpreted the passage as referring to their eschatological function in the purpose of God.

> And those who love the Lord shall be like the pride of pastures. Interpreted [this concerns] the congregation of His elect, who shall be leaders and princes . . . of the flock among their herds.
>
> 4QpPs37 3:4–6 (Vermes' translation)

The Christians certainly shared this freedom in interpreting scripture in terms of themselves and their circumstances. A good example is the quotation from Joel in Acts 2.[1] Joel 2:30 reads, "And I will give portents in the heavens and on the earth, blood and fire and columns of smoke." There is here only one

---

[1]This passage is discussed briefly in chapter 2, p. 35.

set of portents and signs; the reference to both the heavens and the earth simply means something we would express by an adjective like "cosmic." Now the same is true of the Greek version of the text, the Septuagint, which Acts is using. However, Acts 2:19 adds some words to read, "I will show wonders in the heavens *above* and *signs* on the earth *beneath*." Now we have two sets of portents, and when we get to verse 22 we can see why: the signs on the earth beneath are interpreted as referring to Jesus. "Jesus of Nazareth, a man attested to you by God with mighty works and wonders *and signs* which God did through him in your midst." Many more examples of this *pesher* use of scripture in the New Testament could be given, and it is a major element in the development of New Testament theology.


# APOCALYPTIC CHRISTIANITY

## The Source Q

The first literary evidence in the New Testament for the existence of Christian apocalyptic is the source Q, used by the evangelists Matthew and Luke. Q is not itself an apocalypse, but it is dominated by eschatology and by a particular form of the apocalyptic hope. As reconstructed and thematically arranged by Howard Kee, *Jesus in History*, pp. 71–73, the source contained the following material. (All the references given are to the gospel of Luke, because it is generally accepted that Luke edited the Q material to a lesser extent than Matthew, who had a special interest in teaching material.)

### Narrative Material
Healing the Centurion's Slave (Luke 7:2, 6b–10)

### Parenetic Material
Serving Two Masters (16:13)
On Light or Darkness Within (11:34–36)
On Faith and Forgiveness (17:3b–4, 6)

### Eschatological Material

*Eschatological Warning*
Preaching Judgment (3:7–9)
Baptism with Spirit and Fire (3:16–17)
Judging and Eschatological Judgment (6:37–42)
Woes on the Cities Where Jesus Performed Mighty Works (10:13–15)
Judgment on the Scribes and Pharisees (11:39–52)
Fire, Baptism, Sword, and Division (12:49–53)
Inability to Interpret the Signs of this Time (12:54–56)
Repent in View of the Impending Crisis (12:57–58)
Prepare for the Crisis (13:24–29)
Lament over Jerusalem's Impending Doom (13:34–35)
Judgment on the Careless and Preoccupied (17:24, 26–27, 33–37)

*Eschatological Conflict*

Contest with the Devil (4:2–12)
Defeating the Prince of Demons (11:14–22)
Dispelling the Unclean Spirits (11:23–26)

*Eschatological Promise*

The Beatitudes (6:20b–23)
Love of Enemies (6:27–36)
Eschatological Prayer (11:2–4)
What God Will Give (11:9–13)
Seek the Kingdom (12:22–31)
Treasures in Heaven (12:33–34)
A Role in the Kingdom (22:28–30)

*Eschatological Knowledge*

Gratitude for What God Has Revealed (10:21–24)

*Eschatological Discipleship*
Fitness for the Kingdom (9:57–60)
The Kingdom Has Drawn Near (10:2–12)
Fearless Confession (12:2–12)
Bearing the Cross (14:26–27)

*Eschatological Parables*

Three Parables of Watchfulness (12:39–40, 42–46)
Kingdom Compared with Leaven (13:20–21)
The Great Supper (14:16–23)
The Joyous Shepherd (15:4–7)
Investing the Pounds (19:11–27)
The Threatened House (6:47–49)

*Jesus as Eschatological Messenger and Salvation-Bringer*

Jesus' Ministry Fulfills Scripture (7:18–23)
John Is the Forerunner; Jesus Brings the Kingdom (7:24–35)
Law and Prophets Give Way to the Kingdom (16:16–17)
To Receive Jesus Is to Receive God (10:16)
Jesus = The Sign of Jonah: Prophet and Wise Man (11:29b–32)
Sitting at Jesus' Table in the Kingdom (14:15; 22:28–30)
Lament over Jerusalem Ends in Promise of Messiah's Coming (13:34–35; 19:41–44)

It can be seen at a glance that Q is indeed dominated by eschatology. The form of apocalyptic hope that it exhibits is the expectation of Jesus coming from heaven as Son of Man: Luke 11:30; 12:8–9; 12:40; 17:24; 17:26, 30 (each time with a parallel in Matthew). Richard Edwards has shown[2] that of these six sayings four were created by prophets within the Q community itself (the community that produced the source Q): Luke 11:30; 17:24; 17:26, 30. These

[2]Edwards, *The Sign of Jonah*, pp. 49–58.

four he calls "eschatological correlatives." Käsemann had already shown that Luke 12:8–9 is a product of early Christian prophecy; it is one of what he calls "sentences of holy law" and we would prefer to call "eschatological judgment pronouncements." Under these conditions it is more than likely that the sixth, Luke 12:40 ("You also must be ready for the Son of man is coming at an unexpected hour"), is also early Christian prophetic exhortation. The importance of Jesus as Son of Man to the Q community can be seen in the fact that it refers to Jesus as Son of Man not only in connection with his eschatological judgment, but also in his earthly ministry: Luke 7:34; 9:58; 12:10; and their parallels in Matthew.

The origin of the expectation of Jesus coming from heaven as Son of Man is disputed. It is clear that the ultimate origin is Daniel 7:13–14:

I saw in the night visions,
and behold, with the clouds of heaven
there came one like a son of man,
and he came to the Ancient of Days
and was presented before him.

And to him was given dominion
and glory and kingdom,
that all peoples, nations, and languages
should serve him;
his dominion is an everlasting dominion,
which shall not pass away,
and his kingdom one
that shall not be destroyed.

But how we got from that to the sayings in Q is a matter of dispute. There are two possibilities. Either (a) Jesus proclaimed the coming of the Son of Man as eschatological judge without identifying himself with that figure, and then the early church made the identification: Jesus is that Son of Man.[3] Or (b) the early church arrived at the expectation by interpreting the resurrection of Jesus in light of Psalm 110:1 and Dan 7:13–14, and Jesus himself did not speak of the Son of Man as eschatological judge at all. I myself hold the latter view[4] on the grounds that the expectation did not exist as a firm conception for Jesus

[3] This view is represented, for example, by Tödt, *The Son of Man in the Synoptic Tradition*, and Fuller, *The Foundations of New Testament Christology*.
[4] Perrin, *Rediscovering the Teaching of Jesus*, pp. 164–99. My views as to the subsequent development of the Son of Man Christology in the New Testament are to be found in "The Son of Man in the Synoptic Tradition," *Biblical Research*, vol. 13 (1965), pp. 1–23; "The Christology of Mark: A Study in Methodology," *Journal of Religion*, vol. 51 (1971), pp. 173–87; "Towards the Interpretation of the Gospel of Mark" in Betz, ed., *Christology and a Modern Pilgrimage. A Discussion with Norman Perrin* (a special publication of the Society of Biblical Literature, 1971). The last is to be published in a revised and expanded form as a book by S.C.M. Press. Under the title *A Modern Pilgrimage in New Testament Christology*, Fortress Press is planning to publish a collection of my work on New Testament Christology early in 1974.

to use in his message and that, furthermore, all apocalyptic Son of Man sayings fail the test of the criteria for authenticity of sayings of Jesus (these criteria are discussed in chapter 12), while at the same time exhibiting typical characteristics of early Christian prophecy.

The Q community expected the return of Jesus from heaven as Son of Man with power to execute the eschatological judgment (Luke 12:8–9). He would come suddenly and unexpectedly, but he would most certainly come (Luke 12:40). Faced with the need to give form and content to this expectation, prophets in the community reached back into the past history of the Jews and claimed that it would be like Jonah's coming to the Ninevites (Luke 11:30), like lightning striking (Luke 17:24), or like the judgmental catastrophes associated with Noah and Lot (Luke 17:26, 30). Then, with this expectation and with the conviction that the coming was imminent, they set out to instruct and exhort, to challenge and teach people to prepare themselves for it. This dominance of an apocalyptic expectation and the subordination of other activities to the urgency of proclamation and instruction, so much so that almost everything is oriented toward eschatology, justifies us in calling the Q source a document of apocalyptic Christianity. Moreover, the prophets interpret Jesus in categories or texts given to them by the apocalyptic movement, and they regard their sacred meal as an anticipation of that which they will eat with Jesus "in the kingdom of God" (Luke 14:15; 22:28–30).

A very similar orientation is to be found in 1 and 2 Thessalonians, and we could certainly adduce those letters as texts produced by apocalyptic Christianity, but we shall defer that aspect of them until we discuss Paul and deutero-Pauline Christianity.

## The Apocalyptic Discourses:
## Mark 13 and Its Parallels

We come nearer to the actual literary forms of apocalyptic in Mark 13 and in its parallels in Matthew 24 and Luke 21. Apocalyptic discourses, speeches detailing the events to be expected when the End actually comes, are a feature of apocalyptic literature in general. Assumption of Moses 10, which we gave earlier in our description of the apocalyptic hope, is such a discourse, and other examples are 1 Enoch 1:3–9; 1 Enoch 46:1–8; 4 Ezra 6:13–28. These discourses follow the pattern of apocalyptic expectation concerning the End, with variations depending on the particular form of the expectation held by the writer. There is usually a description of the "woes," the climactic catastrophes marking the death throes of human history as now known. This is followed by  an account of the form of God's eschatological intervention, either directly or  through an eschatological redeemer figure. Then there is an account of the final judgment itself and a description of the punishment of the wicked and the eternal blessedness of the people of God that will follow.

Such discourses were written in a certain way. The particular form of the apocalyptic hope held by the writer gave the overall pattern, but the actual content came from two sources: the scriptures, that is, the writings held by the writer to be sacred, and the experience of the writer and the group he represented. The scriptures themselves were used in two ways: they were either directly quoted, or they were alluded to indirectly. Sometimes the writer wished to reinterpret an existing text; sometimes he reached his texts by association of ideas, of words, or even of the *sounds* of words (in the ancient world reading usually meant reading aloud, even to oneself, as in Acts 8:30 when Philip *hears* the Ethiopian reading Isaiah 53). So an apocalyptic discourse is usually a mosaic of scriptural quotations and allusions, together perhaps with some references to the experience of the writer and his community, generally couched in scriptural language.

The Christian apocalyptic discourses vary from this general pattern in that they include sections of parenesis in which the writer exhorts his readers directly out of his text. In this respect the discourses follow the Christian practice of combining parenesis with proclamation.

We now offer an analysis of Mark 13, following in the main that offered by Lars Hartman in *Prophecy Interpreted*.[5]

**13:1–5a** *An introduction to the discourse,* composed by the evangelist Mark to give the discourse its present setting in the gospel as a whole.

**13:5b–8** *The first section of the discourse proper.* It quotes Dan 2:28–29, 45 (LXX: "this must take place"), 2 Chron 15:6; Isa 19:2 (the references to nation against nation and Kingdom against Kingdom), and alludes to Dan 7:21; 9:26; 11:4–27; and perhaps 2:40 at various places.

**13:9–13** *The first parenetical section.* It couches references to the actual and anticipated sufferings of Christians in language deliberately reminiscent of the sufferings of Jesus during his passion but also allusive of various scriptural passages (Dan 7:25; Psalm 119:46; Dan 6:13–24). Verse 11b alludes to Exod 4:11–17, and verse 12 quotes Mic 7:2, 6.

**13:14–20** *The second section of the discourse.* It quotes and reinterprets Dan 11:31 and 12:11 in the reference to the "desolating sacrilege" (in Daniel this is the altar to Zeus set up in the Jerusalem Temple by the Syrians). The command to "flee to the mountains" is a quote from Gen 19:16, as is the command for the man in the field not to turn back in verse 16. In verse 19 the description of the tribulation quotes Dan 12:1.

**13:21–23** *The second parenetical section.* The reference to the false prophets uses language taken from Deut 13:1–5, but the whole addresses itself to concrete problems faced by the Christian church in a period of intense apocalyptic expectation.

**13:24–27** *The third section of the discourse.* Here the quotations are frequent. Verse 24 quotes Joel 2:10 (the sun being darkened) and Isa 13:10

[5]Hartman, *Prophecy Interpreted*, pp. 145–59.

(the moon not giving its light). Verse 25 has the stars falling and the powers of heaven being shaken (from Isa 34:4). The Son of Man reference in verse 26 is from Dan 7:13, and verse 27 is a mosaic of Deut 30:3–4 and Zech 2:10 (in the LXX version). There are allusions to Isa 11:10–12; 27:13; and Dan 7:14 at various places.

Verse 27 ends the apocalyptic discourse proper. The remaining verses 28–37 form a loose-knit, final parenetical section that does not contain a single scriptural quotation but does show a good deal of Christian traditional material. It was almost certainly added to the original discourse by Mark himself.

It is not our purpose here to analyze in any detail the parallel discourses in Matthew and Luke; we are not offering a detailed commentary on these passages but only introducing to the reader this particular early Christian literary form. Briefly, Matt 24:4–31 follows Mark with only minor additions and changes, as does 24:32–36 (= the loose-knit parenesis of Mark 13:28–32). But Matthew then adds a whole series of sayings of various kinds that have parallels in Luke in a different context; i.e., they are from Q—Matt 24:37–51. The Lukan context is the more original, since it is Matthew who arranges teaching material in long discourses. Then Matthew further adds a chapter of eschatological parables (Matthew 25). Luke 21:8–28 is close to Mark's discourse, yet sufficiently different from it to make it possible that he may be following a version of the discourse different from what Mark has. But it is in any case fundamentally the same discourse.

What the original date of this discourse might have been, or what its original form might have been, it is equally impossible to say. It is the nature of apocalyptic writers to interpret and reinterpret texts, even their own, so that any discourse text we have represents the version of it that came from the hand of the particular evangelist concerned. Matthew is conservative in his treatment of Mark's discourse, but then Matthew is no longer an apocalyptic writer; he is on the way to becoming a rabbi, as will appear evident when we discuss him in a later chapter. Luke, on the other hand, has a version so different from Mark's and yet so closely related to it that he may be following a different version of the discourse in the tradition of the church, as noted earlier. But it may also be that Luke, who is by no means becoming in any respect a rabbi, is simply exercising the traditional freedom of a writer dealing with an apocalyptic text. Mark is also an apocalyptic writer, and he must certainly have reworked the discourse he presents. Mark 13:5b–27 is a product of the evangelist Mark, and we shall treat it as such when we come to discuss the gospel of Mark later. Yet apocalyptic discourses are such that so complex a discourse could not have been created by one man at one time in one place, but must have grown and developed over a considerable time. As they stand, then, the apocalyptic discourses in the New Testament are testimony to the continuing element of apocalyptic Christianity and should be read as such. But they are also evidence of the particular concerns of the individual evangelists, and they need also be read in this way.

## The Book of Revelation

The one complete apocalyptic text in the New Testament is the book of Revelation. It is a thoroughly apocalyptic work, and yet in two respects it differs from the usual apocalyptic texts: it is not pseudonymous, and it contains letters to churches located in Asia Minor.

The author identifies himself as "John" and describes himself as having been exiled to Patmos, a small, rocky island in the Aegean Sea about thirty-seven miles southwest of Miletus. Such islands were often used as places of banishment by the Romans, and Christian tradition has it that John was banished there by the emperor Domitian in A.D. 95 and was released some eighteen months later when Nerva became emperor. We have no way of knowing whether this tradition is historically accurate—but surely such a procedure would be entirely normal in the Greco-Roman world. John himself tells us that he was exiled "on account of the word of God and the testimony of Jesus" (Rev 1:9), that is, as a result of persecution of the Christians. The work itself bears out this claim for it is self-evidently written to encourage Christians in a situation of persecution.

The possibility and fact of the persecution of Christians in the Roman Empire during New Testament times is important enough to warrant spending a moment on it. The Roman government was tolerant of local religions but at the same time anxious to guarantee overall loyalty to the Empire. A polytheistic society presented no problems; local inhabitants were asked to formally acknowledge the gods of Rome, and having done so, they were free to continue their local religious beliefs and practices. As monotheists, the Jews could not acknowledge the gods of Rome; yet their special position was recognized, their religion was accepted by the Roman authorities as a legal religion, and they were freed from the requirement. The Christians, however, were no longer Jews, and were therefore in the position of having to refuse to acknowledge the gods of Rome while lacking the protection of a recognized legal religion. Thus, they were liable to persecution at any time: the local Roman official could demand that they acknowledge the gods of Rome; they would have to refuse and be liable to banishment, torture, or even death. This ever present possibility hung over the church from the moment it severed its ties with Judaism and is reflected constantly in the New Testament itself. Moreover, New Testament Christians lived with the memory of the sudden persecution of the Christians in Rome under the emperor Nero, at which time tradition has it that both Peter and Paul perished. John's exile to Patmos was the result of a local persecution, but he clearly anticipated that it could spread to engulf all the churches to which and for which he wrote.

Another element in the persecution of Christians in New Testament times was the widespread tendency for the Roman emperor to be worshiped as a god. This had spread from the East to the West in the Hellenistic world and was more accepted in some places than in others: some emperors demanded it, while others deplored it; similarly, some local Roman authorities pressed for it while others did not. Again, the Jews were in a privileged position the Christians could not share, in that such worship was not required of them.

There was, furthermore, hostility from and possible persecution by the Jews themselves. Jewish communities tended to be tightly knit, with a certain authority over their own members. Paul says that "five times I have received at the hands of the Jews the forty lashes less one" (2 Cor 11:24), which was a Jewish punishment, just as the reference "three times I have been beaten with rods" (2 Cor 11:25) was a Roman one. Similarly, Mark 13:9 speaks of Christians being "beaten in synagogues" and of standing "before governors and kings for my sake"; these, again, are references respectively to Jewish and to Roman persecution of Christians.

Persecution from Jews and Romans was, then, always a possibility for the men and women of the New Testament. John reports that the blood of martyrs had already flowed (2:13; 6:9); the "hour of trial" was threatening all Christendom (3:10); the emperor would demand divine worship (13:4, 12–17; 16:2; 19:20), which Christians would have to refuse (14:9–12). This impending persecution inspires John's apocalyptic vision. We cannot be sure when or where the particular persecution spoken of took place, but most modern scholars incline to the time of the emperor Domitian (A.D. 81–96) and the locale of Asia Minor. This is where early Christian tradition locates John and his book, for he writes his letters to the churches of Asia Minor. The normal practice of dating an apocalyptic work by its recital of recent history in symbols fails in this instance. The clearest reference is to the "Kings" in 17:10, and the writer appears to have lived under the sixth of these. If these were six Roman emperors, beginning with Augustus and omitting the short reigns of Galbo, Otho, and Vitellius, the sixth would be Vespasian, emperor from A.D. 70–79. But Vespasian did not demand worship of himself as a god, and there is no knowledge of a persecution of Christians in Asia Minor during his reign. The conditions implied by the book as a whole simply do not fit. Either the author is reusing an earlier text, or he does not know his emperors.

More important than the date of the work, however, is the fact that the author identifies himself; moreover, he identifies himself as a prophet by describing his work as a prophecy (Rev 1:3). We pointed out earlier that a distinguishing feature of earliest Christianity was the consciousness of the return of prophecy to the community. John of Patmos is such an early Christian prophet, and he describes the ecstatic vision that qualifies him: "I was in the Spirit on the Lord's day . . . " (1:10). The vision itself is an interesting combination of the kind of experience the classical Hebrew prophets claimed as validating their message (for example, Isaiah 6) and the typical visions of apocalyptic writers. John's vision is characteristically apocalyptic; yet at the same time it is shaped by the characteristics of classical Hebrew prophecy. John is an apocalyptic seer, but he is also a prophet, and this "also" is very important to him, just as the possession of the spirit of prophecy was to early Christianity in general.

That John of Patmos can be identified as a prophet is more important to understanding his work than identifying him with some other individual named John in the New Testament. Traditionally it has been claimed that he is the John, son of Zebedee, known to us from the gospel stories, but this is most unlikely. It has also been claimed that he is the "John" of the fourth gospel, but the difference in language and style alone makes this identification quite impossible. However, that he is able to identify himself, and as a prophet (in sharp contrast to the pseudonymity and practice of apocalyptic writers in general), speaks volumes for the vitality, power, and self-confidence of New Testament Christianity.

Another most unusual aspect of the book of Revelation is its letters to seven churches in Asia Minor: Ephesus, Smyrna, Pergamum, Thyatira, Sardis, Philadelphia, and Laodicea (see chapters 2 and 3). This is unparalleled in apocalyptic writing and has to be due ultimately to the impact that Paul's letter writing made on the New Testament church. Paul's letters had become so important that the literary form was imitated even by an apocalyptic writer. The book of Revelation as a whole has the external form of a letter in that it begins with an opening salutation (1:4–6) and closes with a benediction (22:21). The contrast in literary form between the direct address of the letters and the symbolic drama of the remainder of the book is startling, but no more so than the fact that an apocalyptic writer identifies himself and calls his work a prophecy.

The fact that we have here the outward form of a Pauline letter helps us to grasp the essential thrust of the work. It begins with a salutation in the Pauline style: "To him who loves us and has freed us from our sins by his blood and made us a kingdom, priests to his God and Father, to him be glory and dominion for ever and ever. Amen" (Rev 1:5b–6; compare Gal 1:3–5). But then it continues: "Behold, he is coming with the clouds, and every eye will see him, every one who pierced him; and all tribes of the earth will wail on account of him. Even so. Amen" (1:7). This is a classic statement of the early Christian hope for the return of Jesus as apocalyptic judge and redeemer. Similarly, the closing benediction, "The grace of the Lord Jesus be with all the saints. Amen" (22:21), is in the Pauline style, but it is preceded by a prayer for the coming of the Lord, "Come, Lord Jesus" (22:20). However, this is the early Palestinian Christian Eucharistic prayer *Maranatha*, which Paul himself used at the end of a letter: "Our Lord, come! The grace of the Lord Jesus be with you. My love be with you all in Christ Jesus. Amen" (1 Cor 16:22–24). It is a reminder that for all its surface strangeness, the book of Revelation is not to be separated from the rest of the New Testament. The hope it represents is a fundamental feature of a major part of the New Testament.

The nature of an apocalyptic work is such that it necessarily defies exact analysis and a precise outline. Rather it offers a series of dramatic presentations of the author's hope for the future, at the same time reflecting the author's understanding of the past and his reinterpretation of texts he accepts as sacred. The result is that any detailed analysis of the book of Revelation is somewhat arbitrary and in a sense a denial of its very quality as a literary text. An apocalyptic work seeks to stun its readers by the power of its visions so that the reader loses his fear of the present and is caught up in the hope for the future it presents. Nevertheless, as an aid to understanding and appreciating the book as a whole, the following broad analysis of its contents is offered.

**1:1–3**   *Opening address.*

**1:4–20**   *The prophet's vision,* validating his authority to write to the seven churches.

**2:1–3:22**   *The letters to the seven churches.*

**4:1–5:14**   *The prophet's further vision,* validating his message as an apocalyptic seer (this vision shows the influence of Ezekiel 1 and 2).

**6:1–7:17**   *The necessary first stages,* the overture to the coming of the End itself.

**8:1–14:13**   *The preparation for the End,* including an explanation of the status of Christian martyrs.

**14:14–20**   *Interjected prospect of the final judgment.*

**15:1–22:5**   *Vision of the coming of the End itself.*

**22:6–21**   *Concluding postscript.*

## THE VISIONS AND SYMBOLS OF APOCALYPTIC

The visions of the book of Revelation and of apocalyptic in general are strange and arbitrary to the modern reader. But remember that visions play a real part in the general history of religion. A vivid example from recent North American culture is the "great vision" of Black Elk, a holy man of the Oglala Sioux, as reported by him to John G. Neihardt.[6] Here is a scene taken at random from that vision:

> And as I looked and wept, I saw that there stood on the north side of the starving camp a sacred man who was painted red all over his body, and he held a spear as he walked into the center of the people, and there he lay down and rolled. And when he got up, it was a fat bison standing there, and where the bison stood a sacred herb sprang up right where the tree had been in the center of the nation's hoop. The herb grew and bore four blossoms on a single stem while I was looking—a blue, a white, a scarlet, and a yellow—and the bright rays of these flashed to the heavens. I know now what this meant, that the bison were the gift of a good spirit and were our strength, but we should lose them, and from the same good spirit we must find another strength.[7]

Like John of Patmos, Black Elk is given to understanding the past and to interpreting the future by means of a vision.

The component parts of a vision are conveyed to the seer by his own culture. John of Patmos meditated on the scriptures he inherited from his tradition, and Black Elk on the stories told to him; both were surrounded by the artifacts and sacred elements of their people. The differences between the visions are,

---

[6]Neihardt, *Black Elk Speaks*, pp. 20–47.
[7]Ibid., pp. 38–39.

therefore, easy to understand; what should be taken seriously is their similarity as visions.

An important element in the visions of John of Patmos is their relationship to early Christian worship. His authenticating vision comes to him while he is "in the Spirit on the Lord's day" (Rev 1:10), and he constantly quotes what on form critical grounds can be recognized as fragments of confessions, prayers, and hymns, which must come from the liturgy of his church or be modeled on it: Rev. 1:5–6; 4:8, 11; 5:9–10; 7:10, 12; 11:15, 17–18; 12:10–12; 15:3–4; 19:1–2, 5–8; 22:13. Both the fact of John's visions and the reality of the form they take for him are not to be denied. As we have said, such visions are well known in the general history of religion, and the particular form of John's vision came from the culture he inherited, the scriptures on which he meditated, and the liturgy of the church whose worship was a central aspect of his life.

Another aspect of apocalyptic to be taken seriously is its symbolism. We may perhaps illustrate this best with reference to one symbol common to all New Testament apocalyptic, the "son of man" from Dan 7:13. We have already noted that the Q community turned to Dan 7:13, that prophets in that community produced Son of Man sayings to put on the lips of Jesus, and that the apocalyptic discourses also turn to that passage and its central symbol. When one gets to a certain level of experience or expectation, the normal structure of language is simply shattered, and what is experienced or expected can be described only in symbols, often in archetypal symbols that have deep roots in the consciousness of man as man. So it is with the consciousness of evil, sin, and guilt and with the expectation of a cataclysmic, eschatological act whereby evil, sin, and guilt will be no more. The Jewish myth explains the existence of sin as the result of the rebellion of primordial man, Adam, and its natural consequence is the expectation that the act of another representative man would redeem that sin. When Paul says, "as one man's trespass led to condemnation for all men, so one man's act of righteousness leads to acquittal and life for all men" (Rom 5:18), he is reflecting the natural consequence of accepting the myth that sin resulted from the rebellious act of primordial man. In the language of apocalyptic symbolism, the same natural consequence is the idea of the coming of a redeemer figure "like a son of man," a figure human yet more than human, and it is undoubtedly this fundamental propensity of the human mind to think in such terms that accounts for the prominence of Son of Man symbolism in early Christian apocalyptic.

Another example of the human mind's fundamental propensity to embrace myth or symbol when attempting to approach the ultimates of human experience or expectation is Amos Wilder's poetic expression of his experience in the First World War.

> There we marched out on haunted battle-ground,
> There smelled the strife of gods, were brushed against
> By higher beings, and were wrapped around
> With passions not of earth, all dimly sensed.

> There saw we demons fighting in the sky
> And battles in aerial mirage,
> The feverish Very lights proclaimed them by,
> Their tramplings woke our panting, fierce barrage.
>
> Their tide of battle, hither, thither, driven
> Filled earth and sky with cataclysmic throes,
> Our strife was but the mimicry of heaven's
> And we the shadows of celestial foes. [8]

We quote Wilder deliberately because he is consciously sensitive to this aspect of apocalyptic, ancient or modern, Christian or secular; but many other examples could be given.

So in thinking of apocalyptic we have to think of the human mind at a level of ultimacy and at that level turning naturally to the use of myth and symbol. In the case of the ancient Jewish and early Christian apocalyptic the ultimacy came from a total despair of the course of human history and an absolute trust in the purpose of God. The result is the visions and symbols we have been discussing.

## THE ENDURING INFLUENCE OF EARLY CHRISTIAN APOCALYPTIC

The most obvious influence of early Christian apocalyptic is the continuing existence of Christian apocalyptic sects and movements. Throughout Christian history, groups of believers have fed their hopes on New Testament apocalyptic literature and calculated the date of the coming of Jesus as Son of Man, as indeed many still do. Similarly, the Beast whose number is six hundred and sixty-six (Rev 13:18) has been identified with every tyrant in Western history, including Hitler and Stalin. But this is a literalistic and hence necessarily false understanding of the apocalyptic hope.

More important is the enduring influence of the myths and symbols of early Christian apocalyptic itself wherever the New Testament has been read. In modern times historical scholars have had all kinds of problems with the book of Revelation, but poets and artists have found it an unending source of inspiration precisely because it uses images of immense evocative power. Early Christian apocalyptic does not challenge us to gather together on a hillside to await the coming of Jesus as Son of Man, or to identify the Beast; it challenges us to recognize the importance and significance of the myths and symbols it uses so dramatically to express hope in the midst of despair.

---

[8] Quoted by Wilder himself in his article "The Rhetoric of Ancient and Modern Apocalyptic," *Interpretation*, vol. 25 (1971), pp. 436–53. Originally printed in Amos Wilder, *Battle Retrospect and Other Poems*, copyright 1923, Yale University Press. Reprinted by permission.

## FURTHER READING

For the characteristics of apocalyptic, see:

PCB, pp. 484–88, "Apocalyptic Literature" (H. H. Rowley).
JBC, pp. 536–43, "Apocrypha" (R.E. Brown).
IDB, vol. 1, pp. 157–61, "Apocalypticism" (M. Rist).
Kümmel, *Intro.,* pp. 316–18.
Russell, *The Method and Message of Jewish Apocalyptic.*
Barrett, *The New Testament Background: Selected Documents,* pp. 227, 255. A representative selection of texts with introduction and notes.
Hennecke and Schneemelcher, *New Testament Apocrypha,* vol. 2, pp. 579–803. A general introduction and then texts in translation with introduction.

A survey of recent scholarly work on apocalyptic is to be found in *Journal for Theology and the Church,* vol. 6, *Apocalypticism,* Funk, ed.; and *Interpretation,* vol. 25, no. 4 (October 1971) is wholly devoted to the subject of apocalyptic.

For the Qumran Community, see:

JBC, pp. 546–57, "Dead Sea Scrolls" (R. E. Brown).
IDB, vol. 1, pp. 790–802, "Dead Sea Scrolls" (O. Betz).
Vermes, *The Dead Sea Scrolls in English.* The texts in English translation with brief introductions. This is much the best and most convenient readily available translation. Unfortunately, the author did not follow the standard method of designating the texts.

The literature on Qumran and its library is endless: perhaps the best general introduction is Cross, *The Ancient Library of Qumran and Modern Biblical Studies.*

Systematic investigation of the theology of Q was begun by Tödt, *The Son of Man in the Synoptic Tradition,* pp. 232–74. Further studies are:

Kee, *Jesus in History,* pp. 62–103.
Edwards, *The Sign of Jonah,* pp. 41–70.
———, "An Approach to the Theology of Q," *Journal of Religion,* vol. 51 (1971), pp. 247–69.

A recent book on the apocalyptic discourses has rendered all previous work out of date and indeed almost superfluous: Hartman, *Prophecy Interpreted: The Formation of Some Jewish Apocalyptic Texts and of the Eschatological Discourse Mark 13 par.*

For the book of Revelation, see:

*PCB*, pp. 1043–61 (N. Turner).
*JBC*, pp. 467–93 (J. L. D'Aragon).
*IDB*, vol. 4, pp. 58–71 (J. W. Bowman). Most scholars do not share Bowman's convictions with regard to the structure of the work, but his argument is extremely interesting.
Kümmel, *Intro.*, pp. 318–33.
Marxsen, *Intro.*, pp. 274–78.
Fuller, *Intro.*, pp. 184–90.

On the visions and symbols of apocalyptic, in addition to the works mentioned in connection with the source Q above, see:

Wilder, *Early Christian Rhetoric: The Language of the Gospel*, especially pp. 118–28.
_____, "Eschatological Imagery and Earthly Circumstance," *New Testament Studies*, vol. 5 (1958/59), pp. 229–45.
_____, "The Rhetoric of Ancient and Modern Apocalyptic," *Interpretation*, vol. 25 (1971), pp. 436–53.
Hartman, *Prophecy Interpreted*, pp. 248–52.
Beardslee, *Literary Criticism of the New Testament*, pp. 53–63.

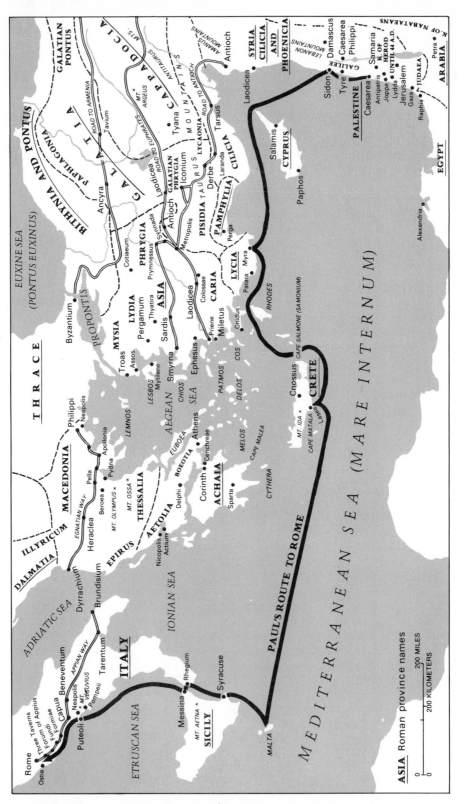

*The world of the apostle Paul.*

# 5

# Paul and His Letters

Paul is a major figure in the New Testament, and his letters make up an important part of it. A leading missionary of the New Testament church, he hammered out an understanding of the Christian faith that is one of the great achievements in Christian theological history. He may be called a man of three worlds: he was the son of a proudly Jewish family, which lived in a strongly Hellenistic Greek environment, and he became a Christian through a dramatic conversion that became the model of piety for centuries. It may be said of him that he was a Hellenist, a Jew, and a Christian, and each of these elements in his personal heritage played an important role in shaping the man who must be reckoned the most important figure in the New Testament church.

Paul was born in Tarsus in Cilicia, a city that rivaled Athens and Rome as an educational center. His letters show that he had a formal Greek education, for he writes Greek well and displays a knowledge of Greek rhetorical devices. At the same time he is always proud of the fact that he came from a family that had deliberately maintained its Jewish heritage in the home. It may even be the case that he also had some formal Jewish rabbinical training. The tradition in Acts 22:3 claims that he had been educated "at the feet of Gamaliel," a famous rabbi of the period, and this may well be true; Paul uses rabbinical techniques, for example, when he argues from scripture in his letters. He himself says that he was a Pharisee, a member of the party within Judaism devoted to the strict interpretation of and obedience to the Law (Phil 3:5). He may even technically have been a rabbi, a recognized teacher with the authority to make legal decisions, but we do not know this with any certainty.

It was this combination of education in and hence real understanding of both Hellenism and Judaism that particularly fitted Paul to assume leadership of the Christian movement as it moved out of Judaism into the Hellenistic world. But there was more to his leadership than his educational background; there was the intensity of his Christian experience. He himself tends to be reticent about the details of his conversion experience (Gal 1:16), but the author of the Acts of the Apostles tells the story three times, which indicates its importance for the Hellenistic Jewish Mission Christianity that Acts represents. Paul could never have become the leader of such a charismatic movement as Hellenistic Jewish Mission Christianity without the gift of a dynamic experience of the risen Christ. In their very language all his letters reflect the vitality and power of that experience, which began at his conversion and continued throughout his life. "At long last," says the famous classical scholar Wilamowitz-Moellendorf, "Greek speaks out of a vivid spiritual experience," [1] and for this reason his letters have nurtured and continue to nurture the evangelical piety of all Christendom.

## PAUL AS A MISSIONARY, FIRST JEWISH, THEN CHRISTIAN

Hellenistic Judaism was itself very much a missionary movement. We saw in chapter 3 that Judaism was very attractive to the Hellenistic world, and the synagogues regularly had their circles of "God-fearers," men attracted to Judaism but resisting full proselytization because they were reluctant to accept circumcision and the dietary laws. In Gal 5:11 Paul asks rhetorically, "But if I, brethren, still preach circumcision, why am I still persecuted?" This leads us to conclude that at one time he had in fact "preach[ed] circumcision," that is, he had been an active missionary for Judaism in the Hellenistic world. This earlier proselytizing for the Jews would account for the readiness and skill with which he took to Christian missionary work and for his vehement resistance to any attempt to have Christians accept circumcision and dietary laws—the major problems he faced in his earlier Jewish missionary activity.

Paul enters the New Testament scene as a bystander at the martyrdom of Stephen in Acts 7:58 and, surprisingly, as a persecutor of the fledgling Christian community in Damascus in Acts 9:1–2. He does not mention the former incident, but the latter is clearly an unforgettable memory for him and for the church at large (Gal 1:13). It is important to note that it was a church in Damascus that he persecuted, a church in the Hellenistic world. In earliest Christianity there were real differences between the churches in Jerusalem (and the strongly Jewish areas of Palestine surrounding Jerusalem) and those in the Hellenistic world in general, even when that world was geographically as close as Damascus. The churches outside Jerusalem and the surrounding areas had often been founded by Hellenistic Jewish Christians driven from Jerusalem by persecution, a persecution occasioned by the fact that they were critical of Judaism and its Law and not by the fact that they recognized Jesus as the Messiah. This is the testimony of the Acts of the Apostles and, as we argued in chapter 2, this testimony is to be accepted. But churches founded by Jewish Christians who were themselves already critical of Judaism—and who had been driven from Jerusalem by persecution on that very ground—would necessarily represent a threat to Judaism itself. They would represent their founders' criticism of Judaism, and in addition to this, they would be attractive to the "God-fearers" precisely because they were critical of those very aspects of Judaism that the "God-fearer" found to be stumbling blocks to full proselytization. If the supposition of Paul's *Jewish* missionary activity is

[1] Quoted by Bornkamm, *Paul*, pp. 9–10.

correct, then we can understand his hostility at that time to a movement that threatened the Judaism he represented, not only by what he would regard as its heterodoxy, but also by its appeal to those "God-fearers" whose full proselytization was the goal of his work.

We consider Paul's conversion in the next section; for the moment let us simply say that "on the road to Damascus" he had an experience that transformed him and his life. The Pharisee became a Christian; the devoted upholder of the Jewish Law became its severest critic; the zealous persecuter of the Christian "way" became its most passionate advocate; the man trained for the Jewish mission in the Hellenistic world became the archetypal Christian missionary.

The actual process of the development of Paul into the Christian apostle of the letters is a complex one, and unfortunately its details are forever lost to us. Paul himself gives an account of it in Gal 1:15–2:21, but that account is written in the heat of controversy and is designed to demonstrate his independence of the Jerusalem church and its authority; biographically it leaves a great deal to be desired. The narrative of the Acts of the Apostles was written from the viewpoint of a later age, was intended to be a dramatized didactic history, and had only very limited access to historical sources. As we pointed out earlier, a group expecting the imminent end of the world does not keep historical records. But it is worthwhile giving in broad outline what we do know, while emphasizing that it is only an outline and that the details are necessarily tentative and the dates only approximate.

The conversion of Paul probably took place in A.D. 32 or 33, some two or three years after the crucifixion of Jesus. We do not know the exact date of the crucifixion of Jesus, however. It was probably either 30 or 33; so the date of Paul's conversion can be as early as 32 or as late as 36. After his conversion Paul spent three years in Arabia, the Gentile district east of the Jordan River, and Damascus (Gal 1:17–18). We do not know what he was doing there, but considering his character, it is most likely that he was already working as a Christian missionary. If he was, his missionary activity must have been unsuccessful, though it apparently aroused enough hostility that he had to flee Damascus (Acts 9:23–25). He then paid a brief visit to Peter, already in many respects the primary leader of the Christian movement, in Jerusalem (Gal 1:18). Paul always refers to Peter by his Aramaic name; they probably always talked to one another in Aramaic. We would give a great deal to know what they talked about, but it was obviously not about the weather, and in view of Paul's vehemence about his gospel not coming from man (Gal 1:12), it is unlikely that the visit was to take part in "a crash course in missionary work with Peter."[2] Paul then went back to his own native district of Cilicia to carry on missionary activity (Gal 1:21–23), and sometime during the next fourteen years Barnabas, a leader of the church in Antioch, brought him to Antioch to help in the Hellenistic Jewish Christian missionary activity in Syria.

At Antioch on the Orontes, the third city in the Roman Empire after Rome and Alexandria, the cultural crosscurrents of the Hellenistic world came sharply into contact. Antioch was the capital of the Roman province of Syria,

[2]Ibid., p. 28.

located on the best land route between Asia Minor and Syria and Palestine, and hence between East and West. Here Greek civilization and philosophy interacted with oriental culture and religion more directly and on more equal terms than almost anywhere else, and the establishment of a Christian community here was therefore an event of the greatest possible importance for the growth and development of the New Testament church. The New Testament itself says that "in Antioch the disciples were for the first time called Christians" (Acts 11:26).

Paul's coming to Antioch marked the beginning of the most important phase of his life and work. Now he had the active support of a strategically located and missionary-minded Christian church, a church that was developing and attracting a whole group of active and potential missionaries. With its support Paul began the missionary work that is the concern of the Acts of the Apostles. Acts 13:3–14:26 reports a first missionary journey that took him and his companions to Cyprus and the southern part of Asia Minor. No trace of this journey is preserved in Paul's letters, and we do not know whether it took place before or after the Council at Jerusalem. Acts has it before and sees the Council as a direct consequence of the success of this journey. But Acts also has it immediately following a visit to Jerusalem by Barnabas and Paul, "the famine visit" of Acts 11:27–30; 12:25. That visit is not mentioned in Galatians, even though Paul is telling under oath the story of his relationship with Jerusalem down to the Council. It is probable, therefore, that the Council was made necessary not by the success of the first missionary journey, but by the success of the work in Antioch itself, and that the missionary journey of Acts 13 and 14 was a result of the Council decision to authorize Paul and Barnabas to go into the Gentile world.

Paul now began the most active phase of his missionary work, deliberately going out into the Gentile world from his base, the Hellenistic Jewish Mission church in Antioch. It is unlikely that this missionary work took the form of the three neatly defined missionary journeys of Acts 13:3–14:26; 15:40–18:22; 18:23–21:17; but the general picture given in Acts is probably correct. Paul would have begun this phase of his work in Cyprus and southern Asia Minor, readily accessible from his base in Antioch. He must have then moved north and west following the overland route from Antioch to the west, and made the momentous decision to go further west into Greece rather than to turn south to the west coastal region of Asia Minor, whose churches are the concern of the book of Revelation, or northeast to the area of Bithynia and the Black Sea. Acts 16:6–10 presents this decision as a result of a direct revelation to Paul; at this point the author seems to have access to something like a travel diary of a companion of Paul's, for he begins to use the first person plural: "we sought to go on into Macedonia."

There followed the central period of Paul's missionary activity carried on in Greece with a lengthy stay in Corinth and in Asia Minor with a lengthy stay in Ephesus, and possibly an imprisonment there. This period lasted some six or eight years, during which the genuinely Pauline letters in the New Testament were written. It ended with a decision to go first to Jerusalem and then to begin a new phase of missionary activity in the western Mediterranean (Acts 19:21; Rom 15:24–29).

The journey to Jerusalem and Rome was begun probably in either A.D. 56 or 58. It took Paul to Rome, but as a prisoner. According to the conclusion of Acts, Paul spent two years in Rome under house arrest, nonetheless preaching "quite openly and unhindered." As we shall see in our discussion of Luke-Acts, this statement is theologically motivated, but it probably is true that Paul was an active missionary even while a prisoner. Our knowledge of Paul ends at this point, since Acts ends here and no genuine letters are preserved from this or any later period; possibly Philippians and Philemon were written during the Roman captivity, although this is by no means certain. Ecclesiastical tradition has it that Paul was released from his captivity, visited Spain, and returned to Rome a second time as a prisoner. But the tradition may well be only a historicization of the plans Paul details in Rom 15:24–29, and it seems most probable that Paul's first imprisonment in Rome ended with his death.

## PAUL AND THE THEOLOGICAL HISTORY OF NEW TESTAMENT CHRISTIANITY

What we know of Paul in the chronological history of New Testament Christianity, like our knowledge of that history altogether, is limited. In terms of the theological history of New Testament Christianity, however, it is different. Paul was a Hellenistic Jew with strong contacts with Jerusalem, and his life as a Christian missionary began, therefore, in the world of Hellenistic Jewish Christianity. But a considerable number of years passed before Paul became a real part of that world, for only after he joined the community in Antioch does the author of Acts know anything about his work. We can make a reasonable hypothesis to account for this.[3]

The conversion of Paul was an intensely personal experience; it came by direct revelation of God and was not mediated by a human agency, such as a preacher. Paul himself insists in Gal 1:15–17 that it was God himself who was "pleased to reveal his Son to me"; Paul "did not confer with flesh and blood" but "went away into Arabia." These words contrast sharply with the three accounts in Acts, 9:3–22; 22:4–21; 26:12–20. In the first two, Paul did more than confer with the Christian leader Ananias and others in Damascus, and all three give the impression that he went from Damascus to Jerusalem. But a legend about an Ananias of Damascus could easily have accrued to the tradition concerning as important an event as the conversion of Paul, and Luke himself has the strongest theological motives to have Paul go directly to

---

[3]In what follows it will be found that we have made only a limited use of the Acts of the Apostles in attempting to reconstruct historical knowledge of the life and work of Paul. Our discussion of the book in chapter 9 shows that as a whole, Acts is too theologically motivated and controlled to have very much value as a historical source. Also, the work uses many literary themes and devices that increase the problems, such as the journey motif. Where Acts has historical value is in the general picture it presents— for the author certainly knows the Hellenistic world and the Christian mission to that world—and in its small incidental details of itineraries and places, which serve no other theological or literary purpose.

Jerusalem and begin his missionary activity there. We have to follow Paul's own account. There is, however, a constant element in all three of the accounts in Acts that is in accord with Paul's, and that is the central dialogue between Paul and the risen Jesus: "Saul, Saul, why do you persecute me?" "Who are you Lord?" "I am Jesus, whom you are persecuting." Furthermore, we know that in this kind of traditional material the central dialogue is the oldest part, the nucleus around which the other details cluster as the tradition is transmitted. We may safely assume that while on the road to Damascus Paul did have a vision of a figure who identified himself as Jesus of Nazareth. He came to understand his vision as a resurrection appearance of Jesus to him, like the appearance to others he lists in 1 Cor 15:3–8, and to interpret it as God's personal revelation to him that Jesus was Messiah, Son of God.

Nor was this the only revelatory vision Paul had. In 2 Corinthians 12 in his debate with his opponents, he speaks of an "abundance of revelations," and Acts 22:17 is likely right in claiming that his call to be a missionary to the Gentiles was the result of a vision in the Jerusalem Temple, though the most probable occasion for that vision was the Council visit when he accepted that particular commission. Further, Acts 16:9 may be correct in that the decision to cross over into Greece was made in response to a vision he had "in the night." Paul believed in revelation by vision, as did the world of which he was a part, but revelation by vision is a private matter.

After the vision that convinced him that Jesus was Messiah, Son of God, Paul probably spent the years before he was brought to Antioch attempting to convince his fellow Jews of this fact, first in Arabia and then in his native Cilicia. He had not yet received the vision that commissioned him to go to the Gentiles, though he may have had intimations of it in his success among the "God-fearers." His success among "God-fearers" is a justifiable supposition since it would have been a reason for Barnabas to bring him to Antioch.

If this hypothesis is correct, Paul truly became a part of Hellenistic Jewish Mission Christianity only after arriving in Antioch; he moved into the world of Gentile Christianity only after the Jerusalem Council and his revelatory vision in the Temple. This accounts for a puzzling feature of his letters; although they are all written within some six or eight years, beginning at least seventeen years after his conversion, they do in fact show very considerable theological development. The earliest of them, 1 Thessalonians, must be considered fairly standard Hellenistic Jewish Mission Christian proclamation and parenesis, and it has little that is distinctively Pauline about it. No more than six or eight years later Romans is very different, but these are the six or eight years of Paul's movement into the world of Gentile Christianity and of his battles both with his Judaizing opponents in Galatia and with his Hellenistic enthusiast opponents in Corinth.

## Paul and His Opponents in Galatia and Corinth

Paul forged his understanding of Christian faith out of conflict with specific groups of opponents; these conflicts play so large a part in his letters that it is worthwhile to consider briefly the two extremes of his opposition: the Judaizers in Galatia and the Hellenistic enthusiasts in Corinth.

## The Judaizers in Galatia

We have seen that there is reason to believe that Paul had been a Jewish missionary in the Hellenistic world and knew at first hand the problems presented to such work by the demand for circumcision and the observance of dietary laws. From the beginning, therefore, he appreciated the immense importance of relaxing these requirements for Gentile converts to Hellenistic Jewish Mission Christianity. From the very beginning, the Hellenistic Jewish Christians in Antioch did not demand them of their Gentile converts, nor did Paul in his own missionary work. A Gentile could become a Christian without also becoming a Jew.

This was the issue the Jerusalem Council faced, and in their farsightedness the leaders of the Jerusalem church, otherwise inclined to a different opinion, accepted the evidence of God's work among the Gentiles in Antioch and agreed that no such demands be made of Gentile Christian converts in the Hellenistic world. But enlightened leaders are one thing, while rank and file members can be something else. There is ample evidence from Galatians and Philippians that members of the Jerusalem Christian church did not accept the Council decision and traveled through the Hellenistic Jewish Mission Christian churches arguing that the only true form of the Christian faith was that in which the Gentile convert became both Christian and Jew.

There was a good deal to be said for the position of these Judaizers: Jesus had been the Jewish Messiah, the leaders of the church in Jerusalem were all Jews, and there was a natural authority about the Christian community in a city that had now also become sacred to the Gentile Christian. Moreover, possibly even Paul himself had wavered on the issue, at any rate as far as Christian community leadership was concerned, because according to Acts 16:3 he circumcised Timothy, a fact that if true may account for the extraordinarily involved syntax of Galatians 2. But in any case, by the time Judaizers turned up in Galatia, Paul was totally unyielding on the issue: the gospel as proclaimed in the Gentile world to the Gentiles was free of any demand for allegiance to Mosaic Law as typified by circumcision.

Paul must have lived with this problem continually in some of his churches, and it may have remained a problem until the Jewish War effectively removed Jerusalem Christianity from the scene. But because he met it head on he worked out aspects of a theology that made sense of the relationship of Christianity to Judaism, developed his characteristic doctrine of justification by faith, and wrote one of the great manifestos of Christian liberty, his letter to the Galatians.

## The Hellenistic Enthusiasts in Corinth

Almost at the other end of the spectrum from the demand that the Christians accept the Jewish Law was the Hellenistic religious enthusiast who declared that he already shared the resurrection life of his risen Lord and was therefore free of any moral obligation. He was already a truly "spiritual man," possessed "knowledge," and had reached "perfection." To him "all things

[were] lawful," and he anticipated no further resurrection in the future. The Hellenistic world tended strongly to think of religion as a manifestation of the power of the deity, of the ability to work miracles, of the experience of all kinds of ecstatic phenomena. The Christian congregation in Corinth moved in this direction and became almost a case study in Hellenistic religious enthusiasm. Paul himself was a man of the Hellenistic world and no enemy of Hellenistic religious enthusiasm, but the developments in Corinth went beyond anything he could accept as genuinely Christian. In his first letter to the Corinthians he wrestles with the problems of religious enthusiasm, striving to strike a balance, and succeeding.

Another feature of the Hellenistic world was the phenomenon of the professional propagandist of a new religion or philosophy. We say "religion or philosophy" because in Hellenism the two had coalesced. Both were ways of successfully coming to terms with the reality of life in the world, and representatives of both sought converts or new adherents on the street corners of Hellenistic cities. These religious or philosophical propagandists, these missionaries, were very much of a type and exhibited the same general characteristics. They proclaimed the power of their divinity or hero or philosopher through stories of his miraculous achievements, including the overcoming of death. They themselves demonstrated the power of their faith or philosophy through miraculous healings, acts of prophecy or clairvoyance, and accounts of their own wonderful experiences. Moreover, they expected to live from the results of their labors. They lived by begging, which was both a livelihood and a means of attracting attention to themselves and their message. In the Hellenistic world, the Christian faith must necessarily have acquired missionaries of this type, and indeed, to many this is how Paul must have seemed. But the similarity was superficial, for when such Christian missionaries appeared in Corinth—attracting wide support in the Christian community precisely because they looked and spoke and behaved as missionaries were expected to—they found in Paul a deep and bitter enemy. The collection of correspondence that is the letter we know as 2 Corinthians is primarily a record of the arrival of a group of "superlative apostles" (2 Cor 11:5) in Corinth, of their initial success, and of Paul's bitter and ultimately successful struggle against them and the understanding of the essential nature of religion that they represented.

## PAUL AS A WRITER OF LETTERS

Of the twenty-seven works that make up the New Testament, twenty-one are called *epistolē*, a Greek word that may be translated either as "epistle" or as "letter." The distinction is important, because in the ancient world a "letter" was a personal communication between individuals, or groups, or individuals and groups; it was a deliberate surrogate for personal conversation and was intended to be direct, personal, and geared to a specific occasion or concern. An "epistle," however, was a deliberate literary creation intended for wide dissemination. Its form as a letter was merely a literary convention; in the ancient world it served the purpose that today would be served by an essay or article, an open letter, a short treatise, or a communication to a journal or newspaper. The letters of the apostle Paul are most emphatically letters, not epistles, and one reason for his impact on New Testament Christianity, and on subsequent Christendom, is that he was an instinctive master of this form of the art of personal communication. Few letters in all antiquity, or for that matter in subsequent literary history, exhibit the person and concerns of the author as vividly as the letters of the apostle Paul.

The letters of Greco-Roman antiquity normally followed a set pattern: a greeting, a thanksgiving and prayer for the well-being of the addressee, the central message, a conclusion, and a final greeting. Paul normally follows this pattern, with suitable Christianizations of the greetings, thanksgivings, and prayers. The one real exception is in his letter to the churches of Galatia, and there he indicates the urgency of his concern when he replaces the normal thanksgiving by the "I am astonished . . . " rebuke of 1:6–9. The central message of the letters shows the characteristic New Testament mixture of proclamation and parenesis, of doctrinal argument and exhortation.

Paul wrote his letters to meet the immediate needs of the congregation he was addressing in a particular situation. This concreteness gives them their existential element of direct confrontation. But with the exception of Philemon, they were not letters to individuals, but to congregations, which meant they would be read aloud at that congregation's meeting. This fact gives them their element of engagement with the group at large and their concern for the common life of the community as a community. The letters were immediately and immensely influential. They were copied and circulated in various churches, and they were imitated in form not only by his own pupils, who wrote in his name, but by many others. The letter form became so important in the New Testament that the apocalypse of John of Patmos not only contains letters, but also has the external form of a letter. The movement toward the bringing together of the New Testament texts into an authoritative canon certainly began with the collection of Paul's letters into a distinct set of texts, the Pauline corpus, a process to which the pseudonymous author of 2 Peter bears somewhat rueful testimony when he speaks of the letters of Paul as being hard to understand but nonetheless of scriptural authority (2 Pet 3:15–16).

## A BRIEF ANALYSIS OF THE GENUINE PAULINE LETTERS

Obviously an "introduction" to the entire New Testament cannot offer a detailed analysis of the letters of Paul, but some general indication of their contents and concerns can and must be given. The importance of Paul to the New Testament as a whole is such that we shall give a more detailed exegetical survey of what from the standpoint of a later time is the most important of those letters, that to the Romans.

The outlines that follow are no more than guides to aid the student in reading the letters themselves. With the structure or outline given below the student will find a great deal of help in the comments given on individual points in the *Oxford Annotated Bible* or in Wayne A. Meeks' *The Writings of St. Paul,* both of which print the text of the Revised Standard Version with introduction and comments.

## FIRST THESSALONIANS

The earliest of Paul's letters, 1 Thessalonians, was written from Corinth about A.D. 51. It represents Paul's version of the characteristic concerns of Hellenistic Jewish Mission Christianity. In its theology it is very close to the synoptic gospel source Q.

In this letter Paul presents the Christian faith as essentially a matter of believing that Jesus is God's Son, that God has raised him from the dead, and that the risen Jesus will shortly return to the earth as judge and redeemer. He presents the Christian life as essentially a matter of preparing oneself for the coming of Jesus as judge and redeemer, and he gives form and content to the expectation of the coming of Jesus, the parousia. The synoptic gospel source Q has the same understanding of the Christian faith and the Christian life, and it also has the same concern to give form and content to the expectation of the parousia. But though 1 Thessalonians is in many respects close to Q and to the characteristic theology of earliest Christianity, it is also distinctively Pauline. In 5:9–10 we find a first statement of themes that were to become characteristic of the Pauline theology: the concept of Jesus offering to man salvation from the wrath of God, and that of Jesus dying "for us so that . . . we might live with him."

**1:1** *Characteristic Christianized greeting.*

**1:2–10** *Thanksgiving.* Paul normally uses this to set the tone of the whole letter and to express his understanding of the situation he is addressing, as he does here. 1:10 is a formula-like representation of the essence of Hellenistic Jewish Mission Christianity.

**2:1–16** Recollection and interpretation of Paul's work in Thessalonica.

**2:17–3:13** An expression of Paul's affection and concern for the Thessalonian Christians.

**4:1–12** *Parenesis.* An exhortation to holiness and love.

**4:13–5:11** *Instruction with regard to the coming of the parousia.* This section is the real concern of the letter. It reiterates the common early Christian apocalyptic hope, but it uses "Lord" rather than "Son of Man" for Jesus as apocalyptic judge and redeemer, and it goes into physical details not found in the words of the Christian prophets of Q or in the apocalyptic discourses of the synoptic gospels. As noted, 5:9–10 is important as a first statement of the themes that came to be characteristic of the Pauline theology.

**5:12–28** *Concluding parenesis.* A characteristic Pauline version of the normal Greco-Roman conclusion and final greeting of a letter.

# GALATIANS

The letter to the Galatians represents the key instance of Paul's controversy with Judaizing opponents. It is difficult to date because we do not know whether Paul used the term "Galatia" to denote the old Celtic tribal kingdom in northcentral Asia Minor or the Roman province that extended further south. These are the so-called "North Galatian" and "South Galatian" theories as to the address of this letter, but the arguments are ultimately indecisive. The theological occasion for the letter, nevertheless, is more important than the geographical region addressed. The similarity of the theme to that of Romans suggests a comparatively late date, and it is often regarded as having been written from Ephesus around A.D. 54.

**1:1–5** *Christianized greeting.* In the greeting itself Paul begins his argument against his opponents in Galatia. He defends the divine nature of his apostleship and gives a terse summary of the gospel that he intends to defend.

**1:6–9** *Amazement and anathema.* At this point in his letters Paul normally offers a thanksgiving for the faith of those he is addressing, but here he plunges immediately into polemic, expressing amazement at the state of affairs in the churches of Galatia and anathematizing the preachers of a false gospel.

**1:10–2:21** *A personal and historical defense of Paul's gospel.* In the first major section of the letter Paul defines and defends his understanding of the gospel against that of his opponents. The section has three parts.

> **1:10–24** *The divine origin of Paul's gospel.* This is an invaluable autobiographical account of Paul's conversion and early activity as a Christian missionary.

> **2:1–10** *The approval of Paul's gospel by the leaders of the Jerusalem Christian community.* This passage is extraordinarily difficult to translate, probably because Paul is wrestling with the fact that he actually circumcised Timothy (Acts 16:3), and it is affecting his grammar. But that was before his controversy with Judaizers. Now he is concerned with defining his mission to the uncircumcised Gentiles who, because of the decision reached in Jerusalem, are free from the need to accept circumcision as they become Christians. His opponents apparently were arguing the opposite, namely that Gentiles who became Christians had also to become Jews by accepting circumcision.

> **2:11–21** *The altercation with Peter in Antioch.* We indicated in our review of the theological history of New Testament Christianity that a major problem following the success of the Christian mission to the Gentiles was organizing table fellowship between Christians who accepted Jewish dietary laws and Christians who did not. Apparently Peter wavered on this issue, but Paul did not. In reflecting on this incident and its significance, Paul reaches one of his great statements on the nature of Christian faith. No doubt Paul's opponents in Galatia

were raising the issue again by claiming that *Christian* table fellowship was possible only on the basis of the observance by all Christians of *Jewish* dietary laws.

**3:1–4:31**   *A defense of Paul's gospel on ground of the Jewish scriptures.* Paul's opponents in Galatia were Judaizers, who strongly emphasized the Jewish Law. Paul now turns to an argument based on that Law and on the scriptures as a whole, no doubt not only to meet his opponents on their own grounds, but also to satisfy himself of the authenticity of his own position. This second major section of the letter is involved and complex, but it may be divided into seven parts.

**3:1–5**   *The gift of the spirit.* Paul here appeals to the very features of Hellenistic religious enthusiasm manifested by Christians in the Hellenistic world that were to be a major problem for him in Corinth. Here they are a validation of the gospel he preached in Galatia.

**3:6–9**   *Abraham as the prototype of justification by faith.* The heart of Paul's gospel as he was eventually to hammer it out was "justification by faith," which essentially involves the ability of a man to stand before the judgment seat of God and be approved. Paul came to believe that obedience to the the Law ("works") could not earn this approval, which is possible only through faith in Christ. He argues on the basis of a typically Jewish, rabbinical use of scripture. Genesis says that Abraham "believed God and it was reckoned to him as righteousness" (Gen. 15:6). This act of belief was *before* the giving of the Law to Moses on Mount Sinai (Exodus 20); so justification by faith takes precedence over justification by works of the Law, even if the latter were held to be possible at all.

**3:10–14**   *The curse on reliance on works of the Law.* Again proceeding by a typically Jewish method of argument from scripture, Paul now strings together a series of quotes to show that anyone who relies on the Law is accursed.

**3:15–18**   *The promise to Abraham has priority over the giving of the Law.* Still following a typically Jewish method of arguing from scripture, Paul turns to Gen 12:7, "To your descendants I will give this land." In the Hebrew Old Testament the word translated "descendants" is a collective noun, and for this reason it is singular and not plural. From this grammatical point Paul argues that Gen 12:7 refers to a single descendant, one person, not a whole people, and that this descendant is Christ. Again, he goes on, since this promise antedated the giving of the Law, it takes precedence over it.

**3:19–29**   *The role of the Law in the interim between the promise to Abraham and its fulfillment in Christ.* The point at issue between Paul and his opponents was that of the function of the Jewish Law. On the basis of his previous exegesis of scripture, Paul now argues that the Law served a temporary purpose between the promise to Abraham and its fulfillment in Christ. But in the fulfillment of the promise in Christ it has been superseded.

**4:1–20**   *The freedom of Christians as Sons of God.* This is a magnificent celebration of the new relationship with God that Christ made possible for the believers. In his use of "Abba! Father!" (verse 6) Paul is aware of the significance of the mode of address that Jesus taught his disciples to use in prayer, and the whole passage is an impassioned plea to the reader not to abandon that which Christ has made possible. A return to the Law, to the "weak and beggarly elemental spirits" (verse 9: probably a reference to stars and planets personified and understood as forces controlling one's life) and to the observance of a calendar of festivals (verse 10) would be such an abandonment. This passage is our clearest indication that Paul's opponents in Galatia were Judaizers, advocating observance of the Jewish Law and festivals together with a typically Hellenistic admixture of astrology.

**4:21–31** *The allegory of Sarah and Hagar.* Paul now returns to the obscurity of traditional Jewish methods of scriptural exegesis to argue from the two sons of Abraham by Sarah and Hagar (Gen 21:2, 9) that those who rely on the Law instead of the promise will be excluded from the inheritance of the true people of God.

**5:1–6:10** *Parenesis.* In a fashion we shall find to be typical of the New Testament Paul now turns to parenesis, exhorting his readers to preserve and to use correctly the freedom they have in Christ.

**6:11–18** *Final "signature."* Even in the closing greetings of the letter, Paul returns to his argument against his opponents, this time with a moving statement of the necessity to share Christ's crucifixion and with the accusation that the return to circumcision is an attempt to escape this necessity.

# THE CORINTHIAN CORRESPONDENCE

First Corinthians has all the appearance of a single whole; it is one long letter addressed to the situation in Corinth at the height of Hellenistic religious enthusiasm. Second Corinthians is, however, a very different matter. It is a collection of fragments from a whole correspondence between Paul and the church at Corinth, probably put together as a unity when Paul's letters were collected into a definite corpus sometime toward the end of the first century.

## First Corinthians

The body of the letter falls naturally into two parts, the first dealing with matters reported to Paul in Ephesus by messengers from a Chloe (1:10–6:20), and the second with questions raised in a letter to him from the Corinthian community (7:1–15:58). The whole is given a unity because the root of both sets of problems lies in the Corinthian religious enthusiasm. The letter was probably written from Ephesus about A.D. 55.

**1:1–3** *Christianized greeting.*

**1:4–9** *Thanksgiving,* characteristically setting the tone of the letter.

**1:10–6:20**   *The matters reported to Paul in Ephesus.* This section of the letter has four main parts.

   **1:10–4:21**   *The factions in Corinth.* The basic problem in the Corinthian church was factionalism. The Corinthian Christians developed a strange view of baptism in which the baptized persons identified themselves with the person who baptized them. Evidently they regarded baptism as a kind of magical rite by which they came to share the power they attributed to the person who baptized them. Moreover, once baptized they felt themselves to be "spiritual" in a way other people were not, to possess "wisdom" in a way other people did not. The quarrels between them were, therefore, quarrels among a spiritual and wise elite, all of whom recognized their distinctiveness from the rest of the world. Paul's argument against this view is fundamentally that the wisdom of the world is folly to God and that what the world would count folly ("Christ crucified, a stumbling block to Jews and folly to Gentiles," 1:23) is in fact the power and wisdom of God. There can, therefore, be no ready determination of what God himself reckons as wisdom or power; each servant of God must work in his own way and only God's final judgment will reveal the truth (4:5).

   **5:1–13**   *Incest and sexual sins in general.* Corinth was notorious for its sexual immorality, and apparently the Christian congregation was too tolerant in this matter. The reference in 5:3–5 is to the kind of act of solemn judgment at the Christian Eucharist isolated and discussed by E. Käsemann in his work on "Sentences of Holy Law in the New Testament."[4]

   **6:1–11**   *Litigation before pagan courts.* Christians will participate in Christ's final judgment of the world, including its magistrates. They must, therefore, fittingly settle their disputes out of court.

   **6:12–20**   *The claim of the enthusiasts that "all things are lawful."* As truly "spiritual" men, the Corinthian enthusiasts were indifferent to things of the body, and one form of this indifference was an extreme libertarianism, including the freedom to visit Corinth's notorious brothels. Against this Paul argues strenuously for a moral spirituality.

**7:1–15:58**   *The questions raised by the Corinthians in their letter to Paul.* The Corinthian Christians had written to Paul asking for guidance on a number of practical matters. He responded as a pastor to his people, and the result is a fascinating account of an early Christian attempt to face the practical problems of living in the world—and perhaps also an illustration of the adage, "The more things change, the more they remain the same." Five particular problems are discussed.

   **7:1–40**   *Marriage and celibacy.* Paul wrestles here with all the problems of marital and sexual relationships, problems complicated in Corinth because one form of the Corinthian spirituality was an asceticism in which newly converted Christians denied their wives and husbands

---

[4]Käsemann, "Sentences of Holy Law in the New Testament," in his collected essays, *New Testament Questions of Today,* pp. 66–81.

their conjugal rights. The full humanity of the apostle is evident in this passage as we see him striving to give advice in matters on which he was by no means an expert. From the standpoint of an overall understanding of Paul, it is important to note that the perspective from which the advice is given is that of the imminent end of the world (verse 26).

**8:1–11:1** *The problems of idolatry.* Living as a Christian in a pagan society presented many problems for the newly baptized Christian's relationship to that idolatrous world. For example, much of the meat sold in the market place came from temples where it had been consecrated to a pagan god. Could the Christian eat it or not? As he attempts to deal with this problem and others in the same area, Paul is in conscious debate with the enthusiasts in Corinth for whom idolatry was a matter of indifference (i.e., since they believed in the true God, idols had no real existence). His argument against them, that the man of strong conscience should concern himself for his weaker brother (8:7–13), is compelling. In the course of this debate with his opponents, Paul defends his apostleship (9:1–27), first on the grounds that he has had a vision of the Lord, and second, that his missionary activity has been successful. He also repudiates the argument that he was not really an apostle because he earned his own living rather than living off the results of his missionary labors, as did the propagandists of religion and philosophy generally in the Hellenistic world.

**11:2–34** *The regulation of Christian worship.* The apostle now turns to a series of problems connected with Christian worship. The first (11:2–16) is the necessity for a woman to cover her head in worship, and it is immediately noticeable how ill at ease Paul becomes in questions concerning women. The second deals with the observance of the "Lord's Supper" (11:17–34). In Corinth the Christian sacred meal was celebrated as a communal meal, but without the necessary observance of the relationship of that meal to the sacrifice of Jesus. The meal must, however, become a solemn celebration of that sacrifice and its significance for the believer.

**12:1–14:40** *The true nature of spiritual gifts.* A major feature of the Corinthian religious enthusiasm was the proliferation of phenomena connected with religious ecstasy: soothsaying, divination, healings and miracles, prophecy and various forms of ecstatic speech (12:8–10). This in itself would not be extraordinary since other religions in the Hellenistic world exhibited the same phenomena. What is noteworthy is Paul's response to the problems created by these phenomena, his insistence on the individuality of the various spiritual gifts and on the centrality of love. Not without reason is 1 Corinthians 13 regarded as a high point in the New Testament.

**15:1–58** *The future resurrection of the dead.* A major problem for Paul in Corinth was that the Christian enthusiasts there believed that at their baptism they already began to share the resurrection life. Paul has to argue carefully for a future resurrection of the dead. A second problem was that for a Greek it was natural to think of the immortality of the soul but not of the resurrection of the body. Paul has also to argue for a future resurrection of the body. A most interesting passage in this section is verses 3–7, where Paul quotes an early liturgical formula, or confession, concerning the death and resurrection of Jesus and where he apparently understands his own vision of Jesus as a resurrection appearance.

**16:1–24** *Some further matters.* Paul concludes his letter by discussing the arrangements he was making concerning the collection for the Christians in Jerusalem (for which he had accepted responsibility at the Jerusalem Council) and for his own future plans. His final greeting is notable for the *Maranatha* ("Our Lord, come!") in verse 22, an Aramaic prayer going back to the earliest days of Christianity in Palestine.

## Second Corinthians

This letter is not a unity but rather a collection of fragments and larger remnants of a whole correspondence between Paul and the church at Corinth when a group of "superlative apostles" had an impact on the Corinthian Christian enthusiasts. The various parts were probably put together when the apostle's letters were circulated as a group toward the end of the first century. They were originally written over a period of time shortly after the writing of 1 Corinthians, around A.D. 56 while Paul was based in Ephesus. The remnants of six letters are in this collection, and to read the first three in their proper order is to become caught up in a very dramatic struggle.[5]

**2:14–6:13; 7:2–4** *Paul's first letter of defense against his new opponents.* This is part of a letter that Paul wrote to defend himself and his authority against opponents who came to Corinth bearing letters of recommendation from Christian communities in which they had previously worked and who rapidly assumed positions of authority in the Corinthian Christian community. Paul calls them "peddlers of God's word" (2:17) and offers in his own behalf a moving account of the humility of the true ambassador for Christ.

**10:1–13:14** *The "painful letter."* Apparently Paul's first letter of defense against his new opponents failed in its desired effect, and he paid a flying visit to Corinth where, however, he found the church in open rebellion against him; one opponent was even able to humiliate him publicly (2:5; 7:12). He returned to Ephesus and wrote a further letter to Corinth "out of much affliction and anguish of heart and with many tears" (2:4). This is traditionally known as the "painful letter," and 2 Corinthians 10–13 is a remnant of it.

In these chapters a picture of Paul's opponents takes shape as he parodies and attacks them, and they represent an aberrant form of

[5]Our analysis is indebted to that in Bornkamm, *Paul,* pp. 244–46. Bornkamm himself gives an excellent picture of Paul's relations with the church at Corinth, pp. 68–77.

Christianity in the Hellenistic world. They boast of their achievements in the name of Christ, and they boast of their Jewish heritage; they are "superlative apostles." They are given visions and revelations as a special sign of their status, and they offer "signs and wonders and mighty works" as proof that Christ speaks through them. Against all this Paul offers the "foolishness" of his own boasting. He appeals to the original effectiveness of the gospel he preached in Corinth, to the fact that he supported himself in Corinth so as not to be a burden on his converts, and to his own Jewish heritage and his sufferings as a servant of Christ. Above all, he appeals to the Corinthian Christians' own sense of what they owe him and his gospel and to the example of Christ himself who was "crucified *in weakness*" (13:4, a deliberately ironic contrast to the power in Christ his opponents claim) but who lives by the power of God.

**1:1–2:13; 7:5–16** *The letter of reconciliation.* Paul sent the "painful letter" to Corinth by the hand of Titus, whom he must have charged with the task of attempting to restore the situation there. The letter and Titus' visit were successful—the Corinthian Christians were probably appalled by the realization of what they had done to the apostle to whom they owed so much—and Paul wrote a letter rejoicing in the resumption of good relations between him and the Corinthian Christian community.

**8:1–24** *A letter of recommendation for Titus.* This is part of a letter of recommendation for Titus as organizer of the collection for the saints in Jerusalem. We have no way of determining its relationship to the remainder of the Corinthian correspondence.

**9:1–15** *A letter concerning the collection for the saints in Jerusalem.* This is part of a letter concerning the collection for the saints. Again, we have no way of determining its relationship to the remainder of the Corinthian correspondence.

**6:14–7:1** *A non-Pauline fragment.* Neither in terms of ideas nor vocabulary does this have any claim to come from the apostle Paul. It appears, rather, to reflect the influence of ideas characteristic of the Qumran community. We have no idea how it came to be included in a collection of Paul's letters to the Christians in Corinth.

# PHILIPPIANS

This letter—or as we shall see, this small collection of letters—is addressed to the Christians in Philippi, the first congregation founded by Paul on European soil (Acts 16:11–15). Through the years Paul maintained a most cordial and indeed affectionate relationship with this congregation as reflected in the correspondence. There are remnants of three letters in this one letter, as follows:

**4:10–20** *Part of a letter of thanks to the Philippians* for the revival of their concern for Paul and the gifts sent to him at the hands of Epaphroditus. Paul appears to be at the beginning of an imprisonment.

**1:1–3:1** *A further letter of thanks* for the concern the Philippians have expressed for Paul, who is now enduring a considerable period of imprisonment. Epaphroditus has been very ill, but is now recovered and will be rejoining the Philippians shortly. This letter characteristically combines thanksgiving and parenesis and includes some of the most moving passages in the Pauline correspondence as well as the great hymn to Christ in 2:5b–11.

**3:2–4:9** *The remnant of a sharply polemical letter warning the Philippians of the dangers of the "circumcision party."* Paul is combating the problem he faced in Galatia, and again he uses among other things an autobiographical statement (3:4–11). The characteristic apocalyptic hope is still present (3:20–21). This letter clearly does not belong with the others and must have been written either before or after them. The attitude of thanksgiving for dangers passed and harmony achieved, which the others breathe, leads to conjecture that this one was written earlier.

The second of these letters was certainly written in prison, and the first probably was also. The only imprisonment reported in Acts is that in Palestine and Rome, but we have already concluded that Acts is not a trustworthy source for historical detail concerning Paul or the early church. The letters themselves assume constant intercourse between the imprisoned Paul and the church in Philippi, a factor difficult to imagine if the distance was that between Philippi and Rome. And the letters breathe the same kind of atmosphere as that of Galatians and the Corinthian correspondence. For these reasons modern scholarship tends to assume that Paul was imprisoned in Ephesus during his long stay there and that this correspondence originated there. Paul himself speaks of facing death in Asia (2 Cor 1:8–10) and of fighting with beasts in Ephesus (1 Cor 15:30–32), and the letters date, therefore, from about A.D. 52–55.

# PAUL'S LETTER TO THE ROMANS

The letter to the church at Rome is unquestionably the most important of Paul's letters, and is to many the most important text in the New Testament itself. It was written about A.D. 57 at the end of the great and creative six or eight years of Paul's work in Greece and eastern Asia Minor, as he was preparing to leave for Jerusalem, planning then to go to Rome and on from there to Spain and the western Mediterranean. For this project he needed the support of the church in Rome, already rivaling in influence that in Antioch, but he had never visited Rome, and the church there did not know him. No doubt he also feared that the controversies he had been embroiled in might have led to a false impression of him and his gospel reaching Rome. So he wrote a letter to the church there, setting out the gospel as he understood and preached it.

The letter to the Romans is Paul's testament, his statement of the faith as he understands it after his work in Hellenistic Jewish Mission Christianity and

Gentile Christianity and after his conflicts with Jerusalem Christianity and with the excesses of Hellenistic religious enthusiasm. It is the mature statement of the man who began as a man of two worlds, Judaism and Hellenism and became a man of three: Judaism, Hellenism, and a distinctive Christianity. Here many major themes of his earlier letters receive a reflective and creative restatement, for example:

- Justification by faith alone and not by works of the Law (Galatians 3 and 4; Philippians 3; Rom 1–4; 9:30–10:4).

- Abraham as the type of justification by faith (Galatians 3; Romans 4).

- Adam as the mythical embodiment of the fall of man and Christ as the head of the new humanity (1 Cor 15:22–28; Rom 5:12–21).

- The sending of the Son of God in the flesh for our redemption and the testimony of the Spirit that we are the children of God (Gal 4:4–7; Romans 8).

The importance of this letter as Paul's major statement of his understanding of the Christian faith warrants our treating it in more detail than the other letters.

## Exegetical Survey of Paul's Letter to the Romans

**1:1–7** *Christianized greeting.* Paul extends this conventional greeting to include a definition of the gospel (verses 3 and 4), which is traditional rather than distinctively Pauline.

**1:8–15** *Thanksgiving.* This sets the tone and indicates the purpose of the whole letter, as it so often does.

**1:16–17** *Summary statement of Paul's understanding of the gospel.* The righteousness of God is an active concept, with God as the acting subject. It refers to the power of God to act in accordance with his own true nature as creator and redeemer, to establish man as righteous before him. This state of acceptance in God's sight is God's own gift; it cannot be achieved by works of the Law, it is accessible only to one act of man, the act of faith. This is the climactic statement of Paul's characteristic doctrine of justification by faith, and one should compare the earlier statement of it in Gal 3:10–11 and Phil 3:9.

*First Major Section: The world's need for justification by faith,* 1:18–3:20

**1:18–32** The judgment of God is revealed against the sin of man.

**2:1–11** The Jews are every bit as much under the judgment of God as are the Gentiles.

**2:12–29** God judges the Jews by the standards of the Law of Moses, and the Gentiles by the "law" of their conscience. But the Jew may not rely on outward observances; true circumcision is a circumcision of the heart.

**3:1–8** The Jews nonetheless have an advantage in that God has directly revealed his will and purpose to them in their scriptures.

**3:9–20** But all men, Jews and Gentiles alike, have fallen under the power of sin.

*Second Major Section: The nature of God's saving act in Christ, and of man's appropriation of that act, 3:21–4:25*

**3:21–26** *Restatement of the doctrine of justification by faith.* Having established that the whole world, Jewish and Gentile, needs justification by faith because it is estranged from God by its sin, Paul now restates the doctrine to include the actual form that the redemptive activity of God has in fact taken: the Cross of Christ. Paul's emphasis on the redemptive power of the Cross of Christ is a major feature of his theology. The crucifixion of Jesus was a stumbling block to the Christian claim that Jesus was the Messiah, the Son of God. How could it be that the Messiah, the Son of God, had been allowed by God to suffer a felon's death on a cross, subject to the power of the Jewish and Roman authorities? The word of his mouth should have had the power to blast them from the face of the earth. Paul must have had this difficulty a thousand times in his years of attempting to convince his fellow Hellenistic Jews that Jesus was the Christ, and he must have spoken out of real personal experience when he said, "We preach Christ crucified, a stumbling block to Jews and folly to Gentiles" (1 Cor 1:23). A crucified redeemer figure was "folly" in the Gentile world, because the characteristic redeemer figures in that world were either heroes of the mystery cults or "divine men." Hellenistic Jewish Mission and Gentile Christianity met this problem by transforming Jesus into a "divine man" and his death into an apotheosis. In the more purely Jewish world the Christians developed a "passion apologetic," an apologetic for the passion and cross of Jesus attempting to show that it was in accord with the will and purpose of God as revealed in the scriptures. But as time went by, the Christians came more and more to accept the fact of the cross as a fact and among themselves to develop an understanding of its meaning rather than an apologetic for its necessity; they moved from a passion apologetic to a soteriology of the cross.

Paul played a major role in the development of a soteriology of the cross, that is, in an understanding of how the Cross of Christ changes forever the relationship between God and man. The Jews, and early Christianity in general, expected the relationship of God and man to be changed by the eschatological act of God, and among Christians the form of this expectation was the return of Jesus from heaven as apocalyptic judge and redeemer when the relationship between God and man would be forever changed. But in Paul's thinking, this change has already taken place in the Cross of Christ. The whole world, Jewish and Gentile, is estranged from God by its sin, but the estrangement is not to be eradicated by an act of God in the future. It has already been eradicated by an act of God in the past: the Cross of Christ.

Paul never tires of this theme. The world is estranged from God by reason of its sin, but God has done something about it. This "something" is the Cross of Christ, and Paul is constantly concerned to find ways of explaining how the Cross of Christ eradicates the estrangement of man from God created by the sin of man. In Rom 3:25 he turns to religious sacrifice and uses the word normally used for the sacrifice that propitiates an angry deity, *hilasterion*, translated in the English Revised Version of the Bible, "whom God set forth to be a propitiation." But God is the acting subject, and how can God be said to propitiate himself? Hence in the Revised Standard Version the translation is "whom God put forward as an expiation," in the New English Bible, "the means of expiating sin," and in Today's English Version, "the means by which men's sins are forgiven." But *hilastērion* is the name the Greek-speaking Jews gave to the "mercy seat" in the Holy of Holies, described in Lev 16:2; 11–17. Paul, also a Greek-speaking Jew, may be saying that the Cross of Christ is the place where the sin of man meets the forgiveness of God. The fact is that we are at a point where language fails us. The fundamental convictions involved are that (a) man is estranged from God and doomed for all eternity because of his sin; and (b) God himself has changed this situation through the Cross of Christ. The fundamental need of man is met by God in the Cross of Christ. This is the deepest conviction of Paul, and, indeed, of New Testament Christianity in general, and the language of direct discourse simply fails us.

The act of God that will eradicate man's estrangement is "to be received by faith" (RSV) and is "effective through faith" (NEB). Paul reaches this view through reflection and as a result of his controversy with the Judaizers in Galatia and elsewhere. Whatever it is that God has done for man in the Cross of Christ, it is effective for any given man only insofar as that man responds to it by the act of faith. "Faith" as Paul understands it is another concept that defies the power of the language of direct discourse. The word means "belief," "trust," "obedience," and what Paul is trying to find words to express is something like the following: just as Jesus gave himself totally to God and man by accepting the necessity for the cross, so must man give himself totally to God-as-revealed-in-Jesus in order to appropriate for himself the power of that cross.

A final point is the meaning of the verb *to justify* and the noun *justification*. The concept is ultimately derived from the law court, and the reference is to an act of judgment. God has given man a standard by which to live—to the Jews his law, to the Gentiles the conscience in their hearts—and ultimately a man must stand before God and be judged by that standard. If he has achieved it he will be declared "righteous," and the divine act of declaring a man righteous is the act of justification: God justifies the man who is righteous in his sight. Paul's whole argument is that no man can achieve the necessary righteousness, and so God has established a new possibility: a man will be justified by God,—i.e., declared "righteous" by him,—if he has faith in Jesus, and this is a possibility for Jew and Gentile alike. The Jew has failed to live up to the law and the Gentile to the conscience in his heart, but God nonetheless declares them righteous in his sight because of the righteousness of Jesus (who more than fulfilled all norms), which they appropriate to themselves by the act of faith.

**3:27–31** *It is faith and not works that matters.* Paul's constant controversy with the Judaizers led him to the oversimplified antithesis: *either* gladly accept by the act of faith what God has done in Christ *or* justify yourself before God by the quality of your own life. It is easy enough to say that it should have been in some respects a question of "both . . . and," but in the heat of controversy contrasting emphases become sharpened to radical antitheses. Paul's argument is that justification must be by faith and not by law, because only the Jews had the law, whereas the purpose of God must be the justification of all men. All men are capable of the act of faith.

**4:1–25** *Abraham himself was justified by faith and thus is the father of all who believe in the God who raised Jesus from the dead.* Paul's position here turns on the fact that it is in Genesis 15 that it is said of Abraham, "he believed the Lord; and he reckoned it to him as righteousness" (Gen 15:6). Not until Genesis 17 is the requirement of circumcision laid on him as on his descendants (Gen 17:11). Faith is anterior and hence superior to circumcision as a means of being justified before God. This is a typically rabbinic method of argument.

### Third Major Section: The new life in Christ, 5:1–8:39

**5:1–5** *The consequence of justification by faith: peace with God and joy in life.*

**5:6–11** *The grounds for the possibility of justification by faith: the Cross of Christ.* In one of his most lyrical passages, Paul expresses his fundamental convictions by using two images: the image of justification, taken as we have seen from the language of the law court, and the image of reconciliation, taken from the world of personal relationships. Both are ways of talking about the plight of man before God—the need for justification, the need for reconciliation—and both are ways of talking about the Cross of Christ—the means by which God has changed the plight of man before him. Men are "justified by his blood" or "reconciled by his death." Two further notes are sounded: (a) the whole work of justification or of reconciliation is a work of God and hence an outpouring of his love of man; and (b) the man who is justified or reconciled by the death of Jesus is further "saved" by Jesus' life. This latter point is Paul's version of the claim of the Corinthian enthusiasts that they knew already the power of the risen Lord, that their life in Christ was already the resurrection life. Paul does not deny this; he is as anxious as anyone to claim that Christians in this life share in the power of Jesus' resurrection and that their lives are already transformed by the power of that resurrection. But there is always for Paul what modern scholars tend to call an "eschatological reservation." However much man now knows of the power and quality of the resurrection life, there is still the resurrection to come. However much man is now justified or reconciled, he still needs to be "saved from the wrath to come," i.e., from the still outstanding, final, eschatological judgment of God. There is in Paul an inevitable element of tension between his ability as a man of the Gentile world to interpret the Christian faith in terms of Greek religious enthusiasm and his necessity as a Jew to think in terms of a Last Judgment. We can understand Paul correctly only if we recognize that for all his enthusiasm for the effectiveness of the Cross of Christ, for all his glorying in the present experience of Christ's risen life, he nonetheless never loses touch with the typical early Christian apocalyptic hope for a second coming of Christ as judge and redeemer. So in this passage, although we are already "reconciled," we still need to be "saved." Logically it is inconsistent, but it has fed the piety of centuries because it has been found to correspond to the reality of Christian religious experience.

**5:12–21** *The myths of Adam and Christ.* In our discussion of the early Christian apocalyptic hope, we said that a reason for its enduring power was the correspondence between the myth explaining the existence of evil in the world as the result of the wrongdoing of a primal ancestor and the myth explaining the removal of evil from the world as an activity of another human or humanlike figure. Paul now develops this correspondence of myths more exactly by claiming that just as the wrongdoing of the one man Adam led to the existence of sin and evil in the world, so also the possibility of the removal of sin and evil from the world is the result of the righteousness of the one man Jesus Christ.

**6:1–14** *Dying and rising with Christ.* In the Gentile world Paul preached to it was natural to think of sharing the power and destiny of a cult hero, a Serapis or a Mithras. In responding to the imagined protest of an opponent with whom he is in dialogue—a characteristic Hellenistic literary device—Paul interprets the Christian initiatory rite of baptism as a sharing in the death and resurrection of Jesus. He then interjects a parenetic passage of exhortation in the characteristic New Testament manner (verses 12–14).

**6:15–7:6** *The two analogies: slavery and marriage.* To drive home his point, Paul turns to two analogies: slavery and marriage. A slave is totally responsible to one master, but only to one. Similarly, a wife is totally responsible to her husband, but only as long as he lives. So Christians were once slaves to sin and married to the Law, but now they are slaves of righteousness, and the Law is dead for them.

**7:7–25** *The meaning and function of the Mosaic Law.* As a Jew Paul inherited the understanding of the Law of God as given through Moses as the supreme gift of God's grace, given to man that he might know and do the will of God in the world and so inherit the blessings of all eternity. But as a Christian he had come to see that under the Law Jesus himself stood condemned, since according to the Law, "cursed be every one who hangs on a tree" (Deut 21:23, quoted in Gal 3:13), i.e., in his crucifixion Jesus was, according to the law, accursed of God. Paul must have maintained this argument in his days of opposition to Jesus and to faith in Jesus. But according to God's direct revelation to Paul, Jesus was not accursed of God; he was God's own Son, and Paul must have begun to question the validity of the Law. In his days as a Christian preacher Paul was forced into controversy with his Judaizing opponents in Galatia and Philippi, and no doubt elsewhere, where the question at issue was the validity of the Law, but where the real issue was the freedom of the Christian mission to be *Christian* (as Paul had come to understand the meaning of that term), and not simply Jewish. So Paul was again forced to question the validity of the Mosaic Law, and indeed to deny it. Now in this passage from Romans, he brings his reflections together, and out of his own experience of the crucified Christ and of the Judaizing controversy fashions his classic statement on the ultimate significance of the Law given by God to the Jewish people as the supreme gift of God's grace: it is a law of sin, not of grace, because it demands of man a standard that cannot in fact be achieved. The man struggling to achieve the standards set him by the Law either becomes conscious of his failure and convicts himself of sin or deludes himself and becomes self-righteous.

It is often supposed that this passage is autobiographical and that Paul was reflecting on his own soul-searching as he attempted to fulfill the Law as a Pharisee. But it seems more likely that the use of the first person singular is a literary device. We have no evidence that Paul thought this way about the Law before his vision of the risen Christ, who should have been accursed of God but was in fact vindicated by him, or before his conflicts with the Judaizers. But the literary device makes it a most powerful passage, because the experience depicted does correspond to the reality of the experience of countless men and women who have conscientiously attempted to fulfill an established code of conduct. "The good that I would I do not: but the evil which I would not, that I do" (Rom 7:19, KJV) is a cry from the heart of conscientious humanity.

**8:1–39** *The new life in Christ in its details.* In what is probably the greatest sustained passage from his letters, perhaps the greatest sustained passage from Christian literature altogether, Paul now depicts the details of the possibilities of the new life in Christ as he understands it in his maturity as a Christian missionary. It is a passage to be read and reflected on by the individual reader rather than commented on by the scholar, and the present writer does not propose to make any remarks whatsoever.

*Fourth Major Section: The place of the Jewish people in God's plan for the salvation of all mankind, 9:1–11:36*

Nothing could have plagued Paul personally more than the problem of his Jewish heritage. He had grown up proudly in the consciousness of being a member of the people of God, the people whom God had chosen to be his people and to whom he had revealed his will and purpose directly in his Law. Yet the people of God had rejected God's own Son. Paul must have spent a lifetime arguing to Jews that Jesus was God's own Son because his life, death, and resurrection had been foretold in the scriptures and trying to explain to Gentiles how it was that the people of God had not recognized the Son of God. Now he was proudly preaching a gospel that claimed a Gentile could be justified on the basis of responsiveness to the dictates of his conscience. What then remained of the superiority of the Jewish people as the people of God? The most natural answer would have been, Nothing! especially when facing the problems created by representatives of the Jewish-Christian church in Jerusalem. Or since the Jews had rejected Jesus, the answer could even have been, Less than nothing!—an answer that would have embodied an attitude that has indeed led to the tragic centuries of persecution of Jews by Christians. But Paul wrestles with the problem on his own terms and comes up with an answer scholars normally discuss under the rubric of the German word *Heilsgeschichte. Heilsgeschichte* means literally "salvation history"; it is used to designate the concept of a history of God's activity directed toward the salvation of humanity as distinct from and yet at crucial points intersecting with *Weltgeschichte,* the secular history of the world and its peoples.

Paul reaches his answer to the rejection of the Son of God by the people of God along the lines of a concept of a *Heilsgeschichte.* Everything that has happened must be in accordance with the will and purpose of God, and that purpose is the salvation of all humanity, Jew and Gentile alike. The Jewish people, however, had finally failed to recognize that righteousness was ultimately attained only by faith, and this failure had led to their rejection of the gospel. They remained obdurate in their insistence on a righteousness attainable by obedience to an external law, "and seeking to establish their own, they did not submit to God's righteousness" (10:3). But God has not rejected them, and the Gentiles should not feel superior to them. The Jewish rejection of the gospel has in practice the consequence that the Gentile now has an opporutnity to hear it, nonetheless, and in the end the Jews will also be saved.

All this is argued in detail and with copious reference to scripture, and yet the modern reader cannot help but feel that there is something very strained about the whole argument. The world of Romans 8 is one world; the world of Romans 9–11 quite another. Romans 9–11 is a testimony to the agony of the spirit of a conscientious Jew who has come to believe that God's own people have rejected God's own Son as well as God's own gospel. A major fact of life in the New Testament is that the Christian mission to the Jews was a miserable failure, while that to the Gentiles was a sensational success, and Romans 9–11 is one Christian Jew's attempt to accept and to understand this reality. It should be read today with sympathy and understanding for the agony of the human spirit that gave rise to it.

### Fifth Major Section: Parenesis, 12:1–15:33

As there is always in the New Testament texts, in Paul's letter to the Romans there is both proclamation and parenesis, and Romans 12–15 is the parenetical section of the letter. It represents Paul rising above the controversies of his mission and the problem of the Jewish people in the purpose of God to pen a passage that gives some indication of how powerful a preacher he must have been. As in Romans 8 one is caught up in the vision of the new life in Christ, so in Romans 12–15 we are challenged by a statement of its responsibilities. Here we have the voice of a great preacher challenging all men at any time and in any place, and as in the case of Romans 8, scholarly comment is ultimately superfluous.

### Appendix: Various greetings, 16:1–27

The last chapter of Paul's letter to the Romans was probably not written to Rome at all. It seems extremely unlikely that Paul, who had never been in Rome, would have had the range of friends and acquaintances there implied by this chapter. Modern scholarship is mostly of the opinion that Paul recognized that his letter to the Romans was a major statement of his theology and that he had a copy sent to Ephesus, with these greetings added.

## THE LETTER TO PHILEMON

This is a kind of appendix to the collection of Paul's letters. It was not written to a church but to an individual, and on a private matter. That matter, however, was slavery, which could never be purely private.

Paul was in prison in Rome (or Ephesus, we cannot be sure which) and there he met a runaway slave, Onesimus, whom he converted to Christianity and who showed promise of becoming a helpful fellow worker and evangelist. But he was a runaway slave; according to Roman law he had to be returned to his master and was liable to severe punishment; anyone who helped him was liable for damages to his master. His master, Philemon, was in this instance, however, a Christian, and so Paul carefully blended punctilious observance of the law with shrewdly conceived appeals to Philemon himself. He offered to pay any damages incurred and he returned Onesimus to his master, but he pleaded that Onesimus might return to him as a valued fellow worker. There can be little doubt that his letter was successful, if only because it was preserved, and there can be no doubt that it represented a practical answer to the difficulty. But in other times and other places Christians were to take a very different attitude to the institution of slavery, and we can only express our conviction that Paul would have reacted differently had he not been able to address his letter to Philemon, "our beloved fellow worker."

# THE IMPACT OF THE APOSTLE PAUL

It is impossible to overestimate the importance of the apostle Paul to the New Testament and to subsequent Christendom. His vision of the nature of Christian faith came at the crucial moment when circumstances were transforming Christianity from an apocalyptic sect within Judaism into a missionary cult within Hellenism and beyond that into a world religion. In this process Paul came to play a major part, not only because he was a leader in the missionary movement, but even more because his view of the nature of Christian faith blended together the three aspects of its heritage—Judaism, Hellenism, and a distinctive Christian experience—into a new whole. Paul's vision of the nature of Christian faith became normative. The author of 2 Peter had to wrestle with it (2 Pet 3:15–16), and we need only to mention such names as Augustine, Martin Luther, and John Wesley to see the impact of Paul on subsequent centuries. Moreover, he trained followers who not only served the church during his lifetime, but who also lived to provide leadership in the next generation. The very existence of Colossians, Ephesians and the Pastorals is eloquent testimony to Paul's continuing influence. Finally, Paul's letter writing provided the impetus toward the formation of the New Testament itself. The first step in establishing the New Testament as a distinctive body of literature was taken when his letters to individual churches were recognized as being important to all churches and were copied and circulated. For Paul himself, "scripture" was what we would call the Old Testament, but it is in no small part due to him that there is now a New Testament.

# FURTHER READING

The literature on Paul is of course extensive, but fortunately two outstanding recent treatments of the apostle are available in English: Bornkamm's *Paul* (in two parts: I, Life and Work; II, Gospel and Theology) and in *JBC*, Fitzmyer's "A Life of Paul" (pp. 215–22) and "Pauline Theology" (pp. 800–27). Bornkamm is slightly more radical and Fitzmyer slightly more conservative, but both are absolutely first-class scholars, and the contrast between them clarifies and focuses attention on the issues at stake. Bornkamm utilizes the insights of his pupils, especially Dieter Georgi, but gives little bibliographical information. Fitzmyer gives excellent bibliographies to all the matters he discusses.

The greatest and most provocative treatment of Paul's theology is by Bultmann in his *Theology of the New Testament*, vol. 1, pp. 190–352. Bornkamm is a pupil of Bultmann's; Fitzmyer writes in deliberate contrast to him.

Other useful treatments are:

*PCB*, pp. 870–81, "The Apostolic Age and the Life of Paul" (W. D. Davies).
*IDB*, vol. 3, pp. 681–704, "Paul the Apostle" (A. C. Purdy).

The "Introductions" have discussions of the chronology of Paul's life and work:

> Kümmel, *Intro.,* pp. 179–81.
> Marxsen, *Intro.,* pp. 17–23.
> Fuller, *Intro.,* pp. 6–15.

For work on Paul and his opponents, see:

> Bornkamm, *Paul,* pp. 18–22, 32–35, 82–84 (at Philippi); pp. 174–76 (restatement in Romans).
> *PCB,* pp. 877–78.

Much excitement in recent years has centered on the discussion of Paul's "divine man" opponents in 2 Corinthians, precipitated by Georgi, *Die Gegner des Paulus im 2. Korintherbrief: Studien zur religiösen Propaganda in der Spätantike,* a truly magisterial work. English-language discussions of this subject are not readily available. Strangely enough, Bornkamm devotes only slightly more than one page to it (pp. 76–77). *PCB, IDB,* and Marxsen's *Intro.* were published too soon to take it into account; *JBC* ignores it; Kümmel, *Intro.,* p. 209, dismisses it in a half sentence; Fuller, *Intro.,* pp. 40–50 offers a brief but sympathetic discussion of it. The only adequate discussion of the matter in English is to be found scattered at various places in Robinson and Koester, *Trajectories Through Early Christianity* (see the references to Georgi in the index), although C. K. Barrett does take it into account in his "Paul's Opponents in II Corinthians," *New Testament Studies,* vol. 17 (1970/71), pp. 233–54.

For Paul as a writer of letters, see:

> *JBC,* pp. 223–26, "New Testament Epistles" (J. A. Fitzmyer).
> *IDB,* vol. 4, pp. 113–15, "Letter" (O. J. F. Seitz).
> Kümmel, *Intro.,* pp. 176–77.
> Marxsen, *Intro.,* pp. 17–29.
> Fuller, *Intro.,* pp. 16–19.
> Funk, *Language, Hermeneutic, and Word of God,* "Language as It Occurs in the New Testament: Letter," pp. 224–74.

For a brief analysis of 1 Thessalonians, see:

> *PCB,* pp. 996–1000, (W. Neill).
> *JBC,* pp. 227–33 (J. T. Forestall).
> *IDB,* vol. 4, pp. 621–25 (F. W. Beare).
> Kümmel, *Intro.,* pp. 181–84.
> Marxsen, *Intro.,* pp. 30–36.
> Fuller, *Intro.,* pp. 19–23.
> Meeks, *Writings,* pp. 3–10.

The first four works listed above all accept 2 Thessalonians as Pauline, whereas the others see it as pseudonymous. This division is representative of responsible New Testament scholarly opinion on the matter.

For Galatians, see:

PCB, pp. 973–79 (J. N. Sanders).
JBC, pp. 236–46 (J. A. Fitzmyer).
IDB, vol. 2, pp. 338–43 (J. Knox).
Kümmel, Intro., pp. 190–98.
Marxsen, Intro., pp. 45–58.
Fuller, Intro., pp. 23–31.
Meeks, Writings, pp. 10–22.

For the Corinthian correspondence, see:

PCB, pp. 954–72 (C. S. C. Williams).
JBC, pp. 254–75 (1 Corinthians: R. Kugelman), pp. 276–90 (2 Corinthians:
    J. O'Rourke).
IDB, vol. 1, pp. 685–98 (S. M. Gilmour).
Kümmel, Intro., pp. 198–215.
Marxsen, Intro., pp. 71–91.
Fuller, Intro., pp. 40–51.
Meeks, Writings, pp. 22–66.

For Philippians, see:

PCB, pp. 985–89 (G. R. Beasley-Murray).
JBC, pp. 247–53 (J. A. Fitzmyer).
IDB, vol. 3, pp. 787–91 (B. S. Duncan).
Kümmel, Intro., pp. 226–37.
Marxsen, Intro., pp. 59–68.
Fuller, Intro., pp. 31–38.
Meeks, Writings, pp. 94–101.

For the letter to the Romans, see:

PCB, pp. 940–53 (T. W. Manson).
JBC, pp. 291–331 (J. A. Fitzmyer).
IDB, vol. 4, pp. 112–22 (F. W. Beare).
Kümmel, Intro., pp. 216–26.
Marxsen, Intro., pp. 92–109.
Fuller, Intro., pp. 51–57.
Meeks, Writings, pp. 66–94.

For the letter to Philemon, see:

PCB, pp. 994–95 (C. F. D. Moule).
JBC, pp. 332–33 (J. A. Fitzmyer).
IDB, vol. 3, pp. 782–84 (M. E. Lyman).
Kümmel, Intro., pp. 245–47.
Marxsen, Intro., pp. 69–70.
Fuller, Intro., pp. 38–40.
Meeks, Writings, pp. 101–04.

*Title page of the book of Thomas the Contender, one of the gnostic texts discovered at Nag Hammadi.*

# 6

# Deutero-Pauline Christianity

Pseudonymity is almost a way of life in the world of the New Testament and also in the New Testament itself. There is no more remarkable example than the six letters supposedly written by Paul, which were not: 2 Thessalonians, Colossians, Ephesians, and the Pastorals (1 and 2 Timothy and Titus). We say categorically "were not," but modern New Testament scholarship is divided on the authenticity or pseudonymity of several of these letters. The Pastorals are accepted by almost all scholars as pseudonymous, Ephesians by most, and Colossians and 2 Thessalonians by some. The present writer is satisfied that all six are pseudonymous, and we proceed on the basis of this opinion, giving arguments for the opinion as each letter is discussed.

That letters are written in the name of the apostle Paul, and indeed that quite elaborate steps are taken to claim his name—2 Thessalonians exactly imitates the greetings of 1 Thessalonians—speaks volumes for the influence of the apostle. The writers were most probably pupils of the apostle who consciously imitated their teacher, wrote in his name, and totally identified themselves with him. This was permissible in the ancient world; indeed, in that world it was an accepted literary practice.

The letters fall into two groups because of their concerns and most probable dates. 2 Thessalonians, Colossians, and Ephesians probably date from the seventies or eighties of the first Christian century and reflect the concerns of the generation immediately following the death of the apostle. The Pastorals are at least a generation later and reflect the concerns of the church at the beginning of the second century. For that reason we will discuss here only 2 Thessalonians, Colossians, and Ephesians, leaving the Pastorals until we discuss emergent Catholicism.

## SECOND THESSALONIANS

Second Thessalonians is so like 1 Thessalonians and yet so different that it must be an imitation of 1 Thessalonians written to meet a later situation.

**119**

Verbal similarities begin with the first verse and continue throughout; yet there are very real theological differences between the two letters, the most important being that of eschatological perspective. In 1 Thessalonians the parousia, the coming of Jesus from heaven as apocalyptic judge and redeemer, is imminent. When Paul speaks of "we who are alive, who are left until the coming of the Lord" (1 Thess 4:15), he clearly expects the event in his own lifetime. But 2 Thess 2:3–12 sets out an elaborate program of what must first happen before that event can occur. Not only has the apocalyptic imagery changed, but the whole tenor of the expectation is different. Another notably non-Pauline feature of the letter is the idea that the judgment of God will be a reward for the persecuted Christians and a persecution of the persecutors (1:5–10). This way of thinking is not only non-Pauline, it belongs to a generation later than Paul's, more poetically expressed in Rev 16:5–7 and 19:2. Furthermore, the generation following Paul tended to ascribe to Jesus attributes and functions that Paul's generation reserved to God, a tendency that was a natural consequence of a developing Christology. So in 2 Thessalonians we read of "our Lord Jesus Christ himself, and God our Father, who loved us and gave us . . . " (2:16), or we find the prayer, "May the Lord direct your hearts to the love of God and to the steadfastness of Christ" (3:5). This is a considerable christological step from "Now may our God and Father himself, and our Lord Jesus, direct our way to you; and may the Lord make you increase and abound in love to one another . . . so that he may establish your hearts unblamable in holiness before our God and Father . . . " (1 Thess 3:11–13). The two are close enough together to be related, but in 2 Thessalonians the Christology represents a later thinking and piety.

The best understanding of 2 Thessalonians, therefore, is to see it as a deliberate imitation of 1 Thessalonians, updating the apostle's thought. The parousia has been delayed beyond anything Paul himself envisaged; the problem of persecution and the response to it is reaching the stage we know from the book of Revelation, itself a text from the end of the first Christian century; and the Christology is significantly advanced from, though clearly related to, that in 1 Thessalonians. The letter, therefore, represents the church coming to terms with the problems of the generation following Paul's though still consciously and immensely indebted to the apostle. The analysis of the letter itself is a comparatively simple matter.

**1:1–2** *Opening greetings,* an imitation of 1 Thess 1:1.

**1:3–12** *Thanksgiving,* together with the awareness of persecution and the expectation that God will reward the persecuted and punish the persecutors.

**2:1–12** *The problem of the delay of the parousia* is dealt with by developing a scenario of things that must come first.

**2:13–3:5** *Thanksgiving and parenesis.* The church must hold fast to the Pauline traditions ("the things which we command," 3:4.)

**3:6–16** *Closing appeals, rebukes, and prayer.*

**3:17–18** *Autographic conclusion.* In itself an argument for pseudonymity, this note is based on the genuine note in Gal 6:11. See also 1 Cor 16:21.

# COLOSSIANS

The authenticity or pseudonymity of the letter to the Colossians is a difficult historical question. Most New Testament scholars who review the evidence and arguments do in fact decide in favor of authenticity. Of the six reference works we are constantly recommending as further reading, only one, Marxsen's *Introduction to the New Testament,* decides for pseudonymity.

The data on which authenticity or pseudonymity has to be decided is not in dispute in the letter to the Colossians; the dispute is in the interpretation of the data. The data itself and the questions it raises may be summarized as follows:

## Factors Indicating Pseudonymity

### Language and style

The vocabulary of Colossians is not homogeneous with the indubitably genuine Pauline letters. There are twenty-five words not found elsewhere in Paul and thirty-four not found elsewhere in the New Testament; so the vocabulary is, to say the least, distinctive. In style, synonyms are heaped together (e.g., 1:9; 1:22) and "the style is cumbersome, verbose and surfeited to opacity with subordinate clauses, participial and infinitive constructions or substantives with *en* (e.g., 1:9–20 [one sentence!]; 2:9–15)."[1] All this contrasts markedly with the normal Pauline style. On the other hand, a number of expressions and stylistic peculiarities in Colossians are found elsewhere in the New Testament only in the genuine Pauline letters.

These linguistic factors could be due to pseudonymity, in part difference from and in part deliberate imitation of genuine Pauline vocabulary and style. Or they could be due to a deliberate use of the opponents' vocabulary and to the very extensive use in this letter of traditional material—hymns, confessions, lists of virtues, household codes, and the like. The letter does employ a great deal of traditional material, and it can be argued that this accounts for the non-Pauline language and style. If this is the case, the non-Pauline language and style are not indications of pseudonymity. But then it could be retorted that such an extensive use of traditional material is itself non-Pauline. In Phil 2:6–11 Paul does quote a hymn, and in Rom 1:3–4 a liturgical formula, and so on, but never to the extent of such material in Colossians. So the argument from language and style seesaws back and forth.

### The absence of Pauline concepts

Several of the concepts particularly characteristic of Paul—righteousness, justification, law, salvation, revelation, fellow Christians as "brethren" (apart from the Greeting)—are noticeably absent from Colossians. Of course, some of

[1]Kümmel, *Intro.,* p. 241.

them are missing from any one genuine Pauline letter; nevertheless, the mortality rate in Colossians is particularly high.

## The presence of concepts not found in the earlier letters

Colossians has a whole series of concepts that are either new in the Pauline corpus or a significant development over anything in the earlier letters. The most important of these are the following.

*Christology.* The Christology of Col 1:15–23 is an advance on anything to be found earlier. In 2 Cor 4:4 (NEB), Christ is the "image" of God, and in Rom 8:29, God predestines Christians "to be conformed to the image of his Son, in order that he might be the first born among many brethren."[2] But in Col 1:15 "He is the image of the invisible God, the first born of all creation." No longer does Christ reflect a likeness to which others can be conformed, but he is now seen as a true representation of God, making visible what heretofore was invisible. He is no longer the first born among the believers who in part share that new birth at their baptism and will share it completely at their resurrection, but rather the first born of all creation. Moreover, he is now the goal of all creation, "all things were created through him and for him" (Col 1:16). In 1 Cor 8:6, God is the goal of creation, "from whom are all things and for whom we exist" "*We* exist," rather than "all things exist," because Paul himself never reaches the pan-cosmic thinking of Colossians, even though in Rom 8:19–23 he is on the way to it. If we argue that these developments in Colossians are because the author is quoting a christological hymn, as indeed he is, it still remains a fact that he is identifying himself with what he quotes, and the differences between Colossians and Romans or the Corinthian correspondence still remain.

*The church as the body of Christ.* In Col 1:18 Christ is the head of the body, the church, where the "body" is a cosmic reality (1:18, 24; 2:19; 3:15), but in Rom 7:4; 12:5; 1 Cor 12:12–31, it is a metaphorical way of expressing mutual interdependence of Christians in the church.

*Steps toward the church as an institution.* Perhaps the most important developments in Colossians are not so much those *from* as those *toward*: developments toward the kind of thinking characteristic of the church becoming an institution rather than of the freer, more charismatic, days reflected in the indubitably genuine Pauline letters. A first instance of this is the references to Epaphras as "a faithful minister of Christ on our behalf," to

---

[2]In the quotations the word translated "image" is always the same word in Greek (*eikon*). But the English translations vary and to make our point we have given the translations that use "image." So 2 Cor 4:4 is NEB (RSV "likeness"), Rom 8:19 is RSV (NEB "likeness"), and Col 1:15 is RSV (NEB also "image").

the gospel "of which I, Paul, became a minister," and to Paul's ministry as "a divine office" in 1:7, 23, 25. These references are a significant step beyond the use of the same Greek word, *diakonos*, in any earlier letter. In Rom 13:4, 5, the word is used of the worldly "governing authorities," in Rom 15:8, of Christ as a "servant" to the circumcision, and in 1 Cor 3:5; 2 Cor 6:4; 11:23, it is used of Paul and others as "servants" of God or of Christ. In these last instances the Revised Standard Version uniformly uses the English word *servant* rather than *minister*. Only in 2 Cor 3:6, which the Revised Standard Version translates, "God who has qualified us to be ministers of a new covenant," do we come even near to the usage in Colossians. But even here there is a significant difference, and a glance at the word in 1 Tim 4:6, "If you put these instructions before the brethren, you will be a good *minister* of Christ Jesus," shows us where the difference lies: the use in Colossians is a move *from* the earlier Pauline letters *toward* the use in the Pastorals.

A further step from the earlier letters toward the Pastorals is the understanding of "Christ Jesus" as the subject of the authoritative tradition the believer "receives" and in which he "lives" (Col 2:6). Here is the understanding of Christian faith as accepting authoritative tradition as the basis for Christian living, which is characteristic of the literature of emergent Catholicism but is foreign to Paul himself. Paul accepts this role of tradition only in connection with the details of Christian living (1 Cor 7:10) or the liturgical practice of the churches (1 Cor 11:23–26), *never* as providing the essence of Christian faith.

One last point is the role of baptism. In Col 2:11 baptism is the Christian equivalent of Jewish circumcision: it is the formal signification of membership in the community. In the earlier letters circumcision is a Jewish rite now abandoned by Christians (Rom 2:25–29; 3:1; 3:30; 4:9–12), and baptism is the dynamic means of entrance into a new and different life (Rom 6:3–11). Moreover, for all that Col 2:11–14 uses the language of Rom 6:3–4, baptism has become much more formal and institutionalized. In Colossians we are on the way toward 1 Peter, itself part of the literature of emergent Catholicism, of the church becoming an institution, where "Baptism . . . now saves you, not as a removal of dirt from the body but as an appeal to God for a clear conscience, through the resurrection of Jesus Christ" (1 Pet 3:21).

A further development from the earlier letters applies both to Colossians and to Ephesians: it is the verb in both letters that expresses the activity of Christ in reconciliation. "In Christ God was reconciling the world to himself" (2 Cor 5:19) is the starting point for the developments in Col 1:19–20 ("to reconcile to himself all things") and in Eph 2:16 ("reconcile us both [Jew and Gentile] to God in one body through the cross"). But 2 Cor 5:19 uses *katallassein*, as the earlier letters uniformly do, whereas Colossians and Ephesians as uniformly use *apokatallassein*. Both verbs mean "to reconcile," but there is a small yet significant difference between them.

Each scholar evaluates the data differently, but for the present writer the cumulative weight of the evidence indicates pseudonymity, and the new concepts developed in Colossians provide the decisive impulse for that conclusion.

## The Situation at Colossae

The church at Colossae fell victim to a form of a heresy that later posed a major threat to Christianity in the second and third centuries: Gnosticism. In its earlier stages Gnosticism was not so much a movement as a mood. Like apocalyptic, its modern name was taken from a central concept: apocalyptic from the Greek *apokalyptō*, "to uncover, reveal"; Gnosticism from the Greek *gnōsis*, "knowledge." Like apocalyptic, Gnosticism despaired of the world and its history. But whereas apocalyptic regarded the world as ultimately under God's control, Gnosticism regarded the world as under the control of spiritual powers hostile to God and, indeed, as having been created by an evil deity locked in eternal conflict with the good deity. The world was irredeemably evil—under the control of evil spiritual powers. Whereas apocalyptic hoped for an act of God that would transform the world, Gnosticism hoped for an act of the good deity that would free man from the evil deity's domain. Apocalyptic expected a redeemer figure who would act by the power of God to transform the world and judge its peoples; Gnosticism expected a savior who would come into the world of the evil deity and impart to men and women knowledge of a means of escaping into the world of the good deity. Apocalyptic expected the flesh of man to be transformed and looked for the resurrection of the body; Gnosticism despaired of the flesh but believed that imprisoned within the flesh of any man was a divine spark that could be liberated by "knowledge," set free to find its true home in the realm of the good deity.

This way of thinking blended together aspects of Greek thought with ideas from the East; even in an eclectic age Gnosticism was especially so. It brought together a radical dualism and a despair of the world. It thought of men imprisoned in the world, longing for the means of salvation by a savior who would come from "above" and impart to them knowledge of the way to escape out of the darkness into the light, out of the unreal into the real. It could be an ascetic movement, despising the world and training the body to rise above it, or it could be a libertarian movement, justifying a wallowing in the things of the world because those things were unreal to men with knowledge of the real. Since the good deity could have nothing directly to do with the world created by the evil deity and yet had to relate to it if men in the world were to find knowledge of the way of salvation, Gnosticism developed an elaborate hierarchy of supernatural beings which served as intermediaries between God and the world.

We may illustrate various facets of Gnosticism by some quotations from a gnostic document, the "Gospel of Truth."[3]

---

[3]The "Gospel of Truth" as we have it is a third-century text, one of the gnostic texts discovered at Nag Hammadi in Egypt in 1946. On this gospel see Hennecke-Schneemelcher, *New Testament Apocrypha*, vol. 1, pp. 233–41 and 523–31. Our quotations are from the translation given in Hennecke-Schneemelcher, pp. 523, 525, and 530.

The Gospel of Truth is joy for those who have received from the Father of Truth the grace of knowing Him through the power of the Word, which has come forth from the Pleroma, (the Word) which is in the thought and mind of the Father (and) which is he whom they call "the Saviour," for that is the name of the work which he is to accomplish for the salvation of those who were ignorant of the Father; for this name "the Gospel" is the revelation of hope, since it is a discovery for those who seek Him.

Therefore if anyone possesses knowledge, he receives that which is his own and draws it back to himself. For he who is ignorant is deficient, and it is a great thing which he lacks, since he lacks what will make him perfect. Since the perfection of the All is in the Father, it is necessary that the All ascend to Him, and that each one receive that which is his own, (the things) which He has written down beforehand, having prepared them to be given to those who came forth from Him.

If anyone possesses knowledge, he is a being from on high. If he is called, he hears, replies, and turns towards Him who calls him in order to ascend to Him, and he knows in what way he is called. Since he knows, he performs the will of Him who called him. He desires to please Him (and) receives rest.

He will speak about the place from which each one has come, and (each) will hasten to return once more to the region from which he derived his true condition, and to be delivered from that place, the place wherein he has been, since he tastes of that place and receives nourishment and growth (therein).

The Gnosticism at Colossae was an early form that had borrowed widely from Judaism, building into its particular way of salvation Jewish elements such as dietary laws and observances of religious festivals and the Sabbath (Col 2:16–17). It also accepted the idea of "elemental spirits of the universe," i.e., supernatural intermediaries between God and the world, who had to be placated because they controlled life in the world and the destiny of man. Therefore one had to know what days were favorable or unfavorable, what was under the control of malevolent supernatural beings and hence taboo, and what was under the control of beneficent beings and hence permitted to the man of "knowledge" (Col 2:20–23).

The author of Colossians meets the problem by claiming, in effect, that Christianity is superior to Gnosticism. Christ is superior to the supernatural beings, as the salvation he offers is superior to that offered by gnostic "knowledge." The author rebukes those falling into the heresy for disqualifying themselves from enjoying the true riches available in Christ. In doing this, the author interprets both Christ and the Christian faith very much in gnostic terms, and the letter is an interesting blend of Pauline and gnostic ideas.

## Exegetical Survey of the Letter to the Colossians

**1:1–14** *Greetings, Thanksgiving, and Intercession.*

**1:1–2** *Greetings.* These are typical of the Pauline style, though somewhat shorter than is usual.

**1:3–14** *Thanksgiving and Intercession.* As we have noted often in Paul himself, and now in the Pauline school, the Thanksgiving indicates something of the concerns of the letter. In verse 7 Epaphras is strongly and emphatically supported in his position in the Colossian church. Nowhere in the genuine letters does Paul show such esteem for a fellow worker as is here exhibited for Epaphras. The Intercession fades over into the Hymn to Christ (1:15–20). For all the periods and paragraphs in the English translations, in the Greek, 1:9–20 is one long sentence.

**1:15–23** *Christology and parenesis.*

**1:15–20** *The christological hymn.* We have already given an analysis of the structure of this hymn, so we have no need to repeat that here. There is, however, a strong case for the hypothesis that originally it was not a hymn to Christ at all but to to a gnostic redeemer, and it has been taken over and Christianized. It is a striking fact that if we take out eight of the total of 112 words in 1:15–20 ("the church," verse 18, "by the blood of his cross," verse 20), there is not a single specifically Christian motif left in the hymn. What we have here is "Gnostic terminology . . . in which the Redeemer, acting as the pathfinder and leader of those who are his, makes a breach in death's domain. Similarly, creation and new creation are invariably linked together in the myth of the Archetypal Man who is the Redeemer."[4] Apart from those eight words, the language and concepts are undeniably such as are found in specifically gnostic texts; indeed, the word translated as "fullness" (*plērōma*, verse 19) is a technical term in Gnosticism. This does not mean that the language and concepts are any less Christian; it simply means that early Christianity was as eclectic as any other religious movement in the Hellenistic world and was "baptizing unto Christ" material offered to it by its cultural environment.

It is possible that we can go even further into the functional context (*Sitz im Leben*) of this hymn, because verses 12–14 contain reminiscences of the baptism of Jesus ("beloved Son," Mark 1:11) and of texts relating to baptism elsewhere in the New Testament.[5] We come close to the dynamics of New Testament Christianity in its "middle period" by envisaging a church adapting a known gnostic hymn to a redeemer to express faith in Christ as *The* Redeemer and using it in baptismal rites. Then the author of Colossians, wishing to

---

[4]Käsemann, *Essays on New Testament Themes*, p. 154. See also the subsequent discussion in Sanders, *New Testament Christological Hymns*, pp. 79–80.

[5]"Deliverance" ("he has delivered us from . . . ") is especially associated with the deliverance of the Jews from Egypt, which in Christianity became a type of baptism (1 Cor 10:2). "Forgiveness of sins" is certainly associated with baptism (Mark 1:4; Luke 3:3; Acts 2:38), and "redemption" is very much a liturgical word (Rom 3:24; 1 Cor 1:30). For detailed arguments see Käsemann, *Essays*, pp. 160–62.

focus attention on Christ as *The* Redeemer, takes it up and uses it in his letter.

**1:21–23** *Parenesis.* In what we recognize as a fashion typical of the New Testament as a whole, the christological hymn is followed by an exhortation to the readers based on it. This concludes on the note of Paul as a "minister of the gospel," which leads into the next section.

**1:24–2:5** *The apostolic office.* In 1:7 Epaphras is "a faithful minister of Christ on our behalf," in 1:23 Paul is a "minister of the gospel," and in 1:25 Paul is a "a minister according to the divine office which was given to me for you." In all this we have come a considerable distance from the freer forms of ministry in the genuine Pauline letters. In its ecclesiastical organization it is a generation later than Paul; we are on the way to what we find in the Pastorals, where the church is an organization with a structured ministry and an official and formal succession.

In this section of Colossians there is another development from Paul at a more personal level. The Paulinist has learned from his teacher: "Now I rejoice in my sufferings for your sake, and in my flesh I complete what is lacking in Christ's afflictions for the sake of his body, that is, the church" (1:24). Let us compare 2 Cor 1:5–6, "For as we share abundantly in Christ's sufferings, so through Christ we share abundantly in comfort too. If we are afflicted, it is for your comfort and salvation . . ." and 2 Cor 4:10 "[We are] always carrying in our body the death of Jesus, so that the life of Jesus may also be manifested in our bodies." The Paulinist is more formal than his teacher, but he has learned from him a preparedness to suffer in and for the ministry of the church.

The Christian message takes on not only specifically gnostic emphases, but also more generally Hellenistic ones. The word of God is the hidden "mystery" now made manifest; the Christian knows "the riches of the glory of this mystery"; he is warned "in wisdom"; he becomes "mature." Though "mystery" turns up at Qumran, this is language characteristic of Hellenistic religion in general. At the same time, definitely Jewish or specifically Christian emphases are also to be found: "the word of God," "the energy which he [Christ] mightily inspires within me," "faith in Christ." This passage is a good example of how different religious traditions came together in what we may call Hellenistic Christianity after Paul.

**2:6–23** *Warning against the false teaching.* It will be noted that we regard this section as beginning at 2:6 (NEB, TEV) rather than 2:8 (RSV).

**2:6–7** *The nature of Christian faith.* Verses 6 and 7 are steeped in the language of Jewish-Christian tradition. In 1 Cor 15:3, Paul speaks of "delivering" what he had also "received," using Jewish technical terms for receiving and passing on tradition. In Col 2:6, the Paulinist takes up a third Jewish technical term, the verb *to walk, to go,* the Hebrew verb from which the Jewish scribes took their term for legally binding decisions, *halachah.* So in Col 2:6, the Paulinist is using technical terms when he says, "As therefore ye received Christ Jesus the Lord, so walk in him" (ERV), and "Christ Jesus" has become the subject of tradition handed on formally in the church and received as authoritative by the church member. We are moving from anything found in the genuine Pauline letters to the concept of Christian faith found in the Pastorals as essentially the acceptance of authoritative tradition.

In Colossians, therefore, Christian faith is understood as accepting "Christ Jesus" as the subject of authoritative tradition and of responding by accepting directions as to how the Christian should "walk." One lives "in him," and one lives by being "built up in him and established in the faith, just as you were taught."

**2:8–15**  *Warning against the false teaching as doctrine.* Since the central element in true Christian faith is "Christ Jesus" as the subject of authoritative tradition, it is essential for the Paulinist to claim that Christ Jesus as understood in orthodox Christian tradition is superior to the spiritual powers and beings who figure so prominently in the gnostic doctrines. This he does by contrasting the gnostic doctrine as "human tradition" concerning "elemental spirits of the universe" with the Christian concept of Christ as the supreme spiritual being. In Christ "the fullness (plērōma) of the deity dwells"; he "is the head of all rule and authority," who, moreover, has proven spectacularly successful in making available to those who believe in him a salvation infinitely superior to anything offered by the gnostic "principalities and powers" over whom, indeed, Christ triumphed in his Cross.

A most interesting aspect of this section is the dynamic blend of developments of Pauline ideas (which the author clearly knows well) with ideas taken from the gnostic teaching itself. We have seen that plērōma, a key word in the Christology of this passage, is a technical term in Gnosticism. Furthermore, Col 2:11–14 must be read against the background of Rom 6:4–11. The differences in the two passages are sufficiently great for us to regard the Colossians passage as written by a Paulinist rather than by Paul himself, but the pupil has understood his teacher and is legitimately developing his insights to meet the needs of a later generation and a different situation. Similarly, Col 2:15 develops for still another situation a metaphor Paul uses in 2 Cor 2:14.

**2:16–23**  *Warning against the false teaching as practice.* The Paulinist now argues against the religious and ethical practices encouraged by the false teaching at Colossae. He argues against the Jewish dietary laws and festival and Sabbath-day observances that the false teaching encourages: "All such things are only a shadow of things in the future; the reality is Christ" (2:17, TEV). This statement is not only telling, it is also a further example of the eclectic blending of Hellenistic and Jewish-Christian ideas in deutero-Pauline Christianity. The distinction between shadow and substance (with the worldly being the shadow and the eternal the substance) is Hellenistic, and indeed Platonic, to the core; but the reality to come in the future is a note from Jewish-Christian eschatology. The Paulinist further argues against "visions" and the "worship of angels" by claiming that they are not proper to the church that is the body of Christ and wholly dependent on its head. Here the church's need for an integrated structure and a disciplined organization come to the fore and necessarily push out the charismatic freedom of an earlier day typified by Paul and his revelatory visions. Finally, in this section the author again takes his point of departure from the Pauline concept of dying with Christ in baptism and holds that this sets the Christian free from an asceticism that would be a form of service to those very elemental spirits to which he died in baptism. This argument applies to a later and different set of circumstances a view that Paul expressed in Gal 2:19–21 and in Romans 6, namely that in baptism the believer died to the Jewish Law and its demands.

**3:1–4:6** *Parenesis.* There now follows a long parenetical section. Col 3:1–4 accepts the claim characteristic of Hellenistic Christian religious enthusiasm as a whole (and apparently a part of the false teaching at Colossae), namely that already in the present the Christian enjoys the power of the resurrection life. The Paulinist tends to accept this, where Paul himself had rejected it (1 Corinthians 15), but he maintains that there is still something that will only be known in the future: "Your real life is Christ, and when he appears, then you too will appear with him and share his glory!" (3:4, TEV.). A similar note of traditional Pauline eschatology is sounded in 3:6, "the wrath of God [i.e., the final judgment] is coming."

Col 3:18–4:1 is the first example in the Pauline corpus of a literary form typical in Hellenistic moral instruction, a household code.[6] Such codes were originally developed by Stoic philosophers and were widely used in the Hellenistic world. They are a feature of the deutero-Pauline literature and emergent Catholicism in the New Testament, but not of the genuine Pauline letters. Except for the references to "the Lord" and the "Master in heaven," this code in Col 3:18–4:1 has no specifically Christian elements. What we have here is most probably the Christianization of a previously existing list of "moral principles governing family life in popular Greek philosophy and Jewish *halacha.*"[7]

**4:7–18** *Final greetings.*


# EPHESIANS

In the case of Colossians, only one of the six reference works recommended as further reading decides for pseudonymity. In the case of Ephesians, however, four of the six decide for pseudonymity, and the other two (*PCB* and *JBC*) recognize the difficulties in maintaining Pauline authorship. Indeed, the difficulties are insurmountable. They may be summarized as follows:

[6]The Germans have a technical term for such lists: *Haustafeln.* Other examples in the New Testament are: Eph 5:2–6:9; 1 Tim 2:8–15; 6:1–2; Tit 2:1–10; 1 Pet 2:13–3:7. There are none in the genuine Pauline letters.
[7]Dibelius, quoted by Marxsen, *Intro.*, p. 183.

## Factors indicating pseudonymity

### Language and Style

There are forty words in Ephesians that are not found elsewhere in the Pauline corpus. Many of them appear in later New Testament writings and in the Christian literature immediately following the New Testament period. Further, synonyms are heaped together in an absolutely non-Pauline manner, e.g., 1:19 has four separate words for "power." Then there is a passion for long, involved sentences, going far beyond anything even in Colossians, e.g., 1:15–23; 3:1–7; 4:11–16. The King James Version and English Revised Version represent this feature of the letter far more accurately than the Revised Standard Version, New English Bible, or Today's English Version which have broken up the sentences as an (admittedly necessary) aid to translating them.

### Relationship to Colossians

A glance at the margin of the Revised Standard Version or of a Greek critical text shows that Ephesians constantly quotes and develops Colossians. About one third of the words in Colossians are found in Ephesians; of 155 verses in Ephesians, 73 have verbal parallels in Colossians; only short connected passages from Ephesians have no parallel in Colossians (e.g., Eph 2:6–9; 4:5–13; 5:29–33). Further, the references to the role of Tychicus in Eph 6:21–22 and Col 4:7 are virtually identical. This dependence on a previous letter is unparalleled in the Pauline corpus, and as an argument for pseudonymity it is reinforced by observation of the fact that Ephesians depends verbally to a great extent on other Pauline letters, except for 2 Thessalonians. The same man could have written the two letters, Colossians and Ephesians, in much the same language within a short time; this is the usual way of arguing for the Pauline authorship of Ephesians, but he would scarcely have reached back into his memory for constant reminiscences of earlier letters written to meet quite different needs.

### Theology

Ephesians repeats the Pauline doctrine of justification by faith (2:5,8–9), but in many respects the theology of Ephesians is simply non-Pauline, even if Colossians is counted among the genuine Pauline letters, (which we, of course, do not). Eph 2:19–22, where Christians are "members of the household of God, built upon the foundation of the apostles and prophets, Christ Jesus himself being the cornerstone . . . " is inconceivable as a statement by the apostle, even if Col 2:7 is reckoned as Pauline, and much more so if it is not. The reference to the "holy apostles" as recipients of special insights into "the mystery of Christ" in Eph 3:4–5 is impossible as a Pauline statement because

Paul never distinguishes apostles in this way and never regards them as "holy" in a way other Christians are not. Ephesians uses the word *church* (*ekklēsia*) uniformly and exclusively for the universal church (Eph 1:22; 3:10, 21; 5:24,25,27). In the genuine Pauline letters and in Colossians (4:16) it is also used for the local congregation. Indeed, the ecclesiology of Ephesians is a striking development toward the understanding of the church as the "Great Church" characteristic of later centuries but not characteristic of Paul. In Eph 3:4–6 the "mystery of Christ" is the unity of Jews and Gentiles in the body of Christ. Not only is this a reflection on an achieved result for which Paul himself was still fighting, but the ecclesiology swallows the Christology. While on the subject of Christology, note that in Ephesians Christ is the subject of the verb *to reconcile* (Eph 2:16), whereas in Col 1:20 God is the subject. In Eph 4:11 Christ appoints the apostles and prophets; in 1 Cor 12:28 God does this. Much more could be said, but we have here enough to indicate why on theological grounds even scholars who accept Colossians as Pauline regard Ephesians as pseudonymous; for those of us who accept Colossians as pseudonymous, the issue is even clearer.

## Literary character of Ephesians

One last point to be made is that Ephesians is not really a letter at all. If we observe a distinction made in our discussion of "Paul as a writer of letters," then Ephesians is not a letter but an epistle. It refers to no particular occasion for its writing; it addresses itself to no particular conflict or problems; it is really "a tract dressed up" as a letter.[8]

## The Occasion for the Writing of Ephesians

Several remarkable features in Ephesians stem from the fact that it is not really a letter at all.

### The lack of an address

Though the opening address parallels the Pauline letters, the best manuscripts and all modern critical Greek texts and responsible translations omit any reference to Ephesus. The address is simply "to the saints who are also faithful in Christ Jesus"; "who are at Ephesus and faithful" (which RSV puts in the margin) was added by a scribe in a later transmission of the text. The possibility is that Ephesians was originally an open letter addressed to the church at large rather than to a particular church, which makes sense of the fact that it is "a tract dressed up as a letter."

[8]Fuller, *Intro.*, p. 66.

## Relationship of Ephesians to other letters attributed to Paul

Ephesians knows and makes extensive use of Colossians; in addition, however, Ephesians shows familiarity with all the other letters attributed to Paul except 2 Thessalonians. Particularly interesting parallels are:

Rom 8:28 = Eph 1:11; Rom 8:29 = Eph 1:4–5.
1 Cor 4:12 = Eph 4:28; 1 Cor 6:9–10 = Eph 5:5;
   1 Cor 11:3 = Eph 5:23; 1 Cor 12:28 = Eph 4:11;
   1 Cor 15:9–10 = Eph 3:8.
2 Cor 1:22 = Eph 1:13; 4:30.
Gal 2:20 = Eph 5:2, 25; Gal 4:4 = Eph 1:10.

In the *Interpreter's Dictionary of the Bible*, volume 2, pages 110-11, from which we have taken these references, G. Johnston gives many, many more. These parallels allow us to suppose that Ephesians was originally written to accompany the collection of Pauline letters while it was circulated as a distinct body of literature, which must have happened sometime in the last quarter of the first century. This possibility has been argued in America by E. J. Goodspeed and in England by C. L. Mitton. It tends to be dismissed in Germany,[9] but the fact remains that it makes a good deal of sense of the contents of the "letter" itself.

## Exegetical Survey of the "Letter"

**1:1–23** *Greeting, Thanksgiving, and Intercession.*
    **1:1–2** *Open greeting.* This of course, is typically Pauline, but it lacks a specific addressee.
    **1:3–14** *Thanksgiving.* It has been said that the most monstrous conglomeration of sentences in the Greek language is found here,[10] and, indeed, any successful translation of it is a tribute to the translator's ingenuity. But the Thanksgiving does make clear the general concern of the "letter," the unity of all men in Christ.
    **1:15–23** *Intercession.* All men everywhere should grasp the magnitude of the hope that awaits them in the church of which Christ is the head.
**2:1–3:21** *The glory of the one holy church.*
    **2:1–10** *By grace are we saved through faith.* The basis for the glory of the church is that all men, including the writer and his readers, are brought into it as they are saved by grace through faith.
    **2:11–22** *We, Jew and Gentile, are reconciled in Christ.* The readers were once Gentiles, "separated from Christ, alienated from the common-

---

[9] Kümmel, *Intro.*, p. 258, "cannot be regarded as probable."
[10] Käsemann, *Die Religion in Geschichte und Gegenwart*, 3rd ed., vol. 2, col. 519.

wealth of Israel, and strangers to the covenants of promise, having no hope and without God in the world"—the rhetoric of this section is magnificent—but now they have been reconciled and brought into the one body of the church by the work of Christ.

In this section we find one of the great christological hymns:

[For] he is our peace,
Who has made both one
And has broken down the dividing wall
    of the fence [the enmity],
In order to make the two into one new
    man in him [making peace]
And to reconcile both in one body to God
[through the cross]

The strophic arrangement has been lost in the text itself because the author quotes and interprets as he writes. A first interpretation is the addition of the words we have put in brackets. This method of interpretation by addition is typically Pauline. As we pointed out earlier, Paul himself interprets the "became obedient unto death" of the hymn in Philippians 2 by adding "even death on a cross." It is possible that the hymn in Ephesians 2 originally had a first stanza celebrating the redeemer's participation in creation as does the hymn in Colossians. Be that as it may, the stanza that is in fact quoted deals with reconciliation, a major theme in deutero-Pauline Christianity.

**3:1–21** *Intercession and doxology.* The fundamental structure of this passage is an intercession begun in 3:1, broken off in 3:2, resumed in 3:14–19, and concluded by a doxology in 3:20–21. The intercession is a prayer for the Gentile members of the church, that they may know all the riches membership in the church offers the believer. Eph 3:2–13 is a parenthetical interruption concerning Paul's mission to the Gentiles, and it testifies to the importance of Paul's work among the Gentiles to a subsequent generation, as the Acts of the Apostles also does.

**4:1–6:20** *Parenesis.* Now the characteristic element of exhortation.

    **4:1–16** *The unity of the faith and of the church.*

    **4:17–32** *The necessity to put off the old and to put on the new.*

    **5:1–20** *Instruction to shun immorality and impurity.* This section develops negatively from a list of vices (verses 3–7) and then positively from a list of virtues (verses 8–20). Such lists of vices and virtues are, like the household codes, characteristic of Hellenistic moral philosophy.

    **5:21–6:9** *The household code.* This is a further and more developed Christianization of a household code such as that found in Col 3:18–4:6.

    **6:10–20** *The armor of God and the warfare of the Christian.*

**6:21–24** *Closing reference to Tychicus, and benediction.*

## DEUTERO-PAULINE CHRISTIANITY AS A MOVEMENT

A major aspect of the importance of deutero-Pauline Christianity is that it shows the influence of the apostle living on in the church. These are Paulinists who were taught by their master, who possessed and meditated on his letters, who developed further some of his ideas, who carefully and conscientiously attempted to meet in his spirit the challenges and needs of the churches, and who wrote formally in his name. It must have been these men who were responsible for the collection of his letters and their circulation as a corpus. The literature they left behind represents the influence of Paul and his ideas a generation or so after his death, and it gives us valuable insights into the nature of the Hellenistic Christianity of that generation.

The problems of the Paulinists in that generation, what we have called the "middle period" of New Testament Christianity, are interesting, and so are the ways they were met. From 2 Thessalonians we learn that a major difficulty was the delay of the parousia. By now Jesus should have come on the clouds of heaven to judge the world, but he had not done so. The Paulinist who wrote 2 Thessalonians meets this problem just as his teacher had, and hence virtually repeats 1 Thessalonians, which he clearly knows well and obviously regards as a tract for his own time and as an answer to the problem he and his church are facing. Yet there are subtle differences between the two letters. Paul himself had expected the parousia in a very short time, whereas the Paulinist knows that it has now been a very considerable time and the parousia is still delayed. So in presenting the scenario for the parousia, the Paulinist attempts to make sense of this delay.

The second problem faced by Hellenistic Christianity after Paul comes to the fore in Colossians—the increasing threat of Gnosticism. At this stage the church freely adopted gnostic ideas and terms and met the danger by an "anything you can do we can do better" claim. Later the threat grew more deadly, and the church had to develop an authoritative body of literature from which gnostic texts were excluded, a canon; an authoritative statement of faith that the Gnostic could not accept, a creed; and a succession of officers who were the source of authority in the church, an episcopate. These structures probably would have developed even without the threat of Gnosticism, but the life and death struggle with that movement as it became a specific Christian heresy encouraged and speeded up the process.

A further insight into the situation of Hellenistic Christianity a generation after Paul can be gained from 2 Thessalonians: the church had to come to terms with the increasing possibility of persecution.

A last such insight gained from 2 Thessalonians is that through this middle period of New Testament Christianity the Christology was developing. The author of 2 Thessalonians attributes to Jesus what the previous generation had attributed only to God. The author of Colossians moves christological thinking a long step forward by taking gnostic insights about the nature and function of a redeemer and applying them to his understanding of Christ, developing particularly the idea of Christ as active in creation, as embodying in himself the fullness (plērōma) of the godhead, and as reconciling everything unto himself as the head of the body, the church. The Paulinist of Ephesians, whose special concern is the single universal church in which Jew and Gentile are one, develops further the concepts of Christ as reconciler and head of the body, the church.

Christ as reconciler is a major theme of Colossians and Ephesians. It is also a major theme in Paul's letters, e.g., Rom 5:10; 2 Cor 5:18–19. Indeed 2 Cor 5:19, "in Christ God was reconciling the world to himself, not counting their trespasses against them," is obviously the point of departure for what happens in Colossians and Ephesians: Col 1:19–20, "For in him all the fulness of God was pleased to dwell, and through him to reconcile to himself all things, whether on earth or in heaven"; and Eph 2:16, "[that he] might reconcile us both to God in one body through the cross." Colossians and Ephesians even use a different form of the verbal root, *apokatallassein*, a verb found only in Christian writers; Paul uses *katallassein*, a verb used in secular Greek of human reconciliation, and indeed so used by Paul in 1 Cor 7:11. The difference is small but significant. Paul always uses the verb metaphorically, one metaphor among others (e.g., justification, redemption, propitiation, or expiation) used to portray the saving work of God in Christ. In Colossians and Ephesians the reconciliation is a metaphysical reality and no longer a metaphor.

A similar development takes place in connection with Christ as the head of the body, the church. Paul himself never speaks of Christ as the head of the body, the church, and when he speaks of the church as the body of Christ (as he does in Rom 12:5; 1 Cor 12:12–26), the expression is a metaphor for the mutual interdependence of Christians in the church. But in Col 1:18, Eph 1:23, and 5:23, the church as the body of Christ is a cosmic reality, and Christ as its head is what gives it life, power, and direction. These are developments beyond Paul, nevertheless taking their point of departure from him.

Another feature of deutero-Pauline Christianity, and indeed of Hellenistic Christianity after Paul altogether, is the increasing use, with only comparatively light Christianization, of Hellenistic religious and philosophical literary material. Paul himself uses Hellenistic literary forms and metaphors, as he uses Jewish rabbinical methods of arguing from scripture, but the hymn in Philippians 2 is a Christian literary product and not a Christianization of a hymn to a gnostic redeemer. Nor is there in the genuine Pauline letters a "household code," as featured so prominently in the parenetical sections of both Colossians and Ephesians. Christianity, as typified by Colossians and Ephesians, was settling down in the Hellenistic world and making increasing use of material presented to it by the cultural environment to which it was increasingly integrated.

The theme of reconciliation in deutero-Pauline Christianity leads naturally to the major theme of Ephesians: the unity of Jew and Gentile in the one body of Christ. In Ephesians "church" invariably means the one universal church, in sharp contrast to Paul's normal use of the word, and the fact that Ephesians is concerned with the one universal church is an important factor in the development of New Testament Christianity. Up until this time the Christian movement had been an apocalyptic sect within Judaism and a cult within Hellenism. Paul took the concept a stage further when in his Corinthian correspondence he addressed "the church of God which is at Corinth . . . together with all those who in every place call on the name of our Lord Jesus Christ" (1 Cor 1:2; compare 2 Cor 1:1). Here the local Christian congregation, still uniformly Paul's concern, was one manifestation of the broader movement of "those who call on the name of the Lord Jesus." But when Ephesians speaks of "the church, which is his body, the fulness (plērōma) of him who fills all in all" (1:22–23), or of "God who created all things; that through the church the manifold wisdom of God might now be made known to the principalities and powers in the heavenly places" (3:9–10), or uses the benediction "to him be glory in the church and in Christ Jesus to all generations" (3:21), then the reference is to the one universal church. Christianity is no longer a sect or a cult within a broader movement but self-consciously the means whereby God works out his purpose in the world, the one all encompassing unit that represents God to men and by means of which men come to God. It is when we come to Ephesians in the New Testament that we must begin to speak of the Christian Church, with a capital C, and no longer of Christian churches. The theme of Ephesians is the Church Universal, the One Body of Christ, and we have now reached the self-understanding that was to characterize and sustain the Christian Church through the long centuries of the Dark and Middle Ages.

Our discussion of Ephesians called attention to the magnificent rhetoric of Eph 2:11–22, magnificent not so much because the author has polished his phrases as because he is here at the heart of his concern: the unity of Jew and Gentile in the Church of God. Jerusalem is now fallen to the Romans, the Temple is no more, there is no longer a Jerusalem church from which emissaries can come arguing that the Christian must also be a Jew. The circumstances that led to Paul's great battles in Galatia, Philippi, and elsewhere are now no more, and the author of Ephesians can celebrate in sonorous phrases the unity of Jew and Gentile in the One Church of God. But even here we catch a glimpse of a major concern of New Testament Christianity in its middle period: the necessity to come to terms with the destruction of the Jerusalem Temple.

> So then you are no longer strangers and sojourners, but you are fellow citizens with the saints and members of the household of God, built upon the foundation of the apostles and prophets, Christ Jesus himself being the cornerstone, in whom the whole structure is joined together and grows into a holy temple in the Lord; in whom you also are built into it for a dwelling place of God in the Spirit.
>
> Eph 2:19–22

This celebrates the unity of Jew and Gentile within the church of God, this church now viewed as the New Temple. In this way the author deals with the catastrophe of the destruction of Jerusalem and its Temple by the Romans.

Eph 2:19–22 also shows the church girding its loins for its own future. The church is "built upon the foundation of the apostles and prophets," Christ Jesus is "the cornerstone." The days of the free, charismatic enthusiasm that provided the dynamism for the beginning of the churches are over; we have a first glimpse of the firm and careful structure that enabled the church to survive and, indeed, to mold the centuries that were to come in the West.

## THE LETTER TO THE HEBREWS

Hebrews has no claim to having been written either by Paul or one of his pupils, and it does not reflect their concerns. But because it was ascribed to Paul in the early church, it is logical for us to consider it at this point.

### General Discussion

The letter to the Hebrews is extraordinarily difficult to fit into any survey of the New Testament. Like Melchizedek of whom it speaks, it is "without father or mother or genealogy" (Heb 7:3), and we would be tempted to add also "without offspring." In the New Testament it has neither antecedents nor descendants and is not part of any movement; it is simply a text of such excellence that it forced its way into the canon of the New Testament, and ascribing it to Paul was only an excuse to include it in the New Testament. As for who wrote it, the famous church father Origen (about 185–254) had the last word, deciding that the name of the author was known only to God. Nor do we know more about the question of whom the text was addressed to. The address "To the Hebrews" was given to it in the early church because the subject matter is addressed to Jewish insights and concerns and says nothing about the original addressees.

Hebrews is known in the New Testament as a letter, but its only characteristic of a letter is that it closes with a greeting (13:22–25). Hebrews is to be understood fundamentally as a sermon. It is a mixture of proclamation and parenesis, and it represents the kind of discourse the Christian church was developing to meet the needs of its members. It is not a missionary sermon designed to convert non-Christians; it is directed to believers who are in need of exhortation, guidance, and comfort.

Hebrews must have been written before A.D. 96 because in that year Clement, bishop of Rome, wrote a letter in the name of the church in Rome to the church in Corinth, a letter known as 1 Clement, and in it he quotes Hebrews (1 Clem 17:1; 36:2–5). It constantly speaks of the Jerusalem Temple, its sacrifices and its High Priest, yet nowhere exhibits an awareness of the destruction of the Temple by the Romans. Some scholars therefore suggest that Hebrews was written before A.D. 70, but this seems impossible in the light of other internal evidence in the text. Heb 2:3 speaks of the message of salvation as being "declared at first by the Lord, and . . . attested to us by those who heard him," which is very close to the language of Luke 1:2 and means that the writer belongs at least to the generation of the author of Luke-Acts, about A.D. 85–90. The references to the Temple are then explicable in that the writer had almost twenty years to adjust to its destruction and saw all that it stood for as realized in Christ. Remember that the writer thought in terms of a heavenly reality and of an earthly copy of that reality, of heavenly substance and earthly shadow. For example, Heb 9:1–5 describes the "earthly sanctuary . . . a tent," but in 9:11, "the greater and more perfect tent (not made with hands, that is, not of this creation)" appears with Christ. Heb 9:23–24 speaks of "the heavenly things" and the "copies of the heavenly things," of "a sanctuary made with hands, a copy of the true one," and this kind of thinking is characteristic of Hebrews altogether. Under these conditions it has been possible for the writer to adjust completely to the destruction of the Temple, so that he can ignore the physical fact as he concentrates on the spiritual reality of which the Temple was always only a shadow and copy.

The writer of Hebrews is thoroughly at home in the world of the Jewish Temple, and he thinks about it in terms of substance and shadow, of reality and copy of reality, thoroughly Greek ideas stemming ultimately from Plato. So he has to be regarded as a product of Hellenistic Judaism; he is a Jew of the Diaspora converted to the Christian faith, and his Greek way of thinking about his Jewish heritage has prepared him to interpret that faith as the revelation of the reality of which Judaism was always a copy.

To whom was Hebrews originally addressed? The writer is a Hellenistic Jewish Christian, and his arguments presuppose that he is writing to others who think as he does, i.e., to a Hellenistic Jewish Christian community. Since Clement of Rome knows and quotes the text within what could only have been a few years of its writing, that community may well have been in Rome. This view is supported by the greetings from "those who come from Italy" in Heb 13:24.

## The Structure of Hebrews

A feature of Hebrews is the careful alternation of proclamation and parenesis that gives it its distinctively sermonic form. It has no introduction, but plunges immediately into proclamation. Its structure is as follows:

> **Proclamation**: Jesus as Son of God and Savior of Men, 1:1–3:6
> **Parenesis**: 3:7–4:13
> **Proclamation**: Jesus as High Priest, first statement of the theme, 4:14–5:10
> **Parenesis**: Christian maturity, 5:11–6:20
> **Proclamation**: Jesus as High Priest, development of the theme, 7:1–10:18
> **Parenesis**: 10:19–39
> **Proclamation**: Jesus as the pioneer and perfector of faith, 11:1–39
> **Parenesis**: 12:1–13:17
> **Closing benediction and greetings**: 13:18–25

## Exegetical Survey

**1:1–3:6** *First aspect of the proclamation: Jesus as Son of God and savior of men.* The preacher dwells on Jesus as Son of God and as savior of men, and, further, as the merciful and faithful High Priest who has expiated the sins of the people. But men are flesh and blood, and so Jesus had to share their nature. Sharing the nature of men and sufferings he has not only redeemed men but can help them since he understands their temptations.

Here we have a major feature of Hebrews. On the one hand, Jesus is the "heavenly" High Priest, making the true sacrifice for the sins of the people; on the other hand, he is of the same flesh and blood as those he sanctifies. In a later generation this was to develop into the Christology of the great creeds, where Jesus is declared to be both truly God and truly man. What we have here is a development from the Jewish way of thinking concerning the High Priest. He represented the people before God, and this he could do because he was one with them. But he also represented God before the people, and in doing this came to be thought of as partaking in some way in the aura of divinity, especially when he came out of the Holy of Holies, which he and he alone might enter and even then only one day in the year. Against this background it is easy to see how the writer of Hebrews, who regards Jesus as fulfilling both functions perfectly as compared to the imperfect fulfillment in the person of the Jewish High Priest, came to use the language he does.

Note also in Heb 2:9 the characteristic Hellenistic myth of the descending-ascending redeemer, as in the New Testament christological hymns.

**3:7–4:13** *First section of parenesis.* This section is built around Psa 95:7b–11. Verses 7b–10 are concerned with the journey of the Israelites through the wilderness, interpreting it as God testing his people. The people failed this testing, hence their failure to reach the perfect "rest" of God (verse 11). The Christians must not similarly fail, and if they can but endure, they will inherit the promised "rest" in which they will share the glory of God's own Sabbath rest.

**4:14–5:10** *Second aspect of the proclamation: Jesus as High Priest* (first statement of the theme).

**5:11–6:20** *Second section of parenesis: Christian maturity.*

**7:1–10:18** *Third aspect of the proclamation: Jesus as High Priest* (development of the theme). The theme of Jesus as High Priest is now developed in various ways, each designed to exhibit the superiority of the high priesthood of Jesus over what it superseded.

    **7:1–28** *Jesus is High Priest after the order of Melchizedek.* The shadowy figure of the priest-king Melchizedek blesses Abraham the father of the Jewish people in Genesis 14, and this is interpreted as indicating that his order is superior to that of any Jewish priesthood.

    **8:1–6** *Jesus has made the one perfect sacrifice.*

    **8:7–13** *He is the mediator of the new covenant that replaces the old, obsolete one.*

    **9:1–14** *The priesthood of Jesus is the perfection of which the Jewish Levitical priesthood had only been the promise.*

    **9:15–22** *The new covenant is superior to the old, since the death that*

> ratified it is a death redeeming men from their transgressions under the old.

**9:23–10:18**   Shadow and substance in regard to the sanctuary and the sacrifice.

**10:19–39**   Third section of parenesis.

**11:1–39**   Fourth aspect of the proclamation: Jesus as the pioneer and perfector of faith. The writer's definition of faith indicates his Hellenistic Jewish heritage. Faith as "the assurance of things hoped for" reflects the Jewish model of promise and fulfillment, and faith as "the conviction of things not seen" reflects the Greek model of appearance and reality.

The idea of listing the heroes of the faith is Jewish. In Sir 44:1 we read, "Let us now praise famous men, and our fathers in their generations," and there follows a list from Enoch to Simon the High Priest (Sir 44:16–50:21). The heroes listed in Hebrews 11 were all faithful men of God, but they did not receive the promise. God had reserved the promise for Christians.

**12:1–13:17**   Fourth section of parenesis.

**13:18–25**   Benediction and greetings.


## FURTHER READING

For 2 Thessalonians, see:

> PCB, p. 1,000 (W. Neill). Treats the letter as Pauline.
> JBC, pp. 227–29, 233–35 (J. T. Forestell). Pauline.
> IDB, vol. 4, pp. 625–29 (F. W. Beare). A good discussion. The letter is treated as Pauline, but with reservations.
> Kümmel, Intro., pp. 185–90. Pauline.
> Marxsen, Intro., pp. 37–44. Deutero-Pauline.
> Fuller, Intro., pp. 57–59. Deutero-Pauline.

For Colossians, see:

> PCB, pp. 990–95 (C. F. D. Moule). "Substantially Pauline."
> JBC, pp. 334–40 (J. A. Grassi). Pauline.
> IDB, vol. 1, pp. 658–62 (G. Johnston). Pauline.
> Kümmel, Intro., pp. 237–45. Pauline.
> Marxsen, Intro., pp. 177–86. Deutero–Pauline.
> Fuller, Intro., pp. 59–65. Pauline.

For Ephesians, see:

> PCB, pp. 980–84. Undecided on question of authorship.
> JBC, pp. 341–49 (J. A. Grassi). Undecided.

*IDB*, vol. 2, pp. 108–14 (G. Johnston). Deutero-Pauline. Has a good discussion of relationship between Ephesians and the Pauline corpus as a whole.
Kümmel, *Intro.*, pp. 247–58. Deutero-Pauline.
Marxsen, *Intro.*, pp. 187–98. Deutero-Pauline.
Fuller, *Intro.*, pp. 65–68. Deutero-Pauline.

All the above discuss the Colossian heresy. In addition, see:

*IDB*, vol. 2, pp. 404–06, "Gnosticism" (R. M. Grant).
Jonas, *The Gnostic Religion*. Certainly the best discussion of Gnosticism.
Bultmann, *Primitive Christianity*, pp. 162–71. Very good, in short compass.
Hennecke and Schneemelcher, *New Testament Apocrypha*, vol. 1, pp. 231–362 (discusses the gnostic gospels—there are many of them) and pp. 511–31 (translation of the Gospel of Thomas; precis of a translation of the Gospel of Truth).
Grant, *Gnosticism: An Anthology* is a very useful selection of texts in translation.

For the letter to the Hebrews, see:

*PCB*, pp. 1008–19 (F. F. Bruce).
*JBC*, pp. 381–402 (M. M. Bourke).
*IDB*, vol. 2, pp. 571–75 (E. Dinkler).
Kümmel, *Intro.*, pp. 273–82.
Marxsen, *Intro.*, pp. 217–22.
Fuller, *Intro.*, pp. 144–50.

*The Chester Beatty papyrus fragment of Mark 8:34–9:8, from the third century* A.D.

# 7

# The Gospel of Mark:
## The Apocalyptic Drama

With Mark we reach the one unique literary form produced by early Christianity: the gospel. Other movements produced letters, chronicles, and apocalypses, but only Christians wrote gospels, and the first Christian to do so was the evangelist Mark. We must therefore consider his achievement very carefully.

## MARK AS A MAN OF THE SYNOPTIC TRADITION

The gospels of Matthew, Mark, and Luke are called the "synoptic" gospels because they can be put side by side and read together; they tell much the same story in much the same way. But they also make extensive use of traditional material, sayings of Jesus and stories about him, that had been circulating in the churches. So we speak of the synoptic tradition, meaning by that the traditional material used by three synoptic evangelists. This traditional material took the literary form of sayings of Jesus and stories about him, but much of the teaching came from prophets and leaders of the church, and many of the stories reflect the situation and concerns of the church. A remarkable feature of earliest Christianity is precisely that the church cast its teaching in the form of sayings of Jesus and reflected its situation and concerns in stories about him.

Mark follows this convention. He too addresses his teaching to the church of his own day in the form of a story of Jesus teaching his disciples. He presents the problem and challenge of discipleship by telling a story about Peter. At one and the same time he is talking about Jesus and Peter and also about the risen Lord and the Christian disciple of the time at which he writes. The Jesus who addresses the disciples in Galilee is addressing the members of the church for which Mark writes.

The gospel narratives blend stories about Jesus' past ministry in Galilee and Judea and the present ministry of the risen Jesus in and through his church.

**143**

There also are previews of the future ministry of Jesus as Son of Man, especially in the gospel of Mark, for when in Mark 2:10 the Son of Man has authority on earth to forgive sins and in 2:28 to abrogate the Sabbath law, he is exercising the authority it was anticipated that he would exercise when he came on the clouds of heaven.

In the gospel of Mark, past, present, and future all flow together. The past of the ministry of Jesus in Galilee and Judea, the present of the ministry of Jesus in and through his church, the future of the ministry Jesus will exercise when he comes as Son of Man all come together in the narrative of Mark's gospel. In this way the evangelist brings to a climax the tradition he inherits and its literary conventions.

## MARK AND THE APOCALYPTIC DRAMA

One reason why Mark can write as he does is that in some respects he thinks in apocalyptic terms. He holds strongly the early Christian apocalyptic hope for the imminent coming of Jesus as Son of Man; moreover, he thinks of himself and his church as caught up in the events that mark the end of history. Mark sees a cosmic drama unfolding, a drama in three acts. Each act involves men who "preach" and who are "delivered up." In Mark 1:7 John is described as "preaching" and in 1:14 he is "delivered up."[1] Then Jesus comes "preaching the gospel of God" (1:14), and he is to be "delivered up" (9:31 RSV, "delivered into the hands of men"; 10:33 RSV, "delivered to the chief priests"). After Jesus is "delivered up" the Christians "preach" (e.g., 1:1, "The beginning of the gospel of Jesus Christ," which implies that Mark is concerned to preach the gospel of Jesus Christ as Jesus preached the gospel of God; and, further, 13:10, where "the gospel must first be preached to all nations"). In their turn the Christians are to be "delivered up" (13:9–13). We may represent Mark's fundamental conception as follows:

(a) John the Baptist "preaches" and is "delivered up."
(b) Jesus "preaches" and is "delivered up."
(c) The Christians "preach" and are to be "delivered up."

When the third act is complete the drama will reach its climax in the coming of Jesus as Son of Man (13:26).

It is because Mark thinks in this way that he can write as he does. For him past, present, and future have flowed and are flowing together in the sequence of events that began when John the Baptist preached, continued with Jesus preaching, continued further with the followers of Jesus preaching, and will end with Jesus coming as Son of Man.

This kind of thinking is characteristic of apocalyptic writers; such writers

---

[1]The Revised Standard Version has "arrested," but the verb is the same one (Greek: *paradidonai*) used of the fate of Jesus in the passion predictions (9:31, 10:33) and in the Gethsemane story (14:21, 41) and of the fate of Christians under persecution in 13:9–13. It means "to deliver up, to betray."

think naturally of a drama that began in the past, continues in the present they and their readers are experiencing, and will reach a climax in the imminent future with the coming of the End. Thinking in these terms, Mark can allow past, present, and future to merge in his narrative since the time represented is the apocalyptic time of history hurrying to its climax and end.

## THE TRADITIONAL MATERIAL USED BY MARK

Before Mark there is no connected narrative of the ministry of Jesus, but he has collected and used a great deal of traditional material. The most extensive unit in this traditional material was probably a passion narrative, an account of the arrest, trial, and crucifixion of Jesus. The church, perhaps in Jerusalem, would have produced such a narrative for apologetic reasons to show that Jesus was indeed the Messiah and that his death had fulfilled scripture. The narrative would have been full of references or allusions to scripture, as indeed Mark 15 is, to help the believer understand that Jesus went to his cross "in accordance with the scripture" and to help the Jew to believe in a crucified Messiah.

Apart from a passion narrative, or perhaps incorporated in it, there would have been also an account of the founding of the "Lord's Supper." The tradition Paul appeals to in 1 Cor 11:23–26 is ample evidence. Probably the traditional account of the meal included some teaching about discipleship. The Lukan account has such teaching (Luke 22:24–27), and the Markan version may have originally had the same setting (Mark 10:42–45). Mark 10:45 has a strong affinity with the "eucharistic word" (Mark 14:24),[2] which may indicate that it was originally found in a eucharistic setting. It is reasonable to suppose that Mark inherited from the tradition of the church both a passion narrative, largely apologetic in tone, and an account of the "Lord's Supper," which interprets the death of Jesus in its significance for the believer and which teaches about discipleship in light of the death of Jesus.

Another connected unit of tradition Mark probably inherited is a cycle of miracle stories portraying Jesus as exhibiting the traits of a Hellenistic "divine man," the stories now in Mark 5 and 7. Further, a cycle of controversy stories in Mark 2 concerning forgiveness of sins, eating with tax collectors and sinners, fasting, and keeping the Sabbath lack evidence of specifically Markan literary traits in the way they are linked together, and Mark may well have inherited them as a unit.

It is also probable that Mark inherited the collection of parables now in Mark 4 as a collection. A careful analysis of the chapter shows that the parables were put together before Mark used them and that he has fitted them into his narrative and added the secrecy motif of verses 10–12.[3] Our earlier discussion of apocalyptic Christianity indicated that the apocalyptic discourse now in Mark 13 was a product of that element of earliest Christianity. This discourse

---

[2]Mark 10:45 and 14:24 both interpret the death of Jesus in terms of the suffering servant passage of Isaiah 53, and both were apparently originally in a Semitic language, either Hebrew or Aramaic.

[3]See especially Jeremias, *Parables of Jesus*, pp. 13–15.

would also have been inherited by Mark as a unit, although he would be responsible for its present setting and for some additions to it.

One last possible pre-Markan unit of tradition is a cycle of stories giving an account of (a) a feeding, (b) a crossing of the lake, (c) a controversy with Pharisees, and (d) teaching concerning bread. Mark has two such cycles of stories:

| | | | | |
|---|---|---|---|---|
| 6:30–44 | Feeding of the five thousand | | 8:1–10 | Feeding of the four thousand |
| 6:45–56 | Crossing of the lake | | 8:10 | Crossing of the lake |
| 7:1–13 | Dispute with Pharisees | | 8:11–13 | Dispute with Pharisees |
| 7:14–23 | Discourse about food and defilement | | 8:14–21 | Incident of "no bread" and discourse about the leaven of the Pharisees |

What is more remarkable is that the gospel of John, normally so different from the synoptic gospels, has the same cycle of tradition:

| | |
|---|---|
| John 6:1–14 | Feeding of the five thousand |
| 6:15 | Attempt to make Jesus a king |
| 6:16–21 | Crossing of the sea |
| 6:22–51 | Coming of the people and discourse on bread |

Possibly Mark inherited two versions of the same cycle of tradition and certainly 6:7–8:21 does not move as smoothly as the other sections, which may indicate that he is using two versions of the same tradition.

Several scholars add other items to the list of pre-Markan units of tradition we have given, and others argue against some of them. But it is generally agreed that some such list is the extent of the connected units of tradition Mark had been able to collect. Apart from these, there are only small or isolated units of tradition, and therefore the organization of the traditional material into an integrated structure is something Mark himself has done. The structure of the gospel of Mark is the work of the evangelist, and it is very important for an understanding of what he was trying to do and to say.

## THE STRUCTURE OF THE GOSPEL OF MARK

When he wrote his gospel, Mark did not have the resources of such externals as divisions and headings to outline the structure of his work. He had to rely on internal indices of the movement of his narrative, and he did so in two ways: by giving geographical references and by offering summary reports. The geographical outline of the gospel is fairly clear: from 1:14 to 6:13 we are in Galilee; from 6:14 to 8:26 beyond Galilee; from 8:27 to 10:52 moving from Caesarea Philippi to Jerusalem; and from 11:1 to 16:8 we are in Jerusalem. From time to time Mark offers his readers reports of what is going on in the narrative. Such summaries are recognized at 1:14–15, 21–22, 39; 2:13; 3:7–12; 5:21; 6:6b, 12–13, 30–33, 53–56; 10:1. They would be expected at transitions in the narrative, and if we observe the coincidence of a geographical shift and a summary, we have the following natural divisions: 1:14–15; 3:7–12; 6:6b.

Note that there are two stories about people being given their sight, the blind man at Bethsaida (8:22–26), and blind Bartimaeus (10:46–52). They occur where the geography shifts, and they also symbolically enclose the section of the gospel where Jesus tries to make his disciples see the necessity for his suffering and its significance for an understanding of discipleship—signally failing to do so (8:27–10:45).

A last aid to a structural analysis of the gospel is that both the apocalyptic discourse and the passion narrative have introductions (13:1–5a and 14:1–2, 10–12), which on linguistic grounds give every indication of having been composed by the evangelist himself.

All this gives the following structure of the gospel of Mark:

| | |
|---|---|
| 1:1–13 | **Introduction** |
| 1:14–15 | *Transitional Markan summary* |
| 1:16–3:6 | **First major section**: the authority of Jesus exhibited in word and deed |
| 3:7–12 | *Transitional Markan summary* |
| 3:13–6:6a | **Second major section**: Jesus as Son of God and as rejected by his own people |
| 6:6b | *Transitional Markan summary* |
| 6:7–8:21 | **Third major section**: Jesus as Son of God and as misunderstood by his own disciples |
| 8:22–26 | *Transitional giving-of-sight story* |
| 8:27–10:45 | **Fourth major section**: Christology and Christian discipleship in light of the passion |
| 10:46–52 | *Transitional giving-of-sight story* |
| 11:1–12:44 | **Fifth major section**: the days in Jerusalem prior to the passion |
| 13:1–5a | *Introduction to the apocalyptic discourse* |
| 13:5b–37 | **Apocalyptic discourse** |
| 14:1–12 | *Introduction to the passion narrative with intercalation, verses 3–9* |
| 14:13–16:8 | **Passion narrative** |

We would argue strongly that the structure we have found is provided by the evangelist himself. We have observed such factors as can be shown to be characteristic of the evangelist and his gospel; this has been deliberate, because recognizing how Mark has structured his gospel is important to understanding the gospel itself and the evangelist and his purpose.

## THE GOSPEL OF MARK AND THE PASSION OF JESUS

It is often said, accurately, that the gospel of Mark is "a passion narrative with an extended introduction,"[4] and W. Marxsen claimed that Mark composed his gospel "backwards" from the passion narrative.[5] Certainly the passion of Jesus looms large in Mark, and our structural analysis bears this out. Every major section of the gospel ends on a note looking toward the passion, and the central section, 8:27–10:45, is concerned with interpreting it:

    3:6    the plot "to destroy" Jesus
    6:6    the unbelief of the people of "his own country"[6]
    8:21   the misunderstanding of the disciples[7]
    10:45  the cross as a "ransom for many"
    12:44  the widow's sacrifice, which anticipates Jesus'

All through the gospel, the passion and the parousia of Jesus stand in a certain tension with each other. For example, our structural analysis shows that the apocalyptic discourse of Mark 13, in which the parousia is the central concern, is parallel to the passion narrative of 14:1–16:8. They both have introductions, neither one is subordinated to the other, and there is an element of carefully organized parallelism in that the events predicted for the Christians in 13:9 are exactly what happens to Jesus in the passion narrative. Furthermore, there is a careful relationship between the uniform "after three days" of the prediction of the resurrection in 8:31 (and 9:31; 10:34) and the "after six days" of the transfiguration in 9:2. Since the transfiguration anticipates the parousia, the sequence would seem to be: after three days, the resurrection; after six days, the parousia. Moreover, 9:9 indicates that the event represented by the transfiguration comes after the resurrection and will be of concern to the disciples then: "he charged them to tell no one what they had seen, until the Son of Man should have risen from the dead." Finally, there are the references to Galilee in 14:28, "*after* I am raised up, I will go before you into Galilee," and in 16:7, "he is going before you into Galilee; there you will see him." We hold these to be references to the anticipated parousia. They are, therefore, a final indication of a consistent movement in the gospel through the passion, including of course the resurrection, to the parousia. Mark is addressing people in a situation like that of the women at the tomb, aware of the resurrection and awaiting the parousia in "trembling and astonishment" (16:8).

---

[4]Originally said by Kähler, *The So-Called Historical Jesus and the Historic Biblical Christ*, p. 80, n. 11.

[5]Marxsen, *Mark the Evangelist*, p. 31.

[6]This is a favorite way of thinking about the ministry of Jesus in light of his passion in the New Testament (compare John 1:11 "He came to his own home; and his own people received him not").

[7]The disciples misunderstand the necessity for the passion, and this note of misunderstanding prepares the way for the interpretation of the necessity for and significance of the passion that dominates 8:27–10:45, and that is also misunderstood.

# THE EVANGELIST AND HIS READERS

From time to time in his gospel, the evangelist indicates the state and status of his readers. Mark 9:9 shows that the "disciples" Mark is addressing are now between the resurrection and the parousia. Mark 14:28 and 16:7 also imply this: the readers know the resurrection and anticipate the parousia. They are like the women at the tomb; indeed, the state of the women represents the state of Mark's readers. But more important than any of these references is the apocalyptic discourse in 13:3–37, which is certainly addressed directly to Mark's readers and must be held to mirror their situation. They are being led astray by false Christs (verses 5–7); they are undergoing tribulation and persecution (verses 8–13); and they are seeing "the desolating sacrilege set up where it ought not to be" (verse 14), which has led to more tribulation and to an increase in the activity of false Christs and false prophets (verses 19–23). But the End is near, the Son of Man will soon be seen "coming in clouds with great power and glory" (verse 26); one must now "Take heed, watch" (verses 33–37).

The readers are, therefore, living in a state of heightened apocalyptic expectation, and this is as it should be, for the parousia is indeed imminent. But at the same time, they are being led astray by false Christs and false prophets. We do not know who these people were, but Kelber's careful exegesis of 13:5b–6, 21–22[8] indicates that they were men claiming to be the Risen Jesus himself, i.e., they were "parousia pretenders." The time envisaged is that of the Jewish War of A.D. 66–70. The war led to an upsurge of apocalyptic expectation among both Jews and Christians and to tribulation for Christians, who to the Romans were Jews and to the Jews were Christians. Many had to flee, and they were all subject to the blandishments of the "parousia pretenders."

The reference to the "desolating sacrilege" is ultimately a reference to the altar of Olympian Zeus set up in the Jewish Temple by the Syrian king Antiochus IV Epiphanes some two centuries before, but the immediate reference is most probably to the desecration and destruction of the Temple by the Romans in A.D. 70. This shattering event would have brought the apocalyptic expectation to a fever pitch—such an event *must* be the beginning of the End—and Mark writes to support this view, to encourage his readers to wait and hope, and to instruct them that as Jesus himself had to go through his passion to his glory, so too they must be prepared for discipleship that involves suffering.

The readers of Mark are, therefore, the men and women of the church caught up in a resurgence of apocalyptic expectation occasioned by the circumstances of the Jewish War, especially by the destruction of the Jerusalem Temple, but led astray by a false teaching. The gospel is written to exhort and to instruct readers who await an imminent parousia in the period immediately following the fall of Jerusalem and the destruction of the Temple.

---

[8]Kelber, "Kingdom and Parousia in the Gospel of Mark" (unpublished dissertation, University of Chicago Divinity School, 1970), pp. 151–59.

# MARK, THE GENTILE MISSION, AND GALILEE

If Mark is concerned with readers who stand between the passion and the parousia, who are reeling under the shock of the destruction of the Jerusalem Temple, and who are to anticipate the parousia in Galilee (14:28; 16:7), is he then concerned with *Palestinian* readers? This would be a natural conclusion to draw and some scholars do so in fact, most notably Marxsen.[9] But there are two major arguments against it: Mark's concern for the Gentile mission (the Hellenistic Jewish Christian mission to the Gentiles) and his symbolic use of "Galilee." We consider each in turn; they are important in determining the readers to whom Mark addressed his gospel, and also to other points in understanding the gospel. It is in fact impossible to separate Galilee from the Gentile mission in Mark's gospel, but we will come at the matter from the two different starting points.[10]

## Mark's Concern for the Gentile Mission

Mark has a strong concern for Gentiles and the Hellenistic Jewish Christian mission to them. This is evident in his explicit references to the conversion of Gentiles: the Jews reject Jesus "the son" and the gospel goes to "others" (12:9–11); "the gospel must first be preached to all nations" (13:10); the elect are "from the ends of the earth" (13:27); "the gospel is preached in the whole world" (14:9). Then there are remarkably many references to Gentiles in the miracle stories in chapters 5 and 7: The Gerasenes are Gentiles, the Decapolis is composed of Greek cities, the woman is a Greek (7:26), and the healing of the deaf mute takes place in the Decapolis. True, Mark is using a cycle of stories developed in the Gentile mission, but that he uses them shows his interest in that mission. Finally, the whole gospel comes to a christological climax when the centurion confesses Jesus as Son of God in 15:39. The centurion is a Gentile, and the title Son of God, itself so prominent in the gospel of Mark, is a Gentile rather than Jewish title.

## Mark's Symbolic Use of "Galilee"

In 14:28 and 16:7 Galilee is the location for the parousia, and as with so much else in connection with the parousia, it is likely to be symbolic rather than literal. The gospel itself seems to treat Galilee symbolically. Jesus is located there explicitly until his rejection in "his own country" (Galilee) in 6:6a. Then his disciples are sent on a mission, presumably to Galilee, but Jesus himself

---

[9]Marxsen, *Intro.*, p. 143, and *Mark the Evangelist*, pp. 92–95, 151–89, 204–06.

[10]In what follows we are indebted to Lightfoot, *Gospel Message of St. Mark*, "appendix"; Boobyer, "Galilee and Galileans in St. Mark's Gospel," *Bulletin of the John Rylands Library*, vol. 35 (1952–53), pp. 334–48; Evans, "I will go before you into Galilee," *Journal of Theological Studies*, vol. 5 (1954) pp. 3–18.

*lead?*

never works there again. So when in 14:28 and 16:7 he is said to "lead" the disciples to Galilee (the verb translated "go before" in the RSV actually means "to lead"), the natural thought is that he is leading them to the place of their missionary activity. But both in chapter 6 and in 14:28 and 16:7 it is extremely unlikely that this missionary activity is considered in strict geographical terms. The fact that Mark is allowing past, present, and future to flow together in his narrative makes it most probable that the references are to the disciples' activity and the place where the Lord has sent them or has led them to, including the Gentile world. Further, there is evidence that in Jewish thinking "Galilee," itself a district of marked ethnic mixing, could be and was a symbol for the work of God in the whole world: Matt 4:15 speaks of "Galilee of the Gentiles"; there is an addition to Isa 8:23–9:6 in the Septuagint that seems to claim that God will pour forth the light of his salvation on "Galilee of the Gentiles"; and in Ezek 47:1–12 the river of life flows from Jerusalem toward Galilee. It is a reasonable claim that in Mark 14:28 and 16:7 "Galilee" has come to symbolize the Christian mission to the world, especially to the Gentile world.

# EXEGETICAL SURVEY OF THE GOSPEL OF MARK

**1:1–13** *Introduction.* Mark defines his work as "the gospel of Jesus Christ, the Son of God" (1:1,11), that is, the "good news" of the divine human drama in which Jesus Christ is the chief protagonist. This drama began with John the Baptist's preaching, continues with Jesus coming into Galilee preaching the Gospel of God, and will continue further with the preaching of the gospel of Jesus Christ, the Son of God, by the church, including the evangelist Mark, and will shortly reach its climax when Jesus comes into "Galilee" again as Son of Man.

A necessary preliminary to the story, a kind of overture to the whole, is the mission of John the Baptist and the baptism of Jesus. Mark provides a brief account of these, carefully leading up to the moment of revelation when the status of Jesus as Son of God is revealed by the voice of God from heaven.

**1:14–15** *Transitional summary.* The drama begins.

**1:16–3:6** **First major section:** *the authority of Jesus exhibited in word and deed.* This section is dominated by the sheer authority of Jesus. He calls Simon and Andrew, and they leave their father immediately to follow him (1:16–20); he exhibits his authority in Capernaum in teaching and healing (1:21–34); he cleanses a leper (1:40–45); he heals a paralytic at Capernaum (2:1–12); he calls another disciple who immediately leaves everything to follow him (2:13–14). Mark 2:15–27 is a series of controversy stories exhibiting the authority of Jesus in various ways: to deny convention by eating with the outcast "tax collectors and sinners"; to disregard fasting regulations; to abrogate the Sabbath law, in both working and healing on the Sabbath. The rubric for this section as provided by the evangelist himself is found in 1:27. "What is this? A new teaching! With authority he commands even the unclean spirits, and they obey him."

This section on the authority of Jesus includes two Son of Man sayings both emphasizing the earthly authority of Jesus as Son of Man to forgive sins (2:10) and to abrogate the Sabbath law (2:28). It will be remembered that in 1:11 the divine voice at his baptism identified Jesus as Son of God. Now he is being identified in his full authority as Son of Man.

In this section there are a number of miracle stories:

| | |
|---|---|
| 1:21–28 | the man with an unclean spirit |
| 1:29–31 | Simon's mother-in-law |
| 1:32–34 | a summary report of many healings |
| 1:40–45 | the leper |
| 2:1–12 | the paralytic at Capernaum |
| 3:1–5 | the man with the withered hand |

These stories have a definite function: to exhibit the authority of Jesus in deeds, just as his teaching and his calling of disciples exhibit it in words. The miracle stories also introduce a theme that will be developed throughout the gospel until it reaches a climax in 14:62, the theme of the "messianic secret."

This theme is introduced in a summary report, "he would not permit the demons to speak, because they knew him" (1:32–34). It was certainly written by Mark himself; so evidently the theme of the demons "knowing Jesus," i.e., knowing the secret of his identity as Son of God (see 3:11–12) and being commanded to keep silent about it is Mark's concern. What he intends to achieve by it will become evident as we trace the theme through the gospel to its climax.

The section ends on a note anticipating the passion, the plot to destroy Jesus (3:6).

**3:7–12** *Transitional summary.* This is the longest of the summary reports composed by the evangelist himself, and it marks the transition from the first to the second major section of the gospel. It also introduces a theme that is important in the next section of the gospel, the miracles of Jesus as exhibiting his power as Son of God. In the first section the miracles are one of several things that exhibit Jesus' authority; here in the transitional summary they are particularly significant in their own right, and their importance is that they exhibit the authority of Jesus as Son of God. This summary also develops the idea of the messianic secret. Whereas in 1:32 the demons simply "knew him," in 3:11 they make their knowledge explicit: "You are the Son of God."

**3:13–6:6a** **Second major section**: *Jesus as Son of God, and as rejected by his own people.* Two themes dominate this section. The first is the power of Jesus as Son of God exhibited through miracles, as in the following references.

| | |
|---|---|
| 4:35–41 | "even wind and sea obey him" |
| 5:1–20 | the Gerasene demoniac: "What have you to do with me, Jesus, Son of the Most High God?" |
| 5:21–24, 35–43 | Jairus' daughter: "they were overcome with amazement." |

5:24b–34 the woman with the hemorrhage: "And Jesus, perceiving in himself that power had gone forth from him . . . "

The miracle stories are longer and more elaborate than in the first section of the gospel, and the emphasis on the supernatural in Jesus' power is more marked. He is shown as a Hellenistic "divine man," with power over wind and sea and with power to raise the dead, as one who is openly confessed as Son of God, the touch of whose garments has the power to heal. There are major questions of the origin of these stories and of the use to which Mark is putting them. But these are best discussed after we have reviewed the very similar stories in the next section of the gospel.

The second theme dominating this section is Jesus' being misunderstood and rejected. He is misunderstood by his friends (3:21); he is in tension with his family (3:31–35); and finally, he is rejected by the people of his own country (6:1–6a). This final rejection is the note of anticipation of the passion on which the section ends.

Mark inserts his parable chapter (4:1–34) in this section. It is inherited from the tradition of the church more or less as a unit,[11] and Mark inserts it here because it is a convenient place and because it enables him to begin a theme that becomes prominent in the next section (6:7–8:21) and dominant in the fourth (8:27–10:45): the theme of the disciples and discipleship.

The disciples appear originally in the first major section of the gospel, where their immediate response to Jesus' call was an aspect of the presentation of Jesus' authority. In this second section they figure more prominently, and characteristic Markan ideas and themes appear in connection with them. The section begins with an account of their formal appointment as a group (3:13–19), and in the parable chapter Mark makes a special point about them. They are privy to "the secret of the Kingdom of God" and so are in an especially privileged position compared to "those outside." In a summary report (4:33–34), again composed by Mark himself as are all of the summary reports, their privileged position is further emphasized: "privately to his own disciples he explained everything." Mark makes a great deal of the privileged position of the disciples and of their total failure to understand Jesus. The latter theme is developed more and more strongly in later sections of the gospel until it reaches a climax in the flight of the disciples (14:50) and the denial by Peter (14:66–72).

Note the careful balancing of the occurrences of christological titles. The introduction established Jesus as Son of God, (1:1 and 1:11), accompanied by the special revelatory circumstances of the heavens opening and the divine voice speaking. The first major section had two occurrences of Son of Man (2:10 and 2:28), and these are now balanced by two occurrences of Son of God (3:11 and 5:7). This careful juxtaposition of titles is a major means whereby Mark presents his christological teaching.

---

[11]Mark has inserted 4:11–12 into the parable chapter. This is evident from the fact that the question in 4:10 now has two answers, 4:11 and 4:13, and that both answers are introduced by "and he said to them," a phrase that is a hallmark of Markan literary composition.

**6:6b** *Transitional summary.* This is the shortest of the transitional summaries in Mark's gospel, but the shift in emphasis between the second and third sections of the gospel is not great.

**6:7–8:21** **Third major section**: *Jesus as Son of God, and as misunderstood by his disciples.* This section does not move as smoothly as do the others, probably because Mark is reproducing two different versions of the same cycle of tradition and finding it difficult to fit them into the overall movement of his narrative. But the two overall themes of the section are clear; indeed, if we accept the thesis that Mark is using a duplicated cycle of tradition, the second, the misunderstanding of the disciples, becomes even clearer.

The first theme of this section is a continuation of the presentation of Jesus as Son of God by reason of his miracles:

6:30–44   The feeding of the five thousand.
6:45–52   Jesus walks on the water, presumably enraptured—"He meant to pass them by" (verse 48).
6:54–56   A summary report emphasizing that Jesus' garments have the power to heal (compare 5:28).
7:24–30   The Syrophoenician woman's daughter, healed at a distance.
7:31–37   The deaf man with a speech impediment. This is much more in the spirit of the stories in the first section (compare 7:37 with 1:27). But Mark can and does link the stories together in the various sections by returning to former emphases (compare 1:27 with 4:41 and 7:37).
8:1–9     The feeding of the four thousand.

Although these stories continue the theme of Jesus as Son of God (e.g., in the deliberate link between 6:56 and 5:28), the title "Son of God" does not occur. Mark is very careful in his use of christological titles. Having balanced the two "Son of Man" references in 2:10 and 28 with the "Son of God" references in 3:11 and 5:7, he does not use another title until the "Christ" of 8:29.

Mark clearly is reinterpreting the miracle stories he presents in these two sections of his gospel. In the form in which he inherited them from the tradition of the church they presented Jesus as a Hellenistic "divine man," and Mark preserves the traits by which they do this. But he then introduces the note of secrecy (3:11; 5:43; 7:36, but not in the story of the Gerasene demoniac, see 5:19). This element of secrecy would strike his readers as startling, because the purpose of such stories is normally precisely to proclaim the power and authority of the "divine man," a tendency that Mark preserves unaltered in the story of the Gerasene demoniac. Mark goes a step further by the careful balancing of the christological titles, whereby Son of God is interpreted in terms of Son of Man, and still further in his narrative structure, which subordinates everything to the passion.

The second theme of this third major section of the gospel is that of the disciples and their misunderstanding of Jesus. The section begins with an account of the mission of the twelve (6:7–13) and of their return (6:30), into which is intercalated the account of the death of John the Baptist (6:14–29). Such intercalation is a favorite compositional technique of the evangelist Mark. Mark does not report this mission of the disciples as a success. He cannot do so, of course, because he is developing the theme of the misunderstanding and failure of the disciples: in 6:51–52 (note "their hearts were hardened," verse 52); in 7:18 (" . . . are you also without understanding?") and in 8:14–21, the climax to this section, (with its final note, "Do you not yet understand?").

**8:22–26** *Transitional giving-of-sight story.* Mark moves from the third section to the fourth, as he does from the fourth to the fifth, with a story of Jesus giving sight to a blind man (8:22–26; 10:46–52). These stories enclose the fourth section of the gospel (8:27–10:45), in which Jesus attempts to lead his disciples to "sight" (i.e., understanding) and fails to do so. They are certainly used in ironic symbolism, and their function here is therefore quite different from the previous functions of miracle stories in the gospel.

**8:27–10:45** **Fourth major section**: *Christology and Christian discipleship in light of the passion.* This is the most homogenous and carefully constructed of all the sections in the gospel. It begins geographically at Caesarea Philippi to the north of Galilee and has the external form of a journey from there to Jerusalem. The stages of the journey are clearly marked by further geographical references: 9:30 Galilee (9:33 Capernaum); 10:1 Judea and beyond Jordan (10:1 is also a summary report, the last such in the gospel); 10:32 the road to Jerusalem. The section is built very carefully around three passion prediction units, which have a fixed pattern: prediction of the passion and resurrection by Jesus, misunderstanding by the disciples, teaching by Jesus concerning discipleship. Each of these follows a geographical reference.

| Geographical reference: | 8:27 | 9:30 | 10:32 |
|---|---|---|---|
| Prediction: | 8:31 | 9:31 | 10:33–34 |
| Misunderstanding: | 8:32–33 | 9:32; 33–34 | 10:35–41 |
| Teaching: | 8:34–9:1 | 9:35–37 | 10:42–45 |

The section has the following structure:

| | |
|---|---|
| 8:22–26 | Bethsaida transitional giving-of-sight story. |
| 8:27 | **Caesarea Philippi**. |
| | 8:27–30    Fundamental narrative of Peter's confession. |
| | 8:31–9:1    **First prediction unit**. |
| | Prediction, 8:31 |
| | Misunderstanding, 8:32–33 |
| | Teaching about discipleship, 8:34–9:1 |

9:2         "After six days . . . ."
            9:2–8            Transfiguration.
            9:9–13           Elijah as forerunner.
            9:14–29          Appended incident and teaching on
                                discipleship.
                             Disciples and boy with the dumb spirit,
                                9:14–27
                             Teaching to disciples, 9:28–29
9:30        **Galilee (9:33 Capernaum).**
            9:30–37          **Second prediction unit.**
                             Prediction, 9:31
                             Misunderstanding, 9:32
                             Teaching about discipleship, 9:33–37
            9:38–50          Appended incident and teaching on
                                discipleship.
                             Nondisciple practicing exorcism,
                                9:38–40
                             Teaching to disciples, 9:41–50
10:1        **Judea and beyond Jordan.** Intercalated units of incident
            and teaching to disciples.
            10:2–12          Divorce.
                             The Pharisees and divorce, 10:1–9
                             Teaching to disciples, 10:10–12
            10:13–16         Receiving the Kingdom of God.
                             The presentation of the children, 10:13
                             Teaching to disciples, 10:14–16
            10:17–31         Entering the Kingdom of God.
                             The man with the question, 10:17–22
                             Teaching to disciples, 10:23–31
10:32       **The road to Jerusalem.**
            10:33–45         **Third prediction unit.**
                             Prediction, 10:33–34
                             Misunderstanding, 10:35–41
                             Teaching about discipleship, 10:42–45
10:46–52    Jericho transitional giving-of-sight story.

Taken together, the three prediction units are extraordinarily interesting. The first summarizes the divine necessity for the passion and is
entirely in the present tense. The second provides a hinge in that the first
part anticipates Jesus being delivered into the hands of men, but still uses
the present tense (RSV is quite wrong in translating 9:31 "The Son of Man
will be delivered . . ."; ERV is more accurate, " . . . is delivered . . .")
and then puts the second half of the prediction into the future tense, "they
will kill. . . ." The third puts the whole prediction into the future and
introduces specific references to Jerusalem and the details of the passion
itself. This care in composition, and Mark has composed the predictions
himself very carefully, provides an element of movement to the plot of the
gospel. In this central section we look back over what has happened to

make the passion necessary—the plots, rejections, misunderstanding, all foreseen by God—we pause for these solemn moments of revelatory teaching, and then we move forward to Jerusalem and the passion itself.

The predictions and the prediction units not only provide the framework for this section of the gospel, they are also the main thrust of the teaching on Christology and Christian discipleship. The first prediction follows Peter's confession of Jesus as the Christ (8:29), and so follows the pattern of interpretation of Christology by juxtaposing titles as in the first and second sections of the gospel. Peter's confession is correct only if "Christ" is understood as the Son of Man who "must suffer," and Peter's reaction indicates that his confession was in fact a false one. The second and third prediction units continue the development of a true Christology by using "Son of Man," and they also implicitly continue the corrective reinterpretation of Peter's confession of Jesus as the Christ. These units provide the key elements to the teaching on discipleship in light of the necessity for Christ's passion: as the master went, so must the disciple be prepared to go. The first unit stresses the need to take up the cross in following Jesus (8:34–37); the second, the necessity for servanthood (9:35); and the third defines servanthood in terms of the cross (10:45). There is, further, more general teaching on discipleship between 10:1 and the third prediction unit, probably introduced here in a general context of teaching to disciples.

The first and second prediction units each have appended to them an incident and teaching to the disciples, and the incidents are curiously related. In the first (9:14–27) the disciples are failures as exorcists, while in the second (9:38–40) a nondisciple is successful as an exorcist using the name of Jesus. In this way Mark pursues dramatically his theme of the misunderstanding and failure of the disciples. The third prediction unit has no such appendix; the ransom saying in 10:45 is the climax of the whole section, in some respects its summary, and so brings it to an end.

The one unit in the section we have not so far discussed is the transfiguration-Elijah unit (9:2–13); it is carefully linked to the first prediction unit by the "after six days" of 9:2, which so significantly contrasts with the "after three days" of the resurrection in 8:31 (and 9:31; 10:34). In Mark's gospel and purpose, the transfiguration is an anticipation of the parousia, especially in 9:9, the command to secrecy "until the Son of Man should be risen from the dead." This indicates that the event symbolized by the transfiguration will be of special importance after the resurrection, and hence this event is the parousia. The same point is made by the contrast between the "after three days" used of the resurrection (8:31; 9:31; 10:34) and the "after six days" used of the transfiguration (9:2). Here is an element of Mark's consistent thrust through the passion, including the resurrection, to the parousia.

The transfiguration is, then, an anticipation of the parousia, and its link to the first prediction of the passion and resurrection prepares the reader to appreciate his own position. Like the disciples, he now stands between the past passion and resurrection and the imminent parousia. The transfiguration unit also furthers Mark's christological purpose by a characteristic juxtaposition of titles. Having presented a confession of Jesus as the Christ, Mark now reminds the reader that Jesus is also the Son of God (9:7), again in a special revelatory manner and with the implication that both need correction and interpretation by a use of Son of Man, a point he makes explicit at his christological climax in 14:61–62.

The discussion of Elijah is added at this point (9:11–13) because of the reference to Elijah in 9:4. It is a convenient moment for Mark to present the early Christian understanding of John the Baptist as Elijah, the forerunner of the Messiah, an understanding of the role of the Baptist that he shares.

The motif of the messianic secret is continued through this section (8:30–9:9).

**10:46–52** *Transitional giving-of-sight story.*

**11:1–12:44 Fifth major section**: *The days in Jerusalem prior to the passion.* The entry (11:1–10) presents all kinds of problems at the level of the historical life of Jesus, but Mark's purpose in presenting the narrative is clear. It fulfills Zech 9:9:

> Lo, your king comes to you;
> triumphant and victorious is he,
> humble and riding on an ass,
> on a colt the foal of an ass.

Already in Jewish exegesis of scripture the irony of the king coming in such a humble fashion is apparent. The Babylonian Talmud preserves a traditional exegesis that claims that if Israel is worthy the Messiah will come in might "upon the clouds of heaven" (i.e., in fulfillment of Dan 7:13); if it is not worthy he will come "lowly, and riding on an ass" (i.e., in fulfillment of Zech 9:9).[12] Mark stresses that Israel was unworthy, and so the Messiah entered Jerusalem in this way.

Mark 11:11–25 is an interesting example of the author's compositional technique, because he interprets the cleansing of the Temple (11:15–19) by intercalating it into the account of the cursing of the fig tree (11:12–14, 20–25). Mark thus comes to terms with the catastrophe of the destruction of the Temple by understanding it as the judgment of God on a place become unworthy and by seeing the tradition of Jesus' cleansing the Temple as anticipating that judgment.

The remainder of the section offers a series of units relevant to the situation of Jesus in Jerusalem immediately before the passion: a parable interpreting the fate of Jesus (12:1–12); a series of three controversy stories, the first two featuring adamantly hostile authorities and the third an individual who can be swayed and become sympathetic (12:13–17, 18–27, 28–34). The contrast is no doubt deliberate. Then there follow two incidents featuring scribes, a denial that Messiahship should be understood in terms of a Son of David, i.e., a warrior leader in the tradition

---

[12]Sanhedrin 98a: The tradition is in the name of Rabbi Joshua ben Levi, about A.D. 250, but it exhibits the kind of understanding possible in Jewish and Jewish-Christian exegesis.

of David (12:35–37), and a denunciation of scribes (12:38–40). The section closes on the widow's sacrifice, which anticipates the sacrifice of Jesus.

**13:1–37   The apocalyptic discourse.** Our structural analysis of the gospel shows that after 12:44 there are no more summaries, no more transitional units or stories, only the twin climax of the apocalyptic discourse with an introduction (13:1–5a) and the passion narrative with an introduction (14:1–2, 10–11). Moreover, the prophecy of the destruction of the Temple (13:2) indicates that Mark is writing after the destruction of the Temple in A.D. 70. Mark wrote the introduction, and it is standard to date an apocalyptic work by the latest historical incident it refers to as prophecy.

In dealing with apocalyptic Christianity in chapter 4, we discussed the composition of the discourse Mark uses in his chapter 13, and earlier in this chapter we took up the situation of Mark's readers as reflected in that discourse. It remains only to be added here that the parenesis with which the discourse ends (13:28–37) is most probably a Markan addition. Certainly this parenesis reflects a particular emphasis in Mark's message to his readers. Similarly, the careful parallel of the apocalyptic discourse and the passion narrative reflects Mark's desire to have his readers see their situation as they watch for the parousia as necessarily and profoundly affected by the passion of Jesus.

**14:1–16:8   The passion narrative.** We discuss this section of the gospel unit by unit.

**14:1–11**   *The introduction.* Here Mark takes a traditional account of an anointing of Jesus in Bethany and intercalates it into the introduction to the passion narrative. The intercalation has the ironic effect of juxtaposing the plots of the authorities and the connivance of Judas Iscariot with an anointing of Jesus as the Messiah ("anointed one").

**14:12–25**   *Jesus' last meal with his disciples.* The parallel in 1 Cor 11:23–26 indicates that Mark is using a traditional account of the Last Supper, but the emphasis on the betrayal is a characteristically Markan emphasis, as is the language in Mark 14:21 ("is betrayed" is *paradidotai* from *paradidonai*, the verb used in the passion predictions, 9:31 and 10:33). This language was traditionally used by early Christians of the passion of Jesus,[13] but Mark develops it, especially in the predictions.

**14:26–31**   *Prediction of the flight of the disciples and the betrayal by Peter.* Again, Mark is moving his readers carefully to the climax of themes very important to him. Note also 14:28, the movement toward the anticipated parousia in "Galilee."

**14:32–52**   *The betrayal and the arrest.* This narrative represents Markan redaction of a traditional narrative and reflects the Markan emphasis on the disciples' failures: they do not watch as they were commanded to do (14:37, 38), and they flee from the scene of Jesus' arrest (14:50). In 14:41 it further reflects the traditional language used of the passion of Jesus, "the Son of Man *paradidotai*. . . ."

[13]Perrin, "The Use of [para] didonai in Connection with the Passion of Jesus in the New Testament," *Der Ruf Jesu und die Antwort des Gemeinde,* pp. 204–12.

**14:53–72** *The betrayal by Peter and an intercalated account of the night trial before the Sanhedrin.* First there is the intercalated account of the night trial before the Sanhedrin (14:55–65). It is evident that Mark himself composed this narrative,[14] and it brings his christological concerns to a climax. The High Priest challenges Jesus as "Christ, the Son of the Blessed," i.e., Son of God (14:61), thus bringing together the two titles that have been separately juxtaposed with Son of Man earlier in the gospel. Jesus accepts the titles, (14:62), thus formally abandoning the messianic secret by using "I am," which is a formula of self-identification for deities, divine men, and redeemers in the Hellenistic world, and indeed in the ancient Near East at a much earlier period, (Exod 3:14–15). Jesus himself uses such a formula earlier in Mark (6:50), as had the "parousia pretenders" of Mark 13:6. Then Jesus goes on to interpret both Christ and Son of God in terms of Son of Man, the last and climactic such reinterpretation in the gospel. The messianic secret is now revealed: Jesus is both Christ and Son of God, but as such has to be understood in light of the emphases associated with Son of Man.

The betrayal by Peter is also a climax, a climax to the presentation of Peter as representative disciple typifying in himself the promise and failure of discipleship as such: the confession (8:29); the misunderstanding (8:32); the leader at the transfiguration (9:5); the responsible person at Gethsemane (14:37). Here he betrays Jesus, as had been predicted after the Last Supper (14:30–31) and then collapses (14:72) in a scene that Aristotle would have recognized as "cathartic."

**15:1–47** *The trial before Pilate and the crucifixion.* This section is probably in the main pre-Markan tradition, and we have already noted how heavily it quotes or alludes to the Old Testament, especially in the crucifixion scene itself where 15:23 = Psa 69:21; 15:24 = Psa 22:18; 15:29 = Psa 22:7; 15:34 = Psa 22:1; 15:36 = Psa 69:21.

An incident of particular importance, in view of earlier elements in the gospel, is the Rending of the Curtain: "And the curtain of the temple was torn in two, from top to bottom" (15:38). The curtain separated the innermost part of the Jerusalem Temple, the Holy of Holies, which only the High Priest might enter and where God was particularly to be experienced, from the remainder of the Temple. Its tearing probably symbolizes in the church's tradition an interpretation of the death of Jesus as removing the last barrier between God and man. But in Mark's gospel it picks up the interpretation of the cleansing of the Temple by means of the fig tree incident (11:13–25) and emphasizes that the Temple not only no longer exists, it is no longer needed. In other words, it is part of Mark's attempt to come to terms with the catastrophe of the destruction of the Temple.

The next verse (15:39) is also very important to Mark, for the

---

[14]Donahue, *Are You the Christ? The Trial Narrative in the Gospel of Mark.* SBL Dissertation Series 10, 1973.

centurion's confession of Jesus as Son of God is the climax of Mark's christological concern. It is the first and only confession of Jesus by a human being in the gospel that is not immediately corrected or reinterpreted, and the reason is that after 14:62 the reinterpretation of a confession of Jesus as Christ or Son of God by a use of Son of Man is complete, the messianic secret is finally revealed, and such a correct confession is now possible. That a Roman centurion makes the confession symbolizes Mark's concern for the Gentiles, also to be seen in his reference to Galilee (14:28 and 16:7).

**16:1–8** *The resurrection.* We are again dealing with specially Markan material, and we saw earlier in 16:7 the movement to the parousia in "Galilee" and the situation of the women as representative of the situation of Mark's readers. Furthermore, 16:7, "tell his disciples *and Peter,*" must be read in the light of 14:72 as implying a restoration of Peter and expressing Mark's hope for a similar happy issue out of the problems afflicting the readers Peter represents in his narratives.

A problem in connection with 16:8 is whether it truly is the ending of the gospel. It seems abrupt, and we can see that the early church regarded it as insufficient, because in the course of transmitting the text of the gospel of Mark two endings were added: a shorter addition to verse 8 and a longer addition that the King James Version has as verses 9–20. All modern translations properly relegate these endings to the margin. Moreover, 16:8 ends with a conjunction, *gar (kai ephobounto gar),* and this is a barbarism not to be found at the end of any other Greek book known to us. It is difficult, however, to imagine that the text of the gospel could have been accidentally mutilated at a sufficiently early period for all our existing textual traditions to reflect it and not have had the mutilation repaired by the author himself or someone close to him who knew the original ending. This is an extraordinarily difficult issue, and commentators are equally divided. The ending as it stands in 16:8 is appropriate to the gospel as a whole with its consistent thrust through the passion to the parousia and its view of the readers as standing between those events. For this reason we incline to accept the gospel as ending at 16:8.

# FURTHER OBSERVATIONS

Having completed our exegetical survey of Mark's gospel, we can make further observations on some of the points touched on in our earlier discussion and exegesis.

## The Major Role of Christology in the Gospel of Mark

The gospel begins with Jesus Christ, the Son of God (1:1), and that Jesus is the Son of God is a main feature of the revelatory scene of the Baptism. Then the two occurrences of Son of Man in the first section (2:10, 28) are balanced by two of Son of God in the second (3:11; 5:7); the titles "Christ" and "Son of Man" juxtaposed in the story of the confession of Peter at Caesarea Philippi (8:27–34) are immediately followed by the use of Son of God at the transfiguration (9:7). Further, Christ, Son of God, and Son of Man are juxtaposed at the trial before the Sanhedrin (14:55–65), and Son of God is the title in the climactic confession by the centurion (15:39). Mark uses Son of Man to correct and interpret a false understanding of Christ and Son of God prevalent in the church for which he writes. The Christology expressed by the use of Son of Man has a threefold emphasis: on authority on earth (2:10, 28), apocalyptic authority at the final judgment (8:38; 13:26), and necessary suffering (8:31; 9:31; 10:33–34, the passion predictions). The threefold christological emphasis expressed by the use of Son of Man in Mark is Mark's answer to the false Christology he is combating and his great contribution to the development of New Testament Christology.

## The Purpose of the Gospel

We are now able to make a statement about the purpose of the gospel in which we will gather points made throughout this chapter. Fundamentally, Mark is an apocalypse in its purpose. For all that he writes realistic narrative, the intent of the evangelist is precisely that of the apocalyptic seers in the discourses in Mark 13 and its parallels or that of John of Patmos in the book of Revelation. He addresses his readers, whom he sees standing between the passion and the parousia of Jesus, to prepare them for the imminent parousia. Like an apocalyptic seer, he views himself and his readers as caught up in a divine human drama, for him the divine human drama that began when John the Baptist "preached" and was "delivered up" and that entered its second act when Jesus came into Galilee preaching the gospel of God. This drama ended its second act when Jesus himself was "delivered up" and rose from the dead, and reached its third act when the church began to preach the gospel of Jesus Christ the Son of God. It is hurrying to the climax of the church being "delivered up" and of Jesus' "coming on the clouds of heaven" to "Galilee."

As preparation for the parousia, Mark seeks to instruct his readers in a correct understanding of Christology and a true understanding of Christian discipleship. This he does not by writing letters to churches and by telling of visions, as did John of Patmos, nor only by putting prophetic words on the lips of Jesus, as in the discourses, nor only by a mixture of remembering, interpreting, and creating Jesus tradition, as in the case of the source Q. Rather, Mark takes the bold and imaginative step of telling the story of the ministry of Jesus so that the concerns of the risen Jesus for his church in the present come to the fore. For him the ministry of Jesus in the past in Galilee and Judea, the ministry of Jesus in the present in the churches for which Mark writes, and the ministry of Jesus that will begin in the future with his parousia in "Galilee," are all the same ministry and can all be treated together in a narrative in which past, present, and future flow together into the one apocalyptic time. He utilized the literary techniques of apocalyptic writers, of the scribes that produced the source Q, and of the editors and transmitters of the synoptic tradition, but he nonetheless created a new literary genre, the gospel: a narrative blend of proclamation and parenesis, of myth and history, a literary type distinctive to early Christianity.

## AUTHORSHIP AND PLACE OF COMPOSITION OF THE GOSPEL

The gospel was originally circulated anonymously; when in the second century it became important to give the gospels authoritative names from the early days of the church, it was ascribed to John Mark, a companion of Paul in Acts (Acts 12:12, 25; 15:37, 39). How valid this ascription was we have no means of knowing. All we know about the author is what we can deduce from the gospel itself. Our earlier discussion shows that he has strong links with Palestine and the Palestinian form of Christian tradition, he shares and indeed strongly expresses the characteristic early Christian apocalyptic hope, he is deeply concerned for the Gentile mission of the church, and he wrote shortly after A.D. 70. If "John Mark" can be held to meet these qualifications, well and good; if not, equally well and good. His name is irrelevant; we have called him "Mark" simply for convenience.

The church's tradition claimed that the gospel of Mark was written in Rome, and again we have no way of judging the validity of this claim. The gospel must have circulated quite rapidly since both Matthew and Luke knew and used it within a generation, which seems to indicate location at an important church center. Moreover, the gospel was accepted into the Christian canon even when it was regarded as little more than an abbreviation of the gospel of Matthew, again indicating the support of an important church center. All that we learn from the gospel itself is that it has a special concern for the Gentile mission and should be located within that mission. Rome is, therefore, a possibility, but then so is almost any other ecclesiastical center outside of Palestine itself. To understand the gospel, however, we need to know far more important things about the author than his name, or about where the gospel was written; so we will concern ourselves with these matters no further.

## THE INTERPRETATION OF THE GOSPEL OF MARK

From the very beginning, the gospel of Mark presented problems to its interpreters because of tensions within the gospel itself: a tension between the purpose of the evangelist and the actual needs of the church within a generation of the writing; and a further tension between the evangelist's purpose and the literary form he chose to express that purpose.

The evangelist followed an apocalyptic purpose, writing within the circumstances of the resurgence of apocalyptic during and immediately after the Jewish War of 66–70. Nevertheless, for all the resurgence of apocalyptic at that time (and at subsequent times of persecution or catastrophe), apocalyptic itself was on the verge of an inevitable decline in the Christian churches. The parousia simply did not take place as was frequently anticipated and expected, and the churches and the Christians were faced with the necessity not only of coming to terms with the delay of the parousia, but also with finding a way of living and working out their faith in a world that continued to exist despite all their hopes, expectations, and prayers to the contrary. In this context the gospel of Mark received its first and perhaps its most dramatic reinterpretation when Matthew and Luke both took it and independently did essentially the same thing with it: they transformed the apocalypse into a foundation myth. They transformed the time of Jesus (which Mark had seen as the same as his own time and that of the parousia, a kind of apocalyptic time), into a kind of Sacred Time. They separated it from all other time by providing it with a beginning, the birth stories, and an ending, the resurrection-ascension (Luke) and the resurrection-commissioning of the church (Matthew). They also made it a Sacred Time by various literary devices that emphasized the element of the sacred and the miraculous in that time. Then they provided the reader with a structured means of relating to that Sacred Time and of living through its power and significance. Now the gospel story became the myth from which Christians lived, as the Jews lived from the myth of the Exodus and as primitive peoples lived from the myth of their totemic ancestors, and so on. It was now the gospel *story*, no longer the gospel as the proclamation of the immediacy and imminence of God's activity, as it has been for Paul and Mark. The apocalypse had become a foundation myth, and apocalyptic time had become Sacred Time, meeting the needs of a generation later than Mark's, and indeed of a hundred generations to come.

The other element of tension was that between the purpose of the evangelist Mark and the literary form through which he expressed that purpose, between his apocalyptic purpose and his realistic narratives. There is no doubt that the narratives of Mark are realistic. They are so realistic that as perceptive a modern literary critic as Erich Auerbach ascribes their realism to the personal reminiscence of an eyewitness and participant.[15] Our discussion has shown that the personal reminiscence is only an echo or shadow, if indeed there is any personal reminiscence at all, but there can be no doubt of the realism of the narratives. With the dwindling of apocalyptic concern in the churches, the apocalyptic purpose of Mark came to be lost, and what remained was the realistic nature of the narratives. In the second and third centuries there was an increasing conflict with Gnosticism, to which we referred in our last chapter, and the gnostic Christian movement did indeed produce many "gospels" expressing its teaching in the "words" of Jesus, especially in "secret" words of Jesus to his disciples, or in post-resurrection revelatory discourses. The more orthodox church combated the gnostic Christian movement by emphasizing the apostolic authority of *its* gospels, and under these circumstances a tradition developed that the gospel of Mark was built up largely of the reminiscences of Peter.[16] So Papias, bishop of Hierapolis around the middle of

---

[15]Auerbach, *Mimesis*, p. 36.

[16]This tradition is discussed in Fuller, *Intro.*, pp. 104–06; Marxsen, *Intro.*, pp. 142–43. Details of the tradition in original texts with translations are to be found in Taylor, *The Gospel According to St. Mark*, pp. 1–8.

the second century, is supposed to have claimed, "The Elder said this also: Mark, having become the interpreter of Peter, wrote down accurately all that he remembered of the things said and done by the Lord. . . ."[17] This tradition is of dubious historical worth, but it is a tribute to the realism of the narratives in Mark's gospel.

This realism provides us with the first clue to the interpretation of Mark's gospel: the narratives are meant to be understood. The evangelist himself takes pains to help his readers by explaining the value of coins (12:42) and by giving the Roman equivalent for the name of a place (15:16).[18] So we must welcome and utilize the patient work of historical scholarship that helps us understand the references and allusions in the narratives. We need to appreciate the significance of the charge of blasphemy in 2:7—the forgiveness of sins was not only reserved to God, it was reserved to God at the End Time—or the force of the plot in 3:6—Pharisees and Herodians were mortal enemies; and much more. We need to know enough about the references and allusions in these narratives for them to become realistic to us and not strange or foreign.

A second clue lies in the fact that narrative functions in a certain way: it draws the reader into the story as a participant. The reader is *there* as the one who took up his cross challenges the disciples to be prepared to take up theirs (8:34), or as he who gave his life interprets the giving as a "ransom for many" (10:45). Similarly, the reader is caught up in the dark hours of the passion and hears Peter's protestations of loyalty (14:26–31), and so shares the catharsis of his breakdown in the courtyard (14:72). The natural function of narrative is to help the reader hear the voices, take part in the action, get involved in the plot. The effectiveness of the evangelist Mark as a preacher is that he has cast his message in a narrative rather than in the direct discourse of a letter or a homily. We appreciate once again the significance of the realism of Mark's narratives, for it enables the reader to be caught up into the narrative as a participant.

Now we can take the important step of recognizing the affinities and differences between Mark and John of Patmos, the author of the book of Revelation. Both are experiencing a period of turmoil and an accompanying resurgence of apocalyptic; one because of the Jewish War and the other because of a time of persecution of the church. Both address their readers directly out of their narrative: Mark by a parabolic discourse, sections of teaching on discipleship, an apocalyptic discourse, and so on; John of Patmos by letters to the churches and interpretations of his visions. Both have essentially the same purpose: to prepare their readers for the imminent parousia. But there is an extremely important difference between them. Mark's narratives are deliberately realistic; John's deliberately symbolic. The one captures the imagination of his readers by drawing them into his narrative as participants, the other by the sheer power of his symbols to challenge, evoke, and sustain.

[17]Eusebius, *Historia Ecclesiastica*, bk. 3, 39.15. Taylor, *The Gospel According to St. Mark*, pp. 1–2.

[18]In the latter instance causing endless difficulties for modern commentators because the soldiers lead Jesus into the *aulē* (courtyard), which is an open space, and Mark explains it as a *praitōrion*, which is a building. Nonetheless, the intent to explain is clear, if not the explanation itself.

We can now recognize that like all apocalyptic, the gospel of Mark needs to be demythologized. The Jesus who comes on the clouds of heaven as Son of Man is probably for Mark already a symbol; certainly he is a symbol for us. He is a symbol of the realities and the possibilities for meaning of human existence in the world. We must allow Mark to catch us up into his narratives as participants and to challenge us with the teaching and example of the Jesus these narratives are concerned to portray, as well as by the example of another kind set by the disciples and opponents, recognizing that in all this we are dealing with symbols of the realities and possibilities of life in the world.

## FURTHER READING

Since the whole chapter is concerned with one book, the further reading is not broken down in accordance with the structure of the chapter, as has been the case previously. Works particularly important at a given place in the chapter are to be found in the footnotes. The references here are more general.

The following three books all discuss the synoptic tradition and the gospel; in this instance Marxsen and Fuller are particularly important.

> Kümmel, *Intro.*, pp. 31–72.
> Marxsen, *Intro.*, pp. 113–45.
> Fuller, *Intro.*, pp. 69–113.

The other three resource books all have sections on the gospel, and *PCB* and *IDB* represent the ongoing attempt in Britain to maintain an essentially historicizing approach to it.

> *PCB*, pp. 799–819 (R. McL. Wilson).
> *JBC*, pp. 21–61 (E. J. Mally).
> *IDB*, vol. 3, pp. 267–77 (C. E. B. Cranfield).

R. H. Lightfoot pioneered what today would be called a redaction critical investigation of the gospel. No one of the books we are about to list is concerned solely with the gospel of Mark, not even the third, but all are important to the study of the gospel.

> Lightfoot, *History and Interpretation in the Gospels.* The Bampton Lectures, 1934.
> ———, *Locality and Doctrine in the Gospels.*
> ———, *The Gospel Message of St. Mark.* Consists of lectures originally given in 1949.

Lightfoot's work and insights were carried further and developed by his pupils, and there is now an excellent commentary on the gospel, deliberately written at a nontechnical level, that embodies them: Nineham, *The Gospel According to St. Mark.*

Recent German language work on the gospel flows from Marxsen, *Mark the Evangelist*. Subsequent developments have been reviewed in Knigge, "The Meaning of Mark," *Interpretation*, vol. 22 (1968), pp. 53–76.

An important recent book taking the evangelist Mark seriously as an author is Weeden, *Mark—Traditions in Conflict*.

The insights and ideas represented in this chapter are, however, very largely those of the present writer and his students. Publication of their work is in progress.

Perrin, "The Son of Man in the Synoptic Tradition," *Biblical Research*, vol. 13 (1968), pp. 1–23.

_____, "The Composition of Mark IX. 1," *Novum Testamentum*, vol. 11 (1969), pp. 67–70.

_____, "The Literary Gattung 'Gospel'—Some Observations," *Expository Times*, vol. 82 (1970), pp. 4–7.

_____, "The Christology of Mark: A Study in Methodology," *Journal of Religion*, vol. 51 (1971), pp. 173–87.

_____, *"What is Redaction Criticism?"* pp. 40–63.

_____, "Towards the Interpretation of the Gospel of Mark," *Christology and a Modern Pilgrimage: A Discussion with Norman Perrin*, pp. 1–78. This is to appear in a revised and expanded form as a book to be published by S. C. M. Press.

Robbins, "The Christology of Mark." Ph.D. dissertation, University of Chicago Divinity School, 1969.

Kelber, "Kingdom and Parousia in the Gospel of Mark." Ph.D. dissertation, University of Chicago Divinity School, 1970. In process of publication in revised form by Fortress Press.

Donahue, *Are You the Christ? The Trial Narrative in the Gospel of Mark*. SBL Dissertation Series 10, 1973.

A scribe at work in a way that has not changed through the centuries.

# The Gospel of Matthew:
## Christianity As Obedience
## to the New Revelation

The gospel of Matthew is the first book in the New Testament because it was found to be the most useful of all the texts for the church's use through the centuries. It is very much a "church book," written specifically to meet the needs of the church as a developing organization, and it succeeded magnificently. It provided a basis on which the church could build its life, a clear set of instructions for procedure in its affairs, and an understanding of its past, present, and future that made sense of its ongoing life in the world.

## THE EVANGELIST AS A MAN OF
## THE HELLENISTIC JEWISH CHRISTIAN MISSION

Like all the gospels, the gospel of Matthew originally circulated anonymously, and its ascription to Matthew, the disciple of Jesus, is no more than a guess. Or perhaps this is more a hope than a guess: the church attempted to give a special authority to the most important of its gospels by ascribing it to a disciple and eyewitness. But the fact that the gospel makes very extensive use of the gospel of Mark, building on it as a foundation, makes it impossible that it should have been written by a disciple and eyewitness.

The evangelist "Matthew" reveals himself to be a man who stands in the tradition of the Hellenistic Jewish Christian mission. He has a deep concern for the mission of the church to the world at large. The climax of his gospel is the scene of the Great Commission, where the risen Jesus commands his disciples to "make disciples of *all nations*" (28:19). Nevertheless, there is no doubt that his concern tends to focus most sharply on the mission of the church to the Jews. Moreover, in developing his own understanding of Christian faith, he is in constant dialogue with what is going on in Judaism at the same time.

The destruction of Jerusalem and its Temple was a shattering problem to both Jews and Christians. For Jews, it meant that the Temple and its worship were no longer available as a way of knowing God in the world and Jerusalem was no longer the center of pilgrimage for the great religious festivals, especially the Passover. Furthermore, the Jewish War had effected a shift in the balance of power and influence among the various sects and parties active in Judaism before the war. The most important of these were the Pharisees, the

**169**

Sadducees, and the Zealots.[1] The Pharisees were the popular religious leaders, devoted to studying and interpreting the Law and obeying it, and to practicing forms of piety such as synagogue attendance, prayer, almsgiving, and punctilious payment of tithes. Since it was difficult to understand how a law written centuries earlier applied to all the circumstances of a changed and changing culture, the Pharisees developed an oral tradition of interpretation of the Law that answered any questions. Fundamentally, the Pharisee understood the Law as revealing the will and purpose of God for men in the world, by obedience to which they achieved the blessing of God (the choice of the masculine is deliberate; a Pharisee regularly thanked God that he had not been born a woman!). The Sadducees, on the other hand, were Jerusalem aristocrats primarily concerned with the Temple, which they controlled, and with the organization of the Jewish state under the authority of the High Priest. They were practical politicians, fully capable of accepting ultimate Roman authority and of accommodating themselves to that authority. The Zealots were the violent revolutionaries. In their zeal for God and his people they took to the sword against their enemies and God's, even when those enemies were among their own people. They were prepared to kill and to die for their beliefs, and they provided the backbone of the final resistance to Rome, holding out in their fortress at Masada after Jerusalem itself had fallen.

Of these three main parties within Judaism, only the Pharisees could survive the Jewish War. The Zealots perished in the fighting and in attempts to start it up again when it was all over. The Sadducees were forced into the dilemma of either active opposition to Rome or betrayal of their own people, and with the destruction of the Jewish state and the Jerusalem Temple, the center of their power and influence, indeed their very reason for being, was gone. The Pharisees, however, had the resources for rebuilding after the holocaust. The Temple was no more, but synagogues could be founded and built. That other pillar of Judaism, the Law, remained, and this was their particular preserve. The forms of piety independent of Jerusalem and the Temple remained, and these had always been the emphasis of the Pharisees. Moreover, while the other parties were discredited by the war—the Sadducees by the failure of politcal compromise with Rome and the Zealots by the failure of violence itself—the Pharisees were able to maintain their standing among the people.

Left in control of a shattered Judaism, the Pharisees rose to the challenge. They set up a new center at Jamnia, in the remote northwest of the ancient territory of Judah, and there they began to settle the canon and text of scripture (determining the extent of what Christians now call the Old Testament), to codify the interpretation of the Law, and in general to systematize matters of belief and practice. The Judaism that survived the centuries into the modern

[1]The Jewish apologist and historian Josephus describes three Jewish sects (in deference to his Hellenistic readers he calls them "philosophies"): Pharisees, Sadducees, and Essenes (*Jewish War*, bk. 2.119, quoted in Barrett, *New Testament Background*, p. 125). It is now generally recognized that the Qumran community, described in chapter 4, was a community of Essenes. The Essenes are not mentioned in the New Testament. Josephus wrote in Rome after A.D. 70 as a deliberate apologist for the Jewish people. Therefore he does not dignify the Zealots, who led the fighting against Rome, by mentioning them in the same context as the Pharisees, Sadducees, and Essenes.

world ultimately stems from the work of the Pharisees at Jamnia. It is usually called rabbinical Judaism, because its center is the authoritative interpretation of the Law by the rabbis. In essence, it is Pharisaism redefined in view of the changes necessitated by the destruction of Jerusalem and the Temple.

Matthew writes his gospel in constant dialogue with the developments going on at Jamnia. The church he writes for is closely related to a synagogue "across the street" in any Gentile city with a strong Jewish element in its population. Since Matthew's gospel also has connections with specifically Palestinian Christian traditions, the city probably was in Syria. Matthew's dialogue seems not to have been with Jamnia directly, but rather with the synagogue and Jewish community as it responded to what was happening there. So the diatribe against "the scribes and Pharisees" in Matthew 23 does not reflect a conflict between Jesus and the scribes and Pharisees of his day, but one fifty years later between Matthew and their descendants spreading their influence from Jamnia.

Though of the Hellenistic Jewish Christian mission, the evangelist Matthew has definite links with earliest Palestinian Christianity. We have called attention to the Palestinian Christian traditions that have been isolated in the gospel of Matthew on form-critical grounds; 5:17–20; 7:22–23; 10:23; 10:41; 19:28–29; 23:8–10; and others. In addition, the evangelist is fond of using the term Son of Man for Jesus in an apocalyptic sense: 10:23; 13:37–41; 16:28 (for Kingdom of God, Mark 9:1); 19:28. This terminology is characteristic of Palestinian Christianity and is another indication of the evangelist's links with the earlier period of Jewish Christianity.

The author of Luke-Acts is also a man of the Hellenistic Jewish Christian mission, but where he represents the movement into the Hellenistic world, the evangelist Matthew represents the continuing links with and concern for the Jewish element in the movement.

## THE EVANGELIST AND THE PROBLEMS OF THE CHRISTIANITY OF HIS DAY

Like all the men of the middle period of New Testament Christianity,[2] Matthew wrestles with the problems of the delay of the parousia and the destruction of Jerusalem and the Temple. But he faces the latter problem in the context of a dialogue with the Judaism developing at Jamnia, which was struggling with the same problem. This gives a special tone to his work and a particular slant to his solution of the problem. Further, he faces the difficulties created by the church in this period becoming "the Church." We saw this happening in the deutero-Pauline letter to the Ephesians, and Matthew must also face the needs of a Christian movement that is becoming a self-conscious entity. It is now separate from the Judaism it came from and as such needs to understand its role in the world and to formulate a policy to guide it.

[2]This phrase denotes the period of New Testament Christianity between the fall of Jerusalem and the "final period" of the development of "emergent Catholicism." The dates would be A.D. 70 to approximately 100, and the period encompasses the writing of the gospels and the deutero-Pauline and Johannine literature. See chapter 3 above.

## The Delay of the Parousia

Matthew maintains the traditional Christian hope of the parousia. He has a fondness for using Son of Man for Jesus in apocalyptic contexts, and, indeed, he is the first evangelist to use the Greek word *parousia* in its technical Christian sense as referring to the return of Jesus as Son of Man: "What will be the sign of your coming [parousia] and of the close of the age?" (Matt 24:3; see also 24:27, 37, 39). That Matthew anticipates the parousia and the end of the age is very clear. But it is more distant for him than for the evangelist Mark. Whereas in Mark all history is hastening to its imminent climax and end, in Matthew there is still a period of time and history left before the end; this is the period of the church. In it the church works and witnesses (24:14; 28:16–20), and at its end the church will be judged (13:36–43). As far as Matthew is concerned, the delay of the parousia allows time for the work and witness of the church, and the parousia itself becomes especially a judgment of the church. Thus he finds a solution to the delay of the parousia in the challenge to understand the role of the church as a self-conscious entity in the world.

## The Fall of Jerusalem and the Destruction of the Temple

Matthew and the Pharisees at Jamnia struggled with the shattering effects of the fall of Jerusalem and the destruction of the Temple. The Pharisees turned to the scriptures, the record of God's past revelation to his people, and organized them into a fixed canon of texts they could interpret and build on. Then they began codifying their interpretation of these texts, and the application of their teachings to the changing situations of life in the world. They were concerned particularly with the Law, the Torah, the first five books of what in Christian hands became the Old Testament, for this was to them God's fundamental revelation of his will to his people. This interpretation and application was first transmitted orally, but under the leadership of Rabbi Judah ha-Nasi it was codified in writing as the *Mishnah* ("teaching"), a process completed about A.D. 200. Once collected in writing, the Mishnah became in turn the basis for further discussion, interpretation, and application. The next development of the Mishnah became known as the *Gemara* ("completion"), and it was added to the Mishnah to make up the *Talmud* ("teaching").

In the first Christian centuries there were centers of Jewish learning both in Palestine and Babylonia. But life for Jews in Palestine became increasingly difficult as the Christians became more influential in the affairs of the Roman Empire; and the emperor Constantine became an active supporter of the Christian religion in A.D. 313. Though the Talmud developed in Palestine and Babylonia, the Palestinian Talmud (known as the *Jerusalem Talmud*) was never completed. The Babylonian Talmud was finished about A.D. 550, and it became and remains the textbook of Judaism, the basis for Jewish life. It is an immense work, covering in encyclopedic fashion every aspect of life that could be imagined or discussed in the five centuries during which it was produced. It is divided into thirty-six tractates, or books, and it contains something like two million five hundred thousand words.

It is interesting to compare the evangelist Matthew with the rabbinic Judaism that produced the Mishnah and Talmud. At the risk of oversimplification, we may say that for both the basis of everything else was the fundamental revelation of the Torah. The rabbis saw the Torah further developed by the teaching of the Mishnah and brought to completion by the Talmud. Matthew, on the other hand, sees the Torah "fulfilled" and redefined in the teaching of Jesus (Matt 5:17–20) and completed in the teaching function of the church (Matt 28:16–20, especially verse 20). For both the rabbis and Matthew, revelation is primarily verbal and always requires authoritative interpretation. By emphasizing this aspect of their religious heritage and developing it further, both managed to come to terms with the fall of Jerusalem.

### The new revelation in the present of Jesus

A major emphasis of the gospel of Matthew is, then, that the present of Jesus is the fulfillment of the past of Judaism. The teaching of Jesus fulfills the Torah, and the events of his life fulfill what the prophets speak of. The most striking example of this latter claim is Matthew's careful use of "formula quotations." These are quotations from the Jewish scriptures always preceded by a formula, such as "all this took place to fulfill what the Lord had spoken by the prophet," or something similar, and always followed by the narration of an incident from the life of Jesus in which the scripture is fulfilled. These are as follows:

| Matthew | Jewish Scripture | Incident from the Life of Jesus |
|---|---|---|
| 1:22–23 | Isa 7:14 | The virgin birth |
| 2:15 | Hos 11:1 | The flight to Egypt |
| 2:17–18 | Jer 31:15 | The massacre of the innocents |
| 2:23 | Isa 11:1 | Jesus dwells in Nazareth |
| 4:14–16 | Isa 9:1–2 | Jesus moves to Capernaum |
| 8:17 | Isa 53:4 | The healing ministry of Jesus |
| 12:17–21 | Isa 42:1–4 | The healing ministry of Jesus |
| 13:35 | Psa 78:2 | Jesus' teaching in parables |
| 21:5 | Isa 62:11; Zech 9:9 | Jesus' entry into Jerusalem |
| 27:9–10 | Zech 11:12–13; Jer 18:1–13; 32:6–15 | The fate of Judas |

Of course, it was a commonplace of Christian apologetic that Jesus fulfilled the Jewish scriptures, but Matthew carries the fulfillment of the Jewish revelation in Jesus to new heights with these careful formula quotations, none of which have parallels in his sources, Mark and Q. They are clearly important to him, and also to us in attempting to understand his gospel. For Matthew it is not a returning to the Torah, but moving forward to the fulfillment of the Torah and the Prophets in Jesus.

Another way Matthew makes this same point is by organizing the teaching of Jesus into five major discourses and by calling attention to them by ending each discourse with a formula, "when Jesus finished these sayings," or the like, as follows:

| Matthew | Subject of Discourse | Formula Ending |
|---------|----------------------|----------------|
| 5:1–8:27 | The sermon on the mount | 8:28 |
| 10:5–42 | The missionary discourse | 11:1 |
| 13:1–52 | Teaching in parables | 13:53 |
| 18:1–35 | Christian community regulations | 19:1 |
| 24:3–25:46 | Apocalyptic discourse | 26:1 |

The careful arrangement of these discourses and their formula endings inevitably recalls the five books of the Torah and necessarily implies that here is the *new* Torah, the new revelation that supersedes the old.

### The new revelation as verbal and as requiring interpretation

The insight that Matthew presents the teaching of Jesus as the new Torah leads us to the recognition that for Matthew, as for the Pharisees at Jamnia, revelation is primarily *verbal,* and as such requires authoritative interpretation with changing times and circumstances. Matthew's attitude becomes clear in 5:17–20, again a passage without parallel in his sources. Here Jesus is said to come to fulfill "the law and the prophets," i.e., the Jewish scriptures.[3] Here greatness in the Kingdom of Heaven depends on keeping the commandments of "the law and the prophets" as fulfilled by Jesus and on teaching men to do so. A similar note is sounded at the beginning of the diatribe against the scribes and Pharisees:[4] "The scribes and the Pharisees sit on Moses' seat; so practice and observe whatever they tell you" (Matt 23:2–3). The passage continues,

[3]The Jewish scriptures are traditionally divided into three parts: "the Law" (Genesis to Deuteronomy); "the Prophets" (Joshua, Judges, Samuel, Kings, Isaiah, Jeremiah, Ezekiel, and the twelve minor prophets); and "the Writings" (Psalms, Proverbs, Ecclesiastes, Song of Solomon, Lamentations, Ruth, Daniel, Chronicles). The last group was achieving canonical status during the New Testament period. Matthew is conservative in this regard, recognizing only "the Law and the prophets"; Luke, on the other hand, has "the law of Moses and the prophets and the psalms" (Luke 24:44), where the third group is recognized and designated by the name of its first book.

[4]A scribe was an interpreter of the Law, generally addressed as "rabbi," whereas a Pharisee was a member of the party or sect of the Pharisees. Many scribes were in fact Pharisees, but the two terms were not synonymous even though the New Testament writers tend to treat them as such.

however, "But not what they do; for they preach, but do not practice." In other words, Matthew honors above all the activity of scribes and Pharisees at Jamnia in interpreting the authoritative revelation; his quarrel with them is about the details of their interpretation and practice. For Matthew the heart of the matter lies in the verbal revelation of "the law" and its authoritative interpretation by "scribes and Pharisees." The Christian revelation is "the law" as definitively interpreted by Jesus: there remains, therefore, the authoritative further interpretation of this revelation by the Christian equivalent of "scribes and Pharisees."

For Matthew that equivalent is "the disciple." An interesting aspect of his presentation of the ministry of Jesus is that he carefully avoids any mention of the disciples of Jesus *teaching*. He regularly summarizes Jesus' activity as "proclaiming the Kingdom," "healing," and "teaching" (4:23; 9:35; 11:1), but when the disciples are commissioned by Jesus (10:1–7), they are to heal and to proclaim the Kingdom, *not* to teach. In the gospel of Matthew only Jesus teaches, and that teaching is the new Torah, the fulfilled revelation. But after the revelation is complete, and the situation has become such that the revelation now needs authoritative interpretation, *then* the disciples begin to teach: "Go therefore and make disciples of all nations, baptizing them . . . *teaching them to observe all that I have commanded you;* and lo, I am with you always, to the close of the age" (Matt 28:19–20, the Great Commission). The commandment in italics sums up the major emphasis of the gospel of Matthew: the teaching of Jesus is the new revelation, and it requires the authoritative interpretation of disciples.

Matthew speaks of "disciples" because he is bound by the literary conventions imposed by the form of a gospel. This convention limits him to terms that are realistic in the situation of Jesus and his ministry. But he also readily uses the term because the Greek word for disciple, *mathētēs*, means "learner." There can be no doubt that he is thinking of a Christian equivalent to the Jewish "scribes and Pharisees." He does not object to the *function* of a "scribe and Pharisee." On the contrary, he applauds it: "Therefore every scribe who has been trained for the kingdom of heaven is like a householder who brings out of his treasure what is new and what is old" (Matt 13:52). A scribe is an official interpreter of the revelation; in Matthew's view, the need is for scribes "trained for the kingdom of heaven" for official interpreters of the revelation as fulfilled in Jesus Christ.

## THE CHURCH AND THE CHURCH'S BOOK

Matthew is much concerned with the Christian church as an entity distinct from the Judaism it came from. This can be seen, for example, in that he is the only evangelist to use the Greek word for church, *ekklēsia*: "And I tell you, you are Peter, and on this rock I will build my church" (16:18) and "If he refuses to listen to them, tell it to the church" (18:17). Both these instances are important to understanding the gospel of Matthew.

The first of them, 16:18, occurs in Matthew's version of the incident at
Caesarea Philippi. In Mark 8:27–9:1 we have a firmly structured incident:

8:27–29   Peter's confession
8:30      Command to secrecy
8:31      First passion prediction
8:32–33   Peter's misunderstanding and Jesus' rebuke
8:34–9:1  Teaching on discipleship

Mark is Matthew's source; yet the incident has been very significantly edited
and redacted by Matthew:

16:13–16  Peter's confession
16:17     Blessing of Peter
16:18–19  Commissioning of Peter as the founder of the Christian church
16:20     Command to secrecy
16:21     First passion prediction
16:22–23  Peter's misunderstanding and Jesus' rebuke
16:24–28  Teaching on discipleship

What has happened is that Matthew has combined two quite different
traditions: a confession by Peter, which he takes from Mark, and a blessing and
commissioning of Peter by Jesus, which he inserts between the confession and
the command to secrecy. Where this second tradition came from we do not
know, but it has been plausibly suggested that it is the remnant of an account
of a resurrection appearance to Peter,[5] otherwise lost to us. The effect of the
conflation of the two traditions is to focus the reader's attention on Peter's role
in the church and on the authority of the church on earth, emphases foreign to
the original Markan narrative and yet characteristic of Matthew. Matthew has
another version of the saying that appears in 16:19 in his discourse on
Christian community regulations in 18:18. The second occurrence of the word
*ekklēsia* in Matthew, 18:17, is in the discourse on Christian community
regulations, 18:1–35. This discourse has a core in Mark 9:42–50, but Matthew
expands and develops it until it is an embryonic "church order" regulating the
life of the Christian community, the church. All communities require such
regulations and Matthew is responding to this need.

Whereas Mark had called his work a "gospel" (1:1), Matthew calls his a
"book," "The *book* of the genesis of Jesus Christ, the Son of David" (1:1).
Indeed, Matthew rarely uses "gospel" except when following Mark; he is not
preaching the gospel, but organizing an interpretation of the revelation given
in Jesus Christ, the Son of David. His goal is to build a church on the
foundation stone of Peter that will guard and interpret the revelation, going out
into all the world to make "disciples from among all nations" (28:19–20).

---

[5]For example, Fuller, "The 'Thou Art Peter' Pericope and the Easter Appearances,"
*McCormick Quarterly*, vol. 20 (1966/67) pp. 309–15.

But the final guarantee of the church is not the primacy of Peter nor the efficiency of the regulations nor even the trustworthiness of the interpretation; it is the presence of the risen Christ among its members. The gospel ends with the promise of the risen Lord to the disciples: "and lo, I am with you always, to the close of the age" (28:20). Moreover, in the discourse on community regulations this same note is sounded: "For where two or three are gathered in my name, there am I in the midst of them" (18:20).

Matthew is providing the basis for the church's life—the new revelation in Jesus Chirst, Son of David. The revelation is essentially verbal, "teaching," and as such it requires authoritative interpretation. To this task the church is commissioned to go into all the world as bearer and interpreter of this revelation. In this task the church will be strengthened by the risen Lord in its midst, until that final movement when it, like all the world, will be confronted by the judgment of the Son of Man and his angels. It can readily be seen how in the gospel of Matthew the church came to find "its book."

# EXEGETICAL SURVEY OF THE GOSPEL OF MATTHEW

The gospel of Matthew is built on the foundation of the gospel of Mark, but Matthew has edited and redacted Mark so that all is changed. As Matthew presents his "book," it falls naturally into five parts.

1. *Introduction, 1:1–4:17.* This part explains who and what Jesus is: the new revelation of God.

2. *The ministry of Jesus to Israel, 4:18–13:58.* As the new revelation of God, Jesus fulfills the old revelation and hence, fittingly comes first to the people of God who nevertheless reject him.

3. *The ministry of Jesus to his disciples, 14:1–20:34.* Rejected by the old people of God, Jesus turns to the new people of God, his disciples, and prepares them for their work in the world.

4. *Jesus in Jerusalem, 21:1–25:46.* The drama now approaches its climax as Jesus is involved in a final clash with Judaism and teaches his disciples concerning the final judgment.

5. *The passion, resurrection, and great commission, 26:1–28:20.* The drama reaches its climax in the passion and resurrection of Jesus and in his commissioning of his disciples.

## Introduction, 1:1–4:17

**1:1–1:17** *Genealogy.* "The book of the origin of Jesus Christ, the son of David," is the superscription of the whole gospel. Among the Jewish rabbis, Son of David became a favorite title for the expected Messiah. It emphasized the Messiah's descent from David and his coming as fulfilling God's promise to David in 2 Samuel 7. Matthew, in dialogue with developing rabbinical Judaism, uses the title frequently of Jesus (1:1; 9:27; 12:23; 15:22; 20:30; 21:9, 15; 22:42, 45), strengthening the claim that Jesus is the Jewish Messiah.

The genealogy traces the descent of Jesus back through David to Abraham, the father of the Jewish people, thus stressing his significance as the fulfillment of the Jewish heritage.

**1:18–2:23** *The birth and infancy of Jesus.* A series of stories on every aspect of the birth and infancy of Jesus as fulfillment of Jewish scriptural prophecy.

**3:1–4:17** *The prelude to the ministry.*

**3:1–6** *John the Baptist in the wilderness* (= Mark 1:1–6).[6] Matthew brings John the Baptist into close contact with Jesus, giving him exactly the same message as Jesus (3:2 = 4:17) and making his ministry also a fulfillment of prophecy. As Jesus' immediate precursor, he shares in the act of fulfillment. He is described in terms reminiscent of the description of Elijah in 2 Kings 1:8.

**3:7–10** *John's warning to Pharisees and Sadducees.* Matthew depicts Judaism united in its opposition to John, as later he depicts it as equally united in its opposition to Jesus. John's language here is echoed by Jesus in 7:16–20 and 12:33.

**3:11–12** *John predicts the coming of Jesus* (= Mark 1:7–8). These verses reflect the Christians' belief that their baptism is superior to John's. The idea of the separation of the good from the evil at the last judgment is dominant in Jesus' eschatological teaching in Matthew 24–25. Matthew is further paralleling John the Baptist and Jesus. This part of John's message has no parallel in Mark.

**3:13–17** *The baptism of Jesus* (= Mark 1:9–11). Although Matthew carefully parallels John the Baptist and Jesus in several ways, he also carefully subordinates John to Jesus by adding verses 14–15, which have no parallel in his source, the gospel of Mark.

**4:1–11** *The temptation of Jesus* (= Mark 1:12–13). Mark 1:12–13 simply mentions the temptation of Jesus in the wilderness, while both Matthew and Luke (Luke 4:1–13) share a tradition in which Jesus meets the temptations by quoting Deuteronomy (Matt 4:4 = Luke 4:4: Deut 8:3; Matt 4:7 = Luke 4:12: Deut 6:16; Matt 4:10 = Luke 4:8: Deut 6:13). The passages in Deuteronomy reflect the Jewish interpretation of their people's journey through the wilderness as a testing by God to determine their fitness to inherit the Promised Land

---

[6]We give the parallels from Mark or Luke (indicating Q material) where appropriate, but not where the parallels are weak or scattered through the source.

(Deut 8:2–3). A parallel is drawn between the testing of Israel and of Jesus, with the necessary implication that the Jews failed whereas Jesus, who is the fulfillment of Judaism, succeeded.

**4:12–17** *Jesus goes to Galilee and begins to preach* (= Mark 1:14–15). Mark 1:14–15 makes this the beginning of the apocalyptic drama, but Matthew makes it the conclusion to his introduction. Verse 14 is one of Matthew's formula quotations. In verse 17 Jesus takes up the message that John had proclaimed. The preliminaries are complete; the new revelation can now begin.

## The New Revelation: The Ministry of Jesus to Israel, 4:18–13:58

**4:18–22** *The call of the four fishermen* (= Mark 1:16–20). The ministry begins with the challenge to "follow" Jesus, as it will end on the note of "Go and make disciples . . . " Note that Matthew does not call these men "disciples" until 5:1 when they begin to listen to the teaching, the verbal revelation.

**4:23–25** *Summary of the characteristic activity of the ministry* (= Mark 1:39).

**5:1–7:29** *The First Book of the New Revelation: the Sermon on the Mount.* This takes place on a mountain, whereas the comparable discourse in Luke is on a plain. Matthew is stressing the parallel to Moses receiving the Torah on a mountain, the previous revelation now being superseded (Exod 19:3–6). The first book of the new revelation concerns the personal aspects of Christian piety and behavior.

> **5:3–12** *The Beatitudes* (= Luke 6:20–23). "Blessed" in the sense used here refers to the fortunate, happy condition of a man blessed by God. The reference is to the blessed conditions that will obtain after Jesus has returned as Son of Man. These are eschatological blessings, and Matthew is using them to set the whole teaching in the context of eschatological expectation.

> **5:13–16** *Salt and light: the disciples' special status* (= Luke 14:34–35; 11:33).

> **5:17–20** *The essential nature of Christian faith: obedience to the new revelation.* This is a key passage in Matthew's gospel; it expresses the evangelist's understanding of the essence of Christian faith: obedience to the new revelation as it is interpreted by the Christian equivalent of "scribes and Pharisees." In Judaism, obedience to the revelation in the Torah was expressed by the concept of "righteousness." Righteousness was the quality of obedience a man must have achieved to be able to stand before God, and "the righteous" are those who have achieved it. For Matthew the quality of the Christian's obedience to the new revelation must exceed that of the "scribes and

Pharisees" to the old. By this means they will "enter the Kingdom of Heaven," i.e., enter into that state of blessedness Jesus will establish for the "righteous" when he comes as Son of Man.

**5:21–48** *The antitheses* (partial parallels only in Mark and Luke). In a series of antitheses Matthew expresses aspects of the new revelation in contrast to the old. In each instance the new is an intensifying or radicalizing of the old.

**6:1–18** *Instruction on almsgiving, prayer, and fasting* (Matt 6:9–13 = Luke 11:2–4). Almsgiving, prayer, and fasting are forms of Jewish piety independent of the Temple. Even while the Temple stood the Pharisees emphasized them, and after its destruction they developed them still further. Matthew is here in dialogue with the developments going on at Jamnia, and his acrimonious tone indicates its intensity. Matthew is close enough to the Pharisees to quarrel violently with them and denounce them vigorously. Note his constant use of the epithet "hypocrites," which occurs as a refrain throughout the denunciation of the "scribes and Pharisees" in Matthew 23.

**6:19–34** *Various images describing the truly righteous man.*

**7:1–12** *Various maxims illustrating the new righteousness.*

**7:13–27** *Warnings designed to stress the necessity for obedience to the new revelation.* These warnings constitute the ending to the Sermon. They end it on a note of eschatology as the Beatitudes had begun it on a similar note.

**7:28–29** *Formula ending to the first book of the new revelation.*

**8:1–9:34** *The miracles of Jesus.* Matthew characteristically arranges his material in blocks. He follows his first revelatory discourse with a block of nine miracle stories presented in groups of three, interwoven with teaching on discipleship. In 4:23 the summary of the characteristic activity of Jesus' ministry had stressed healing, and eight of the nine miracles are healing miracles.

**8:1–17** *The first three healings: the leper, the centurion's servant, and Peter's mother-in-law.*

**8:18–22** *First discipleship section: sayings on discipleship.*

**8:23–9:8** *The second group of three miracles: the stilling of the storm, the healing of the demoniac, and the cure of the paralytic.* The stilling of the storm deserves special comment because here we see Matthew's own understanding most clearly.[7] Matthew's source is the account of the same miracle in Mark 4:35–41, and it is instructive to observe his redaction of that source. In Mark the story has the natural form of a miracle: Jesus and his disciples embark in a boat, accompanied by other boats; a great storm arises; the disciples appeal to Jesus, and he calms the storm. The following dialogue ends on a

[7]We are now following Bornkamm, "The Stilling of the Storm in Matthew," in Bornkamm, Barth, Held, *Tradition and Interpretation in Matthew*, pp. 52–57.

note of wonder. In Matthew there is no mention of any other boats. The dialogue takes place *before* the storm is calmed, and Jesus is addressed as "Lord" (Mark: "teacher"); he in turn addresses the disciples as "men of little faith," a frequent reproach by Jesus in this gospel (6:30; 8:26; 14:31; 16:8), and only in this gospel. Matthew has redacted the traditional miracle story to make it an allegory of the church. The one boat is the little ship of the church, beset by the storms of persecution, and the disciples are the members of the church who fail because of their "little faith" and need the presence of their Lord to help them, which presence they have.

**9:9–17**  *Second section on discipleship: the call of Matthew, eating with "tax collectors and sinners," fasting.* Eating with "tax collectors and sinners" is important in the Hellenistic Jewish Christian mission because in Palestine they were ostracized and treated as *Gentiles.* Since table fellowship between Jews and Gentiles in the Christian church was a major problem in the mission, Jesus' attitude to "tax collectors and sinners" was for Matthew an important aspect of teaching on discipleship. Fasting was also important because it was a form of piety stressed by the Pharisees at Jamnia.

**9:18–34**  *The third group of healings: the ruler's daughter and the woman with a hemorrhage, the two blind men, the dumb man.*

**9:35–11:1**  *The Second Book of the New Revelation: the Missionary Discourse.* Matthew has inherited from Mark 6:6b–11 an account of a teaching journey by Jesus, followed by the commissioning of "the twelve" for a missionary journey. The teaching journey further summarizes the activities characteristic of Jesus' ministry—preaching, teaching, and healing—and the commissioning of "the twelve" becomes the occasion for the second revelatory discourse. The discourse itself contains originally disparate elements (10:5–42). Matt 10:5–6 reflects the Christian mission to the Jews rather than the Hellenistic Jewish Christian mission. In 10:7 Matthew gives to the disciples the exact proclamation of Jesus (4:17), and John the Baptist (3:2). John the Baptist, Jesus, and now the Christian church are the succession of the new revelation. Notice, however, that the disciples are *not* commissioned to teach, as they are when the revelation is complete. Matt 10:9–16 seems to be a development from some traditional "handbook" for the missionaries of the Hellenistic Jewish Christian mission, since Luke 10:4–12 has a similar set of instructions.

**11:1**  *Formula ending to the second book of the new revelation.*

**11:2–13:58**  *The Jews refuse to believe in Jesus.* Matthew ends his account of the mission of Jesus to Israel by focusing attention on Jesus himself, developing a Christology, and interweaving with it an account of the Jewish rejection of Jesus. It is a skillful ironic blend of Jesus as the Jewish Messiah and his rejection by the Jews themselves.

**11:2–6** *John the Baptist's question* (= Luke 7:18–23). Jesus is the Christ (Messiah) as his ministry testifies.

**11:7–15** *Jesus' testimony to John* (= Luke 7:24–30). John is the Elijah expected by the Jews to come as the forerunner to the Messiah.

**11:16–19** *Parable of the Children in the Market Place* (= Luke 7:31–35). Neither John the Baptist nor Jesus have been recognized or accepted by the Jews.

**11:20–24** *Woes on the Galilean cities* (= Luke 10:13–15). The cities that have rejected Jesus will be judged accordingly.

**11:25–30** *The "thunderbolt from the Johannine sky"* (= Luke 10:21–22). These verses are astonishing because their style is associated with the gospel of John rather than Matthew. Yet they represent a major Matthean christological statement: Jesus is the revealer of knowledge of God, a knowledge that he reveals to his intimates. "Yoke" is a metaphor much used by the Jewish rabbis of obedience to the Law, the "yoke of the Torah." Matt 11:25–30 therefore contrasts the burden of the old revelation to the ease and joy of the new.

**12:1–14** *Jesus in controversy with Pharisees* (= Mark 2:23–28; 3:1–6). Matthew here gives two stories of Jesus in controversy with Pharisees, taken from a collection of five such stories in Mark 2:1–3:6. He had given the other three earlier (9:1–8, 11–13, 16–17), interpreting them as dealing mainly with discipleship.

**12:15–21** *Jesus as servant of God.* A further christological statement is made by a formula quotation.

**12:22–24** *A healing and two reactions* (= Mark 3:19b–22). A healing evokes two reactions: the crowd in general begins to think Jesus may be the Son of David; the Pharisees denounce him as an emissary of Beelzebub.

**12:25–37** *Jesus denounces the Pharisees* (= Mark 3:23–30). The opposition between Jesus and the Pharisees sharpens. Matthew expands and intensifies the tone of his Markan source.

**12:38–42** *The sign of Jonah* (= Luke 11:29–32). Jesus rejects a Pharisaic request for a "sign" that would vindicate his authority and denounces "this evil and adulterous generation." The sign will be the sign of Jonah; that is, Jesus' resurrection will be his vindication over "this generation" that rejected him.

**12:43–45** *Further denunciation of "this generation"* (= Luke 11:24–26).

**12:46–50** *The true family of Jesus* (= Luke 8:19–21). Matthew turns from the compatriots of Jesus, who rejected him, to the true family of Jesus, those who accepted him and his revelation.

**13:1–50** *The Third Book of the New Revelation: the Parables of the Kingdom.* Like Mark, Matthew has a collection of parables, but he makes special use of them. He has just called attention to the false and true family of Jesus as those who reject and accept his revelation. Now Jesus addresses the parables of the Sower, the Weeds, the Mustard Seed, and the Leaven to "the crowds," i.e., the Jews (13:1–33). Matthew concludes this half of his parable chapter with a formula quotation (13:34–35). Jesus then turns to the "disciples," the true family, and gives them the explanation of the Weeds and the parables of the Pearl and the Net.

The Sower (13:1–9) with its explanation (18–23 = Mark 4:1–9; 13–20) interprets the ministry of Jesus as rejection and acceptance. The intercalated verses (10–17 = Mark 4:10–12) contrast those who accept Jesus with those who reject him and add a formula quotation. The parable of the Weeds (13:24–30) continues the theme of acceptance and rejection, this time in the context of the coming "harvest," i.e., final judgment of God. The parables of the Mustard Seed and the Leaven (13:31–33 = Mark 4:30–32 = Luke 13:18–21) in Matthew's context and use are means of interpreting the Jewish rejection of Jesus and of holding out the hope of ultimate acceptance, if not by all the Jews then certainly by the world at large.

Matt 13:36 is the watershed of the chapter. We are no longer concerned with the Jews who rejected Jesus, but with those who accepted him, the disciples. In this new context the parable of the Weeds is interpreted as an allegory of the earthly ministry of Jesus as Son of Man and of his coming apocalyptic judgment. Notice the Matthean promise of blessing to the "righteous" in verse 43, and compare it with 5:20. In Matthew, the parables of the Treasure in the Field and the Pearl refer to the blessing that awaits the "righteous," those who accept Jesus' revelation and obey it. The parable of the Net is a restatement of Matthew's characteristic view of the judgment that will separate the evil from the righteous.

**13:51–52** *The Christian scribe.* As a climax to his parable chapter, Matthew adds this description of the ideal of acceptance and obedience, the scribe "trained for the kingdom of heaven."

**13:53–58** *The climactic rejection.* Matthew ends his third revelatory discourse and turns to the climax of his theme of the rejection of Jesus "in his own country and in his own house."

## The New Revelation: Jesus Instructs his Disciples, 14:1–20:34

The ministry to Israel now having reached the climax of the rejection of Jesus by "his own," Matthew turns to the second stage of the new revelation, which occurs in the relationship between Jesus and his disciples.

**14:1–16:12** *Preliminary instruction.* In this section Matthew is closely following his source, the gospel of Mark.

**14:1–12** *The death of John the Baptist* (= Mark 6:14–29). Matthew abbreviates the story as it occurs in Mark, and he subordinates other elements in the story to his theme of John's death being the occasion for the withdrawal of Jesus with his disciples.

**14:13–21**   *The withdrawal of Jesus and the feeding of the five thousand*
(= Mark 6:30–44). Matthew is still abbreviating Mark's narrative in
the interest of his withdrawal theme. In Matt 14:19 the disciples play
more of an intermediary role than they do in Mark 6:41; they are
becoming the church that mediates the sacraments.

**14:22–33**   *The walking on the water* (= Mark 6:45–52). Again Matthew
is abbreviating Mark, in this instance to make room for the
redactional insertion of the incident of Peter also walking on the
water (Matt 14:28–31). Peter becomes a paradigm of the "disciple"
who has "little faith" and so needs the help of his "Lord"; compare
8:23–27, another sea miracle. Matthew ends the account with a
formal confession of Jesus as the Son of God (verse 33). In Matthew's
thinking the story has become a paradigm of the relationship between
Jesus and his followers in the Christian church, and so a formal
confession is in place here.

**14:34–36**   *Healings at Genneseret* (= Mark 6:53–56).

**15:1–20**   *Dispute with "scribes and Pharisees" about the tradition of the
elders* (= Mark 7:1–23). In the dispute with the scribes and Pharisees
Matthew is following Mark (12), but he uses it as a starting point for
instruction of the disciples.

**15:21–39**   *A group of three miracles* (= Mark 7:24–8:10). Matthew is still
following Mark closely, shortening somewhat as he goes. The one real
change is that a healing of a deaf mute in Mark 7:31–37 is generalized
into a healing of many sick persons in Matt 15:29–31.

**16:1–4**   *The sign of Jonah* (= Mark 8:11–13). This is another version of
the pericope found earlier in the gospel (12:38–40). Matthew has
added verses 2–3, taken from Q (= Luke 12:54–56), and the reference
to Jonah. He also has the request coming from "Pharisees and
Sadducees" (Mark: "Pharisees") to depict a universal Jewish opposition to Jesus (Compare 3:7).

**16:5–12**   *Warning against the teaching of Pharisees and Sadducees*
(= Mark 8:14–21). Again from Mark, with "Pharisees and Sadducees"
substituted for Mark's "Pharisees and Herod."

**16:13–20:34**   *The predictions of the passion and resurrection and instruction
on life in the Christian community.* This section is Matthew's equivalent
of Mark 8:27–10:52 (he omits 8:22–26). In general, he follows Mark but
adds considerable material, and the additions transform Mark's teaching
on discipleship into instruction on life in the Christian community.

**16:13–28**   *Caesarea Philippi* (= Mark 8:27–9:1). We pointed out earlier
that Matthew adds the blessing and commissioning of Peter to the
narrative in Mark 8:27–9:1. Further changes are the addition of "and
then he will repay every man for what he has done" (verse 27) and the
modification of Mark's "before they see the Kingdom of God come
with power" to "before they see the Son of Man coming in his
Kingdom." These changes introduce the Matthean understanding of

discipleship, as living the life of obedience to the new revelation in the church until the coming of Jesus as Son of Man, into the Markan understanding of discipleship, as preparedness to accept suffering as one followed Jesus to his cross and awaited the parousia. These changes are characteristic of the whole section.

**17:1–8** *The transfiguration* (= Mark 9:2–8). This reproduces Mark with the significant addition of verses 6–7, where Jesus reassures the disciples in their fear. We saw in 8:23–27 and 14:22–33 that this is a very important theme to Matthew, representing his understanding of the reality of life in the church.

**17:9–13** *The coming of Elijah* (= Mark 9:9–13). Matthew adds his verse 13 to Mark's narrative, stressing the identification of John the Baptist and Elijah.

**17:14–20[8]** *The healing of the epileptic boy* (= Mark 9:14–29). Matthew shortens Mark's narrative to make room for verse 20, which introduces another of his favorite themes, the disciple in the church as a man of little faith (see also 6:30; 8:26; 14:31; 16:8).

**17:22–23** *The second prediction* (= Mark 9:30–32). Matthew abbreviates the prediction and then breaks up the carefully structured Markan prediction unit by introducing his fourth revelatory discourse.

**17:24–27** *The temple tax.* An early Christian legend, reproduced here by Matthew because it features the prominence of Peter, the foundation stone of the church, in verse 24.

**18:1–35** *The Fourth Book of the New Revelation: Christian Community Regulations.* In this discourse Matthew follows Mark where he can, but he adds material from Q and special material of his own to make the whole a revelatory discourse.

**18:1–5** *Greatness in the Kingdom* (= Mark 9:33–36; 10:15; 9:37). Matthew uses the latter part of Mark's second prediction unit to introduce the discourse.

**18:6–9** *On temptations* (= Mark 9:42–48).

**18:10–14** *The parable of the Lost Sheep.* Matthew interprets the "little ones" of Mark 9:42 as members of the Christian community and then uses the parable of the Lost Sheep to reassure them that God will take care of them. The parable has a quite different application in Luke 15:3–7.

**18:15–22** *Two community regulations.* In verses 15–20 Matthew greatly expands a saying from Q (= Luke 17:3) by adding references to the need for witnesses to the church, to the authority of the church (18:18 = 16:19), and to the promise of the presence of the risen Lord in the church. All told, 18:15–20 is a major Matthean statement about the church. In verses 21–22 Matthew reproduces a regulation

---

[8]Verse 21 is omitted in the earliest Greek texts and relegated to the margin in the best modern translations.

concerning the necessity for reconciliation within the community from Q (= Luke 17:4).

**18:23–35** *The parable of the Unmerciful Servant.* Matthew brings his discourse to a close by using the parable of the Unmerciful Servant to reinforce the regulation concerning the necessity for reconciliation within the Christian community. Note the characteristic emphasis on the eschatological judgment in verse 35.

**19:1–20:34** *The journey to Jerusalem.* Matthew concludes his revelatory discourse with a characteristic formula and resumes his close following of Mark as he portrays the journey of Jesus from Galilee to Jerusalem. As in Mark, the journey features teaching on discipleship, and the differences reflect the different understandings of discipleship by Matthew and Mark.

> **19:1–12** *Marriage and divorce* (= Mark 10:1–12). Matthew now gives his characteristic formula for ending a discourse and then goes on to reproduce a pericope from Mark as a community regulation on marriage and divorce. Note the addition of "except for unchastity" in verse 9, which brings the teaching into line with that of the strictest Jewish rabbi of the period, Rabbi Shammai, and the addition of verses 10–12, introducing the note of celibacy into the life of the church.

> **19:13–15** *The blessing of the children* (= Mark 10:13–16).

> **19:16–30** *The rich young man* (= Mark 10:17–31). The Markan incident is made into a community regulation by the addition of verse 28, which introduces the eschatological promise for those who will accept the challenge to leave all for the sake of discipleship.

> **20:1–16** *The parable of the Laborers in the Vineyard.* Matthew inserts this parable into the Markan narrative to illustrate the theme of the reversal of values in the coming Kingdom of the Son of Man (verse 16). But the parable fits that purpose uneasily, and it is an example of a parable of Jesus steadfastly resisting an attempt to serve a later and different context.

> **20:17–28** *The third prediction unit: prediction-misunderstanding-teaching* (= Mark 10:32–45). This essentially reproduces Mark's third prediction unit. In our discussion of the gospel of Mark we saw how carefully structured were the three prediction units (Mark 8:27–9:1; 9:32–37; 10:32–45) with their constant theme of prediction-misunderstanding-teaching on discipleship. Matthew broke up the first two by various insertions, but he left the third practically intact. Even in Mark the third unit has what are to all intents and purposes Christian community regulations (Mark 10:42–44); so as it stands the narrative serves Matthew's particular purpose.

> **20:29–34** *The healing at Jericho* (= Mark 10:46–52). In Mark this is a transitional giving-of-sight pericope, but Matthew simply reproduces it with a characteristic doubling of the healing as

blind Bartimaeus becomes two blind men. Matthew is fond of healings in pairs (8:28–34; 9:27–31).

## Jesus in Jerusalem, 21:1–25:46

This section narrates Jesus' activity in Jerusalem before the beginning of the passion itself. For the most part Matthew follows Mark 11:1–13:37, but with some very significant changes and additions.

**21:1–23:39** *The final clash between Jesus and the Jews.*
- **21:1–11** *The triumphal entry* (= Mark 11:1–10). Matthew follows Mark in the main, but he adds the formula quotation in verses 4–5 and changes one animal to two to make the narration agree exactly with his own understanding of the quotation.
- **21:12–17** *Jesus in the Temple* (= Mark 11:11a, 15–19, 11b). Mark intercalates the cleansing of the Temple into the fig tree incident to interpret the cleansing by means of the fig tree. Matthew has no such purpose; so he restores what must have been the original unity of the cleansing. Note that verses 14–16 have no parallel in Mark, they represent Matthew's characteristic emphasis on the healing ministry of Jesus.
- **21:18–22** *The fig tree incident* (= Mark 11:12–14, 20–25). What in Mark had been a testimony to the judgment of God on the Temple and a way of coming to terms with the fact of its destruction becomes in Matthew an example of the power of faith.
- **21:23–27** *The question of Jesus' authority* (= Mark 11:27–33). This follows Mark in narrating a clash between Jesus and the Jewish authorities.
- **21:28–32** *The parable of the Two Sons.* The true son of God is he who accepts Jesus as his revelation.
- **21:33–46** *The parable of the Wicked Tenants* (= Mark 12:1–12). In the main this follows Mark, but the addition of verse 43 stresses that the Christians and not the Jews are now the heirs of God.
- **22:1–14** *The parable of the Marriage Feast* (= Luke 14:16–24). Matthew interprets the parable as testimony that after the Jews rejected Jesus and killed him, the heritage passed to the Christians. But even the Christian must have the wedding garment of true obedience.
- **22:15–46** *Three questions in dispute between Jesus and his opponents* (= Mark 12:13–37). Matthew now follows Mark in narrating three questions that cause disputes between Jesus and the Jews: Tribute to Caesar, the Resurrection, and the Great Commandment. Since his source already had a strong element of conflict between Jesus and his Jewish opponents, Matthew engages in no significant redaction, except that he carefully omits the sympathetic answer of the scribe and Jesus' praise of him in Mark 12:32–34. For Matthew there can be no mitigation of the conflict between Christians and Jews. In verse 46

he formally brings to an end all debate between Jesus and his opponents. The rejection is complete and the conflict over; there remains now only the working out of the consequences.

**23:1-36** *The woes against the Pharisees.* Mark 12:38-40 has a warning against the scribes; in Matthew it becomes a carefully organized diatribe against his opponents, the scribes and Pharisees at Jamnia, and their influence. It is not their *function* he is against, very much to the contrary, but their practice.

**23:37-39** *The lament over Jerusalem* (= Luke 13:34-35). This is a Christian lament over Jerusalem that interprets its destruction as the judgment of God for its rejection of his emissaries and which anticipates a restoration at the parousia. A saying developed in the church to help Christians come to terms with the destruction of Jerusalem, it is used by both Matthew and Luke.

**24:1-25:46** *The Fifth Book of the New Revelation: the Apocalyptic Discourse.* The apocalyptic discourse proper, Matt 24:1-36, in the main follows Mark 13:1-32. But Matthew omits Mark's ending of the discourse and goes on to add apocalyptic teaching that he takes from Q (Matt 24:37-51 = Luke 17:26-27, 34-35; 12:39-40, 42-46) and then a series of parables (the Ten Maidens, Talents, Last Judgment). As Matthew interprets them, the first two are concerned with the coming of the Son of Man and his judgment (25:13, 29-30), and the third directly describes that judgment.

The third parable, the Last Judgment, is the last element of the teaching of Jesus in the gospel, and it sums up many prominent themes: the need for "righteousness" to enter the Kingdom; righteousness consisting of an obedience expressed in deeds; the fact that the Son of Man will repay everyone according to his deeds; the need for mercy, especially to those who are weak. It is thus a fitting climax to Matthew's presentation of the teaching of Jesus.

## The Passion, Resurrection, and Great Commission, 26:1-28:20

**26:1-27:66** *The passion and death of Jesus.* In his account of the passion and death of Jesus Matthew follows Mark closely, with only minor redactional changes. We follow our division of the Markan narrative.

**26:1-16** *The introduction* (= Mark 14:1-11). The only real change here is the introduction of a fourth passion prediction in verse 2, which links the narrative more closely to the previous teaching of Jesus.

**26:17-29** *Jesus' last meal with his disciples* (= Mark 14:12-25). In verse 25 Matthew makes the reference to Judas the betrayer more explicit. This is simply a legendary accretion to the narrative.

**26:30-35** *Prediction of the flight of the disciples and the betrayal by Peter* (= Mark 14:26-31).

**26:36–56** *The betrayal and the arrest.* Matthew makes minor editorial changes that heighten the theme of the fulfillment of scripture: adding verses 52–54 and rewriting verse 56 (= Mark 14:49b) to read, "But all this has taken place, that the scriptures of the prophets might be fulfilled."

**26:57–75** *Betrayal by Peter and intercalated account of the night trial before the Sanhedrin* (= Mark 14:53–72). The only significant change is that Matthew edits the dialogue between Jesus and the High Priest to make it a formal statement of the person of Jesus before the spiritual head of Judaism: "I adjure you by the living God, tell us . . . You have said so . . . " (verses 63–64).

**27:1–2** *Jesus is delivered to Pilate* (= Mark 15:1).

**27:3–10** *The fate of Judas.* Only Matthew has this narrative of the fate of Judas as fulfilling a formula quotation.

**27:11–66** *The trial before Pilate and the crucifixion* (= Mark 15:2–47). Matthew introduces several editorial changes in this narrative. In verse 19 he emphasizes the innocence of Jesus, and hence by implication, the guilt of the Jews, and in verses 24–25 he makes the guilt of the Jews explicit. In verse 43 he uses Psa 22:8 to add to a narrative already saturated with allusions to that Psalm. Then in verses 52–53 he inserts a whole series of supernatural events, including a temporary resurrection of "the saints" to stress the fact that God is at work in these events and that new life will emerge from the death of Jesus. Finally, in verses 62–66 he adds the incident of the Guard at the Tomb. This is a late composition, very probably by Matthew himself, designed to forestall a possible claim that the resurrection was a lie because the disciples had stolen the body of Jesus.

**28:1–20** *The resurrection of Jesus and the Great Commission.* At this point Matthew begins to go beyond Mark, necessarily so since Mark has no account of the resurrection as such, only of the women at the tomb.

**28:1–10** *The empty tomb* (= Mark 16:1–8). The main changes here are that verses 2–4 further emphasize the supernatural nature of these events, and in verses 9–10 Matthew goes beyond the Markan ending to provide an appearance of Jesus and an explicit command of the risen Lord himself for the disciples to go into Galilee.

**28:11–15** *The report of the guard.* This is a narrative loaded with anti-Jewish polemic.

**28:16–20** *The Great Commission.* This climax to the gospel of Matthew relates the intended reader to what the gospel has narrated. Jesus has given the new revelation to his disciples, and it is now their responsibility to go into the world and make new disciples. Thus the reader becomes a "disciple," heir to the new revelation and to the task of interpreting and obeying it, as well as making further disciples. In this way the reader appropriates the revelation to himself and locates his place in the scheme of things. There will be an extended interval between the passion and the parousia, and during this interval he is to accept, interpret, and obey the revelation, and at the same time persuade others to do the same. But he will not be alone in this task; always the risen Lord will be with him, to the close of the age.

The narrative is not so much a resurrection appearance as an account of the risen and exalted Lord commissioning the church and its members. Certainly it represents the message of the evangelist Matthew to his readers, as it reveals the convictions that inspired his writing of the gospel: Jesus as the medium of the new revelation that fulfills and decisively reinterprets the old; the disciple as recipient of the revelation he is to obey so that the quality of his obedience exceeds that of the scribes and Pharisees. These are the themes that have dominated the gospel. But now new elements are added. Jesus explicitly claims the authority that had before been his only implicitly (verse 18). Now, for the first time, the disciples are commissioned to "teach," to interpret the revelation. Now also the church is given the baptismal confession that will separate it from the world and dedicate it to its Lord (verse 19). Finally, the gospel ends on a note sounded earlier (8:25–26; 14:27; 18:20): the distinguishing mark of the church and the source of its power and authority is the presence of the risen Lord in its midst.

## THE INTERPRETATION OF THE GOSPEL OF MARK BY THE EVANGELIST MATTHEW

The material in the gospel of Matthew comes from three sources: the gospel of Mark, the sayings source Q (indicated in our exegesis by = Luke), and a separate source or sources of material peculiar to Matthew. Matthew may have composed some of this last material himself. But whatever the source, it is organized on the basis of the structure of the gospel of Mark. Matthew diverges from that structure by making additions and insertions, or by rearranging related material, such as teaching or miracles, into large blocks. But by and large he organizes his gospel on the basis of the structure of the gospel of Mark, and from 14:1 to 28:10 he follows Mark's order exactly.

The fundamental changes in the gospel of Matthew compared to Mark are the birth stories at the beginning and the resurrection appearance and commissioning scene at the end. Mark himself gives only enough of an introduction to locate the story and identify the characters before he plunges into the first act of his three-act apocalyptic drama. But Matthew does not think in terms of a three-act apocalyptic drama, but rather of the time of Jesus as a special, sacred time. By adding a genealogy and a series of stories on the birth and infancy of Jesus, by emphasizing Jesus as the new revelation fulfilling the promise of the old and superseding it, he is able to set the time of Jesus off from all previous time as the time of fulfillment.

The time of Jesus is then a special kind of time—of fulfillment, of revelation—and Matthew makes this point over and over in various ways. He uses the formula quotations to claim the time of Jesus as the time of fulfillment. He organizes the teaching of Jesus into five discourses, each ending with a formula, and the first taking place on a mountain, to claim that the teaching of Jesus is the new verbal revelation, the new Torah. Though he abbreviates miracle stories, he consistently heightens the sense of the miraculous, having two or many healed where in his source only one was healed, to stress the awesome nature of Jesus and his ministry.

But Matthew not only separates the time of Jesus from all previous time, he also separates it from all following time. Whereas Mark had deliberately involved his readers in the story and left them at the empty tomb awaiting the parousia in fear and trembling, Matthew just as deliberately separates his readers from the story by the Great Commission, in which Jesus appears as the risen and exalted Lord. The Great Commission envisages a time before the parousia, which will be of a different order from the time of Jesus. The revelation has now been given, and the need is for interpretation of that revelation and obedience to it. Now the disciples are to go out into all the world and make disciples; now, for the first time, the disciples are to *teach*, to interpret the revelation. Moreover, they are to organize into a church with a distinctive rite and formula of initiation: baptism in the name of the Trinity. Finally, the disciples will constantly be helped and their teaching authenticated by the presence of the risen Lord in their midst.

In our previous chapter we claimed that despite its realistic narrative the gospel of Mark was essentially an apocalypse. We can now claim that at the hands of Matthew the apocalypse became a foundation myth. In the gospel of Matthew the time of Jesus is separated from all preceding and succeeding time and becomes what can only be called Sacred Time, the time of fulfillment and revelation. Moreover, the Christian church is constituted on the basis of this Sacred Time—the Sacred Time of Jesus is the time of Christian origins—and lives out of the relationship to that time. The life of the church, and the life of Christians in the world, is made possible by the interpretation of the revelation, and by the concept of the presence of the risen Lord in the church and of the fellowship of the community of believers with him. This may well be called foundation myth: a myth of origins to which the involved group relates by carefully organized means.

# THE INTERPRETATION OF THE GOSPEL OF MATTHEW

The evangelist Matthew has a distinctive theology and view of the church. Both are built on essentially Jewish models. The concepts of the fulfillment of a previous promise, of a verbal revelation authoritatively interpreted, of a carefully organized and structured community of believers—for all these Matthew is indebted to his Jewish heritage. One could, of course, find parallels in the varied religious communities in the Hellenistic world, but the fact is that Matthew inherited them from Judaism, and he developed them in debate with the changes in Judaism going on at Jamnia. But Matthew's views are not simply Christianized Judaism. He is indebted to his distinctively Christian heritage at many points, especially for the concept of the risen Christ present in the church. Even though Jewish rabbis were to come to speak of the presence (shekinah) of God wherever two or three gathered to study the Torah, the Matthean view of the risen Lord present in the church, helping, sustaining, and guiding the "disciples" has its roots in the Hellenistic Christian concept of the presence of the Lord in the cultic worship of the community. Matthew is always a man in the tradition of the Hellenistic Jewish Christian mission.

By the intent of its author, the gospel of Matthew cries out for the interpretation it has in fact received through the centuries: as a text enshrining a revelation subject to authoritative interpretation within the Christian community. Its author expected this "book of the origin of Jesus Christ" to become the subject of authoritative interpretation within the church. More than that, this is what happened to the whole of the New Testament of which it became the first book. The centuries have treated it as the enshrinement of revelation and authoritatively interpreted it within the church, which would have delighted the evangelist himself. Even today, whenever it is claimed that "the Bible says . . . ," expression is being given to the stance and attitude of the evangelist Matthew.

## FURTHER READING

Kümmel, *Intro.*, pp. 72–86.
Marxsen, *Intro.*, pp. 146–54.
Fuller, *Intro.*, pp. 113–18.
*PCB*, pp. 769–98 (K. Stendahl).
*JBC*, pp. 62–114 (J. L. McKenzie).
*IDB*, vol. 3, pp. 302–13 (F. C. Grant).

Recent work on the gospel is dominated by Günther Bornkamm and his pupils, who pioneered the redaction critical approach to the gospel.

Bornkamm, Barth, Held, *Tradition and Interpretation in Matthew.*
Bornkamm, "The Risen Lord and the Earthly Jesus: Mt 28:16–20," *The Future of our Religious Past* (ed. James M. Robinson), pp. 203–29.

Other useful studies include:

Davies, *The Setting of the Sermon on the Mount.*
Fenton, *The Gospel of St. Matthew.*
Kingsbury, *The Parables of Jesus in Matthew 13.*
Suggs, *Wisdom, Christology and Law in Matthew's Gospel.*

Thompson, *Matthew's Advice to a Divided Community.*

Strecker, "The Concept of History in Matthew," *Journal of the American Academy of Religion,* vol. 35 (1967), pp. 219–30.

Kingsbury, "The Jesus of History and Christ of Faith in Relation to Matthew's View of Time—Reactions to a New Approach," *Concordia Theological Monthly,* vol. 37 (1966), pp. 500–10.

*A pilgrim journeying towards Jerusalem.*

# 9

# The Gospel of Luke and
# the Acts of the Apostles:
## The Idea of Salvation History

There is a sense in which the collection of the New Testament texts into one unit has done a grave disservice to two of them, the gospel of Luke and the Acts of the Apostles. As their introductions show, Luke and Acts were originally written to be read together as a single work in two volumes. But when the New Testament texts were collected, the four gospels were put in a group separate from the remainder, and the gospel of Luke was separated from the Acts of the Apostles. This separation led to the title "gospel" being given to the first volume and "Acts of the Apostles" to the second. The title "gospel" was influenced by the title of the gospel of Mark, which the author himself called a "gospel" (Mark 1:1); the title "Acts of the Apostles" came about simply from the contents of the second volume. As far as we know, the author did not entitle his two-volume work, though he does refer to it as "a narrative of the things which have been accomplished among us" (Luke 1:1). We treat the two-volume work as the unity it is intended to be and refer to it as Luke-Acts.

## THE AUTHOR AS A MAN
## OF THE HELLENISTIC JEWISH CHRISTIAN MISSION

Luke-Acts was written in the generation immediately following the fall of Jerusalem, in what we are calling the middle period of New Testament Christianity. The author knows and uses the gospel of Mark, which we have dated shortly after A.D. 70. Furthermore, his view of the church and its faith shows movement toward the institutionalism and theology characteristic of the later period of emergent Catholicism. So a date of A.D. 85, plus or minus five years or so, is appropriate.

By this time the characteristic phases of the Christian movement before the fall of Jerusalem no longer existed as distinct entities; we find only Gentile Christianity more or less concerned with the Judaism it ultimately descended from. In the deutero-Pauline letters, Christianity was becoming a real part of the Hellenistic world and moving toward the institutionalism of emergent

**195**

Catholicism. In the gospel of Matthew, Christianity was also moving toward emergent Catholicism, but in dialogue and in dispute with Judaism. Both the deutero-Pauline letters and the gospel of Matthew make creative use of the traditions of an earlier period. In his turn, the author of Luke-Acts is also moving toward emergent Catholicism, and his concern is particularly with the relationship between the church and the Roman Empire, though he also uses the earlier traditions of Hellenistic Jewish Mission Christianity.

The speeches in Acts are examples of the preaching of Hellenistic Jewish Mission Christianity. Paul's Sermon in Acts 13 is not a report of a speech delivered on a specific occasion, but a sample of what Paul must have said many times to Jews and "God-fearers." Similarly, the speech in Athens (Acts 17:16–31) is not so much a record of one attempt to convert the intellectual center of the Hellenistic world as a sample of what Paul and others must have tried a hundred times as they preached to the Gentile world whenever and wherever they found opportunity. In the same way, Peter's speech in Acts 2 or Stephen's in Acts 7 are samples of how Hellenistic Jewish Christianity came to understand itself and its break with Judaism. In the ancient world it was customary for authors of historical works to put speeches on the lips of the main characters in which they, the authors, represented their understanding of the narrative's events and of the speaker's role. The speeches in Acts certainly represent the author's understanding of what was going on in the narrative, but he also has access to some traditions from the past (the past of Hellenistic Jewish Mission Christianity rather than of Palestinian Christianity) as well as knowing the missionary preaching of his own day. So the speeches he writes are examples of the characteristic preaching of Hellenistic Jewish Mission Christianity, and they reflect its traditions.

In presenting Peter as one whose rebuke can bring Ananias to death (Acts 5:3–5), and Simon to penitence (8:14–24), or Paul as one whose garments have the power to heal and whose name has power over demons (19:11–15), the author is reflecting the tendency of his movement to think of its heroes as "divine men." Hellenistic Jewish Mission Christianity claimed Peter as a supporter, Paul as its hero, and Jesus as its savior; all three have the aura of divinity, are human and yet more than human, and they are presented as "divine men" according to the conventions of the Hellenistic world.

## THE AUTHOR AND THE PROBLEMS OF THE CHRISTIANITY OF HIS DAY

Though the author of Luke-Acts is a product of and utilizes the traditions of the Hellenistic Jewish Christian mission, the problems of the churches he represents were different from those of Paul and his colleagues, or if not different then a distinct development from them. Consider the account of the Jerusalem Council in Acts 15. The probable historical occasion for this "summit conference" was the success of the mission to the Jews, "God-fearers," and Gentiles in Antioch and other predominantly Gentile communities, which contrasted dramatically with the comparative failure of the mission to the Jews in Palestine and other predominantly Jewish communities. The decision of this conference, historically speaking, was to commission Paul and his companions to go to the Gentiles, to the predominantly Gentile communities, and to send Peter to the Jews, to the predominantly Jewish communities. The result was the first organized Christian mission to the Gentile world, the mission of Paul and Barnabas to Cyprus and the southern part of Asia Minor, which Acts 13–14 depicts as the occasion for the Jerusalem Council when it was its consequence. In Acts 15, however, the concern of the conference, as reflected in its decision, is to find a procedure to regulate social relationships between Jews and Gentiles in a Christian community. As Galatians 2:11–21 testifies, they became a problem in the Hellenistic Jewish Christian mission *after* the Jerusalem Council, and Acts 15:23–29 can be seen as a compromise solution to a problem created by Paul's missionary activity as authorized by the Jerusalem Council. The account in Acts represents the later phase of a compromise solution to a problem raised by the sheer success of Paul's missionary activity.

But though the social relationship of Jew and Gentile in the Christian church is a problem for the author of Luke-Acts, it is not major, nor is it the occasion for his writing his two-volume work. His major concerns are the delay of the parousia, the fall of Jerusalem and the destruction of its Temple, and the need to help the church normalize its relations with the Roman Empire and its members settle down to Christian witness in a continuing world.

## The Delay of the Parousia

Like all the authors of the middle period of New Testament history, the author of Luke-Acts wrestles with the delay of the parousia, Jesus' return on the clouds of heaven, which should have happened and did not. His solution is to defer the expectation to the indefinite future and to make sense of the extended interim by regarding it as the time of the church, the time of the church's work and witness in the world.

The author defers the time of the parousia by his treatment of certain key passages in the gospel of Mark, one of his sources. Mark 1:14–15 has Jesus coming into Galilee and proclaming, "The time is fulfilled, and the Kingdom of God is at hand," a proclamation intended to arouse a fervent expectation that the End is imminent. Luke 4:14 simply says, "Jesus returned in the power of the Spirit into Galilee." The element of imminent expectation has neatly been removed. Mark 13:16 is a reference to the false claim that the parousia had already taken place: "Many will come in my name, saying, 'I am he!' and they will lead many astray." Luke 21:8 significantly modifies this passage to "Many will come in my name, saying, 'I am he!' and, 'The time is at hand!' Do not go after them." The imminent expectation of the gospel of Mark has now itself become a false teaching. The very next verse tells the same story. Mark 13:7 allows for a brief interim before the parousia: "this must take place, but the end is not yet." Luke 21:9 extends this brief interim: "the end will not be at once." This tendency persists throughout Luke-Acts; the parousia is indefinitely postponed.

The author of Luke-Acts also makes theological sense of the extended interim period; it is the period of the "witness" of the church. This is very clear in the words of the resurrected Jesus to the disciples: "You shall be my witnesses in Jerusalem and all Judea and Samaria and to the end of the earth" (Acts 1:8). Now that is both a geographical and an ethnic progression. Judea surrounds Jerusalem and is still Jewish. The movement outward from Jerusalem toward Rome brings one to Samaria, regarded as only half-Jewish, and still moving toward Rome one comes to Gentile Syria and eventually to "the end of the earth," Rome itself. The Acts of the Apostles does indeed follow this geographical and ethnic progression, and very significantly, it ends on the note of Paul witnessing "openly and unhindered" in Rome (Acts 28:31). The extended time before the parousia is for the author of Luke-Acts the period of the church and her witness in the wide world.

A good example of the consequences of this viewpoint is Luke's treatment of the teaching on discipleship found in Mark 8:34–9:1. In Mark this teaching deals with the urgent demands of the brief period before the parousia; it is an interim ethic. But Luke 9:23–27 introduces a series of subtle changes. The disciple must now take up his cross *daily;* the Son of Man will come, but not "in this adulterous and sinful generation"; the martyr witnesses will be sustained by a vision of the Kingdom of God, but they will not see it come "in power." The effect is to change the tone of the whole passage so that it becomes concerned with an ongoing witness in a world that has a long history before it.

## The Destruction of Jerusalem and the Temple

The treatment of Jerusalem in Luke-Acts is a very special feature of the two-volume work. Though the gospel follows Mark in using the spelling *Ierosolyma* at 13:22 (= Mark 10:32) and 19:28 (= Mark 11:1), the author infinitely prefers *Ierousalēm*, which Luke-Acts uses some sixty-three times out of an approximate total of seventy-four uses in the whole New Testament. Our author has both a special concern and a special word for Jerusalem. He uses almost exclusively a form of the city's name not used frequently elsewhere in the New Testament, and he refers to the city many times.

We can approach the question of what Luke-Acts has to say about Jerusalem by observing a very important element in the composition of the gospel. If we compare the structure of the gospel with the structure of Mark, its source, we see that one major change is the insertion of a long, rambling travel narrative (Luke 9:51–18:14). It begins with a statement of Jesus' intent, "When the days drew near for his ascension he set his face to go to Jerusalem" (9:51),[1] and the rest of the gospel's narrative is about the fulfillment of that intent. Jesus goes up to Jerusalem and there endures the passion, which in Luke-Acts climaxes in the ascension, the act of Jesus being taken up into heaven: "While he blessed

---

[1]This is our own translation. RSV says, "When the days drew near for him to be received up"; NEB, "when he was to be taken up into heaven"; TEV, "would be taken up into heaven." The Greek text uses *anamlēmpsis,* the technical term for "ascension" in Greek, hence our translation.

them, he parted from them and was carried up into heaven.[2] And they returned to Jerusalem with great joy and were continually in the temple blessing God" (24:51–53). The Acts of the Apostles exhibits the same compositional feature as Luke; it too has a long, rambling travel narrative beginning with a statement of intent. Acts 19:21 reads, "Paul resolved in the Spirit to pass through Macedonia and Achaia and go to Jerusalem, saying, 'After I have been there, I must also see Rome,'" and from that point the narrative is about Paul's journey to Jerusalem and Rome, ending with Paul preaching in Rome "quite openly and unhindered" (28:31).

So the narrative of Luke-Acts leads quite deliberately from Jerusalem, the place of Jesus' passion-ascension, to Rome, the place of Paul's preaching. That it is deliberate can be seen not only in Luke 9:51 and Acts 19:21 but also in many other references—Luke 9:31 (compare Mark 9:4); 9:53; 23:27–31—all emphasizing Jerusalem as the place of the passion. In Luke-Acts all the resurrection appearances take place in or near Jerusalem. But after the ascension the thrust is consistently from Jerusalem to Rome (Acts 1:4–6, 8). Each of the three accounts of Paul's conversion (9:1–30; 22:3–21; 26:9–23) has him begin his witnessing in Jerusalem immediately after his conversion. It is important that Paul, the exemplary witness, carry the gospel from Jerusalem to Rome; hence the references to Jerusalem in the conversion accounts, and hence 19:21 and the ending in 28:31. In fact, Paul did not go to Jerusalem immediately after his conversion, and his journey to Rome ended with his death. But to the author of Acts, the gospel events must climax in Jerusalem, the gospel must be brought from Jerusalem to Rome, and the gospel must take root in Rome. To portray all this in his narrative he has to take liberties with the historical events—limit the resurrection appearances to Jerusalem, have Paul go to Jerusalem immediately after his conversion, give the impression that Rome posed no problems for Paul's preaching—good examples of myth distorting history. The myth is needed because Jerusalem is fallen, and the needs of the myth distort the facts of history. According to Matthew and John, there were resurrection appearances in Galilee; Paul himself denies going to Jerusalem after his conversion (Gal 1:17); and Rome martyred him. But none of this matters compared to the needs of the myth.

The author of Luke-Acts interprets Jerusalem as the place of the passion of Jesus and regards its destruction as a consequence of that; Rome is the new center of gravity for Christians. Jerusalem and its Temple are gone, but the preaching of the gospel in the world of which Rome is the center remains.

## The Relations between Christians and the Roman Empire

In our earlier discussion of apocalyptic Christianity we saw that persecution was an ever present possibility for New Testament Christians, as true in the

---

[2]Most modern translations relegate the second half of this verse to the margin. However, the reference forward to the ascension in 9:51 indicates that the gospel was intended to end on this note by its author; so we include the second half of the verse despite the ambiguous textual evidence.

middle period of New Testament Christianity as in the earlier or later periods. But in Luke-Acts persecution is only a part of the whole problem of relations between the Christians and the Empire. As the author thinks of the long period of history before the parousia, he has also to consider Christians living within that history, and that means living within historical circumstances dominated by Rome and the Roman Empire. As long as Christians expected the world to pass away shortly, they could revile Rome and its Empire in anticipation of its imminent destruction, as John of Patmos does in Revelation 18. But to live in the Empire for a considerable period of time, they must come to terms with it, as the author of Luke-Acts and no doubt the churches he represents try to do.

To help his readers do so, the author of Luke-Acts consistently presents Roman authorities as sympathetic to the Christian movement: Pilate finds no fault in Jesus (Luke 23:4); in Cyprus the proconsul "believes" (Acts 13:12); Gallio, proconsul of Achaia, takes Paul's side against the Jews (Acts 18:14–15); and so on. The Christians' difficulties are not the hostility of Roman authorities but the machinations of the Jews (Acts 13:28; 14:2, 19; 18:12, etc.). At the same time the Christian movement is consistently represented as descended directly from, and indeed the proper fulfillment of, Judaism, especially in the speeches in Acts, (e.g., 13:16–41). Not only was this the theme of Christian preaching to Jews, it also implied a claim that Christians share the Jews' privilege of having their faith declared a "legal religion" by the Romans, with its implications of toleration and freedom to practice their rites. Thus the author attempts to present Roman authority to Christians, and the Christians to Roman authorities, in the best possible light, in the hope of fostering good relations between them.

## THE IDEA OF SALVATION HISTORY

The great contribution by the author of Luke-Acts to the New Testament is the idea of *salvation history*,[3] a term that has to be explained rather than defined. The author thinks in historical terms—in terms of a remote past and an immediate past, a present and an immediate future, and a distant future. The remote past of the time of the first man (taking the genealogy of Jesus back to Adam, Luke 3:38) and the distant future of the parousia mark the limits of history, but within those limits history is an affair of taxation and censuses, of emperors, governors, kings, and high priests (Luke 2:1; 3:1–2). But it is also the word of God coming to men and the Spirit of God descending on them. This is the crux of the matter: the concept of a history of the world in which God may be known, a history that is both a history of men and their affairs and a history

---

[3]This term is derived from Conzelmann, whose book *The Theology of St. Luke* dominates all contemporary discussion of Luke-Acts. Conzelmann himself writes in German and uses the term *Heilsgeschichte*, which the English translation of his book renders as "redemptive history." We prefer to use "salvation history" to avoid any suggestion that history itself is redemptive. In the thought of the author of Luke-Acts it is not that history is redemptive but that redemption has a history.

of God's affairs with men. As the history of God's affairs with men, of God's activity on man's behalf, it is *salvation* history, the history of man's salvation at the hand of God. There is then a world history, a history of men and their affairs in the world, and a salvation history, a history of God and his activity directed toward the salvation of man. These two run side by side, and at certain points they intersect, but salvation history is not exhausted in world history. The salvation history of God's activity on behalf of man began before the creation of man and before the beginning of world history, and it will continue after the parousia has brought world history to an end. Even now it transcends world history, for it is the history of that realm from which the Spirit comes and to which Jesus ascends after his resurrection. Neither the term *salvation history* nor the language we are using to describe it is native to the author of Luke-Acts himself, but neither the term nor the description is inappropriate.

Viewing history in the context of salvation history, the author of Luke-Acts thinks of it as divided into three distinct epochs. There is first the era of "the law and the prophets," down to and including the mission of John the Baptist (Luke 16:16). There is the era of "the proclamation of the Kingdom of God," the time of Jesus and of the church (Luke 16:16; Acts 28:31). This second era is further subdivided, for it begins with the descent of the Spirit on Jesus at his baptism and is divided at the cross where Jesus returns the Spirit to the Father (Luke 23:46). Then there follows an interim period in which Jesus is raised from the dead and reveals to the disciples the secret of the second part of the era of the Kingdom of God, an interim culminating in the ascension (Acts 1:1–11). This is followed by the period of the church, inaugurated by the descent of the Spirit at Pentecost (which is a baptism, Acts 1:5) and epitomized by Paul preaching the Kingdom of God "openly and unhindered" in Rome (Acts 28:31). This era will end with the parousia (Luke 21:25–28), which will be at some indefinite point in the future (Luke 21:9; Acts 1:7).

The whole conception may be represented as follows:

**First era**:    The time of "the law and the prophets," from Adam to John the Baptist.

**Second era**:    The time of the proclamation of the Kingdom of God by Jesus, from the descent of the Spirit on Jesus to the return of the Spirit to the Father at the Cross.

**Interim period**:    The time of the resurrection, revelatory teaching to the disciples by the risen Jesus, and the ascension.

**Third era**:    The time of the proclamation of the Kingdom of God by the church, from the descent of the Spirit at Pentecost to the parousia.

We will now say something about each of these divisions.

## The Time of "the Law and the Prophets"

The key to understanding this epoch is Luke 16:16. "The law and the prophets were until John; since then the good news of the Kingdom of God is preached" is certainly crucial to understanding the thought of the author of Luke-Acts. He has made the text very much his own with its distinction between the time of the law and the prophets and that of the preaching of the Kingdom of God; consider his use of "kingdom of God" in Acts 1:3; 19:8; 28:23. Interestingly enough, he does not have the phrase in his equivalent to Mark's reference to Jesus coming into Galilee saying, "The kingdom of God is at hand" (Mark 1:15 = Luke 4:14), because he has an account of Jesus in Nazareth immediately following, which serves as a frontispiece for his whole gospel (Luke 4:16–30) and makes the same point in much greater detail.

For the author of Luke-Acts the time before Jesus is the time of "the law and the prophets"; it is the time of anticipation, of promise, and as such, very different from the time of Jesus. It is particularly interesting that he relegates John the Baptist to that past time. Whereas Matthew goes to considerable pains to draw parallels between John the Baptist and Jesus, the author of Luke-Acts goes to even greater pains to remove John from the scene before the ministry of Jesus begins. In Luke 3:18–20 John is shut up in prison before the Spirit descends on Jesus at his baptism (3:20–22). Whereas for Matthew John the Baptist begins the new time of fulfillment, for Luke he is the climax of the old time of promise. In the gospel of Luke, the genealogy of Jesus is traced back to Adam, the first man (in Matthew, to Abraham, the father of the Jewish people), so we have in effect an era stretching from Adam to John the Baptist to which the birth and infancy of Jesus belong.

The old era ends and the new begins not with the birth of Jesus but with the descent of the Spirit on him at his baptism. For the author of Luke-Acts, this is the turning point; the birth and infancy of Jesus is full of promise, but it is not part of the time of fulfillment.

## The Time of the Proclamation of the Kingdom of God by Jesus

With the descent of the Spirit on Jesus at his baptism, a new era begins, which in Luke 16:16 is a time when "the good news of the kingdom of God is preached." The synagogue scene at Nazareth (Luke 4:16–30), which the author deliberately presents to the reader as a means of understanding the time of Jesus, describes a time when prophecy is fulfilled, specifically Isa 61:1–2. That prophecy concerns the coming of the Spirit of God, proclaiming the good news to the poor, their release to the captives, recovery of sight by the blind, setting the oppressed at liberty, and "the acceptable year of the Lord." These themes dominate the presentation of the time of Jesus in the gospel of Luke. Here we find the parables of the Lost Sheep, the Lost Coin, and the Lost Son (Luke 15). In this gospel is told the story of the tax collector who beats his breast; cries out to God, "God, be merciful to me a sinner!"; and goes down to his house, justified (Luke 18:9–14). Here too the poor widow successfully importunes an unjust judge (Luke 18:1–8), and paradise is promised to the penitent thief on his cross (Luke 23:43). The gospel of Luke is the gospel of the poor and the outcast, of Jesus' concern with them, and of God's gracious dealing with them through Jesus.

The author of Luke-Acts also emphasizes that the time of Jesus is free of Satan's malevolent activity. After the temptation of Jesus the devil "departed from him until an opportune time" (Luke 4:13; compare Matt 4:11), and that opportune time does not come until Jesus is in Jerusalem, the place of his passion and death, where "Satan entered into Judas called Iscariot, who was of the number of the twelve" (Luke 22:3).

The time of Jesus presented by the author of Luke-Acts has been appropriately called "the center of time."[4] It is the central time, the hinge of history, in which both the meaning of the past and the course of the future are revealed. The author recognizes that he and the people he is writing for are involved in the ongoing flow of history in the world, but in effect he is claiming that one epoch in that history, the time of Jesus, is also the decisive epoch in salvation history, the time when the good news of God's activity on behalf of man and man's salvation was proclaimed in the world. Now the world lives out of its relationship to that time of proclamation; now men and women know salvation as they relate to the center of time and history.

## The Interim Period of Jesus' Resurrection, Revelatory Teaching to the Disciples, and Ascension

Between Jesus' act of committing his spirit to God at the cross and the return of the Spirit to the church at Pentecost, there is an interim period of resurrection, teaching, and ascension. Luke stresses the resurrection of Jesus more than either Mark or Matthew. Mark has no resurrection appearances at all, and Matthew has one and then the commissioning scene. But Luke has the appearance on the Emmaus road (24:13–35), the appearance in Jerusalem itself (24:36–43), and also mentions an appearance to Peter (24:34). Further, Luke-Acts has a period in which the risen Jesus is with his disciples, teaching them (Luke 24:44–49; Acts 1:6–8), and then the ascension is an event separate from the resurrection, (Luke 24:51, RSV margin; Acts 1:9). As far as we know, the author of Luke-Acts is the first man to conceive of the ascension as separate from the resurrection. Normally in the New Testament it is an aspect of the resurrection-ascension conceived of as one act. But Luke needs a separate ascension to have a place in his narrative for the revelatory teaching of the risen Jesus to his disciples. This teaching is very important. It is in Luke 24:44–49 and Acts 1:4–8 that the heart of the Lukan understanding of things is revealed. Here we find the necessity for repentance and forgiveness of sins to be preached by the disciples, who are "witnesses." Here we find, further, the "beginning from Jerusalem" and the moving "to the end of the earth," and

---

[4]This is Conzelmann's phrase. The German is *Die Mitte der Zeit*, which in the translation of Conzelmann's book is rendered as "the center of history."

finally the baptism with the Spirit that will make it all possible. These themes are crucial to the author of Luke-Acts, and they are all given in this interim period of revelatory teaching.

## The Time of the Proclamation of the Kingdom of God by the Church, from Jerusalem to Rome

The *time of Jesus,* the center of time, is the time of the work of the Spirit through *Jesus,* the time of preaching the good news of the Kingdom of God. The *time of the church* is the time of the work of the Spirit through the *church,* the time of the proclamation of the Kingdom of God in the form of the church preaching repentance and the forgiveness of sins, the time of witnessing from Jerusalem to Rome. This time of the church will continue until the parousia, and it is the time of the author of Luke-Acts and of his readers. Just as the gospel of Mark ends symbolically with the reader's situation in mind, so also does Acts. Paul preaching and teaching in Rome "quite openly and unhindered" symbolizes the situation of the church in the world and also the situation of the reader in the world.

The presentation of the time of the church in Acts is extraordinarily realistic. For all the legendary elements, for all that Peter and Paul are "divine men" in accordance with the practice of religious propaganda in the Hellenistic world, the narratives of Acts are full of elements taken directly from the life and experience of the church in that world. Baptism, the laying on of hands and the experience of the Spirit, revelation by dreams and visions, the receptiveness of "God-fearers" to the gospel and the hostility of Jews—all this and more is taken by the author directly from the experience of the church in which and for which he was writing. Furthermore, the author carefully draws parallels between the time of Jesus and the time of the church. In particular he makes Jesus himself a model, or paradigm, of Christian piety. Jesus is empowered by the Spirit, as is the believer, and he prays and attends worship regularly as the believer should also. Moreover, the death of Jesus is not "a ransom for many," but Jesus is "one who serves" (Luke 22:27; compare Mark 10:45). The author of Luke-Acts consistently plays down the differences between Jesus as the Christ and other men. A good example is the reply to the question of the High Priest. In Mark 14:62, Jesus accepts the titles of "Christ" and "Son of the living God" by using the formula "I am." But in Luke 22:70, when Jesus is asked if he is the Son of God, he replies, "You say that I am." A very striking parallel between Jesus and the believer is that drawn between the passion of Jesus and the fate of Stephen, the first martyr. In his account of the trial of Jesus, Luke has no reference to the false witnesses found in Mark (Luke 22:66–71; compare Mark 14:56–64). But in Acts 6:13–14, false witnesses appear at Stephen's trial with the testimony that Mark has them give at the trial of Jesus. At his stoning Stephen cries with a loud voice, "Lord, do not hold this sin against them" (Acts 7:60), just as Jesus had cried from his cross, "Father, forgive them; for they know not what they do" (Luke 23:34).

The effect of these parallels between the time of Jesus and that of the church, and between Jesus and the Christian believer, is to make it possible for the believer to relate directly to the time of Jesus and to Jesus himself as the model of Christian piety. The author of Luke-Acts is carefully providing his readers with an understanding of their place in salvation history and of their role in the world. The believer lives by the power of the spirit as he "preaches repentance and the forgiveness of sins" and joins in the worldwide witness of the church.

# THE STRUCTURE OF LUKE-ACTS

Important factors in the structure of Luke-Acts are the introductions to each volume (Luke 1:1–4; Acts 1:1–5), the careful parallelism of the baptism and descent of the Spirit in each volume, the parallelism of the journey motif of Jesus to Jerusalem and Paul to Rome, and the great significance of the teaching of the risen Jesus (Luke 24:46–49; Acts 1:8). At critical moments in the geographical progression of the narrative of Acts, there are formula-like summaries of the action: 2:43–47; 5:42; 9:31; 12:24; 15:35; 19:20. Coming where they do in the plot of the narrative, they provide us with the clues to its structure.[5] The following structure then emerges for the two-volume work:

GOSPEL OF LUKE

> Introduction to the two volumes, 1:1–4
> **Book One**: **The Ministry of the Spirit through Jesus**
> Introduction to the Ministry of the Spirit through Jesus, 1:5–4:13
> The Ministry in Galilee, 4:14–9:50
> The Journey of Jesus to Jerusalem, 9:51–19:27
> Jesus in Jerusalem 19:28–21:38
> The Passion Narrative, 22:1–23:49
> Burial, Resurrection, Ascension, 23:50–24:53

ACTS OF THE APOSTLES

> Introduction to the second volume, 1:1–5
> **Book Two**: **The Ministry of the Spirit through the Church**
> Introduction to the Ministry of the Spirit through the Church, 1:6–26
> Descent of the Spirit on the Church, 2:1–42
> > SUMMARY, 2:43–47
> The Church in Jerusalem, 3:1–5:41
> > SUMMARY, 5:42
> The Movement into Judea and Samaria, 6:1–9:30
> > SUMMARY, 9:31
> The Movement into the Gentile World, 9:32–12:23
> > SUMMARY, 12:24

---

[5]We shall note that similar formula-like expressions are used elsewhere in the narrative of Acts to mark divisions within it. Our contention is that the combination of a formula summary and a geographical shift mark the major divisions in the narrative.

## EXEGETICAL SURVEY OF LUKE-ACTS

Because of the limitations of space it will not be possible in this exegesis to do
more than indicate the outline and flow of the narrative and call attention to
particular emphases and concerns of the author. We give the parallels to Mark
or Matthew where the parallelism is close.

### Introduction to the two-volume work, Luke 1:1–4

The introduction is couched in the conventional language of Hellenistic
literature and indicates that the author is deliberately attempting to compose a
literary work. Note that he calls his work a "narrative" and wants to put
matters into "an orderly account." But note also that his orderly account is a
careful blending of secular history and salvation history.

### Book One: The Ministry of the Spirit through Jesus

#### Introduction to the ministry of the Spirit through Jesus, 1:5–4:13

**1:5–80** *The birth of John the Baptist and the announcement of the birth of
Jesus.* This introduction is written in a Greek characteristic of the
Septuagint, the Greek translation of the Hebrew scriptures. The first
epoch of salvation history is approaching its climax and end.

**2:1–52** *The birth and infancy of Jesus.* Now salvation history and world
history approach the point of intersection. Whereas Matthew concentrat-
ed in his infancy stories on the fulfillment of scriptural prophecy, Luke is
concerned particularly with the promise that Jesus holds for the future,
and his infancy stories are designed particularly to interpret the "center of
time" of salvation history in advance (e.g., 2:30–32, 34).

**3:1–18** *Activity of John the Baptist* (= Mark 1:1–8 = Matt 3:1–12). This is
close to Mark and Matthew and hence in general from Mark and Q. But
Luke tones down the note of apocalyptic urgency in John's proclamation
and adds the general ethical teaching of verses 10–14.

**3:19–20** *The imprisonment of the Baptist.* This is a remarkable passage. In the service of his understanding of the periodization of salvation history, Luke has John shut up in prison *before* the baptism of Jesus.

**3:21–22** *The descent of the Spirit on Jesus* (= Mark 1:9–11; Matt 3:13–17). What in the other gospels is the baptism of Jesus becomes in Luke the descent of the Spirit on him. Note the characteristic introduction of "and was praying" in verse 21.

**3:23–28** *The genealogy of Jesus* (= Matt 1:1–16). Here the descent of Jesus is traced back to Adam, the first man, and not, as in Matthew, only to Abraham.

**4:1–13** *The temptation of Jesus* (= Mark 1:12–13; Matt 4:1–11).

*The ministry in Galilee, 4:14–9:50*

**4:14–15** *The first preaching in Galilee* (= Mark 1:14–15). Luke carefully omits the eschatological content of Jesus' preaching.

**4:16–30** *The synagogue scene* (= Mark 6:1–6). What in Mark is an account of the rejection of Jesus by "his own" in Galilee is in Luke a carefully staged introduction to the whole ministry of Jesus. Here is a first statement of themes sounded constantly throughout the gospel; this scene is designed to introduce the reader to the whole ministry of Jesus and to help him understand it.

**4:31–41** *The Sabbath day at Capernaum* (= Mark 1:21–34). Luke here follows Mark with only minor modifications.

**4:42–44** *A preaching journey* (= Mark 1:35–39). Verse 43 represents Luke's view of the ministry.

**5:1–6:11** *Incidents of the ministry in Galilee* (= Mark 1:40–3:6). With the exception of the miraculous catch of fish, which is a hint forward to the worldwide mission of the church (5:1–11), Luke is with minor variations following Mark.

**6:12–16** *The call of the twelve* (= Mark 3:13–19). This follows Mark in general, but note the characteristic Lukan emphasis on Jesus spending the night in prayer before choosing the twelve.

**6:17–19** *Jesus heals the multitudes* (= Mark 3:7–12).

**6:20–49** *The Sermon on the Plain.* This is Luke's equivalent of Matthew's Sermon on the Mount, though it lacks Matthew's characteristic understanding of it as the first book of the new revelation. That both Matthew and Luke have such a sermon indicates that the tradition of bringing together teaching material and giving it a brief narrative setting was already a feature of the sayings source Q. Like Matthew, Luke also gives the sermon an eschatological setting, the Beatitudes (6:20–23), as Q must therefore have done. Luke, the gospel of the poor and outcast, characteristically adds a series of woes on the rich and happy (6:24–26). The remainder of the sermon parallels various places in Matthew; it is Q material, and probably in the same order.

**7:1–8:3** *Further incidents of the ministry in Galilee.* Now we have a series of incidents reflecting Luke's interests and concerns. The Centurion's Slave emphasizes the faith of a Gentile (7:1–10); the Widow's Son portrays Jesus' concern for a widow (7:11–17); the Baptist's Question (7:18–23) echoes the key note of the Nazareth synagogue scene; Jesus' testimony to John the Baptist stresses the subordinate role of the Baptist (7:24–35); the Woman with the Ointment highlights Jesus' concern for a sinner (7:36–50); and the Ministering Woman his preparedness to help and be helped by women (8:1–3). Some parts have parallels in Matthew (Luke 7:18–35 = Matt 11:2–19), but the configuration and concerns are those of Luke and his gospel.

**8:4–18** *The parable of the Sower and the purpose of parables* (= Mark 4:1–29). Here Luke follows Mark's parable chapter except that he omits Mark's parable of the Seed Growing Secretly and transposes the Mustard Seed to a different setting (Luke 13:18–19). Also, the three sayings in 8:16–18 are from Mark 4:21–25, but Luke has doublets of them at 11:33; 12:2; and 19:26, each time with a Matthean parallel. Clearly, different versions of these sayings were known to Mark and to the Q community.

Luke 8:16 is particularly interesting. Mark 4:21 has a saying about a lamp being put on a stand. Matt 5:15 has a version in which the lamp "gives light to all in the house"; "he is thinking of a reform within Judaism; Luke's lamp is placed, as in a Roman house, in the vestibule, that those who enter [i.e., the Gentiles] may see the light!"[6] The reinterpretation of traditional sayings in accordance with the interests and concerns of the evangelists is a complex and fascinating process.

**8:19–21** *Jesus' true relatives* (= Mark 3:31–35).

**8:22–25** *The stilling of the storm* (= Mark 4:35–41).

**8:26–39** *The Gerasene demoniac* (= Mark 5:1–20).

**8:40–56** *Jairus' daughter and the woman with the hemorrhage* (= Mark 5:21–43).

**9:1–6** *The mission of the twelve* (= Mark 6:6b–13).

**9:7–9** *Herod thinks Jesus is John, risen* (= Mark 6:14–16).

**9:10–17** *The return of the twelve and the feeding of the five thousand* (= Mark 6:30–44). Luke is here following Mark, with some transpositions of order, but he omits Mark's account of the fate of the Baptist (Mark 6:17–29), because he has John in prison before the baptism of Jesus.

**9:18–27** *Caesarea Philippi* (= Mark 8:27–9:1). Like Matthew, Luke omits the healing of the blind man at Bethsaida (Mark 8:22–26). Neither of them have Mark's interest in carefully setting off a long section on the passion and discipleship. Luke's version of Mark's first prediction unit introduces a characteristic emphasis on Jesus at prayer (9:18), and he omits the misunderstanding and rebuke of Peter, most probably in the interest of honoring a hero of the church. Also, the eschatological note of Mark 9:1 is minimized in Luke 9:27.

[6]Caird, *The Gospel of St. Luke* (Pelican Gospel Commentaries), p. 119.

**9:28–36** *The transfiguration* (= Mark 9:2–8). Luke follows Mark but omits the eschatological note of the reference to the coming of Elijah in Mark 9:9–13.

**9:37–43a** *The healing of the epileptic boy* (= Mark 9:14–29). Luke abbreviates Mark's narrative and omits the reproach to the disciples in Mark 9:28–29.

**9:43b–48** *The second prediction unit* (= Mark 9:30–37). Luke greatly abbreviates Mark at this point, almost obliterating the passion prediction. This is a consequence of his particular understanding of the passion, which we discuss later in connection with his passion narrative.

**9:49–50** *The strange exorcist* (= Mark 9:38–41). Again, an abbreviation of Mark.

### The journey to Jerusalem, 9:51–19:27

Luke begins this section with a key verse: "When the days drew near for him to be received up, he set his face to go to Jerusalem" (9:51). The reference is actually to the ascension—"received up" (RSV) is a translation of the technical term for the ascension in Greek—and from this point forward the gospel moves towards Jerusalem and the ascension. Luke 9:51–18:14 is a long, rambling section loosely organized around the journey to Jerusalem, until in 18:15 Luke rejoins Mark's narrative at Mark 10:13. The material in this section of Luke is partly from Q and partly from Luke's own special traditions. We will content ourselves with calling attention only to some features which particularly represent the characteristic concerns of this gospel.

**10:1–20** *The mission of the seventy.* Only Luke has this mission, probably a symbolic anticipation of the church's mission to the Gentiles, since in Jewish thinking seventy was the traditional number of Gentile nations.

**10:29–37** *The parable of the Good Samaritan.* The parable reflects Luke's concern for the outcast since the Jews regarded the Samaritans with real hostility (compare 9:51–56).

**10:38–42** *Mary and Martha.* The characteristic approach to women of the Jesus in Luke's gospel.

**12:13–21** *The parable of the Rich Fool.*

**14:7–14** *Teaching on humility.* The characteristic attitude toward wealth and concern for the poor.

**15:1–32** *The Lost Sheep, the Lost Coin, and the Lost Son.* This is one of the great chapters in the New Testament. In these three parables Luke presents what he believes to be Jesus' intense concern for the lost. The sheep is lost from the flock, the coin from the woman's meager store, the boy from the land and standards of his father. But all are found again and in this Luke sees, no doubt correctly, a symbol of God's love and concern for the lost and the outcast as epitomized by Jesus and to be echoed by the believer.

**16:19–31**   *The Rich Man and Lazarus.* The concern for the poor.

**18:1–14**   *The parables of the Unjust Judge and the Publican.* Characteristic piety in the form of prayer, encouraged by the stories of a poor widow who successfully importunes an unjust judge and a tax collector who successfully prays for mercy.

**18:15–19:27**   *Jesus draws near to Jerusalem.* Luke now rejoins Mark's narrative. The blessing of the children (18:15–17 = Mark 10:13–16) would obviously appeal to Luke, as would the story of the rich young man (18:18–30 = Mark 10:17–31). Mark's third prediction unit (Mark 10:32–45) is itself composite, since the teaching on discipleship was probably originally in a Eucharistic setting, where Luke has it (Luke 22:24–27). Luke 18:31–34 has the third prediction of the passion, and 18:35–43 the healing of the blind man with only minor variations from Mark. Luke 19:1–10 has the story of Zacchaeus, only in Luke and characteristic of his concern for the ministry of Jesus to the outcast, in this instance a tax collector.

## Jesus in Jerusalem, 19:28–21:38

This basically follows Mark 11:1–13:37. Luke 19:39–44 adds a prediction of the destruction of Jerusalem, which interprets that catastrophe as a judgment on the city, "because you did not know the time of your visitation." Luke maintains the apocalyptic discourse of Mark 13 because he accepts the parousia (Luke 21:25–38). He even adds a note of his own (Luke 21:34–36) that stresses the universal nature of the event. We have already noted how he redacts the chapter to take out the note of imminence.

## The passion narrative, 22:1–23:49

This is rather different from the account in Mark 14:1–16:8, and it has been suggested that Luke is following another source. But the general framework of his narrative is from Mark, and the divergencies can be explained partly by his use of special material at some points and partly by a particular interpretation of the passion that causes him to undertake a rather extensive redaction of the Markan narrative in some places.

Luke understands the passion of Jesus as the legal murder of Jesus by the Jews, achieved despite a favorable attitude to Jesus by the Roman and Herodian authorities. The Jews and the Jews alone bear the guilt for the death of Jesus. A second major deviation from Mark is that Luke does not regard the cross as an atonement for sin: the death of Jesus is not the basis for man's salvation. In Luke's version of the Last Supper the cross of Jesus is interpreted as an act of service, not as in Mark 10:45 a "ransom for many." There is even doubt as to whether the words of interpretation of the bread and wine at the Supper—a body "given for you" and blood "poured out for you"—belong in the original text of the gospel (Luke 22:19b–20).[7] The Lukan passion narrative has to be reviewed with some care.

**22:1–2**   *The conspiracy against Jesus* (= Mark 14:1–2).

**22:3–6**   *Satan returns to the scene* (= Mark 14:10–11). This is Luke's account of Judas Iscariot's agreement to betray Jesus, with the special note on the return of Satan, who was absent from Luke's narrative since the Temptation (4:13).

**22:7–13**   *Preparation for the Supper* (= Mark 14:12–16).

**22:14–38**   *The Last Supper* (= Mark 14:17–25, but with significant variations). Luke begins his account of the Supper with the institution of the Eucharist and follows it with the announcement of the traitor, an inversion of the order in Mark. In itself this is of no great moment. More important is that Luke 22:15–16 has the reference forward to eating in the Kingdom of God before the words of interpretation, 22:17–19a (?19b–20), whereas Mark has the reverse order. It is entirely possible that Luke is minimizing the impact of the words of interpretation by deliberately preceding them with the reference to the future of the Kingdom of God.

Luke 22:24–27 is his version of Mark 10:42–45, and it is certainly independent of what Mark represented. The two versions of the teaching developed separately in the tradition of the church, and Luke chooses this one rather than what is in Mark because it avoids the ransom saying of Mark 10:45. Verses 28–30 seem to be from Q; Matt 19:28 has the saying in a different context. Verses 31–34 and 35–38 are special Lukan tradition, and the latter verses seem out of place in this context.

**22:39–53**   *Jesus in Gethsemane* (= Mark 14:26–52). A somewhat abbreviated version of Mark's narrative.

**22:54–71**   *The trial before the Sanhedrin and Peter's denial* (= Mark 14:53–72). Luke finishes the account of the denial before beginning the trial, whereas Mark intercalates the trial into the denial story.

**23:1–5**   *Jesus before Pilate* (= Mark 15:1–5). Luke develops Mark's account in accordance with his wish to stress the positive attitude of Pilate to Jesus and the guilt of the Jews.

**23:6–12**   *Jesus before Herod.* A further demonstration of Luke's emphasis: the innocence of Jesus, the guilt of the Jews, the favor of the authorities toward Jesus.

**23:13–25**   *The sentencing of Jesus* (= Mark 15:6–15). Luke adds verses 13–16 to Mark's narrative, reiterating his emphases.

**23:26–32**   *The road to Golgatha.* Luke adds verses 27–31, the lamenting of the women of Jerusalem, to Mark 15:21.

**23:33–43**   *The crucifixion* (= Mark 15:22–32). Particular Lukan emphases are the prayer for forgiveness (verse 34), and the Penitent Thief (verses 39–43).

[7]The textual evidence indicates that Luke 22:19b–20 was added to the original text in the course of its transmission in the church. NEB and TEV relegate these verses to the margin.

**23:44–49** *The return of the Spirit to the Father* (= Mark 15:33–41). Luke rewrites the account of the death of Jesus in accordance with his concept of the role of the spirit in salvation history. The centurion's confession becomes a declaration of the innocence of Jesus, not a confession of his status as Son of God, as it is in Mark 15:39.

### Burial, resurrection, ascension, 23:50–24:53

**23:50–24:11** *The burial of Jesus and the empty tomb.* Basically follows Mark 15:42–47; 16:1–8.

**24:13–35** *The road to Emmaus.* This is the first of the Lukan resurrection appearances, and verses 19–21 represent Luke's view of Jesus.

**24:36–49** *The risen Christ in Jerusalem.* This is the gospel version of the risen Jesus' teaching to his disciples. A further version is given in Acts 1:6–9, and Luke uses the opportunity of the repetition to develop slightly different emphases each time. These two sets of teaching are the key to the Lukan enterprise, and our overall exegesis of Luke-Acts builds heavily on them.

**24:50–53** *The ascension.* In accordance with 9:51 the reference to the ascension should be read in verse 51b and not relegated to the margin as in the Revised Standard Version.

### Introduction to the second volume (Acts of the Apostles), Acts 1:1–5

## Book Two: The Ministry of the Spirit through the Church

### Introduction to the ministry of the Spirit through the church: the risen Lord and his disciples, Acts 1:6–26

**1:6–11** *The risen Lord with his disciples.* This is Luke's second version of the interim period of special revelation. Note the emphasis on the empowering by the Spirit, the work of witnessing, and the geographical progression from Jerusalem to the end of the earth (Rome). This is a statement of the theme of Acts. Note further that the expectation of the parousia is still maintained (verse 11).

**1:12–26** *The replacement of Judas.* The author of Luke-Acts is moving toward the church as an institution, and the fact that it is headed by a formal group of twelve apostles is important to him. Note the emphasis on prayer in verse 24, no doubt deliberately reminiscent of Jesus at prayer before the appointment of the twelve in the gospel.

## The descent of the Spirit on the church, 2:1–42

This descent of the Spirit had already been interpreted as a baptism in 1:5 and so carefully parallels the beginning of the ministry of Jesus. The gift of tongues symbolizes the worldwide mission of the church. We have already pointed out that Peter's speech in verses 14–36 and 38–39 is built on an example of the *pesher* method of the interpretation of scripture in the early church. As it stands in its present context, the speech represents Luke's understanding of things. Note especially the emphasis on the humanity of Jesus (verse 22), the guilt of the Jews (verse 23), the resurrection of Jesus and the witness of the church (verse 32), the subordination of Jesus to God (verse 36), and repentance and the forgiveness of sins (verse 38).

The section closes with a summary, 2:43–47.

## The church in Jerusalem, 3:1–5:41

The witness of the church begins in Jerusalem, in accordance with the programmatic statement in 1:8. Luke may be drawing on early traditions about the church in Jerusalem, but he clearly stamps them with his own emphases and concerns, especially in the speeches: 3:12–26 (Peter at Solomon's Porch), 4:8–12 and 5:29–32 (Peter before the Sanhedrin). Here, for example, Jesus is understood as a prophet (3:22); there is also an emphasis on the resurrection (3:26; 5:30) and on the guilt of the Jews (4:11; 5:30). For the most part, however, the legends are about the early days of the church, developed in the church for the edification of the believers. Such legends are common to all religious movements.

The section closes with a summary, 5:42.

## The movement into Judea and Samaria, 6:1–9:30

Following on the programmatic statement in 1:8, the witness now moves outward to Judea, the territory immediately surrounding Jerusalem, and Samaria. Here we begin to have some contact with the history of the early church as distinct from myths and legends about it. Behind the narrative of the dispute between Hellenists and Hebrews in Jerusalem (6:1–6) and the persecution of the church in Jerusalem (8:1) there lies the reminiscence of a real division in the church and the persecution of one part of it and not another. For all its legendary overlay and its reworking by the author of Luke-Acts in his understanding of things, this section of Acts does echo the historical origins of the Hellenistic Jewish Christian mission.

Stephen's speech (7:2–53) must be regarded as an example of the exegesis of scripture and the interpretation of events by which Hellenistic Jewish Mission Christianity justified its break with Judaism. We noted earlier the parallels the author of Luke-Acts carefully draws between the passion of Stephen, the proto-martyr, and that of Jesus. In 8:1 Paul appears for the first time, and there can be no doubt that he did in fact persecute the church in some such manner as is here depicted. Luke 8:4–24 is a collection of legends about the origin of the Hellenistic Jewish Christian mission remarkable in that it associates Peter firmly with that movement and presents both Philip and Peter as Hellenistic "divine men." Luke 8:25 is a summary reflecting a division in the narrative, not major since it is not associated with a geographical shift, but a division nonetheless. It is followed by the incident of Philip and the Ethiopian Eunuch (8:26–39). Then comes a summary of Philip's further activity (8:40), making it probable that the author of Luke-Acts has deliberately inserted this narrative here. It certainly represents two of the author's characteristic concerns. The eunuch was an outcast since the Jews would not have accepted a mutilated man as a proselyte, and the quotation from Isaiah 53 carefully avoids any interpretation of the death of Jesus as an atonement for sin.

Luke 9:1–30 is the first of the three accounts of the conversion of Paul in Acts (see also 22:3–21; 26:9–23). That this event is narrated three times indicates its importance to the author of Luke-Acts and the Hellenistic Jewish Mission Christianity he represents. We have already discussed the conversion of Paul, and here we need only note that the account is deliberately redacted in line with the programmatic statement of 1:8. Paul's witness did not begin in Jerusalem as all three accounts of his conversion insist it did, but the program announced in 1:8 is here dominant for our author. The myth is distorting the history.

The section closes with a summary, 9:31.

### The movement into the Gentile world, 9:32–12:23

Still following the programmatic statement of 1:8, the narrative now moves to an account of the first Christian witness in the purely Gentile world. The author of Luke-Acts emphasizes the role of Peter in this movement, as he had previously emphasized the role of Peter in the beginning of Hellenistic Jewish Mission Christianity. In part the author wants to bring Peter and Paul, the two great heroes of early Christianity, into essential agreement with each other. But that Peter did in fact take part in the Hellenistic Jewish Christian mission is attested by his appearance in Antioch and Paul's passionate altercation with him there (Gal 2:11–21).

Characteristically Lukan themes recur in Peter's speech (10:34–43) and the foundation of the church at Antioch (11:19–21). The latter marks the true beginning of the Christian mission to the purely Gentile world, and the fact—and it probably is a fact—that "in Antioch the disciples were for the first time called Christians" (11:26) is symbolic testimony to the importance of this moment in the history of New Testament Christianity.

The section closes with a summary, 12:24.

### The movement to the "end of the earth" (1): Paul's first missionary journey and its consequence, the Council at Jerusalem, 12:25–15:33

A feature of Acts is the presentation of Paul's missionary work in the form of three missionary journeys: 13:13–14:28; 15:36–18:21; 18:23–19:19. Clearly Paul must have undertaken missionary journeys; however, in view of the fondness of the author of Luke-Acts for the literary theme of "journeys" (Luke 9:51 and Jesus' journey to Jerusalem; Acts 19:21 and Paul's journey to Rome) these missionary journeys in Acts are probably a literary device around which the author organizes his presentation of Paul's work.

The first "missionary journey" features the first major speech by Paul in Acts, at Pisidian Antioch, 13:16–41. It rehearses themes characteristic of Luke-Acts: the guilt of the Jews, an emphasis on the resurrection, the witness of Christians, the proclamation of the forgiveness of sins as the heart of the Christian message, and so on. It represents the mind of the author of Luke-Acts far more than it does anything appropriate to the Paul of the New Testament letters. We have already indicated our reasons for believing that this Council was the start of Paul's missionary journeys into the world beyond Antioch and that the "decree" of 15:29 represents a solution to a problem that arose as a consequence of Paul's work rather than during the course of it. At the same time, the activity and experiences depicted here in connection with Paul and Barnabas must have been typical of Hellenistic Jewish Christian missionaries in general as known to the author of Luke-Acts.

This section ends with a summary, 15:35.

### The movement to the "end of the earth" (2): Paul's second missionary journey, the movement into Europe, and the decision to go to Rome, 15:36–19:19

This section of Acts is dominated by Paul's decision to carry the Christian witness from Asia into Europe, presented as a direct consequence of the activity of the Spirit, and it leads to Paul's decision to go to Rome (19:21), which in Acts structurally parallels Jesus' decision to go to Jerusalem in Luke 9:51. Paul's experiences as presented here must have been very like those of most Hellenistic Jewish Christian missionaries, as Paul's speech at Athens (17:22–31) no doubt represents typical Christian preaching to the Hellenistic world. Note also the characteristic themes of the favor of the Roman authorities toward the Christians and the guilt of the Jews (18:14–17).

The section ends with a summary, 19:20.

### The journey of Paul to Rome, 19:21–28:16

We now find in Acts the same long, rambling travel narrative beginning with the chief protagonist's resolve that is in the gospel of Luke beginning with

9:51. It is a literary device obviously dear to the author of Luke-Acts. The narrative has been composed of a mixture of traditions and legends about the work of the apostle Paul on which the author of Luke-Acts has imposed his own understanding of things—as for example in the second and third accounts of the conversion of Paul (22:3–21; 26:9–23), where Paul's Christian witness always begins in Jerusalem and moves toward Rome.

A feature of this section of Acts is long passages written in the first person plural, the so-called "we passages." These had first appeared in the previous section of the work (16:10–17), but now they are extensive (20:5–15; 21:1–18; 27:1–28:16). Possibly the author of Luke-Acts is relying on a source in the form of a travel diary kept by a companion of Paul's on his journeys. Certainly the narrative in these sections is extremely realistic.

### Paul in Rome, 28:17–31

Luke-Acts ends with the establishment of Paul and his mission in Rome and the programmatic note of Paul preaching the gospel "openly and unhindered" there. It is the climax of the narrative as depicted in 1:8 and represents the situation of the readers of Luke-Acts as the author understands that situation.

## THE INTERPRETATION OF THE GOSPEL OF MARK BY THE AUTHOR OF LUKE-ACTS

The author of Luke-Acts uses the gospel of Mark as a major source, that use revealing clearly his own emphases and concerns. We may begin with Christology, with the presentation and understanding of the person of Jesus. The evangelist Mark wants to present Jesus as Christ and Son of God and to interpret those designations by a careful and systematic use of Son of Man, leading up to the climactic interpretation of Jesus as Son of Man in 14:62 and the climactic confession of him as Son of God by the centurion in 15:39. In the gospel of Luke all this changes. The confession of the centurion becomes in Luke 23:47 simply a declaration, "Certainly this man was innocent," and the formal acceptance and reinterpretation of the titles "Christ" and "Son of God" by Jesus in Mark 14:61–62 is in Luke 22:67–70 an indiscriminate use without any sensitivity to the nuances of meaning attaching to these titles. The author of Luke-Acts does not have either the same Christology or the same christological concerns as the evangelist Mark. In Luke-Acts Jesus is predominantly understood as a prophet (Luke 24:19), he is always carefully subordinated to God (Acts 3:22), and he becomes Lord and Christ only at his resurrection (Acts 2:33, 36).

It is interesting to consider the interpretation of Mark's predictions of the passion and resurrection (Mark 8:31; 9:31; 10:33–34) in Luke (Luke 9:22; 9:44; 18:31–33). In all the predictions Mark stresses the authority of Jesus in that Jesus is said to "rise again" or "rise." But in Luke 9:22 the verb goes into the passive voice, and it is said that Jesus will "be raised." Luke-Acts emphasizes the resurrection throughout but as the act of God on behalf of the man Jesus. The impact of the gospel of Mark is strong enough for Jesus simply to "rise" in Luke 18:33, but the concern of the author of Luke-Acts in general is to subordinate Jesus to God and to stress the resurrection as an act of God's power, for example, as in Acts 2:33,36; 4:10; 5:30, and elsewhere.

Examining Luke's interpretation of Mark's predictions of the passion and resurrection leads to Luke's understanding of the passion of Jesus altogether. For Mark, the passion and death of Jesus is the means of man's salvation. Jesus comes "to give his life as a ransom for many" (Mark 10:45), and his cross is a sacrifice in which his blood is "poured out for many" (Mark 14:24). None of this survives in the gospel of Luke. In Luke's equivalent to Mark 10:45 (Luke 22:27), the cross of Jesus is simply an act of service and not the means of man's salvation, and Luke's account of the Last Supper omits the word of interpretation of the wine, Luke 22:19b–20 having little claim to being part of the original text of the gospel of Luke. Moreover, this understanding of the cross of Jesus as determinative for man's salvation was reached in early Christianity by interpreting that cross in terms of the great suffering servant passage of Isaiah 53, which Mark 10:45 and 14:24 certainly allude to. But when this passage comes up in Acts 8:32–33, it is most emphatically not used to interpret the death of Jesus as an atonement for sin.

The author of Luke-Acts simply does not understand the passion and death of Jesus in the same way as does the evangelist Mark. For Mark the death of Jesus is the means of man's salvation, the gospel of Jesus Christ is the proclamation that the cross of Christ has made possible the salvation of man, and Christian discipleship is following Jesus in the way of his cross. For the author of Luke-Acts the death of Jesus is an act of legal murder by the Jews, and the gospel as preached by Jesus and the church is a proclamation that if men will repent and turn to God they will receive the forgiveness of their sins. The death of Jesus does not have the role in Luke-Acts it has in the gospel of Mark, and in Luke-Acts Christian discipleship is a witnessing to the resurrection of Jesus rather than a following of Jesus in the way of his cross.

But the major difference between Mark and Luke-Acts is, of course, the sheer existence of the Acts of the Apostles itself. Mark could not possibly have written any such volume since he was anticipating an imminent parousia and envisaging his readers as preparing themselves for that event. The author of Luke-Acts, however, sees the parousia as deferred to the indefinite future and his readers as necessarily settling down to a long period of witnessing in the world. Under these circumstances an Acts of Apostles becomes necessary to help its readers understand how they came to be in their present position and give them a paradigm they can follow. This is the twofold purpose of Acts: it helps the readers understand their place and function in the world and its history by explaining to them the origin and development of the movement of which they are a part, and it helps them fulfill their function by giving them a model. In the Acts of the Apostles the almost legendary heroes of the early days of the church are deliberately presented as models of Christian witness in the world. Historically speaking, there were all kinds of differences between

Peter and Paul, but in Acts they speak with one voice, share the same concerns, preach the same gospel; and the voice, concerns and gospel are those of the church of Luke's own time. Or perhaps it would be more accurate to say they are the voice, concerns, and gospel as Luke hopes they will become in his own time.

Both the gospel of Mark and the Acts of the Apostles are didactic history, a history of the past told to instruct the reader in the present. But they go about their task differently. The evangelist Mark puts his message on the lips of the authoritative figure of Jesus, who is Christ, Son of God and Son of Man. The author of Luke-Acts presents his message through the heroes of the church, Peter and Paul, who become models to be imitated, paradigmatic figures whose example should be followed. But the use of model figures does not end with the presentation of Peter and Paul in the Acts; it is extended to the figure of Jesus in the gospel of Luke. A remarkable feature of the gospel of Luke is the way Jesus is presented as a model of Christian piety, and the way parallels are carefully drawn between the practice of Jesus in the gospel and that of the apostles in the Acts. These parallels are then extended by implication to the readers of Luke-Acts, and the readers find themselves at one with Peter, Paul, Stephen, *and Jesus* in the world. For this reason the author of Luke-Acts plays down the christological emphases of his source, the gospel of Mark, and also avoids any soteriological emphasis in connection with the cross. The Jesus of the gospel of Luke is the first Christian, living out of the power of the spirit of God in the world. He is not the Jewish Messiah whose death ransoms men from the power of sin over them.

It is interesting to compare the different and yet sometimes similar reinterpretations of the gospel of Mark by the evangelist Matthew and by the author of Luke-Acts. The similarity is that both carefully separate the time of Jesus from all preceding or succeeding times. Matthew does so by birth stories at the beginning and the commissioning scene at the end; Luke by the descent of the Spirit at the beginning and the ascension at the end. Moreover, the similarity continues in that both emphasize the special nature of the time of Jesus; for both the time of Jesus is the time of fulfillment. Matthew does this with his constant use of formula quotations; Luke with his insistence on the absence of Satan between the temptation of Jesus and the plot to betray him, and also with the various portrayals of the time of Jesus as the center of time, distinct both from the time of "the law and the prophets" before it and the time of the preaching of "repentance and the forgiveness of sins to all nations" after it. There is a sense, therefore, in which both Matthew and Luke transform what is essentially the apocalypse of Mark into a foundation myth of Christian origins.

But if Matthew and Luke both transform the apocalypse of Mark into a foundation myth, they go very different ways in portraying how their readers may relate to this foundation myth. For Matthew, the means is an authoritative interpretation of the verbal revelation that occurred in the Sacred Time of Jesus. For Luke, the means is an imitation of the Jesus of the Sacred Time, because for him Jesus is quite simply the first Christian. Luke sees Jesus as the primary example to be imitated, as he sees the heroes of the Christian church as secondary examples to be imitated. For him, Christian faith means essentially the imitation of Jesus and following the example of those heroes of the early church who did successfully imitate him.

## THE INTERPRETATION OF LUKE-ACTS

The author of Luke-Acts is the father of all presentations of the life of Jesus in which Jesus is an example to be imitated and the early church is a challenge to and exemplar of what is expected of Christians in the world—and of what Christians may expect of their life in the world. The author of Luke-Acts deliberately presents Jesus and the heroes of the early church as models of the challenge and possibilities of Christian existence in the world. Whereas the evangelist Matthew encouraged the interpretation of the gospel as a verbal revelation to be authoritatively interpreted, the author of Luke-Acts encourages the interpretation of that gospel as an example to be followed in the world. What Jesus, Peter, Stephen, and Paul did, so may and must we also do: that is the message and challenge of the author of Luke-Acts.

## FURTHER READING

All our resource books discuss Luke-Acts:

Kümmel, *Intro,* pp. 86–134.
Marxsen, *Intro,* pp. 155–62; 167–73.
Fuller, *Intro,* pp. 118–32.
PCB, pp. 820–43; 882–926 (G. W. H. Lampe).
JBC, pp. 115–64 (C. Stuhlmueller);165–214 (R. J. Dillon and J. A. Fitzmyer).
IDB, vol. 3, pp. 180–88 (V. Taylor); vol. 1, pp. 28–42 (H. J. Cadbury, and particularly important).

The interpretation of Luke-Acts presented by the present writer stands generally in the tradition represented by Dibelius, Haenchen, and Conzelmann.

Dibelius, *Studies in the Acts of the Apostles.*
Haenchen, *The Acts of the Apostles.*
Conzelmann, *The Theology of St. Luke.*

An interesting and stimulating collection of recent essays is *Studies in Luke-Acts,* edited by Keck and Martyn.

Rylands Greek Papyrus 457, a fragment of
John 18. Known also as P⁵², it is the oldest
surviving New Testament text (middle of
the second century).

# 10

# The Gospel and Letters of John:
## The Literature of the Johannine School

Traditionally, five of the texts in the New Testament are regarded as having been written by the apostle John: the fourth gospel, the three letters of John, and the book of Revelation. The last, however, has at best only a tenuous relationship to the others and is so representative of apocalyptic Christianity that we do not discuss it further here. Neither in style nor in content does it have a claim to a place in the "Johannine corpus," the collection of literature attributed to the apostle John. But the other four texts exhibit a unity of style and content that shows that they certainly belong together, whatever the details of their origins may turn out to have been. They use the same language in the same way. They present stark contrasts between light and darkness, truth and falsehood, life and death, faith and unbelief. Striking indeed is the fact that the long discourses attributed to Jesus in the gospel and the contents of the first letter exhibit a habit of thinking in what has been called a "spiral structure": "The author states a thought, contemplates it from every angle, and apparently finishes up where he started. Yet, there is a slight but perceptible movement to another thought, and the process is repeated."[1] Above all, even the most casual reader can sense that here he is in the presence of someone who has meditated long and earnestly on the verities of the Christian faith: on God, who is light and in whom is no darkness at all; on Jesus Christ his Son whom he sent into the world to save it; on the Christian life as essentially the recognition of being loved and the act of loving. Every line of the gospel and letters of John breathes the spirit of this meditation, and this quality has made them the fundamental literature of Christian mystics through the long centuries of Christian history.

In reading the literature about the gospel and letters of John, we are struck by the frequent images of artistic and especially musical composition. Amos Wilder, a scholar extremely sensitive to literary forms, says that in John's gospel "we have a kind of sacred drama or oratorio,"[2] and the *Oxford*

[1]Fuller, *Intro.*, p. 178.
[2]Wilder, *Early Christian Rhetoric*, p. 30.

**221**

*Annotated Bible* says of the first letter that its various themes "are frequently reintroduced, and often blend into one another, like the leading refrains of a great musical composition."[3] This imagery extends even to individual parts of the gospel. Bultmann speaks for many commentators when he describes the prologue to the gospel (John 1:1–18) as an "overture . . . singling out particular motifs from the action to be unfolded."[4] The gospel and letters of John give the impression of carefully composed wholes, of being a response to the internal dynamics of the genius and vision of the author rather than to the external dynamics of a concrete historical situation and need. As a consequence, it is extraordinarily difficult to answer any historical questions about these works. While we can say with some certainty what circumstances called forth the gospel of Mark and can identify the "scribes and Pharisees" with whom the evangelist Matthew was so furiously in dialogue, and even have a fairly clear idea of the issues that impelled the author of Luke-Acts to write a two-volume work rather than a one-volume gospel, it is very difficult to make similar statements about the gospel of John. Recently some progress has been made, and this progress will be reflected in what follows. But our comments in this instance are very much more tentative than they were in our discussions of the synoptic gospels.

## HISTORICAL QUESTIONS
## CONCERNING THE GOSPEL AND LETTERS

### Authorship

The gospel itself identifies its author as "the disciple whom Jesus loved" (John 21:20–24; compare 19:35) but does not name him. Church tradition identified him as John, the son of Zebedee, one of the inner group of disciples singled out for special mention in the gospel of Mark. He was supposed to have lived to a great age in Ephesus and to have written the gospel there. The author of the second and third letters identifies himself simply as the "presbyter" ("elder"), and there is a presbyter John who is a shadowy figure in early Christian tradition. Before considering the identity of the author, though, we have to examine the unity of authorship of the gospel and letters of John and the integrity of the gospel itself.

### *The unity of authorship of the gospel and letters*

Are the gospel and letters from the same author? They have a unity of general style, tone, and thought that seems to indicate they are, especially in the case of the letters and the discourses in the gospel. But a closer

[3]*Oxford Annotated Bible*, p. 1482.
[4]Bultmann, *The Gospel of John*, p. 13.

examination reveals a poverty of style in the first letter compared to the gospel—"the author works to death a few favorite constructions, and his vocabulary is more limited than that of the gospel"[5]—and some real differences in thought. The latter aspect of the matter is particularly important since these differences concern eschatology and the sacraments. The author of the letter has a strong hope for the future, a version of the traditional Christian hope for the parousia (2:17, 18, 28; 3:2, 3; 4:17), and he has a great interest in the sacraments of the church (2:12, 20, 27; 3:9; 5:1, 6). In the gospel of John the main thrust is toward a denial of the hope of the parousia, on the grounds that the first coming of Jesus was the decisive event and no further coming, no further judgment, is to be expected (3:16–21, 36, and elsewhere). But throughout the gospel are individual sayings that express the more traditional Christian hope (5:27–29; 6:39–40; 44b, 54; 12:48). Similarly with the sacraments: the gospel as a whole puts its major emphasis on the idea that men are brought to faith by their response to the church's proclamation (3:31–36 and elsewhere), and has no particular concern for the sacraments. Yet the words "water and" in 3:5 make that verse an unmistakable reference to baptism, where no such reference exists apart from those two words; 6:51b–58 makes the discourse on the bread of life sacramental, whereas without those verses it is not; and 19:34b–35 introduces an allusion to baptism as it interrupts the continuity of the narrative.

These indications suggest that the gospel has been redacted from an original text with no future parousia hope or concern for the sacraments, and that such hope and concern were introduced into the gospel by the author of the first letter.[6] If this is the case (and it is all very tentative), the main text of the gospel is by one author and the first letter by another. Are either of these authors the "presbyter" who wrote the second and third letters? There are similarities of language and thought, yet there are small subtle differences.[7] We simply do not know; the most we can say is that probably at least two authors are involved in the gospels and letters of John, and perhaps three. What is important is that the similarities of style, tone, and thought point to the existence of a Johannine "school." Whether the final form of these texts is the work of one author, or two, or three, their ideas, theology, contents, tone, and style have taken shape not in the mind of one man, but in a group, probably formed of one strong leader and a few intimate followers.

## The integrity of the text of the gospel

Though it is possible that the original gospel of John had been redacted by someone with more interest in the parousia hope and sacraments of the

---

[5]Fuller, *Intro.*, p. 178.

[6]Suggested by Marxsen, *Intro.*, p. 262, who sees the author of 1 John as a member of a group who redacted the original text of the gospel in the interests of the church's views on eschatology and the sacraments.

[7]The differences are listed in Kümmel, *Intro.*, p. 315, but Kümmel himself dismisses them as "too trivial to be taken seriously."

church, there is no textual evidence for this redaction of the gospel. We do not know of any text of the gospel ever circulated that did not include the references to the future hope and sacraments of the church. If the redaction took place—and we think it did—it occurred before any text of the gospel actually circulated outside the immediate members of the Johannine school.

Equally, we know no text of the gospel ever circulated that did not include chapter 21. Yet that chapter is all but universally recognized to have been a supplement to the original text of the gospel.[8] In the first place, 20:30–31 reads like the original ending to the gospel. Then in 21:2 the sons of Zebedee, who are missing in chapters 1–20, suddenly appear. Further, like the commissioning scene in Matthew 28, the resurrection appearance of Jesus in chapter 21 takes place in Galilee, whereas in chapter 20 the appearances are located in Jerusalem, as in Luke-Acts. The traditions are here in conflict. John 21:24 seems designed to identify the "disciple whom Jesus loved" as the author of the gospel, and it could not have come from the author of the gospel itself. So, in any case, 1:1–21:23 has to be differentiated from 21:24–25. But the differentiation should come earlier, at the beginning of chapter 21, because in addition to the factors we have already mentioned there are some important differences between the Greek of chapter 21 and that of chapters 1–20.[9] It seems probable, therefore, that chapter 21 was added to the original chapters 1–20 of the gospel, but before the text of the gospel had actually circulated outside the immediate group of the Johannine school.

A natural question is whether the same person, who may possibly have been the author of the first letter, added chapter 21 and the redaction in the interest of the parousia and the sacraments. This is another question whose answer we simply do not have, but it is interesting that in 21:22 the traditional Christian parousia hope is implied.

Most responsible modern translations relegate the story of the adulteress (7:53–8:11) to the margin, because the best Greek manuscripts do not include it at all; when it does appear, it is either marked with asterisks or other signs to indicate that it is dubious, or it is included' at different places. Some manuscripts have it after John 7:36, others after John 21:24, others after Luke 21:38. It is a traditional story about Jesus that circulated in the church and that various scribes inserted at various places throughout the New Testament as they transcribed it. It so happened that the texts from which the King James Version was translated had it at John 7:53–8:11, but it is not written in the Johannine style and has no claim to a place in John. Indeed, it has no claim to a place in the text of the New Testament at all, which is in some ways tragic, since it is one of the most challenging of all the stories told about Jesus.

## The Gospel of John and Its Sources

Does the gospel of John use sources? We leave for our next section the question

---

[8]Kümmel, *Intro.,* p. 148.
[9]Given in Kümmel, *Intro.,* pp. 148–49.

of the use of the synoptic gospels or of synoptic gospel traditions. But there is one source whose use must be recognized: a signs source.[10]

In 2:11 Jesus' miracle at Cana is described as "the first of his signs." Further signs are mentioned in general terms in 2:23, and in 4:54 the healing of the official's son at Capernaum is described as "the second sign that Jesus did when he had come from Judea to Galilee." Then 12:37 says, "Though he had done so many signs before them, yet they did not believe in him," and this note is sounded again in the closing summary of the gospel proper, 20:30–31: "Now Jesus did many other signs in the presence of the disciples, which are not written in this book; but these are written that you may believe. . . ." The possibility that in his narrative up to 12:37 the evangelist has used a source other than the synoptic gospels or the tradition represented by those gospels is strengthened since all the other miracles in John that are not paralleled in the synoptic gospels occur before 12:37: the healing at the pool of Bethzatha (5:1–9); the healing of the blind man (9:1–12); the raising of Lazarus (11:1–44). These miracles are generally on a grander and more elaborate scale than those in the synoptic gospels and seem to go further in presenting Jesus as a Hellenistic "divine man." Throughout the gospel until 12:37–38, and again in 20:30–31, the miracles are presented as intending to call forth faith: 2:11; 4:53; 6:14; 7:31; 11:45, 47b–48; 12:37–38; 20:31. Whereas in the synoptic gospels the emphasis is on faith as the prerequisite for miracles (e.g., Mark 6:5–6), here in the gospel of John miracles induce faith. These references not only contrast with the synoptic gospels, they also contrast with the remainder of the gospel of John itself. In 2:23–25 as in 4:48, Jesus repudiates the kind of faith induced by signs. The conversation with Nicodemus contrasts such faith unfavorably with rebirth "from above" and "of the spirit" (3:2, 3, 5–6). These factors make it very probable that the author of the gospel of John is using as a source and *reinterpreting* a book of signs that presents Jesus as a Hellenistic "divine man" whose miracles induce faith.

A further source has been offered in connection with the discourses in the gospel. Long extended discourses are a striking feature of the gospel and Bultmann suggests that they derive from gnostic revelation discourses.[11] But the language and style of these discourses is so thoroughly Johannine and their thought so integral to the gospel and letters as a whole that the hypothesis of a discourse source has not found general acceptance.[12]

But the author of the gospel of John had a model for his discourses. Hellenistic religion in general knows many discourses in which a revealer deity explains who and what he is in a speech using the formula "I am. . . ." One is known in connection with the Egyptian goddess Isis.[13]

[10]The thesis that John uses a signs source has been argued strongly and carefully by R.W. Fortna, *The Gospel of Signs: A Reconstruction of the Narrative Source Underlying the Fourth Gospel* (1970).

[11]Bultmann, *The Gospel of John*, passim.

[12]Marxsen is a member of the "Bultmann school" and hence sympathetic to Bultmann's views. So his judgment that Bultmann's suggestion of a discourse source is "by no means so certain as is the use of the 'signs source'" is particularly important (*Intro.*, p. 253).

[13]Quoted from Grant, *Hellenistic Religions*, pp. 131–32.

I am Isis, the mistress of every land, and
I was taught by Hermes, and with Hermes
I devised letters, both the sacred and the
demotic, that all things might not be written
with the same letters.
I gave and ordained laws for men . . .
I divided the earth from the heaven . . .
I made an end to murders . . .

Another is found in connection with Poimandres, a revealer figure in Hellenistic literature roughly contemporary with the Johannine literature.[14]

[The revealer appears to the speaker in a vision] "Who are you?" I said. "I am Poimandres," said he, "the Mind of the Sovereignty. I know what you wish, and I am with you everywhere . . . Keep in mind the things you wish to learn and I will teach you."

The idea of a revelatory discourse in the first-person singular using the formula "I am . . . " has provided the gospel of John with its immediate model. Within the general framework of the model, the development is, however, thoroughly Johannine.


## The Gospel of John and the Synoptic Gospels


Was the gospel of John written with a knowledge of the synoptic gospels, or any one of them? That question has never been answered by a consensus of scholarly opinion. There are obvious and immediate differences between John and the synoptics in style and presentation of material. The long discourses on themes characteristic of Christian piety, which are not pieced together out of separate sayings as are the discourses in the synoptics but evolve as complex monologues or dramatic dialogues, are a good example. Then the chronological and topographical framework of the gospel is different. John envisages a ministry of Jesus beginning with the joint activity with the Baptist and featuring several extended ministries in Jerusalem. The synoptics have Jesus begin his ministry only after John was imprisoned, and it lasts one year and includes only one visit to Jerusalem. Further, only a limited number of incidents in John have parallels in the synoptics: a call of disciples (1:35–51); the healing of the official's son (4:46–53); a feeding followed by a sea miracle (6:1–21); Peter's confession (6:66–70); the triumphal entry into Jerusalem (12:12–15); the cleansing of the Temple (2:13–22); the anointing at Bethany (12:1–8); the Last Supper with a prophecy of betrayal (13:1–11); and the general story of the passion itself. By the same token, John has incidents unknown to the synoptics: the wedding at Cana (2:1–11); the narratives concerning Nicodemus (3:1–21) and the Samaritan woman (4:7–42); the healing at the

[14]Dodd, *The Interpretation of the Fourth Gospel*, pp. 10–53; Barrett, *New Testament Background*, pp. 80–90. Our quote is from Barrett, p. 82.

pool of Bethzatha (5:1–9);[15] the healing of the man born blind (9:1–12); and the raising of Lazarus (11:1–44), which is the direct cause of the plot to put Jesus to death (11:45–53). Furthermore, there are no parables in John, while parables are a major feature of the teaching of Jesus in the synoptic gospels.

This combination of agreement and disagreement between the gospel of John and the synoptic gospels makes the question of John's knowledge of the synoptic gospels very difficult.

## Differences in style and presentation

The differences in style and presentation are real, but they are due to the meditative and reflective character of the material in the gospel of John. Let us take the parallels and contrasts between John 12:25–26 and Mark 8:34–35.

| John 12:25–26 | Mark 8:34–35 |
|---|---|
| He who loves his life loses it, and he who hates his life in this world will keep it for eternal life. If anyone serves me he must follow me; and where I am, there shall my servant be also; if any one serves me the Father will honor him. | If any man would come after me, let him deny himself and take up his cross and follow me. For whoever would save his life will lose it; and whoever loses his life for my sake and the gospel's will save it. |

The parallels of the theme of following Jesus and losing and saving one's life indicate a relationship between the two. The differences are so great, however, that we might conclude that the texts were not related to one another directly but to a common tradition that had undergone independent development in different directions before each evangelist used it. But then we note that the differences between John and Mark represent interests characteristic of John, what in the synoptic gospels we would call redactional concerns: "hating life in this world"; "eternal life"; "where I am, there shall my servant be also"; "the Father will honor him." When we recognize that the Johannine material has gone through a considerable period and process of reflection and meditation it is by no means evident that John 12:25–26 does not exhibit knowledge of Mark 8:34–35.

## Differences in the order of events

The differences in the order of the events between John and the synoptic gospels (really between John and Mark since Matthew and Luke in general

---

[15]Note, however, the striking parallels between the command to the paralytic here and that to the paralytic at Capernaum in Mark 2:9. They are verbally identical.

follow the order of Mark) are also not grounds for denying John's knowledge of the synoptic gospels. John is simply not following the order of Mark; down to 12:37–38 he is probably building around his signs source; 13–17 are thematic discourses and a prayer; from 18:1 onward we have the passion narrative. Whether he *knows* the order of Mark is a different matter, dependent on the sequence of agreements with Mark and whether John knows a passion narrative independent of that in Mark.

### Sequence of agreements with the Markan order

Despite the great differences between John and Mark, the following events occur in the same sequence: the work of the Baptist, Jesus' departure to Galilee, the feeding of a multitude, walking on the water, Peter's confession, the departure to Jerusalem, the entry into Jerusalem and the anointing (order of these two transposed by John), the supper with predictions of betrayal and denial, the arrest and the passion narrative. Apart from the fact that the gospel story necessarily climaxes in a passion narrative, this is an impressive list and can be weakened only by supposing an independent cycle of tradition linking the feeding and the walking on the water,[16] which would depend on a prior decision on other grounds that John does not know Mark. We have taken the list from C. K. Barrett's *The Gospel According to St. John*, pages 34–36, where Barrett considerably strengthens the case by pointing to a whole series of verbal similarities between John and Mark in precisely these passages that occur in the same order.

### The passion narrative in John and Mark

The similarities and differences we have mentioned neither demonstrate that John knew the gospel of Mark nor necessarily deny it. In the passion narrative, however, the correspondence between the two gospels becomes much closer. For a long time the general opinion of New Testament scholars was that the passion narrative existed as a connected unit before the gospel of Mark was written, and it was easy and natural to think that John had known and used a version of that pre-Markan narrative rather than the gospel of Mark. But today the tendency is to ascribe more and more of the composition of the passion narrative to the evangelist Mark himself[17] and to doubt the very existence of a pre-Markan and non-Markan passion narrative extensive enough to have been the basis for the gospel of John. A particular consideration is the fact that the trial before the High Priest (John 18:19–24) is set in the context of the denial by Peter (18:15–18, 25–27), as it is also in the gospel of Mark. But there is a strong case that Mark himself originally composed this account of

[16] As for example in Fuller, *Intro.*, p. 82, n. 2.
[17] See especially Kelber, Kalenkow, Scroggs, "Reflections on the Question: Was There a Pre-Markan Passion Narrative?" *The Society of Biblical Literature One Hundred Seventh Annual Meeting Seminar Papers*, vol. 2, pp. 503–85.

the trial at night before the Jewish authorities and then set it in the context of the story of Peter's denial. If this is so, the evangelist John must necessarily have known the gospel of Mark.[18]

### Verbal similarities between John and the other gospels

For all the differences between the gospel of John and the other gospels, there are some verbal parallels at various points. In John and Mark there is the command to (different) paralytics in John 5:8 = Mark 2:11, "Rise, take up your pallet and go home." Equally striking are John 6:7 = Mark 6:37, "bread (worth) two hundred denarii," and John 12:3 = Mark 14:3, "a pound (jar) of costly ointment of pure nard." In all three, only John and Mark among the gospels share this wording.[19] In John and Luke the argument really turns on the account of the anointing (John 12:3–8 = Luke 7:36–50). All the names in John occur in Luke at various places, and John's version of the anointing (Mary anoints Jesus' feet and wipes them with her hair, itself a not very reasonable process) is explicable if John knew the gospel of Luke, where the woman wipes Jesus' feet with her hair and then anoints them. In Mark 14:3–9, by contrast, the woman anoints Jesus' head, and there is no mention of her hair. The references to the woman anointing the feet and drying them with her hair that Luke and John have in common may indicate that John knew the Lukan account.

These are the considerations on which a decision as to whether the evangelist John knew the other gospels must be based. Obviously, they do not point overwhelmingly in one direction or the other, but they have convinced the present writer that the gospel of John shows knowledge of the gospel of Mark, and perhaps also of the gospel of Luke.

### The Date of the Gospel and Letters of John

In attempting to date the gospel there are three factors to take into account. The earliest text we have of any part of the New Testament is a fragment of the gospel of John. It is a papyrus fragment containing parts of John 18:31–33, 37–38, discovered in Egypt, and scholars consider it to have been written in the first half of the second century.[20] The gospel must have been written early enough for it to have circulated in Egypt early in the second century. A date later than A.D. 100 is, therefore, out of the question.

There is also a comment in the story of the healing of the man born blind in chapter 9; where we read, "the Jews had already agreed that if anyone should confess him to be Christ, he was to be put out of the synagogue" (9:22). This is to be considered a reference to a benediction introduced into Jewish synagogue

[18]Donahue, *Are you the Christ? The Trial Narrative in the Gospel of Mark*, makes a convincing argument for the supposition that Mark composed the trial scene and intercalated it into the denial story in his gospel. If this is the case then John must have known Mark since he also has the trial scene and he has it in the same place.

[19]Kümmel, *Intro.*, p. 144, lists other parallels.

[20]Brown, *The Gospel According to John*, vol. 1, LXXXIII with references.

worship by the rabbis meeting at Jamnia after the fall of Jerusalem.[21] It ran as follows:

> For the apostates let there be no hope
> And let the arrogant government be
> speedily uprooted in our days.
> Let the Nazarenes [Christians] and
> the Minim [heretics] be destroyed
> in a moment.
> And let them be blotted out of the
> Book of life and not be inscribed
> together with the righteous.
> Blessed art thou, O Lord, who humblest
> the proud!

The reorganization of Judaism that became necessary after the catastrophe of the Jewish War needed to establish the unity of the Jewish community and guard it against the threat of heresy. The worldwide Jewish community no longer had the geographical center of Jerusalem and its Temple; it was urgent to establish a center of theological belief and religious practice and to protect that center against the corrosion of heterodoxy and heresy. The benediction was one way of achieving this end, because its presence in the synagogue liturgy would force out of the synagogue community those who knew themselves to be designated Nazarenes or Minim. The most plausible date for the composition of this benediction and its introduction into the synagogue liturgy is A.D. 80–90.[22] So if John 9:22 is a reference to the benediction, as it seems to be, the gospel has to be dated at or after that time.

A third factor is whether the author of John knew of the synoptic gospels. The dates of the synoptic gospels are reasonably certain: Mark shortly before or more probably shortly after A.D. 70, and Matthew and Luke a generation later. If John does know Mark and Luke, its date has to be toward the end of the period 80–100, but if not, it can be much earlier. Since the present writer holds that John does know Mark and perhaps also Luke, he naturally inclines to a date toward the end of the first century.

It therefore seems probable that the gospel of John is to be dated about A.D. 90, and the close relationship between the gospel and letters would indicate a similar date for the letters.

## Displacements Within the Text of the Gospel

The careful reader of the gospel of John is struck by a number of inconsistencies in the narrative. For example, 3:31–36 simply does not fit the theme of the testimony of the Baptist but reads more like a follow-up of 3:16–21. Is it possible that 3:22–30 is out of place and should be read as following 2:12? Again, in 6:1 it is presupposed that Jesus is in Galilee, though

---

[21]In our consideration of this benediction and its relationship to the writing of the gospel of John we are indebted to Martyn, *History and Theology in the Fourth Gospel.*
[22]Brown, *John*, vol. 1, LXXXV.

in 5:1 he is already in Jerusalem. Should chapters 5, 6, and 7 be read in the order 6, 5, 7? John 7:15–24 is concerned with the plot against Jesus' life reported in 5:18 and reads like the natural continuation of 5:47, whereas 14:1, 25–31 is also a very natural sequence. Did 7:15–24 originally follow 5:47? In 14:31 Jesus says "Rise, let us go hence," yet the discourses continue for three more chapters. Does 14:31 belong after 17:26 as the conclusion of the discourses?

There is no doubt that the flow of the narrative would be improved by answering these questions in the affirmative and making the necessary transpositions. However, once we begin to do this the question becomes, where do we stop? Bultmann, for example, in *The Gospel of John* comments on the text in an order that is extraordinarily complex, and one has the feeling that equally good arguments could be made for a different arrangement. In a text as reflective and meditative in character as the gospel of John, narrative consistency is not to be expected, and if there are displacements within the text they do not affect our general understanding of it. In our exegetical survey we shall accept only the first of the possibilities mentioned here.

## THE STRUCTURE OF THE GOSPEL[23]

The gospel of John falls naturally into five main parts:

1. **Introduction**: **Prologue and Testimony**, 1:1–51. In the prologue (1:1–18) a christological hymn is presented with comments, and then a series of incidents bring John the Baptist on the scene to give his testimony to Jesus, testimony confirmed by some of his disciples.

2. **The Book of Signs**, 2:1–12:50. Even before the general recognition of the use of a "signs source" in this part of the gospel, C. H. Dodd recognized the essential nature of these narratives by giving it this title.

3. **Farewell Discourses and Prayer for the Church**, 13:1–17:26. These discourses and the prayer are found in the context of the Lord's Supper (13:2; compare 1 Cor 11:20), and they meditate on the nature, meaning, and significance of the passion of Jesus.

4. **Passion Narrative**, 18:1–20:30.

5. **Epilogue**: **The Appearance in Galilee**, 21:1–25

Dodd points out that there is a characteristic Johannine pattern of narration.[24] It consists of the following elements, as seen in chapter 5:

ACTION: 5:1–9 (healing at Bethzatha)
DIALOGUE: 5:10–18 (Sabbath healing)
MONOLOGUE: 5:19–40
APPENDIX: 5:41–47

[23]In what follows we are deeply indebted to Dodd, *The Interpretation of the Fourth Gospel*.
[24]Ibid., p. 400.

Or it can be, as in chapter 6:

> ACTION AND DRAMATIC DIALOGUE: 6:1–23 (feeding of the multitude)
> DIALOGUE TENDING TO MONOLOGUE: 6:24–59 (bread of life)
> TWO BRIEF CONCLUDING DIALOGUES: 6:60–65, 66–71

Or it can be, as in chapters 9 and 10:

> ACTION: 9:1–7 (healing at Siloam)
> DIALOGUES: 9:8–41 (trial scene and two brief colloquies)
> MONOLOGUE: 10:1–18
> BRIEF CONCLUDING DIALOGUE: 10: 19–21
> APPENDIX: 10:22–39

The farewell discourses and prayer follow this pattern, except that in this instance we have the action, the passion narrative, coming last and not first.

> OPENING DRAMATIC SCENE: 13:1–30
> DIALOGUE: 13:31–14:31 (on Christ's departure and return)
> MONOLOGUE: 15:1–16:15 (on Christ and his Church)
> CONCLUDING DIALOGUE: 16:16–33
> APPENDIX: 17:1–26 (the prayer for the Church)
> ACTION: 18:1–20:31 (the passion narrative; anticipated in 13:1–3)

This is a very important structural observation, and we take it seriously as we attempt the following exegetical survey of the gospel, though at some points our analysis differs slightly from Dodd's; for example, our experience with the other gospels has led us to pay particular attention to transitional passages.

## EXEGETICAL SURVEY OF THE GOSPEL OF JOHN

### Introduction: Prologue and Testimony, 1:1–51

*Prologue, 1:1–18*

The prologue consists of a hymn with comments. As reconstructed and translated by R. E. Brown, the hymn reads as follows.[25]

In the beginning was the Word;
the Word was in God's presence,
and the Word was God.
He was present with God in the beginning.

[25]Excerpts from *The Gospel According to John* by Raymond E. Brown, copyright © 1970 by Doubleday & Company, Inc. Brown's translation and discussion of the hymn are in vol. 1, pp. 3–23.

Through him all things came into being,
and apart from him not a thing came to be.
That which had come to be in him was life,
and this life was the light of men.
The light shines in darkness,
for the darkness did not overcome it.

He was in the world,
and the world was made by him;
Yet the world did not recognize him.
To his own he came;
Yet his own people did not accept him.
But all those who did accept him
he empowered to become God's children.

And the Word became flesh
and made his dwelling among us.
And we have seen his glory,
the glory of an only Son coming from the Father,
filled with enduring love.

And of his fullness
we have all had a share—
love in place of love.

The comments on this hymn are in effect the testimony of the Baptist
(verses 6–8), the reference to being born "of God" (verse 13), further testimony
of the Baptist (verse 15), and the evangelist's climactic summary (verses
17–18). These comments all represent important themes to the evangelist,
which are further developed in the gospel: the testimony of the Baptist
(1:19–42); being born of God is the theme of the dialogue with Nicodemus
(3:1–15); while verses 17–18 are a summary of the whole gospel, not only of the
prologue. The hymn itself presents features foreign to the gospel—in the gospel
after the prologue Jesus is never called the Logos nor is the phrase *grace and
truth* found—but its presentation of Jesus as the pre-existent redeemer who
manifested his glory in the world matches exactly the major aspects of the
gospel's presentation of Jesus. In its presentation of Jesus as the redeemer who
descends to the world the hymn shares the emphasis of the other christological
hymns we discussed in chapter 3.

*Testimony, 1:19–51; 3:22–30*

The theme of testimony, prominent in the comments on the hymn in the
prologue is now developed with regard to John the Baptist, and with regard to
some of his disciples who become disciples of Jesus. Originally, 3:22–30
followed 1:51. It has been accidentally displaced.

**The Book of Signs, 2:1–12:50**

The first major section of the gospel, the Book of Signs, is built on the skeleton
framework of seven miracle stories or "signs." These are as follows:

- Changing water into wine at Cana (2:1–11)
- Curing the official's son at Cana (4:46–54)
- Curing the paralytic at Bethzatha (5:1–15)
- Miraculous feeding in Galilee (6:1–15)
- Walking on the water (6:16–21)
- Curing the blind man in Jerusalem (9)
- Raising of Lazarus in Bethany (11)

In addition, there is a series of three consecutive thematic concerns:[26]

(a) From Cana to Cana—Jesus manifests his glory in various ways and elicits various responses (2:1–4:42)

(b) Jesus and the principal feasts of the Jews (5:1–10:39)

(c) Jesus moves toward the hour of his glorification (11:1–12:50)

With these observations as our starting point and with Dodd's compositional insight as our guide, we offer the following exegetical survey of the Book of Signs.

### Manifestation and response, 2:1–4:42

ACTION

*The first sign: the miracle at Cana*, 2:1–11. It is explicitly stated that this is the first of the signs through which Jesus manifested his glory, and that it elicited the response of faith (verse 11).
   Transition, 2:12.
*The anticipation of the final sign: the cleansing of the Temple in Jerusalem*, 2:13–22. The cleansing of the Temple is not itself a sign, but it anticipates the climactic sign, the resurrection. In turn, the resurrection elicits the response of faith (verse 22).
   Transitional summary, 2:23–25.

DIALOGUE

*Jesus and Nicodemus*, 3:1–15. This dialogue is built on the theme of the new birth (compare the theme of being born "of God" in the prologue). It climaxes in a Son of Man saying (verses 14–15), which is itself a major statement of the Johannine theology.

MONOLOGUE

*The power of the Son to give eternal life to the believer*, 3:16–21. The evangelist now moves into a monologue developing the theme of the Son's power to give eternal life to the believer, stated in the preceding verse. The traditional Christian future eschatology has been replaced by an

---

[26]On this we are indebted to Brown, *John*, vol. 1, CXL–CXLI.

eschatology realized in the present (a realized eschatology): "This is the judgment . . . " (verse 19). The farewell discourses parallel the same theme (12:46–48), where, however, the traditional eschatology has been restored ("the word that I have spoken will be his judge on the last day," 12:48).

A *displaced section of monologue;* 3:31–36. John 3:22–30 originally belonged after 1:51. But what about 3:31–36, obviously part of a monologue by the Johannine Jesus on the theme of witness, testimony, and belief? It does not fit well after 3:21; perhaps it originally belonged after 3:15, where it would certainly fit better, but we cannot be sure.

ACTION

*Jesus moves to Samaria,* 4:1–6.

DIALOGUE

*Jesus with the woman,* 4:7–21. The dialogue turns on two themes, "living water" and worship "in spirit and truth." Water is a universal symbol for life, and worship is a universal religious practice. John develops them in his characteristic dualism by contrasting "this" and "living" water, false worship and true.

MONOLOGUE

*The coming of the true worship,* 4:22–26. The second theme of the dialogue now develops in a short but characteristic monologue culminating in an interchange between Jesus and the woman and in a Messianic claim by Jesus. The theme of living water is not further developed here; the evangelist will return to that later.

APPENDIX

*Further dialogue and testimony in Samaria,* 4:27–42.

*Transition to Galilee,* 4:43–45.

*The second sign: the official's son in Capernaum,* 4:46–54. While in Cana, Jesus heals an official's son from a distance. This second sign in Cana marks the end of the first section of the Book of Signs. It ends as it had begun—in Cana and with a sign.

## Jesus and the Jewish festivals, 5:1–10:39

The second section of the Book of Signs explores the significance of Jesus as understood in the symbolism and meaning of the great Jewish religious festivals and observances.

**Jesus and the Sabbath,** 5:1–47. The Sabbath is a weekly observance, built on Gen 2:3: "so God blessed the seventh day and hallowed it, because on it God rested from all his work which he had done in creation." The Jews kept, and still keep, this day of the week free from work for religious observance, to link themselves ever more closely with God. This observance led to the question of what was to be considered "work" on the Sabbath, which is the background for such synoptic gospel controversy stories as Mark 2:23–27, the Plucking of the Grain. In the fourth gospel, however, the aspect of controversy between Jesus and the Jews as to what "work" was lawful on the Sabbath has been transformed into a meditation on the fact that Jesus "works" as God "works," to give life to the dead and to judge.

*Transitional verse, 5:1.* This verse speaks of a "feast," i.e., a religious festival, but the term is used broadly, since the concern is not with an annual religious observance but with the Sabbath.

ACTION

*Jesus heals a lame man on the Sabbath, 5:2–9.* The exact parallelism between the command to this paralytic and that to the paralytic in Capernaum in Mark 2:9 is striking; it is cause for arguing that John knew the gospel of Mark. But the meditative character of the Johannine narrative is such that it leaves in the dark how far and in what ways this story is related to Mark 2:1–12. All the narratives in the Book of Signs have been so transformed into vehicles for meditation on the significance of Jesus for the believer that historical questions about them are all but impossible to answer.

DIALOGUE

*A series of dialogues between the Jews, the man, and Jesus, 5:10–18.* By means of these dialogues, the evangelist introduces the theme of the relationship between Jesus and God. Jesus is the Son of the Father, and equal with God.

MONOLOGUE

*Jesus' relation to God, 5:19–47.* This monologue explores the relationship of Jesus and God. Jesus is the Son of God, and as such his actions are identical with those of God: he judges, and he gives life to the dead.

**Jesus and the Passover,** 6:1–71. The Passover celebrates the deliverance of the Jewish people from Egypt. It is observed annually by a meal in which the food eaten and the wine drunk symbolize this deliverance and anticipate the final eschatological deliverance. The Christian Eucharist was based on the Passover and uses much of the same symbolism. The evangelist John now explores the significance of Jesus in terms of Passover and Eucharistic symbols.

ACTION

*The feeding of the multitude, 6:1–14*
    Transitional verse, 6:15
*The walking on the water, 6:16–21.*
    The two incidents of a miraculous feeding and a sea miracle undoubtedly come to John through the tradition of the church, and probably through the gospel of Mark, which has them in exactly the same sequence: Mark 6:30–44 (feeding); 45–51 (walking on the water). John's gospel maintains them because they both have parallels in the narrative of the deliverance from Egypt: the Jews miraculously crossed the sea (Exod 14:21–25) and were equally miraculously fed in the wilderness (Exod 16:13–16, "It is the

bread which the Lord has given you to eat." In Exod 16:31 this bread is called *manna*).

DIALOGUE

A *dialogue between Jesus and the Jews on the bread that God gives to man,* 6:22–34. John follows his usual pattern of introducing the theme of the ensuing monologue by means of a dialogue. The theme is the "bread of life," and it evokes both the manna of the wilderness and the bread of the Eucharist.

MONOLOGUE

*Jesus as the bread of life,* 6:35–40.

DIALOGUE

*The bread of life is the flesh of Jesus, the bread of the Eucharist,* 6:41–59. The theme of Jesus as the "bread of life" is developed in a monologue, which in turn is followed by a dramatic dialogue. The manna the Jewish people ate in the wilderness has become a symbol of the life-giving power of God to his people, which is now fulfilled forever in Jesus. The life-giving power of Jesus is in turn symbolized in the bread of the Christian Eucharist.

APPENDIX

*Jesus and his disciples,* 6:60–70. In its theme, this passage is strikingly reminiscent of the misunderstanding and confession in Mark 8:14–21.

*Transition to the feast of Tabernacles,* 7:1–13. Jesus is now to be considered in light of the symbolism of a further major Jewish festival, the feast of Tabernacles.

**Jesus and the feast of Tabernacles,** 7:14–10:21. The feast of Tabernacles was held in the autumn. It was originally an agricultural festival celebrating the harvest, but in the course of time it came also to celebrate the constant renewal of the covenant between God and his people. This latter fact makes it natural to take up here the theme of Jesus as the one who fulfills the old covenant as the Jewish Messiah. So in this section the evangelist explores the messianic claims of Jesus and also makes extensive use of the literary device of dramatic dialogues between Jesus and his Jewish opponents about those claims.

ACTION

*Jesus in the Temple at Tabernacles,* 7:14.

DIALOGUE

*The claim of Jesus to be the Christ,* 7:15–36. This is a series of three dramatic dialogues. The first (verses 15–24) concerns the authority of Jesus to heal on the Sabbath; the second (verses 25–31) the claim of Jesus to be the Christ by the signs he has done; the third (verses 32–36) introduces the theme of the death of Jesus. This last will loom larger and larger from this point on in the gospel, until it dominates everything else as the theme of the farewell discourses.

ACTION

*Jesus makes a personal claim to be the Living Water, 7:37–39.* At the feast of Tabernacles, water was ceremoniously carried from the Pool of Siloam to the Temple as a reminder of the water miraculously supplied in the wilderness (Num 20:2–13) and as a symbol of the coming of the Messiah as the "water of life" (Isa 12:3). The evangelist has the opportunity to return to the theme of Jesus as the water of life, which he had first stated in the dialogue between Jesus and the woman of Samaria in chapter 4.

DIALOGUE

*The Jews dispute among themselves concerning the claim of Jesus to be the Christ, 7:40–52.* Unlike the previous dialogues, these do not feature Jesus at all but present the Jews in dispute among themselves concerning the validity of his claims.

[The adulteress story, 7:53–8:11, is not part of the original text of the gospel.]

ACTION

*Jesus makes a personal claim to be the Light of the World, 8:12.* A further feature of the symbolism of the feast of Tabernacles was the ceremonious lighting of lamps in the Temple court. The evangelist can return to the theme of Jesus as the Light of the World, a theme first stated in the prologue (1:4–5, 9).

DIALOGUE

*The validity of Jesus' claims, 8:13–20.* The Jews are presented as disputing with Jesus the validity of the claims he is making. This dialogue concludes on a further note of anticipation of the passion (verse 20).

ACTION

*Jesus condemns the Jews, 8:21.* The theme of the death of Jesus understood as his going where he cannot be followed (i.e., back to the heavenly region he came from) is developed at length in the farewell discourses (13:31–14:7). Here is its first statement in the context of a condemnation of the Jews, who cannot follow him. In the farewell discourses, the disciples are promised that they will be able to follow him.

DIALOGUE

*Jesus and the Jews who do not believe in him, 8:22–30.* Jesus is here presented as debating vigorously with, and condemning, the Jews who did not believe in him.

ACTION

*Jesus and the Jews who did believe in him, 8:31–32.* Jesus is now presented as making promises to the Jews who did believe in him.

DIALOGUE

*Jesus and the natural claims of the Jews on God, 8:33–59.* This dialogue begins with the Jews who did believe in Jesus and ends with those same Jews taking up stones to throw at him: here is the evangelist wrestling with the problem of the Jewish rejection of Jesus. Jesus himself had had some success in his mission to the Jewish people—he had attracted disciples— yet the Jews had finally engineered his crucifixion. Similarly, the Christians had had some success in their mission to the Jews, especially among the Greek-speaking Jews of the Dispersion, yet the Jews at Jamnia had finally produced the benediction that drove the the Christian Jews out of the Jewish community. The evangelist anguishes over this tragic pattern in the literary form of a dialogue between Jesus and his Jewish contemporaries.

ACTION

*Jesus gives sight to a man born blind, 9:1–7.* Continuing the theme of Jesus as the Light of the World, the evangelist now presents an account of Jesus giving light to a man born blind.

DIALOGUE

*The fate of Jesus and his followers in the Jewish community, 9:8–41.* In many ways this is the most interesting and complex of the dialogues in the fourth gospel. But the complexities can be unraveled once we realize that what is at issue here in this series of dialogues is the fate of Jesus and his followers in the Jewish community.[27]

The first dialogue is between the man and his neighbors (verses 8–12). It reflects the original impact of Jesus on his Jewish contemporaries and the questions it gave rise to.

The second dialogue is between the man and the Pharisees (verses 13–17). Here the Pharisees represent not only the Jewish authorities who finally condemned Jesus, but also those at Jamnia who produced the benediction banning the Christian Jews from the synagogue.

The third dialogue is between the Jews and the man's parents (verses 18–23). It reflects the problems and divisions within the Jewish community produced by Jesus and his followers and their claims. As we indicated above, verse 22 refers to the benediction against the Nazarenes and the Minim, which came into use in Jewish communities toward the end of the first century A.D.

The fourth dialogue concerns the man himself and his fate at the hands of the Jewish authorities (verses 24–34). It reflects the fate of the Jewish convert to Christianity as the evangelist knows it; perhaps even the fate of the evangelist himself.

The fifth dialogue mirrors the further fate of the man who, now rejected by the Jewish community, finds his new home in the community of those who come to faith in Jesus (verses 35–41). The members of this community in turn reject the community that had rejected them.

These dialogues reveal the actual situation of the evangelist and his readers, just as Mark 13 revealed the situation of the evangelist Mark and

---

[27]In what follows we are heavily indebted to Martyn, *History and Theology in the Fourth Gospel.*

his readers. John and his readers are Hellenistic Jewish Christians who have been rejected from the synagogue community in their city as a consequence of the introduction of the benediction against Nazarenes and Minim.

CONCLUDING MONOLOGUE

*Jesus as the Shepherd and the Sheepgate,* 10:1–18. The evangelist closes this section with a monologue and a dialogue on the messianic claims of Jesus and the response of the Jews. The monologue concerns Jesus as the Shepherd and the Sheepgate. The discourse is an involved allegory in which various images on the care of sheep appear in connection with Jesus. In verses 1–6 Jesus is the shepherd responsible for the sheep and to whom the sheep are responsive. In verses 7–10 he is the gate through which sheep enter and leave their fold. Verses 11–15 introduce the theme of Jesus as the good shepherd prepared to die for his sheep, and Jesus is contrasted in this respect with other "shepherds." Finally, in verses 16–18 Jesus is the shepherd who lays down his life not only for his flock, the Jewish people, but also for the Gentiles.

CONCLUDING DIALOGUE

*The Jews disagree as to the claims of Jesus,* 10:19–21. The section concludes with a dialogue on the varied responses of the Jews to Jesus. This dialogue no doubt reflects the experience of the evangelist as he became a Christian in his own Jewish community.

**Jesus and the feast of Dedication,** 10:22–39. The feast of Dedication celebrates the rededication of the Temple in 164 B.C. after its desecration by Antiochus Epiphanes, who erected an altar to the Greek god Zeus in the Jerusalem Temple. This is the "abomination of desolation" to which such frequent reference is made in Jewish and Christian apocalyptic (e.g., Mark 13:14). Since the festival celebrated a major victory of the people of God against their enemies and was seen as a renewal of the covenant between God and his people, it becomes a suitable occasion for the evangelist to return to his theme of the messianic claims of Jesus.

ACTION

*Jesus at the feast of Dedication,* 10:22–23.

DIALOGUE

*The climactic claims of Jesus and the response of the Jews to them,* 10:24–39. In this dialogue the evangelist presents Jesus as summarizing the claims he has already made for himself. He is the Shepherd and the Giver of Life; he and the Father are one. At the same time a new note is introduced in accordance with the symbolism of the rededication of the Temple, which lies behind the feast of Dedication: Jesus is the one consecrated by God and sent into the world (verse 36). Similarly, the negative response of the Jews is also summarized, and it is presented as reaching a climax. The Jews attempt to stone Jesus (verse 31) as they had before in 8:59; they also attempt to arrest him (verse 39) as they had before in 7:30, 32, 44; 8:20.

*Transition: The end of the public ministry of Jesus, 10:40–42*

The thought of the evangelist is now turning more strongly to the cross, and the last section of his Book of Signs deals with the meaning of the death of Jesus. So this transitional passage marks the end of the public ministry of Jesus; from this point forward we are concerned only with the death of Jesus and its meaning. But the evangelist John thinks in a circular manner. We pointed out that the first part of the Book of Signs began and ended in Cana. Similarly, Jesus appeared on the scene for the first time in this gospel at the place where John was baptizing (1:29–34), and his public ministry must end at that same place, as it does in these transitional verses.

*Jesus moves toward the hour of his glorification, 11:1–12:50*

This is the last section of the Book of Signs. Jesus is still presented as working and teaching in public, but in the mind of the evangelist the public ministry is over, and now everything is dominated by the Cross. In this section, therefore, the evangelist begins the meditation on the death of Jesus and its meaning.

ACTION

*The raising of Lazarus, 11:1–44.* For the reader who comes to the gospel of John after a reading of the synoptic gospels this is a most startling narrative. Not only is it a major miracle of Jesus about which the synoptic gospels appear to know nothing; but also it is presented as the actual occasion for the crucifixion (verses 45–53). Moreover, the Martha and Mary of this story appear also in the gospel of Luke (Luke 10:38–42), where, however, there is absolutely no mention of Lazarus. The historical problems in connection with this story are all but insurmountable, and the best that scholars can do is suggest that the evangelist John is meditating upon an element of early Christian tradition otherwise lost to us.[28] But when all is done and said, the existence of this story alone is evidence that the gospel of John is simply not written at the level of history as "what actually happened." The evangelist is concerned rather with history as the believer's historical existence in the world and the difference that belief in Christ can make to that existence. At this level the story comes alive as a dramatic presentation of Jesus as the resurrection and the life to those who believe in him.

REACTION

*The Jewish authorities condemn Jesus to death, 11:45–53.* The normal pattern of the Johannine literary construction is shattered by the nearness of the Cross. So here we have the reaction of the Jewish authorities to the raising of Lazarus rather than the dialogue and monologue that would normally follow the action.

[28]Brown, *John,* vol. 1, pp. 427–30.

*Transition: Will Jesus come to Jerusalem for the Passover?* 11:54–57. The evangelist dramatically heightens the tension of his narrative in this transitional section.

ACTION

*The anointing at Bethany,* 12:1–8. This scene relates both to Mark 14:3–9, the anointing at Bethany, and to Luke 7:36–38, an anointing of Jesus in Galilee. In the gospel of John, as in Mark, the anointing anticipates the burial of Jesus.

*Transition: The tension in Jerusalem heightens,* 12:9–11.

ACTION

*Jesus enters Jerusalem in triumph,* 12:12–19. This parallels the synoptic gospel accounts of the same incident (Mark 11:1–10; Matt 21:1–9; Luke 19:28–38). In John, however, the incident is interpreted as an anticipation of the glorification of Jesus (verse 16).

ACTION

*The Greeks come to Jesus,* 12:20–22. The evangelist has been concerned thus far in his narrative with Jesus and the Jews, which no doubt reflects his personal position as a member of a Jewish community who became a Christian. But now he turns to Jesus and the Greeks in an incident referring to his being a Christian in a Greek city and preaching the gospel to the Greek world.

DIALOGUE

*The meaning of the Cross,* 12:23–36. The evangelist now returns to his favorite literary device and explores the meaning of the Cross in a dialogue between Jesus and the voice from heaven and between Jesus and the crowd.

*The ending of the Book of Signs,* 12:37–50. The evangelist brings his Book of Signs to an end with a summary of the meaning of the signs of Jesus, meditating on their meeting with the reactions of both nonbelief and belief.

## Farewell Discourses and Prayer for the Church, 13:1–17:26

In this third major section of the gospel the evangelist explores the meaning of Christ for the believer and the church in a series of discourses and a prayer by Jesus at the Last Supper. They probably originated as a series of meditations at the celebration of the Christian Eucharist.

OPENING DRAMATIC SCENE

*The Last Supper,* 13:1–30. This is the Johannine version of the Last Supper between Jesus and his disciples, narratives of which we also find in 1 Cor 11:23–26; Mark 14:17–25; Matt 26:20–29; Luke 22:14–38. Unlike those, John does not mention the "Eucharistic words," words of interpretation spoken by Jesus over the bread or the wine, and he has an incident of foot washing the other narratives do not. We have no idea why the Eucharistic words are missing. Earlier we suggested that the evangelist has no concern for the sacraments and puts his emphasis elsewhere, and the omission of the Eucharistic words may be part of this general trend. On the other hand, these "words" were especially sacred to Christians and the evangelist may have regarded this aspect of the narrative as too sacred to be written down. The matter of the washing of the feet lends itself more readily to an explanation. The evangelist thinks in plastic terms; it is natural for him to cast his thought in the imagery of incident and dramatic dialogue. So here he dramatizes the sacrifice of Jesus and its significance by means of an acted parable of humility and service. The humility of the action is the more striking in light of the evangelist's concentration on the passion of Jesus as his "glorification."

DIALOGUE

*Christ's departure and return,* 13:31–14:31. In this dialogue between Jesus and his disciples, the evangelist explores the glory of the relationship between the believer and the glorified Christ.

MONOLOGUE

*Christ and the beliver,* 15:1–16:15. The evangelist now turns to the pattern of the Christian believer's life in the world. The believer *abides* in Jesus (15:1–11); he enters into a relationship of *love* with the fellow believer (15:12–17); and he *separates* himself from the world (15:18–27). In this last connection we are introduced to a particular Johannine conception, the *parakletos,* the Paraclete (15:26: RSV, "Counselor"; NEB, "Advocate"; TEV, "Helper"). In Greek, the word means "the one called beside," and in John's thinking it represents the thought that the risen Lord is spiritually present to the believer as that believer wrestles with the problems of Christian existence in the world.

DIALOGUE

*Jesus and his disciples,* 16:16–33. Turning now from monologue to dialogue, the evangelist explores the relationship of the risen Lord with those who believe in him. As is uniformly the case in these discourses, the Lord who speaks is the Jesus who died and rose again from the dead, who came from the Father and returned to him, and whose spiritual presence can now be known by the believer in the world.

MONOLOGUE

*Christ's prayer for his church,* 17:1–26. This is the evangelist's climactic statement of the significance of Jesus for the believer. It falls naturally into three parts. In part one (verses 1–5), the prayer is concerned with Jesus himself, with his death as his glorification, and with his power to give eternal life to those who believe in him. In part two (verses 6–19), the thought turns to the believer who is still in the world. Jesus is now glorified, but the believer still has to live out his life in the world and to represent Christ in the world. Finally, part three (verses 20–26) considers the corporate body of believers, the church, and the prayer is that the church may know the indwelling love of God as it fulfills its mission in the world of leading that world to belief in God.

## The Passion Narrative, 18:1–20:31

The fourth major section of the gospel of John is the passion narrative. John covers the same ground as do the synoptic gospels, and we note the parallels between John and Mark. But the narrative in John has its own particular emphases. In the first place it has a distinctively apologetic tendency. The Jews are presented as "the sole villains of the plot," while Pilate becomes "a sympathetic figure, earnestly interested in Jesus' welfare."[29] Second, the Jesus of the Johannine passion narrative is a sovereign figure. In this narrative, "Jesus goes through the passion not as a victim, but as a sovereign and super human Being who at any moment could bring the process to a halt."[30]

**The betrayal in the garden,** 18:1–11 (compare Mark 14:32–48). John omits any reference to the prayer of Jesus, but then he has just completed the great prayer for the church. The saying of Jesus "Rise, let us be going" (Mark 14:42) is found earlier in John (John 14:31).

**Jesus before the high priest and Peter's denial,** 18:12–27 (compare Mark 14:53–72). The narrative follows the structure in Mark, even to the extent of intercalating the trial scene into the account of the denial by Peter. But compared with the Markan narrative there are some new elements. There is the informal appearance before Annas (18:12–14), which has the effect of bringing Jesus before two high priests: "the high priest then questioned Jesus . . . " (verse 19) and "Annas then sent him bound to Caiaphas the high priest" (verse 24). The historical fact was that Annas was deposed from the high priesthood by the Romans in A.D. 15, but he remained enormously influential, and it may well have been that the Jews continued to grant him the courtesy of the title, if only as a protest against the Roman power to appoint and depose the chief representative of the Jewish people before God. In itself then, there is nothing intrinsically improbable about the Johannine narrative of the two hearings, and it may be that John here does have access to a tradition about the appearance of Jesus before Jewish authorities that is otherwise lost to us. At the same time, however, it is obvious from the comment in verse 14 that John's interest is in the symbolic significance of the high priest as the chief representative of the people before God. With dramatic irony he puts on the lips of Caiaphas the key to understanding the meaning of the death of Jesus.

Another new element in the Johannine narrative is the appearance of "another disciple" who was "known to the high priest" and who brings Peter into the courtyard (verses 15–16). This disciple appears again in 20:2–10, where Mary Magdalene runs to Peter "and the other disciple" to tell them that Jesus'

---

[29]Ibid., vol. 2, p. 787.
[30]Ibid.

body is not in the tomb. In that context the "other disciple" is identified as "the one whom Jesus loved" (20:2), and this brings us to other references to the "beloved disciple," of which there are five in the gospel. In 13:23–26 the disciple "whom Jesus loved" is intimately close to Jesus at the Last Supper. In 19:25–27 Jesus from the cross commits his mother to the care of "the disciple whom he loved." In 21:7 "that disciple whom Jesus loved" recognizes the resurrected Jesus, and in 21:20–23 there is a dialogue between the risen Jesus and Peter about "the disciple whom Jesus loved, who had lain close to his breast at the supper." Finally, in 21:24 this disciple is identified as the ultimate source for the tradition in the gospel of John: "This is the disciple who is bearing witness to these things, and who has written these things; and we know that his testimony is true."

The identity of this "other disciple," the "disciple whom Jesus loved," is one of the many fascinating problems in the gospel of John. Traditionally he has been identified with John, the son of Zebedee, who constantly appears in the synoptic gospel accounts together with Peter and James as a special intimate of Jesus (e.g., Mark 9:2, the transfiguration, and Mark 14:32–33, the agony at Gethsemane). The case for this traditional view has recently been carefully reargued by R.E. Brown,[31] but it remains difficult to accept for three reasons. In the first place, the gospel of John simply does not read as if it were based on the reminiscences of an eyewitness; its dependence on a signs source and its style and concerns are such as to cause one to think more readily of a second-generation Christian meditating on the significance of Christ for the believer. Second, the narrative of this gospel is so heavily loaded with symbolism that it is possible that this "other" disciple "whom Jesus loved" is a symbolic figure representing ideal discipleship. This possibility is increased to the point of probability by a third consideration, namely, that this disciple is never mentioned by name.[32] There is no conceivable reason for this if he is John, the son of Zebedee.

**Jesus before Pilate,** 18:28–19:16 (compare Mark 15:1–15). This narrative is particularly interesting for its presentation of Pilate as a sympathetic figure earnestly interested in Jesus' welfare and of "the Jews" as the real villains of the plot. One gets a very strong impression that the author is himself a Jew reacting bitterly to the treatment of Jesus by his own people. The bitter note of rejection in John 19:15 is an echo of that in Matthew's gospel (Matt 27:25). There is no evidence that John knows the gospel of Matthew; it is rather the case that both John and Matthew are reacting equally strongly to a situation in which they feel themselves, as Jews, personally involved.

**The crucifixion,** 19:17–37 (compare Mark 15:22–41 and Luke 23:33–49). This narrative is close to Mark's with the exception of the mention of "the disciple whom he loved," and the reference to the giving up of the spirit (verse 30), which is reminiscent of Luke 23:46.

---

[31]Ibid., vol. 1, XCII–XCVIII.
[32]This point is made by Bultmann in *The Gospel of John*, pp. 483–85.

**The burial,** 19:38–42 (compare Mark 15:42–47). All the gospels stress the role of Joseph of Arimathea in the burial of Jesus (Mark 15:43; Matt 27:57; Luke 23:50), but John is alone in introducing the figure of Nicodemus, whom he carefully identifies as the one who had come to Jesus by night (verse 39; compare 3:1–15; 7:50–52).

**The discovery of the empty tomb,** 20:1–10 (compare Mark 16:1–8). All the gospel narratives diverge dramatically after the point at which Mark ends: the discovery of the empty tomb and the astonishment of the women. In Matthew the women run to tell the disciples and are met by the risen Jesus on the way, (Matt 28:9–10); then the risen Lord appears to the disciples in Galilee. In Luke the women tell of their discovery of the empty tomb, but they are not believed until a series of resurrection appearances in and around Jerusalem convinces the disciples that "The Lord has risen indeed!" (Luke 24:36). In John's gospel Mary Magdalene tells Peter and the "other disciple" of the empty tomb, and Jesus appears to her and to the disciples both in Jerusalem (20:19–23, 26–29) and in Galilee (21:1–14).

**The appearance to Mary Magdalene,** 20:11–18. The gospel of John puts a major emphasis on the spiritual presence of Jesus with the believer. Both in 6:62–63 and 16:7 the evangelist emphasizes the eventual return of Jesus to the heavenly realm from which he came and the consequent possibility of his spiritual presence with the believer. Now he returns to this note in the story of the appearance to Mary Magdalene as Jesus tells her that he is about to ascend to the Father. That will make possible his spiritual presence with the believer and the promise of that presence is the point of the next story.

**The appearance to the disciples as a group,** 20:19–23. The evangelist now dramatizes the possibility of the spiritual presence of Christ with the believer through this story of the risen Lord appearing to his disciples and breathing on them. Both in Hebrew and Greek the word for "spirit" is the same as the word for "breath."

**The appearance to Thomas,** 20:24–29. In this story the evangelist brings his gospel to a climax by dramatizing doubt so as to highlight the possibility of belief. "Thomas has become here the personification of an attitude,"[33] and by means of this story of his coming to faith the evangelist presents a paradigm of the possibility for all men everywhere to reach the point of saying to the risen Jesus, "My Lord and my God."

**The purpose of the gospel,** 20:30–31. The evangelist climaxes his work with a statement of its purpose: to bring the reader to belief in Jesus and to the life that belief makes possible.

## Epilogue: The Appearance in Galilee, 21:1–23

Surely the evangelist intended his gospel to end at 20:31, and chapter 21 has been added as an epilogue by another writer. The language is not quite that of

[33]Brown, *John,* vol. 2, p. 1031.

the vangelist; yet the epilogue certainly echoes his concerns. It emphasizes the role of Peter, it uses the imagery of shepherd and sheep, and it features "the disciple whom Jesus loved." In many respects it is like the prologue to the gospel (1:1–18), which also shares the concerns of the gospel and yet at the same time differs in language from the text of the gospel itself. R.E. Brown makes the interesting suggestion that both the prologue and the epilogue may have been added to the main text of the gospel by the same redactor.[34]

The purpose of the epilogue seems to be ecclesiastical. The author is now concerned with the ongoing life and work of the church in the world and appears to feel that from this viewpoint something needs to be added to the gospel narrative. In particular, four matters concern him. He knows a tradition of a resurrection appearance to the disciples in Galilee as they were fishing, and he preserves it as a supplement to the accounts of the appearances in Jerusalem (verses 1–8). Second, he is concerned with the Christian sacred meal, the Eucharist, and he presents here an account of a meal between the risen Lord and his disciples (verses 9–14), which is deliberately evocative of the Eucharist (Jesus "takes the bread" and "gives" it to the disciples in a solemn manner, verse 13). The Eucharist celebrated in the church is interpreted as a solemn meal between the risen Lord and those who believe in him. Third, there is the restoration of Peter after his denial of Jesus (verses 15–19). The gospel of Mark already hinted at the restoration of Peter and of a resurrection appearance to him: "tell his disciples *and Peter* that he is going before you into Galilee; there you will see him" (Mark 16:7). The epilogue to the gospel of John develops this theme further. Finally, the author of the epilogue identifies the "disciple whom Jesus loved" as the ultimate author of the gospel. As we have said, we do not know whether this disciple is a historical or an ideal figure.

## THE FIRST LETTER OF JOHN

Most of what we wish to say about 1 John has already been said at various places in this chapter and now only needs to be brought together. It is probably not from the same author as the main text of the gospel. We noted the poverty of the style of this letter compared to that of the gospel and the real differences in thought between them on eschatology and the sacraments. At the same time we joined Bultmann, Marxsen, and others in holding that it was possible that the author of 1 John had redacted the main text of the gospel. The text of 1 John exhibits a balance of proclamation and parenesis, and it may be analyzed as follows:

**1:1–4**  *Proclamation.* The eternal life has been made manifest.

**1:5–2:17**  *Parenesis.* Right behavior depends on true knowledge of God.

**2:18–27**  *Proclamation.* True knowledge of God depends on recognizing that Jesus is the true and only Son of God. He rewards with eternal life those who abide in him now.

**2:28–3:24**  *Parenesis.* Those who abide in him now and exhibit the love that naturally flows from that relationship have no need to fear his parousia.

[34]Ibid, vol. 1, XXXVIII.

**4:1–6** *Proclamation.* Jesus Christ actually came in the flesh as the Son of God.

**4:7–5:5** *Parenesis.* To abide in God is to be "of God," and to be "of God" is to exhibit love in the world. "We love because he first loved us."

**5:6–12** *Proclamation.* Jesus Christ is the Son of God, and acceptance of him is the means to eternal life.

The *Oxford Annotated Bible* has said that 1 John is not really a letter at all, but "in form and content it resembles a theological treatise or sermon, written with obvious affection and concern for the spiritual welfare of those to whom it is addressed."[35]

One last point about 1 John is the "docetism" it is in part directed against. The Christology of the Johannine writings stresses Jesus as the Son of God who came into the world to empower and glorify those who accept him. Nevertheless, the gospel and letters of John show a strong dualism, a strong sense of the contrast between above and below, light and dark, good and evil, the spirit and the flesh. Under these conditions it was natural that Christians particularly influenced by these writings and their authors should be susceptible to the view that the world and the flesh were essentially evil and that the heavenly redeemer could not truly have come in the flesh, but must have maintained his heavenly nature while only appearing to be in the flesh. This way of thinking was natural in the Hellenistic world, and when it was applied to Jesus it became the christological heresy "docetism." The homily we know as the first letter of John is designed in no small part to combat it.

## THE SECOND AND THIRD LETTERS OF JOHN

These are true letters written by a member of the Johannine school who calls himself the "presbyter" (elder). The word came to designate a given official in the church, e.g., 1 Tim 5:17 "Let the elders who rule well . . . " and probably the author is simply referring to himself by the title of his office in the church. The letters have no formal structure.

One interesting question is the kind of authority the author exercises over the churches he writes to. It seems to have been moral or even spiritual rather than formal, for the writer could not do much about Diotrephes, "who likes to put himself first," except appeal to his readers on moral grounds (3 John 9–12). This fact, together with the very nature of the gospel and letters of John themselves, indicates that the writer's authority stems primarily from his function as a preacher prominent in the conduct of Christian worship. It is perhaps not too much to say that in the second and third letters of John we have a much-loved leader of Christian worship and celebrator of the Eucharist attempting to extend his influence into matters of doctrine and polity.

The second letter of John is notable for its reference to churches as "the elect lady" and the "elect sister" and to the members of the churches as "her

35 *Oxford Annotated Bible,* p. 1482.

children" (2 John 1, 13). This indicates that the Christian church is now a definite and separate entity in the Hellenistic world and that individual churches are coming to be recognized as integral units in that entity. We are now in the middle period of New Testament Christianity. The second letter of John also continues the argument of the first letter against docetism (2 John 7–11).

The third letter of John reflects the authority of the writer as moral or spiritual rather than formal and, like 2 John, it emphasizes the importance of the physical presence of the writer in exercising such authority as he may possess (3 John 13; compare 2 John 12). For the rest, the letter testifies that the Christian churches are recognizing that they are separate entities in the world and as such, have a definite responsibility for Christians who come to them from another place (3 John 5–8). This hospitality to other Christians was to become an important sociological factor in the development of the church.

## THE EVANGELIST JOHN, HIS GOSPEL, AND HIS SCHOOL

After our exegetical surveys of the gospel and letters of John we are now able to make some further tentative statements about these texts and their authors. As far as the gospel is concerned, it is evident that the author is or was a member of the Jewish community in a predominantly Greek city. His concern for Christian Jews and their exclusion from the Jewish community (John 9:22; 12:42; 16:2) indicates his Jewish background, as does his intense desire to explore the meaning of Jesus in terms of the symbolism of the Jewish festivals, (John 5:1–10:39). At the same time, there is an equally unmistakable wish to interpret the meaning of Jesus to the believer in terms that would be realistic to the Greek world, symbolized by the story of the Greeks coming to Jesus in John 12:20–22, but evident throughout the gospel. So the evangelist is a Christian Jew living somewhere in a major population center in the Hellenistic world. Ephesus is that center according to ancient Christian tradition, but almost any city in Syria or Asia Minor would meet the requirements, and recently Alexandria in Egypt has been suggested as a possibility.[36] We do not know where the gospel of John originated, except that it was somewhere in the Hellenistic world where Greek culture was dominant but where there was a strong Jewish community.

We are on somewhat firmer ground when we claim that the gospel and letters of John are not the product of an individual but of a "school." The main text of the gospel was redacted in various ways, and certainly a second author was involved in the letters, perhaps even a third. As we consider the gospel and letters, the homogeneity of style, thought, and emphasis, with sometimes marked and sometimes subtle differences, indicates the activity of a close-knit group rather than a single person. The differences in literary form seem to make the same point. One person could indeed have written the gospel, the first letter (which is not really a letter at all, but a theological homily), and the second and third letters (which are indeed letters). But when these differences

---

[36]Martyn, *History and Theology*, p. 58.

in literary form are linked with differences in style and thought, it becomes probable that we are dealing with related members of a closely knit group.

The existence of a Johannine "school" is in itself an extremely likely possibility in the cultural conditions of the first century. Jewish rabbis regularly attracted disciples who became responsible for developing and applying their teaching. Both Rabbi Shammai and Rabbi Hillel, slightly older contemporaries of Jesus, are known to have founded schools, and they were not the only rabbis to do so. In the Greek world there were schools of popular moral philosophy, named either after a viewpoint (e.g., Stoic or Cynic) or a person (e.g., Plato, Aristotle, or Epicurus). Within Christianity itself there was the tradition of Jesus and his disciples, and in chapter 6 we discussed the school of Paul and his followers. The existence of a Johannine school is, therefore, in itself most likely, and the literary features of the gospel and letters of John make it virtually certain. The gospel and letters are the literary product of a tight-knit group that shared a common vision of the nature and meaning of Christian faith.

## FURTHER READING

Kümmel, *Intro.* Gospel, pp. 134–75; Letters, pp. 305–16.
Marxsen, *Intro.*, pp. 251–69.
Fuller, *Intro.*, pp. 168–83.
*PCB*, Gospel, pp. 844–69 (C. K. Barrett); Letters, pp. 1035–40 (G. Johnston).
*JBC*, Gospel, pp. 414–66 (B. Vawter); Letters, pp. 404–13 (B. Vawter).
*IDB*, vol. 2, Gospel, pp. 932–46 (J. N. Sanders); Letters, pp. 946–52 (G. B. Caird).

There is voluminous literature about the gospel and letters of John. Good surveys of the literature are:

Howard and Barrett, *The Fourth Gospel in Recent Criticism and Interpretation.* (Barrett revised Howard's volume to bring the survey down to the work of Bultmann.)
Robinson, "The Johannine Trajectory" in Robinson and Koester, *Trajectories through Early Christianity*, pp. 232–68. Surveys the situation since the work of Bultmann.

Important recent studies include the following:

Dodd, *The Interpretation of the Fourth Gospel.*
Fortna, *The Gospel of Signs: A Reconstruction of the Narrative Source Underlying the Fourth Gospel.*
Käsemann, *The Testament of Jesus.*
Martyn, *History and Theology in the Fourth Gospel.*

Among the many commentaries available the following are particularly important:

Barrett, *The Gospel According to St. John.*
Brown, *The Gospel According to John.* 2 vols. (The Anchor Bible). Massive and encyclopedic.
Bultmann, *The Gospel of John.* Bultmann's commentary on the letters is available in German in the Meyer series, and an English translation is promised in the Hermeneia series published by Fortress Press.
Dodd, *The Letters of John.* Moffatt New Testament Commentary.
Hoskyns and Davey, *The Fourth Gospel.*
Lightfoot, *St. John's Gospel.*

It will be evident from our own presentation that we are particularly indebted to Dodd's *Interpretation of the Fourth Gospel*, to Martyn's *History and Theology in the Fourth Gospel*, and to the commentaries of Bultmann and Brown, respectively.

*Wall painting of a Eucharistic banquet from the catacomb of Priscilla, in Rome (early third century).*

# 11

# The Church on the Way
# To Becoming an Institution:
## The Literature of Emergent Catholicism

Traditionally, the letters in the New Testament are divided into two groups: "the Pauline epistles" (including Colossians, Ephesians, the Pastorals, and Hebrews) and "the Catholic epistles" (James; 1, 2 Peter; Jude; and 1, 2, 3 John). The latter group is called "Catholic" because the letters are addressed to the church in general rather than to a particular congregation or individual. We have preferred to group the letters according to literary and historical considerations. In chapter 5 we grouped together the letters actually written by Paul and then in chapter 6 those written in his name by pupils and immediate followers, including Hebrews in this group for convenience. In chapter 10 we grouped 1, 2, and 3 John with the gospel of John because the four texts have literary and theological connections as products of the Johannine school. We now consider the Pastorals, James, 1 and 2 Peter, and Jude together because they are the common products of the final period of New Testament history. We follow the order of the New Testament except that we put Jude before 2 Peter because 2 Peter reproduces Jude almost in its entirety. Furthermore, the connection between Jude and 2 Peter has led us to discuss 2 Peter before the Pastorals, although we recognize that, of the texts accepted into the New Testament canon, 2 Peter was probably the last to be written. The Pastorals and 2 Peter stand together as the most complete representatives of what we are calling "emergent Catholicism," and so the order of their treatment is comparatively unimportant.

The final period of New Testament history is marked by the growing institutionalization of the church. In the period roughly A.D. 100–140 the Christian movement is approaching the end of the first century of its existence. Though old problems—for example the delay of the parousia—continue to exist, new difficulties and needs are developing.

The major characteristic of this period is that the Christian movement has settled down to the task of being the church in the world. The parousia is no longer immediately expected, the Christians have learned to adjust to the destruction of Jerusalem and the Temple, and relations with Judaism and the

**253**

Roman Empire are assuming an established norm. The church, therefore, now has to develop its own institutions in order to be the church in the world. After almost a hundred years the Christian movement exists in its own right without having to define itself over against other movements. But the sheer fact of existing in its own right creates a new set of demands. A religious movement needs a creedal or confessional basis that makes clear what it stands for. Further, a movement stemming ultimately from Judaism, with its consciousness of revelation enshrined in written texts, needs its own texts defined carefully from other texts. To survive and function in the world the movement also requires an organizational structure, a decision-making apparatus, and a definition of the function of its officers and servants. To meet these needs the Christian church at the end of the New Testament period was rapidly establishing a creed, a canon, and an organized ordained ministry.

Some Christian literature of this period did not find a place in the final canon of the New Testament: a letter written by Clement, bishop of Rome, to the church at Corinth; letters written by Ignatius, bishop of Antioch, to various churches as he was on his way to martyrdom in Rome; and the Didache ("Teaching of the Lord to the Gentiles by the Twelve Apostles"), a church order from Syria. We do not discuss these in any detail, but we refer to them, especially in our concluding summary of the characteristics of emergent Catholicism.[1]

Our procedure in this chapter is to discuss the texts in the order James, 1 Peter, Jude, 2 Peter, the Pastorals. Then we offer a summary of the characteristics of emergent Catholicism and some remarks on the interpretation of its literature.

## THE LETTER OF JAMES

Despite the fact that it begins with greetings, James is not a letter but a homily. Nor may we call it a sermon, because there is absolutely no proclamation within it. Unlike 1 John and Hebrews, it does not alternate and weave together proclamation and parenesis, but consists of nothing but parenesis. In its 108 verses it has 54 verbs in the imperative![2]

Parenesis, or moral exhortation, is a feature of the literature of the ancient world—Hellenistic, Jewish, and Christian. "Household codes" existed in Hellenistic moral philosophy and were borrowed by Christians. In the Jewish world the teaching of the rabbis and such books as Proverbs and Sirach, both virtually without proclamation, were popular. Before the writing of James, there were in the New Testament collections of ethical teachings ascribed to Jesus in the gospels (especially Matthew's Sermon on the Mount) and the parenetical sections of the Pauline and deutero-Pauline letters. We have every reason to believe that there was a strong tradition of parenesis in the Christian

[1]Information about these texts is readily available in *IDB* under "Clement, Epistles of," vol. 1, pp. 648–49; "Didache," vol. 1, pp. 841–43; "Ignatius, Epistles of," vol. 2, pp. 678–80.

[2]Marxsen, *Intro.*, p. 226.

movement and that it borrowed freely from Hellenistic and Jewish parenetical material, as well as vigorously developing its own. The existence of a vigorous Christian parenetical tradition is important because a consequence is that verbal similarities between James and other New Testament texts do not mean that James necessarily knows those texts; all may have depended on a common parenetical tradition.

James shows knowledge of a parenetical tradition that uses sayings ascribed to Jesus in the gospels: 5:12 (compare Matt 5:36–37); 1:5, 17 (compare Matt 7:7–12); 1:22 (compare Matt 7:24–27); 4:12 (compare Matt 7:1); 1:6 (compare Mark 11:23–24). There is, further, parenetical material also used in 1 Peter: Jas 1:2–3 (compare 1 Peter 1:6–7); Jas 4:1–2 (compare 1 Pet 2:11). It is not that James necessarily knows the gospels or 1 Peter, but rather that there is a Christian parenetical tradition into which sayings ascribed to Jesus in the gospels have been taken up, although not in the form of sayings of Jesus, and of which both James and 1 Peter make use.

A further feature of James, as incidentally also of 1 Peter, is that the author uses Hellenistic Greek literary rhetorical devices. There are plays on words: 4:14, "That appears for a little time and then vanishes" (Greek: *phaino-mēne/aphanizomenē*); 1:1–2, "greeting/joy" (*chairein/charan*); 2:4, "made distinctions/become judges" (*diekrithēte/kritai*); and others. There is alliteration: 1:2, "you meet various trials" (*peirasmois/peripesēte/poikilois*); 3:5, "little member/great things" (*mikron/melos/megala*). James also uses the Hellenistic literary device of the diatribe, presenting an argument in the form of a dialogue between the writer and an imaginary interlocutor: 2:18–26; 5:13–15.[3]

Moral exhortation is very much the same throughout the various elements in a given culture. By the same token parenesis itself has little doctrinal concern, and James, a wholly parenetical work, has almost nothing distinctively Christian about it. Jesus Christ is mentioned only twice (1:1; 2:1), and both verses could be omitted without any harm to the flow of thought in the text. When the "coming of the Lord" is mentioned (5:7) there is nothing to denote the specifically Christian hope of the parousia; it could equally be a reference to the coming of the Lord God. "Faith" in this text is not specifically Christian faith but rather the acceptance of monotheism (2:19). These facts have led some scholars to suggest that the text is a Jewish homily lightly Christianized. But a number of features seem to speak of a Christian origin, especially the evidence of contacts with Christian parenetical tradition already noted and the discussion of "faith and works" in 2:14–26. The latter seems to presuppose an awareness of Paul's teaching in Galatians 3 and Romans 4. The discussion of faith and works in Jas 2:14–26 caused Martin Luther to contrast James unfavorably with the main texts in the New Testament as "a right strawy epistle in comparison with them, for it has no evangelical matter about it";[4] and this passage remains a problem.

Who is the James who identifies himself as the author of this homily? The tradition has been to identify him with James, the brother of Jesus. But the

---

[3]Kümmel, *Intro.*, p. 289, with other examples of the literary style of the homily.
[4]Kümmel, *Intro.*, p. 285.

comparatively late date of the homily, its use of Hellenistic Greek rhetorical devices, its lack of specific references to Jesus, and its failure to exhibit any of the conservatism with regard to the Jewish Law we know to have been characteristic of Jesus' brother all make this quite impossible. Probably the author himself intended the identification, and the homily is therefore deliberately pseudonymous.

## Structure

This homily defies the categories of our approach to the New Testament in more ways than one. Not only is it purely parenetical, it also has no discernible structure. It simply moves from theme to theme as the mind of the homilist takes him, on the principle of association of ideas or sometimes merely on catchwords. In our exegesis we follow the analysis given in Kümmel, *Introduction to the New Testament*, page 284, which recognizes the nature of the text. The insights we used in our structural analysis of other texts in the New Testament simply do not apply to the homily of James.

## Exegetical Survey

**1:1** *Address.*

**1:2–18** *Trials.* Rejoice over trials because trials are a way of being tested before God, and endurance in them leads to the rewards that only God can give.

**1:19–27** Both hear and do the word of God.

**2:1–12** Show no partiality, but fulfill the royal law of love.

**2:13** *The necessity of mercy,* a verse attached by a catchword to the preceding.

**2:14–26** *Faith and works.* This passage is obviously concerned either to controvert the Pauline doctrine of "justification by faith" or, more probably, to argue against an irresponsible development of that view that denied the necessity for "works" at all. Paul and the homilist see "faith" in very different terms. For Paul faith is a dynamic relationship to the risen Lord allowing man to appropriate for himself that which God has wrought for man through Jesus. For the homilist it is subscription to a sound monotheism. The two views could scarcely be further apart within the same tradition, and the difference characterizes those between emergent Catholicism and the earlier periods of the New Testament history. Paul himself would never have denied what the homilist is saying, because it would have been self-evident to him that faith must have consequences in one's behavior in the world. The homilist is arguing against the libertarians of his own day, whose view of faith was no doubt closer to the homilist's than to Paul's. There can be no direct comparison between James and Paul because they come from very different periods in New Testament history.

**3:1–12**   Watch your tongue.

**3:13–18**   Abandon earthly wisdom and seek heavenly wisdom.

**4:1–10**   Seek the peace that comes only from God.

**4:11–12**   Do not speak evil against one another.

**4:13–16**   The plans of merchants are subject to God.

**4:17**   Appended by catchword: the necessity of doing right.

**5:1–6**   Woes upon the rich.

**5:7–11**   The judgment of God is imminent.

**5:12**   Swear not.

**5:13–18**   The power of prayer.

**5:19–20**   Be concerned for the erring brother.

The homily has no formal conclusion.

## THE FIRST LETTER OF PETER

In the First Letter of Peter the proclamation is not so much a challenge to accept some aspect of the Christian faith as it is a recognition that those being addressed have already accepted that faith. Thus, for example: "without having seen him you love him" and "as the outcome of your faith you obtain the salvation of your souls" (1:4–9); or "having purified your souls by your obedience to the truth" (1:22) and "To you therefore who believe" (2:7); or "You are a chosen race . . . now you are God's people . . . now you have received mercy" (2:9–10). Another feature of this proclamation is the constant baptismal theme: being born again or being like sheep who had been straying "but have now returned to the Shepherd and Guardian" of their souls (2:25); or the salvation of Noah by water as a type of the salvation of the readers by baptism (3:20–21). Hence the very plausible suggestion that the fundamental thrust of 1 Peter is that of a baptismal homily.

Another feature of this letter is that there seems to be a real difference in the references to suffering and persecution after 4:11. In 1:6; 3:14; and 4:1, "trials," suffering "for righteousness' sake," and "abuse" are real possibilities the readers must contend with. But in 4:12 the readers are actually enduring a "fiery ordeal," and in 5:8 they are warned that their "adversary the devil prowls around like a roaring lion, seeking some one to devour." This has led to the equally plausible suggestion that up until 4:11 we are dealing with the general possibility of suffering, but that after 4:11 we are in a concrete situation of persecution. Moreover, the reference to the one adversary seems to require that the persecution be general and not simply local, and 4:14–16 seems to indicate that Christians were being persecuted simply because they were known to be Christians. The first certain reference we have to systematic and widespread persecution of Christians *as Christians* is from the reign of Trajan (A.D. 98–117). 1 Pet 4:12–5:11 seems to require conditions that as far as we know first obtained under Trajan, whereas 1:3–4:11 seems to anticipate only the general possibility of suffering for one's faith.

These considerations lead to the conclusion that 1:3–4:11 is based on a baptismal homily the author was in the habit of using, and which at a time of real persecution, probably under Trajan, serves as a reminder to his readers of the spirit in which they first became Christians. He then adds 4:12–5:11 as a reflection on their current situation and circulates the whole to comfort his readers in the face of persecution.

A feature of 1 Peter, as of the homily of James, is the use of Hellenistic Greek rhetorical devices: the play on words, e.g., "perishable/imperishable" (*phthartēs/aphthartou*) (1:23); carefully paralleled clauses, e.g., "whoever . . . as/whoever . . . as" (4:11); the series of similar compound words, e.g., "imperishable, undefiled and unfading" (all words constructed in Greek in the same way, with the alpha-privative) (1:4); and others. Furthermore, 1 Peter is written in excellent Greek, and all quotations from and allusions to the Jewish scriptures come without exception from the Greek translation of those scriptures, the Septuagint. This evidence, together with the fact that the most probable date for the circumstances envisaged in 4:12–5:11 is the reign of the emperor Trajan, 98–117, makes it impossible that the letter should have been written by the apostle Peter. It is best understood as a letter written at the end of the first century by someone who used the pseudonym of the apostle.

## Structure

It is difficult to recognize a structure in 1 Peter because so much of it is parenesis, and even where there is some small proclamation celebrating what God has done or some aspect of the significance of Jesus, there is always parenesis interwoven with it. We can recognize the opening greeting (1:1–2), the baptismal homily (1:3–4:11), the exhortation to stand fast in the face of persecution (4:12–5:11), and the closing greetings (5:12–14). Beyond that, however, the most we can do is try to follow the writer's train of thought.

## Exegetical Survey

**1:1–2**   *Opening greetings.*

**1:3–4:11**   *The baptismal homily.*

> **1:3–9**   *An opening blessing.* It was customary in Jewish worship to bless God for what he had done on man's behalf. Here we have a Christian development of that liturgical practice. Note how the author moves from "him" to "us" to "you" as his thought moves from God to Christians in general and then to the group he is addressing.

> **1:10–12**   *Christian salvation as the fulfillment of prophecy.*

> **1:13–2:10**   *An exhortation to holiness.* Parenesis based upon "[You shall] be holy, for I am holy" (Lev 11:44–45). Interwoven with the parenesis is reflection upon the significance of Christ: he is the lamb of God; he is the precious stone. Both these concepts are developed from Old Testament passages much used in the New Testament, the lamb from

Isaiah 53 and the stone from Psa 118:22. Here the latter has led to other scriptural passages mentioning stones.

**2:11–3:12** *An exhortation on the obligation of Christians.* A long parenetical section dealing with the relation of Christians to the world. It begins with an emphasis on maintaining good conduct among the outsiders (2:11–12) and moves to the necessity for accepting the authority of earthly rulers (2:13–17). In this latter passage we see the practical necessity for Christians to adjust to the realities of life in the world. Just as the author of Luke-Acts speaks to the subject of the Christian's relationship to the Empire, so the author of 1 Peter finds it necessary to speak to the Christian's relationship to those institutions of authority to which he is personally subject. Next the writer turns to a household code, a summary of duties and responsibilities. Here the code itself becomes the basis for homiletical development.

A remarkable feature of this development is the use of Isaiah 53. Let us compare 1 Pet 2:21–25 with Isaiah 53.[5]

| **1 Pet 2:21–25** | **Isaiah 53** |
|---|---|
| 21. (Christ) also suffered for you leaving you an example that ye should follow his steps. | 4. he . . . is pained for us |
| 22. Who did no sin neither was guile found in his mouth. | 9. he did no sin nor guile was in his mouth |
| 23. Who when he was reviled, reviled not again; when he suffered, threatened not; but committed himself to him that judgeth righteously; | (7. As a lamb before his shearers is dumb, so opens he not his mouth) (11. the Lord also is pleased to justify the just one) |
| 24. Who his own self bare our sins in his body upon the tree, that we, having died unto sin, might live unto righteousness; by whose bruise ye were healed. | 11. and he shall bear their sins (compare 4–6) |
| | 5. by his bruise we were healed |
| 25. For ye were going astray like sheep | 6. all we like sheep have gone astray |

The parallels are too close to be accidental. 1 Pet 2:21–25 is to all intents and purposes a meditation upon Isaiah 53 as fulfilled in the crucifixion of Jesus.

[5]We are now following Hoskyns and Davey, *The Riddle of the New Testament*, pp. 57–59, and quoting the ERV as the most literal modern translation.

**3:13–4:6** *Further exhortation.* This passage deals in general with Christians preparing to suffer for their faith, and in their prospective suffering to follow the example of Christ. The passion of Jesus as an example for individual Christians to follow in their suffering is a major theme of the literature of the early church concerning martyrdom, and it is prominent in this passage.[6]

**4:7–11** *The End is at hand.* The baptismal homily climaxes on the note of anticipation of the parousia, but even this is interwoven with parenesis.

**4:12–5:11** *The persecution parenesis.* The suffering that was thought of as prospective in the baptismal homily has now become actual persecution. The writer exhorts his readers to stand fast and reiterates many of the themes of his homily.

**5:12–14** *Closing greetings.*


# THE LETTER OF JUDE

If the letter of James is a homily, then the letter of Jude is a polemic, a polemic against a group of heretics within the church who are creating dissidence. These heretics appear to have been Gnostics, because the word used of them and translated as "worldly" in verse 19 is *psychikoi,* a technical term used by Gnostics. They were certainly libertarians; despising the world of the flesh they saw no fault in abandoning themselves to fleshly practices (verses 8 and 12). The writer simply denounces these heretics; he does not discuss their views or argue against them, but calls them all kinds of names and threatens them with dire examples of punishment taken from Jewish scriptures. "Jude's method of dealing with the false teaching is the least creative in the New Testament."[7]

The author calls himself Jude, the brother of James, which would make him also the brother of Jesus, and tradition has affirmed this (Mark 6:3). But the letter looks back on the time of the apostles as in the past (verse 17), and this, together with features of emergent Catholicism in the letter, make such an authorship impossible. The letter is pseudonymous, as is all the literature of emergent Catholicism in the New Testament.

The most interesting features of this letter are the characteristics of emergent Catholicism it exhibits. The letter speaks of "the faith once for all delivered to the saints"; faith is the acceptance of authoritative tradition, and the writer denounces the heretics and admonishes the faithful on the authority of that tradition. There is also evidence of a developing Christian liturgy. In verses 20–21, "pray in the Holy Spirit; keep yourselves in the love of God; wait for the mercy of our Lord Jesus Christ" testifies to the liturgical development of a trinitarian formula. The closing benediction is a magnificent piece of liturgical language, so different in style and tone from the remainder of the letter that the writer has probably taken it from the liturgy of his church.

[6]On the problem of the "descent into hell" in 3:19, see especially Fitzmyer, *JBC*, p. 366.
[7]Fuller, *Intro.*, p. 161.

## Structure

This polemical letter defies structural analysis beyond the obvious fact that it opens with a greeting and closes with a doxology. The writer simply denounces the heretics and warns his readers against them.

## Exegetical Survey

**1–2** *Address and salutation.*

**3–4** The emergence of false teachers makes it an urgent necessity to contend for the faith once and for all delivered to the saints.

**5–7** *Scriptural instances of sin and punishment.* The writer warns his readers that God punishes sin, using as examples the tradition of God punishing the unfaithful Israelites in the wilderness (compare 1 Cor 10:1–11; Heb 3:7–4:11) and the fate of the rebellious angels (Genesis 6) and of Sodom and Gomorrah (Genesis 19). The reference to the fallen angels seems to exhibit an awareness of how this myth was developed in the apocalyptic works Enoch, Jubilees, and 2 Baruch.

**8–16** *Denunciation of the false teachers.* The reference to the archangel Michael in verse 9 is a reference to a legend in an apocalyptic work, the Assumption of Moses, where Michael digs a grave to bury Moses, and Satan appears and unsuccessfully claims the body. Cain (Genesis 4) and Baalam (Numbers 22–24) figure prominently in both Jewish and Christian tradition. Korah led a rebellion against Moses (Num 16:1–11). "Love feasts" are a form of the Christian sacred meal in which the cultic aspect was blended into a regular communal meal. In Corinth, and no doubt elsewhere, this blending led to excesses and loss of the cultic aspect (1 Cor 11:20–22), and the communal meals were eventually separated from the cultic Eucharist. The reference to the wandering stars is from the apocalyptic book of Enoch. The quote in verses 14–15 is from Enoch 1:9.

**17–23** *Attitude required of the faithful.* If verse 19 is a quotation, we do not know its source. It may represent the author's understanding of apostolic teaching and is notably apocalyptic in tone.

**24–25** *Closing doxology.*

## Jude's use of apocalyptic texts

A remarkable aspect of Jude is its use of apocalyptic texts. Apocalyptic flourished in both Judaism and Christianity throughout the New Testament period, and its Jewish and Christian forms were closely related. Jude is eloquent testimony to this relation because he is aware of the myth of the fallen angels in Jewish apocalyptic in general, and he knows the myth of the burial of Moses from a Jewish-Christian apocalypse, the Assumption of Moses. He also alludes to a major apocalyptic work, the book of Enoch, in the matter of the wandering stars, and he explicitly quotes Enoch 1:9. His own understanding of apostolic faith is notably apocalyptic. The letter shows that apocalyptic is still a living force in the period of emergent Catholicism. Nevertheless, when Jude is reused in 2 Peter 2, the author of 2 Peter is careful to remove all references and allusions to apocalyptic works which were excluded from the Jewish canon of scripture.

# THE SECOND LETTER OF PETER

The Second Letter of Peter is, together with the Pastorals, the most thoroughgoing representation in the New Testament of the views of emergent Catholicism. Furthermore, 2 Peter 2 is based on Jude 4–16. This evidence makes it impossible for the apostle Peter to have written it, and it is universally recognized as pseudonymous. The writer knows the synoptic gospel account of the transfiguration (1:17–18); he knows 1 Peter (3:1) and the letters of Paul as a collection and as scripture (3:15–16). He is probably the latest of all the New Testament writers, and a date about A.D. 140 would be appropriate.

This "letter" has a double purpose: to reiterate the hope for the parousia against a growing skepticism and to combat false teachers in the church. The two have a single root in that the false teachers were most probably Christian Gnostics who emphasized knowledge of salvation now and eventual translation to the heavenly sphere, despised the world and the body, and therefore had no concern for a future parousia. The sheer passage of time and the continuing delay of the parousia had undoubtedly sharpened their polemic against the traditional Christian hope.

Although 2 Peter has an opening greeting, it has no further literary characteristics of a letter. Its main text is a manifesto, a strong statement of what the author regards as correct and authoritative teaching against false and disruptive teaching in the church. It opens with a greeting we would find in a Christian letter, but the greeting, like the pseudonymity, is characteristic of emergent Catholicism itself.

## Structure[8]

The structure of 2 Peter is simple.

> Salutation, 1:1–2
> Exhortation to holiness, 1:3–21
>> 1:3–11    Exhortation
>> 1:12–18    The certainty of the promise is grounded in the revelation the apostle encountered.
>> 1:19–21    An appeal to scriptural prophecy

[8]In the remainder of our discussion of 2 Peter we are deeply indebted to Käsemann, "An Apologia for Primitive Christian Eschatology," now in his collected essays, *Essays on New Testament Themes*, pp. 169–95.

Attack upon the false teachers, 2:1–22
True teaching concerning the day of the Lord, 3:1–10
Parenesis and concluding doxology, 3:11–18

## Exegetical Survey

**1:1–2** *Salutation.* The salutation is important for an understanding of the author's viewpoint and the emergent Catholicism he represents. It sees faith as something originally obtained by the apostles and now available to those who stand in succession to them.

**1:3–21** *Exhortation to holiness.*
  **1:3–11** *Exhortation.* Note the characteristic Hellenistic emphasis on the corruption of the world and on escaping it to partake of the divine nature (verse 4). It is only a short step from this to the Gnosticism of the false teachers. The list of virtues in verses 5 and 6 is a Christianization of the kind of lists of virtues popular in the Hellenistic world. Verse 11 represents a Hellenizing of much earlier Christian language about "entering the Kingdom of God."
  **1:12–18** *The certainty of the promise is grounded in the revelation encountered by the apostle.* This is a difficult passage, but its general meaning seems clear. The apostles were eyewitnesses to the transfiguration of Jesus and so eyewitnesses of his majesty—i.e., they saw him partake of the divine nature on one occasion in anticipation of the moment after his resurrection when he would partake of it fully. Having been granted this vision, the apostles can testify to the reality of the promise that Christians also will one day partake of that divine nature.
  **1:19–21** *An appeal to scriptural prophecy.* The promise is also guaranteed by the scriptures. All scripture is understood as prophecy, not only particular books or passages, and a very high, albeit somewhat mechanical, view of the inspiration of scripture is presented. In such a view the question of canonicity is crucial, and we shall see that 2 Peter is in fact our earliest witness to the development of a definite, distinct, and limited view of the canon of Christian scripture.

**2:1–22** *Attack on the false teachers.* This is based on Jude 4–16. It portrays the false teachers in Jude's language and uses many of his examples. It is interesting that 2 Peter carefully purges Jude of all references to works outside the canonical scriptures, as the Jewish canon was by this time coming to be defined. Jude has a reference to the myth of the burial of Moses from the Assumption of Moses, an allusion to the book of Enoch in the reference to the wandering stars, and a quotation from Enoch 1:9. The myth of the burial of Moses, the wandering stars, and the quotation are all missing in 2 Peter. It is not that the author of 2 Peter has an objection to apocalyptic; far from it. His objection is to the use of books now regarded as suspect insofar as a canon was developing among the Jews and as it should be accepted by Christians.

**3:1–10** *True teaching concerning the day of the Lord.* This section begins with a renewal of the pseudonymous claim to Petrine authorship, which is at the same time a recognition that, for the writer, 1 Peter was already achieving the status of scripture (verse 1). It continues with a clear recognition of the sacredness of the apostolic age, which is now past (verse 2). The present of the writer is separated from that age as "the last days" (verse 3; compare Jude 17–18 where we have exactly the same distinction between the apostolic age and "the last time"). The scoffing of the false teachers is met by claiming that God's time is different from man's and that the parousia is imminent in God's time and certain in man's. It is an ingenious argument, but it loses the dynamic of the imminence of the parousia in Mark or of the attempt to make theological sense of the delay of the parousia in Matthew or Luke. Verse 10 represents a theme known to us from the synoptic gospels (Matt 24:43 = Luke 12:39) and from 1 Thess 5:2, except that it is considerably embellished.

**3:11–18** *Parenesis and concluding doxology.* The most interesting element in this concluding passage is the references to Paul's letters. In verses 15–17 they are clearly known as a collection and regarded as "scripture." We are approaching a Christian canon that excludes Jewish apocalyptic works that the Jews themselves were excluding from their canon and that includes Christian writings. The Christian writings embrace at least the synoptic gospels (see 2 Pet 1:17 and its reference to the Transfiguration—this is scriptural because 2 Peter does not use nonscriptural material in this way), 1 Peter (see 2 Pet 3:1), and a collection of the letters of Paul. Another important aspect of these references is the characterization of the letters of Paul as "hard to understand, which the ignorant and unstable twist to their own destruction . . . " (verse 16). This seems to imply that the false teachers the author is directing his polemic against are using the letters of Paul, or some aspects of them, as a basis for their position. The remainder of this passage is parenesis based on reiterating the expectation of the "day of the Lord" in 3:1–10.

# THE PASTORAL LETTERS: 1 TIMOTHY, 2 TIMOTHY, TITUS

These letters are known as the "Pastoral Letters" because of their obvious pastoral concern for churches and their ministry. They purport to be written by the apostle Paul, but this is impossible on the following grounds:

*Vocabulary.* While statistics are not always as meaningful as they may seem, of 848 words (excluding proper names) found in the Pastorals, 306 are not in the remainder of the Pauline corpus, even including the deutero-Pauline 2 Thessalonians, Colossians, and Ephesians. Of these 306 words, 175 do not occur elsewhere in the New Testament, while 211 are part of the general vocabulary of Christian writers of the second century. Indeed, the vocabulary of the Pastorals is closer to that of popular Hellenistic philosophy than it is to the vocabulary of Paul or the deutero-Pauline letters. Furthermore, the

Pastorals use Pauline words in a non-Pauline sense: *dikaios* in Paul means "righteous" and here means "upright"; *pistis*, "faith," has become "the body of Christian faith"; and so on.

*Literary style.*  Paul writes a characteristically dynamic Greek, with dramatic arguments, emotional outbursts, and the introduction of real or imaginary opponents and partners in dialogue. The Pastorals are in a quiet meditative style, far more characteristic of Hebrews or 1 Peter, or even of literary Hellenistic Greek in general, than of the Corinthian correspondence or of Romans, to say nothing of Galatians.

*The situation of the apostle implied in the letters.*  Paul's situation as envisaged in the Pastorals can in no way be fitted into any reconstruction of Paul's life and work as we know it from the other letters or can deduce it from the Acts of the Apostles. If Paul wrote these letters, then he must have been released from his first Roman imprisonment and have traveled in the West. But such meager tradition as we have seems to be more a deduction of what must have happened from his plans as detailed in Romans than a reflection of known historical reality.

*The letters as reflecting the characteristics of emergent Catholicism.*  The arguments presented above are forceful, but a last consideration is overwhelming, namely that, together with 2 Peter, the Pastorals are of all the texts in the New Testament the most distinctive representatives of the emphases of emergent Catholicism. The apostle Paul could no more have written the Pastorals than the apostle Peter could have written 2 Peter.

The Pastorals are, therefore, pseudonymous and the question is why the author, whom we will call the Pastor, following R. H. Fuller, chose to write in the name of the apostle Paul. Vocabulary, style, viewpoint, and concerns in the three letters are sufficiently homogeneous to make it virtually certain that they were written by the same person. The answer probably is that the author believed himself to be in the tradition of Paul; he may have been a second- or third-generation member of the Pauline school. Perhaps also the false teachers against whom he writes were using Pauline material in their teaching, and he wished to present a true understanding of Paul against this.

The affinity of perspective between the Pastorals and 2 Peter, and of language between the Pastorals and second-century Christian literature in general, indicates a date for these letters somewhere in the first half of the second century, perhaps around A.D. 125.

The form of the Pastorals as letters must have been a stratagem by the Pastor. They were directed to the church at large or to churches in a particular area, and the address to individuals known to be companions of Paul is a literary device to lend plausibility. Despite their literary form, like 2 Peter, they are essentially manifestos, written in response to the threat of a spreading Gnosticism within the church. Furthermore, they are also an answer to the growing need for organizational structure in the church.

The structure of the Pastorals is simple; the Pastor argues against the false teachers and urges organizational structure on the church. He urges on

"Timothy" or "Titus" correct behavior and practice as ordained ministers of the church. He characteristically holds up the false teachers as bad examples to avoid and the apostle Paul (according to his literary device, himself) as a good one to follow. The structures are too simple to warrant separate discussion; so we proceed immediately to the exegetical survey, in the course of which the structure will become evident.

## Exegetical Survey of 1 Timothy

**1:1–2** *Salutation.*

**1:3–20** *Attack on the doctrine of the false teachers.* The false teaching is apparently a form of Gnosticism with a strong Jewish element. The reference to "myths and endless genealogies" (verse 4) would fit the gnostic tendency to speculate about the hierarchy of heavenly beings, and the reference to the Law in verses 8–9 indicates the Jewish element. Faith in this passage has become a synonym for "the Christian religion." In verse 5, "sincere faith" can be read as "sincere profession of the Christian religion" (see also 5:8; 6:10, 21). Moreover, that faith has become a matter of accepting doctrinal propositions (verse 15).

**2:1–3:16** *A church order: part one.* Reflecting emergent Catholicism's concern with the organizational structure of the church, 1 Timothy includes what is to all intents and purposes a church order, divided into two parts, 2:1–3:16 and 4:11–6:19. The first part covers worship in the church (2:1–15) and the ordained ministry (3:1–16).

  **2:1–15** *Worship in the church.* The regulation to pray "for Kings and all who are in high positions" and the grounds given for it (2:1–2) reflect the concern of emergent Catholicism for the world outside the church and for the good reputation of Christians in that world.

  **3:1–16** *The ordained ministry.* In emergent Catholicism the bishop is becoming the chief officer of the church, which we also find in the letters of Ignatius. The office of deacon is mentioned in the New Testament only here, and perhaps in Rom 16:1 where Phoebe is a "deaconess." This section climaxes in one of the great New Testament christological hymns (3:16), no doubt taken by the Pastor from the liturgy of his church.

**4:1–10** *An attack on the ethics of the false teachers.* The writer contrasts the ethics of the false teachers with the behavior expected of the true teacher.

**4:11–6:19** *A church order: part two.* In the form of instructions to "Timothy" the Pastor develops the ideal of a Christian minister (4:11–5:2). He details regulations concerning widows, who are also a recognized group in the church in the letters of Ignatius (5:3–16), and elders. Earlier in the New Testament *elder* is synonymous with *bishop* (Acts 20:17, 28), but now the bishop is separated as the chief officer (5:17–22). There follow some further instructions to the ideal minister (5:23–25; 6:3–19), and to slaves (6:1–2).

**6:20–21** *Conclusion.* Even in his concluding greeting the Pastor continues his polemic against the false teachers. The reference to "what is falsely called knowledge" strengthens the case that the false teaching was a form of Gnosticism.

## Exegetical Survey of 2 Timothy

This was perhaps the first Pastoral written; certainly it is most concerned with creating an impression of personal relationship between Paul and "Timothy," showing a desire to authenticate the manifesto comparable to the "This is now the second letter I have written to you" of 2 Peter 3:1. The Pastor seems to have drawn his material for this from Acts.[9]

**1:1–2** *Salutation.*

**1:3–2:13** *Exhortation to witness on the basis of the example of Paul.* Verses 13 and 14 of chapter 1 exhibit the view of Christian faith characteristic of emergent Catholicism. In essence it is the "pattern of sound words" which was heard from the apostles, and which is to be guarded and followed. Note also 2:2, which has a similar understanding, and 2:8, alluding to Rom 1:3; the Pastor knows a collection of the Pauline letters.

**2:14–4:8** *Exhortation to good behavior in all respects.* The Pastor now turns to the behavior expected of the true minister of God. Characteristically, the false teachers are examples to avoid and the apostle Paul an example to follow. In this section we learn more about the false teaching: it is "godless chatter" (2:16); it holds that "the resurrection is past already" (2:18); it features "myths" (4:4). We also learn more about the characteristics of emergent Catholicism: it regards its time as the last time, separate from the time of the apostles (3:1; compare Jude 18; 2 Pet 3:3); it is coming to regard scripture in a very formal way as "inspired by God" and "profitable" (3:16).

**4:9–18** *Paul's personal situation.* This has been constructed to add verisimilitude to the pseudonymity.

**4:19–22** *Closing greetings.*

## Exegetical Survey of Titus

**1:1–4** *Salutation.*

**1:5–9** *The ordained ministry.* This section is not a church order such as we find in 1 Timothy but rather some directions with regard to bishops and

---

[9]On the general relationship of the Pastorals to Acts, apart from the question of the personal references being taken from Acts, see Moule, *The Birth of the New Testament*, pp. 220–21. On the question of the Pastor's use of Acts in his personal references to Paul, see Fuller, *Intro.*, pp. 139–40.

elders. It seems to equate the two offices, whereas 1 Timothy separated them. Either Titus is considerably earlier than 1 Timothy or, more likely, the situation with regard to the relationship between the two offices was still fluid, and separation of the two was only beginning to take place at the time of the writing of the Pastorals.

**1:10–16** *An attack on the false teaching.* The false teaching apparently had some connection with Crete (1:12) and certainly with Judaism (1:14).

**2:1–3:7** *Exhortation to a proper Christian behavior.* Here is the kind of moral teaching standard in the literature of emergent Catholicism (compare 1 Pet 2:11–3:7). Note also the renewed parousia hope and the description of Jesus as "our great God and Savior" (2:13; compare 2 Pet 1:1).

**3:8–11** *Renewed attack on the false teaching.*

**3:12–14** *Personal notes.*

**3:15** *Closing greetings.*

# THE CHARACTERISTICS OF EMERGENT CATHOLICISM

In the era of emergent Catholicism the church needed organization and structure. At the same time, it was faced with a threat from within, the growing influence of Gnosticism, and with the need to relate to those outside, especially those in positions of influence or power. In meeting these various needs the church developed the characteristics of emergent Catholicism.

## The Apostolic Tradition

Perhaps the most obvious characteristic of emergent Catholicism is its concern for the apostolic age and its reliance on the idea of apostolic tradition. The church is now separated from the age of the apostles by a considerable period, and the tendency is to look back on that time as one of perfection, as the golden age of the church, as the time of revelation by God through Jesus to the church in the persons of the apostles. This process begins in the legends of the early church in the Acts of the Apostles, but the author of Luke-Acts himself deliberately stresses the parallels between that heroic age and his readers'. The writers in the period of emergent Catholicism, however, characteristically see themselves and their readers as separated from the age of the apostles. That time was the time of revelation and perfection; theirs is the time of apostasy; of falling away. These are the "last days," and they are days of trial and corruption (Jude 17–18; 2 Pet 3:3; 2 Tim 3:1–5).

In many respects this understanding is strikingly parallel to the apocalyptic writers' understanding their days as the last days of a history hastening to its close. The representatives of emergent Catholicism shared the Christian apocalyptic hope of the parousia. Yet there is nonetheless an important difference. The apocalyptic writers looked to the future *and lived out of that future;* the representatives of emergent Catholicism looked to the future *but lived out of the past,* the past of the apostolic age. An apocalyptic writer's expectation of the future dominates his whole understanding of things; a representative of emergent Catholicism, such as the author of 2 Peter, has an expectation of the future but is dominated by the past of the apostolic age, and the tradition he believes comes to him out of that past.

The concept of an apostolic tradition is, therefore, essential to emergent Catholicism, and this tradition must be guaranteed both in its origin and transmission. If it is to carry the authority of the apostles, then the apostles must themselves be the guarantors of the origin of the tradition. But if it is to carry the authority of the apostles into the "last days," there must be a separate agent guaranteeing its purity in transmission. That agent is the Holy Spirit; as the apostles are guarantors of the origin of the tradition, so the Spirit is the guarantor of its transmission (Jude 3; 2 Peter 1:12–18; 2 Tim 1:14).

In these circumstances these writers have a particular way of meeting the false teaching. They do not argue the issues or debate with the false teachers. Instead they confront the teaching and the teachers and, standing squarely on the authority of the apostolic tradition, denounce both as not being in accord with the apostolic truth.

## The Concept of Faith

Emergent Catholicism conceived of revelation as given in the past of the apostolic age and handed on in the church as an object, sacred to be sure but nonetheless an object. It follows from this that its concept of faith is very different from that of earlier periods of the church's history. It is no longer a dynamic belief in the imminent coming of Jesus as Son of Man, nor is it a similarly dynamic relationship to the risen Lord; it has become the acceptance of a revealed truth that can be expressed in propositional sentences. It is even a synonym for the Christian religion. The gospel of Matthew prepares for this with its concept of obedience to a verbal revelation authoritatively interpreted; and Hebrews, where faith is "the assurance of things hoped for, the conviction of things not seen" (Heb 11:1), represents a transitional stage. But in the literature of emergent Catholicism, faith becomes the acceptance of monotheism (Jas 2:19), the acceptance of authoritative tradition (Jude 20), something originally obtained by the apostles and available to those who stand in true succession to them (2 Pet 1:1–2), and a synonym for the Christian religion (1 Tim 1:5). The key passages are, however, 2 Tim 1:13–14 with its "pattern of sound words" to be guarded and passed on; 2 Tim 2:2 with a similar emphasis; and the propositional statements scattered through the Pastorals that are "sure"—i.e., part of the structure of faith, the adjective coming from the same root as the noun "faith" (1 Tim 1:15; 3:1; 4:9; 2 Tim 2:11; Tit 3:8).

## The View of Scripture

The emphasis on authoritative apostolic tradition and on the Spirit as its guardian leads naturally to a high view of the written deposit of that tradition and of its Jewish counterpart, scripture. In 2 Pet 1:20–21, scripture does not come "by the impulse of man, but men moved by the Holy Spirit spoke from God," and in 2 Tim 3:16, "All scripture is inspired by God. . . ." This view of scripture naturally brought with it a concern for defining what constituted scripture and what did not. The concern for a canon was intensified by the successful Jewish definition of their scriptures in this period (about A.D. 90, at Jamnia) and also by the fact that the gnostic false teachers depended on their own "scriptures," which were often "secret" books or writings (for example, the gnostic gospel of Thomas, whose opening reads: "These are the secret words which the living Jesus spake"). Motivated by their own high view of scripture, challenged by the successful Jewish promulgation of a canon, and confronted by the necessity for authoritative writings with which to confront the gnostic false teachers and their secret books, the representatives of emergent Catholicism took the first step toward defining a Christian canon of scripture.

The most dramatic example is the contrast between Jude and 2 Peter 2. Jude makes indiscriminate use of the texts the Jews were accepting into their canon—what Christians were to call the Old Testament—and the texts the Jews were rejecting; in this instance apocalyptic texts. Jude is here typical of earlier phases of the Christian movement. But when Jude is used as the basis for 2 Peter 2 all reference to anything outside the Jewish canon of scripture is carefully removed. The author of 2 Peter is paying eloquent testimony to the force of the Jewish example. In his own work he takes significant steps toward a Christian equivalent. By his treatment of Jude he has already revealed himself to be the first Christian writer to accept the Jewish canon of the Old Testament. Similarly, he is the first Christian writer to refer to Paul's letters as "scripture" (2 Pet 3:15–16), and in his treatment of the transfiguration of Jesus (2 Pet 1:16–19) and in his reference to "the second letter that I have written to you" (2 Pet 3:1), he is also prepared to accept the gospels and 1 Peter as "scripture," and incidentally is not too reluctant to put his own letter in that category.

## An Ordained Ministry

A natural outgrowth of emergent Catholicism's concern for the organizational structure of the church was its emphasis on a regular ordained ministry. There is in its literature, especially in the Pastorals, the beginning of the separation of the offices of bishop and elder (1 Tim 3:1–7), explicit instructions for the offices of deacon (1 Tim 3:8–13) and elder and bishop, apparently here synonymous (Tit 1:5–9), and a reference to the actual act of ordination to the ministry of the church, the laying on of hands (2 Tim 1:6).

## The Concern for "Those Outside" the Church

The church settling down to the task of witnessing in the world must necessarily deal with its relations with the world at large, as the author of

Luke-Acts dealt with the Roman Empire and its authorities. In the literature of emergent Catholicism, there is a parallel concern for authorities—governors, kings, etc.—and also for the good reputation of Christians and the church among "those outside" (1 Pet 2:11–17; Tit 2:7–8; 3:1–2).

## The Epistolary Form

Outstanding in the literature of emergent Catholicism in the New Testament is the deliberate use of the form of the letter. Only one of the texts is actually a letter (1 Peter), and the bulk of that is a baptismal homily. Of the others, James is a homily and the remainder—Jude, 2 Peter, and the Pastorals—are manifestos. Why then are they all given, artificially, the form of letters? The answer is probably twofold. In the first place, at this time the letters of Paul were known and were being circulated as scripture. To imitate the literary form was to present the churches with something familiar and hence more likely to be accepted. In the second place, and actually much more important, imitating the form of a letter provided an opportunity for pseudonymity—an opportunity to write in the name of a man from the apostolic age—and pseudonymity is crucial to this literature.

## Pseudonymity

We have already discussed pseudonymity in the New Testament at several points,[10] but since pseudonymity is a major characteristic of the literature of emergent Catholicism, we must now give the subject closer attention. We discuss, first, pseudonymity in the New Testament apart from the literature of emergent Catholicism, and then we turn to the phenomenon in that literature itself.

### Pseudonymity in the New Testament
### apart from the literature of emergent Catholicism

The synoptic gospels and the Acts of the Apostles are not pseudonymous; they are anonymous. They were originally circulated without any author's name, and the names they now bear were ascribed to them in the early church. Similarly, the literature of the Johannine school first circulated anonymously, except that the writer of the second and third letters identifies himself as "the elder," and the author of the appendix to the gospel, chapter 21, identifies the evangelist as "the disciple whom Jesus loved." The apocalyptic author of the book of Revelation identifies himself as "John" with no further qualification, and we have no reason to doubt that a John "of Patmos" was in fact the author of the book, though we have every reason to doubt that we may identify him with any other "John" known to us from the early days of the church.

[10]A brief general discussion of the authorship of the books of the N.T. is given in chapter 1, pp. 6–8. The pseudonymity of the deutero-Pauline literature is discussed in chapter 6, p. 119 (general), pp. 119–20 (2 Thess), pp. 121–23 (Col), pp. 129–32 (Eph).

Outside the literature of emergent Catholicism, pseudonymity confronts us in the New Testament only in the case of the deutero-Pauline letters: 2 Thessalonians, Colossians and Ephesians. These are in a sense a special case, for they are an instance of pupils deliberately writing in the name of the master. This was a wholly acceptable practice in the ancient world—Plato wrote in the name of Socrates—and need occasion no further comment. Analagous to the pseudonymity of the deutero-Pauline letters is the quite remarkable gospel practice of putting everything in the form of sayings of Jesus and stories about him, even when the contents come from the church.

## Pseudonymity in the literature of emergent Catholicism

It is in the literature of emergent Catholicism that pseudonymity becomes a major factor in the New Testament. Every single text in the literature of emergent Catholicism is pseudonymous! Neither James nor Jude, the brothers of Jesus, nor Peter nor Paul, are the authors of the texts claiming their names in this literature. There is no single text in this literature that bears the name of its author; all without exception are written in the name of a figure from the apostolic age.

In claiming authorship, the other Christian literature of this period is also interesting. Clement of Rome does not write to the church at Corinth in his own name, but in the name of the church at Rome. The letter begins, "The church of God which sojourns in Rome to the church of God which sojourns in Corinth," and the actual author is nowhere mentioned in the letter. Ignatius of Antioch writes in his own name, but he is writing personal letters to churches and to an individual (Polycarp). The Didache is technically "The Teaching of the Lord to the Gentiles by the Twelve Apostles." In other words, in this period there was a reluctance to write in one's own name; the important thing is not oneself, but the church one represents, or still more, the apostolic tradition in which one stands. Ignatius is the exception, but then his letters are distinctly personal letters; they are not homilies, manifestos, or incipient church orders.

We say "Ignatius is the exception," but what we should perhaps say is that Paul, Ignatius and John of Patmos are all the exceptions. Of all the literature we are discussing—the New Testament literature plus 1 Clement, the letters of Ignatius and the Didache—only these few intensely personal texts are written in the names of their authors. Paul writes personal letters to churches he has founded, to an individual he knows, and to a church from which he hopes to get support. John of Patmos writes an account of a personal revelation granted to him. Ignatius writes personal letters to churches and to an individual, Polycarp, known to him. The gospels and Acts are anonymous, as are 1 John, Hebrews and the Didache. The second and third letters of John are written by someone who identifies himself with his office in the church, and 1 Clement is written in the name of the church in Rome. The deutero-Pauline letters are written in the name of Paul, and the literature of emergent

Catholicism is written in the names of men from the apostolic age, including Paul.

We can see that the pseudonymity of the literature of emergent Catholicism is not something exceptional that must be accounted for; rather, it is part of a pattern. What we need to do in the early Christian literature is distinguish the highly personal from the remainder. Paul and Ignatius are writing very personal letters, and John of Patmos is giving an account of a personal revelation granted to him. But the others do not think of their work in this way. They are writing by the authority of the risen Lord, or of the church, or of an office within the church, or of their teacher, or of the apostolic age. So anonymity or pseudonymity is the rule; it is personal authorship that is the exception.

Once we recognize this, the pseudonymity of the literature of emergent Catholicism becomes readily understandable. The writers viewed themselves as defenders of a faith once and for all delivered to the apostles and transmitted in the church by means of an apostolic tradition. So they wrote in the name of apostles and even went to considerable lengths to establish "authenticity," as when the Pastor carefully constructs situations in the life of Paul out of which to write. The apostolic age and the apostolic tradition is the source of their inspiration and their authority. To write in the name of a man from the apostolic age is for them a natural next step.

## THE INTERPRETATION OF THE LITERATURE OF EMERGENT CATHOLICISM

The interpretation of this literature depends very much on the personal standpoint of the interpreter (as does the interpretation of any literature). One who shares the concern of the writers for the apostolic age and apostolic tradition will find that these texts speak directly to him, as will one who shares the concern of the authors for proper order and sound doctrine. Others will perhaps see these texts as representing the church hammering out a new vision of its faith and purpose in drastically changing historical circumstances, which is what in fact they do represent, and will find that they speak to a similar situation of drastically changing historical circumstances.

## FURTHER READING

We are immensely indebted to the work and insights of Ernst Käsemann, especially his epoch-making essay on 2 Peter, "An Apologia for Primitive Christian Eschatology," now found in his collected *Essays on New Testament*

*Themes,* pp. 169–95. Further, J. C. Beker's contributions to *IDB* on Jude, 2 Peter, and especially the Pastorals were of considerable help.

For the Letter of James, see:

*PCB,* pp. 1022–25 (L. E. Elliott-Binns).
*JBC,* pp. 369–77 (T. W. Leahy).
*IDB,* vol. 2, pp. 794–99 (A. E. Barnett).
Kümmel, *Intro.,* pp. 284–92.
Marxsen, *Intro.,* pp. 226–32.
Fuller, *Intro.,* pp. 151–55.

For the First Letter of Peter, see:

*PCB,* pp. 1026–30 (C. E. B. Cranfield).
*JBC,* pp. 362–68 (J. A. Fitzmyer).
*IDB,* vol. 3, pp. 758–66 (J. C. van Unnik).
Kümmel, *Intro.,* pp. 292–99.
Marxsen, *Intro.,* pp. 233–38.
Fuller, *Intro.,* pp. 155–60.

For the Letter of Jude, see:

*PCB,* pp. 1041–42 (G. H. Boobyer).
*JBC,* pp. 378–80 (T. W. Leahy).
IDB, vol. 2, pp. 1009–11 (J. C. Beker).
Kümmel, *Intro.,* pp. 299–302.
Marxsen, *Intro.,* pp. 239–40.
Fuller, *Intro.,* pp. 160–62.

For the Second Letter of Peter, see:

*PCB,* pp. 1031–34 (G. H. Boobyer).
*JBC,* pp. 494–98 (T. W. Leahy).
*IDB,* vol. 3, pp. 767–71 (J. C. Beker).
Kümmel, *Intro.,* pp. 302–5.
Marxsen, *Intro.,* pp. 241–45.
Fuller, *Intro.,* pp. 162–67.

The great work on this letter is, however, Käsemann's essay.

For the Pastoral Letters, see:

*PCB,* pp. 1001–7 (A. J. B. Higgins).
*JBC,* pp. 350–61 (G. A. Denzer).
*IDB,* vol. 3, pp. 668–75 (J. C. Beker).
Kümmel, *Intro.,* pp. 258–72.

Marxsen, *Intro.*, pp. 199–216.

Fuller, *Intro.*, pp. 133–44. (Especially valuable for a discussion of the Pastor's creation of circumstances in the life of Paul as background to his letters.)

Four representations of Christ: a Byzantine mosaic from
the church of "Nea Moni," Chios (eleventh century); paintings
by Antonello da Messina (c. 1430–1479) and Georges Rouault
(1871–1958); and a scene from the movie Godspell (1973).

# 12

# The Presupposition of the
# New Testament: Jesus

The ministry and message of Jesus is the presupposition for everything else in the New Testament. Had Jesus bar ("son of") Joseph from Nazareth not proclaimed his message concerning the Kingdom of God to the men and women of Galilee and Judea, had the Romans not executed him as a politically dangerous revolutionary, had some of those who heard him in his lifetime not come to believe that God had raised him from the dead, there would have been no Christian church and no New Testament. It is equally true that the books of the New Testament were produced for the service of the church by Christians who were far more interested in the living Lord they believed present in their midst and whom they expected to come soon on the clouds of heaven "to judge the quick and the dead" than they were in the historical Jesus bar Joseph from Nazareth. On this the modern view differs radically from that of the ancient church, and we must say something further about it.

## THE FIGURE "JESUS" IN THE NEW TESTAMENT

In earliest Christianity the figure of Jesus was central to the belief and expectation of the group. But by our standards this figure was extremely complex. In part he was the Jesus who had lived and proclaimed his message in Galilee and Judea—whom we would mean by the "historical Jesus." But in still larger part he was the risen Lord present in the Christian communities; still conducting his ministry to them and through them. The early Christians took the extraordinary step of recording his teaching-through-prophets in the form of Jesus' speaking to his disciples in Galilee and Judea, recording their arguments with their fellow Jews in the form of Jesus disputing with scribes and Pharisees, and recording the success and failure of the Christian mission in terms of people coming to Jesus from various places in and around Palestine. Then, finally, the Jesus they spoke and wrote of was the one whom they expected suddenly to appear "on the clouds of heaven" to judge and redeem, to destroy and remake, and they created a whole tradition portraying him already in his earthly ministry as exercising the authority that would be his when he came as Son of Man. In other words, earliest Christianity created a Jesus tradition—a tradition of sayings of Jesus and stories about him—based partly on actual reminiscence of his ministry and teaching, partly on experience of him in their present, and partly on an expectation of him in the future. But in all this the *form* was the form of sayings and stories of Jesus in what we would call his earthly ministry.

When in due course the authors of the various books of the New Testament came to write about Jesus, they were heirs to this complex way of thinking about him, and they added new dimensions and emphases. Paul concentrates his attention almost exclusively on the crucifixion and resurrection of Jesus and is virtually uninterested in his life; the unknown author of Hebrews sees Jesus as the fulfillment of whatever is truly valid about Jewish Temple worship; the evangelist Matthew sees him as the embodiment of the new and final revelation of God to his people; and so on. Only the author of Luke-Acts comes close to a modern historical interest when he depicts Jesus in his ministry as a paradigm of Christian piety. But he was in turn reinterpreting traditional materials so that though he has something approaching a modern historical concern, his gospel is just as far from being a life of Jesus in any modern sense as are the others.

Furthermore, earliest Christianity also treated Jesus as the Hellenistic world in general treated its heroic figures: it developed legends increasingly depicting him as a man of miraculous knowledge and power. There are legendary stories in the gospels, such as the Stilling of the Storm (Mark 4:35–41) and the Walking on the Water (Mark 6:45–52) and many more in the later apocryphal gospels.

This varied treatment of the figure of Jesus in the New Testament makes the task of arriving at historical information about him very difficult, but some progress is possible. We will now say something about how that progress has been made, and for the sake of convenience we will treat the life and the message of Jesus separately.

## The Life of Jesus from a Historical Standpoint

### The outline of the story of Jesus in the gospels

Serious historical presentations of the life of Jesus emerged in the nineteenth century,[1] and the writers took the obvious step of building on the framework of the narrative outline in the gospels. With the development of the "Markan hypothesis," that the gospel of Mark was the earliest gospel and fundamentally a historical presentation of the ministry of Jesus, the outline of that gospel came more and more to be used in this way.[2] The outline seemed reasonable

---

[1]The classic account of this movement is, of course, Schweitzer, *The Quest of the Historical Jesus.*

[2]For a discussion of this hypothesis and its rise and fall, see Perrin, *What Is Redaction Criticism?*, pp. 3–13.

when it was treated as historical: a beginning in Galilee; the gathering of disciples on the one hand and the rise of opposition on the other; the movement toward Jerusalem and the intensive private instruction of the disciples; the final ministry in Jerusalem and the narrative of the passion. But then in 1901 William Wrede published his book *Das Messiasgeheimnis in den Evangelien (The Messianic Secret in the Gospels)* and showed that those who saw history in the gospel of Mark were reading that history into the gospel; the evangelist himself was motivated by theological concerns and his outline was dogmatic rather than historical.[3] In 1919 Karl Ludwig Schmidt's *Der Rahmen der Geschichte Jesu (The Framework of the Story of Jesus)* showed that the evangelist had in fact constructed his own outline, and this began the movement toward the kind of understanding of the gospel and its outline we presented in chapter 7. Clearly, if this understanding of the gospel and its outline is correct, and it does represent a consensus of contemporary scholarly opinion, the outline of the gospel of Mark has no historical value.

But if that is true of the Markan outline, it is certainly true of the outlines of the gospels of Matthew and Luke. We saw in chapters 8 and 9 that these gospels follow the outline of Mark in general, and where they differ they do so for theological reasons. Their outlines, therefore, also have no historical value. The gospel of John is even more intensely theologically motivated than Mark, and its outline also has no historical value. Though in some respects where the gospel of John differs from the synoptic gospels it could be historically correct (e.g., in implying more than one visit to Jerusalem), this does not make the outline any less theological or more historical in purpose. The several visits to Jerusalem by Jesus are theologically motivated; they provide the evangelist with the opportunity to introduce the symbolism of some of the major discourses.

The most that can be argued for the gospel outlines is that some aspects of the story they tell have an element of inherent historical probability. For example, it is inherently probable that Jesus was baptized by John the Baptist and that his ministry had some connection with that of the Baptist. Whether the connection was that of Jesus beginning his ministry while John was still at work (according to the gospel of John) or only after John was "delivered up" (according to the synoptic gospels) we do not know, but that there was some continuity between the two ministries is inherently probable.

Other aspects of the story of the life of Jesus can be accepted on the basis of extrapolation from known historical data. A calling and training of disciples is certain in view of the role of Peter and others in the early church, and some kind of table fellowship between Jesus and the disciples as a group is extremely probable considering the role of sacred meals in earliest Christianity. Other elements of the story can be accepted on the basis of extrapolation from aspects of the teaching of Jesus that are established as authentic: that Jesus proclaimed the Kingdom of God, that he had a special concern for the group known as "tax collectors and sinners," that he did not attempt to lead a revolt against Rome, and so on.

---

[3]Wrede's work is presented and discussed in Perrin, *What Is Redaction Criticism?*, pp. 7–13.

### The Old Testament and events in the life of Jesus

A further problem for historical research into the life of Jesus is that so many of the events portrayed in the gospels are narrated as the fulfillment of Old Testament texts, or their details are allusions to the Old Testament. This is especially the case in the "formula quotations" in the gospel of Matthew, but it is a phenomenon in all the gospels. Good examples from the pre-Matthean stage of gospel writing are the Triumphal Entry and the Crucifixion in Mark. The former (Mark 11:1–10) fulfills Zech 9:9, and almost all the narrative details in the latter (Mark 15:22–37) are from the Psalms.

This phenomenon inevitably raises the question as to whether the details of the events, or even the events themselves, have been built up out of the Old Testament and whether, therefore, they "actually happened." To add narrative details from the Old Testament to interpret an event or even to create an event from an Old Testament text to interpret a person or movement would be quite in keeping with ancient Jewish practice, and certainly Christians did both of these things. We can see Matthew adding the detail of the second animal from Zech 9:9 to his account of the triumphal entry (Matt 21:7; compare his source, Mark 11:7), and it would be all but universally agreed that the birth and infancy stories in Matthew's gospel were created from the Old Testament texts they are held to fulfill. On the other hand, Jesus did enter Jerusalem as a pilgrim and he *was* crucified. Each event or narrative detail in which there is a quotation from or an allusion to the Old Testament—very many indeed—has to be investigated on its own merit.

## The Historical Reconstruction of the Message of Jesus from the New Testament

Though it is virtually impossible to say very much about the life of Jesus on the basis of the New Testament, the same is not true of his message. Here our resources are greater, and historical scholarship has arrived at satisfactory criteria for determining the authenticity of material attributed to the Jesus of the New Testament.

For the sake of convenience we summarize here what we have said in earlier chapters and, indeed, in some part earlier in this chapter. The New Testament writers present us with material put on the lips of the Jesus of the gospels by the church. But this Jesus is not the historical Jesus and the material attributed to him in fact had a long and complex history of transmission in the tradition of the church before it reached the form in which we find it. It came in part from Jesus himself, but also from anonymous prophets and scribes in the community, and even from the evangelists themselves. It had constantly been edited and interpreted in response to the changing needs and insights of the communities of Christians through which it passed. Our problem is, therefore, twofold: we have to find a way of working back through the tradition to the earliest form of the material we can reach, and then we have to devise criteria for determining whether in that form it can be attributed to the historical Jesus.

As we pointed out in chapter 1, an important consequence of form criticism has been the growing ability to trace the history of material that existed in the tradition of the church before the present books of the New Testament were written. Since the rise of redaction criticism the matter has become somewhat more complex, but the work has become surer since we have a firmer starting point for determining the final stage of redaction by the evangelist himself. Though it is a complex process, it is indeed possible to go back through the work of the evangelist and the tradition of the church and to reconstruct the history of the tradition of the church. This is an essential first step on the way to rediscovering the message of Jesus. Once we have reached the earliest form of the saying or parable, we then search for criteria for authenticity.

### Criteria for authenticity

A remarkable feature of work on this subject is that R. H. Fuller and the present writer, working independently of each other, arrived at virtually identical conclusions.[4] Fuller has four criteria, Perrin three. They may be tabulated as follows.

(a) Fuller: Distinctiveness
Perrin: Dissimilarity

(b) Fuller: The cross-section method
Perrin: Multiple attestation

(c) Fuller: Consistency
Perrin: Coherence

(d) Fuller: Linguistic and environmental tests
Perrin: Assumed this, but did not define it.

*The criterion of dissimilarity.*   Dissimilarity is the fundamental criterion. Sayings and parables may be accepted as authentic if they can be shown to be dissimilar to characteristic emphases of both ancient Judaism and early Christianity. A good example of this is the use of "Father" (Aramaic: *Abba*) in addressing God. It is found in the Lord's Prayer (Luke 11:2) and on Jesus' lips in the Gethsemane story (Mark 14:36). It is a familiar mode of address that the Jews at the time of Jesus did not use for God, preferring "Our Heavenly Father," or something similar. Matthew (6:9) and the church following him revert to the Jewish mode of address.[5]

The obvious problems with the criterion of dissimilarity are that it misses material in which Jesus is at one with his Jewish heritage and the later church at one with him, and that by concentrating on what is different it may present a distorted picture of the message of Jesus. On the other hand, it is a relatively certain criterion, and its judicious use has led us to the distinctive elements in

[4]Fuller, *Intro.*, pp. 94–98; Perrin, *Rediscovering the Teaching of Jesus*, pp. 39–47.
[5]For a further discussion of this example and for other examples, see Perrin, *Rediscovering*, pp. 40–43.

such fundamental things as Jesus' proclamation of the Kingdom, his use of parables and proverbial sayings, and the prayer he taught his disciples. Moreover, it is only a starting point; its use must always be supplemented by the use of other criteria.

*The criterion of multiple attestation.* This criterion tends to determine the authenticity of themes or concerns rather than of particular sayings, and it is immensely important because it tends to focus attention on themes or concerns that occur most frequently in the message of Jesus. Briefly, themes or concerns may be accepted as authentic if they occur in different literary forms within the tradition. So, for example, the concern for "tax collectors and sinners" is authentic because it is attested to in sayings, parables, and controversy stories, and that Jesus had a distinctive eschatology is evident from the fact that a particular view of the End Time is stamped on Kingdom sayings, proverbial sayings, and parables.

*The criterion of coherence.* This criterion grew out of a desire to go beyond the rather narrow limits of what can be established through dissimilarity and multiple attestation. Material may be accepted as authentic if it coheres with, or is consistent with, material established as authentic by other criteria. The validity of this criterion is self-evident.

*The criterion of lingustic and environmental tests.* This criterion tends to be negative rather than positive. Material is rejected if it is incompatible with the languages or environment of the ministry of Jesus. The interpretation of the parable of the Sower in Mark 4:13–20, for example, cannot be authentic because it uses language from the technical vocabulary of the early church,[6] and the teaching on divorce in Mark 10 cannot go back to Jesus in its present form because it presupposes Roman and not Jewish divorce law. The criterion does not work in the opposite direction. Material cannot be accepted as authentic only because it reflects the linguistic or environmental circumstances of the ministry of Jesus for the obvious reason that the earliest Palestinian church shared those circumstances.

## JESUS IN SOURCES OTHER THAN THE NEW TESTAMENT

Thus far we have been discussing the use of New Testament material in our attempt to reach the historical Jesus. To begin here is justifiable because the New Testament is the major source for any possible historical knowledge of Jesus. But there are other sources and we must examine them to see whether they offer us any help in our quest for the historical Jesus.

[6]On this see Jeremias, *The Parables of Jesus,* pp. 77–79. It is important to note that the argument is not based simply on the fact that the language is Greek; the decisive point is that the particular Greek terms used in this passage reflect the technical vocabulary of the early church. Greek may well have been in use in Palestine at the time of Jesus and hence spoken by him. See Fitzmyer, "The Languages of Palestine in the First Century A.D.," *Catholic Biblical Quarterly,* vol. 32 (1970), pp. 501–31.

## Non-Christian Sources

There are references to Jesus in both ancient Roman and ancient Jewish literature. The first of the Roman sources[7] is a work of the historian Tacitus written in A.D. 112–113. He describes a great fire in Rome in the summer of A.D. 64 while Nero was emperor, and he says that the emperor used the Christians as scapegoats to account for the fire. He then gives a brief account of the sect.

> The founder of this sect, Christus, was given the death penalty in the reign of Tiberius [A.D. 14–37] by the procurator Pontius Pilate; suppressed for the moment, the detestable superstition broke out again, not only in Judea where the evil originated, but also in the city [i.e., Rome] to which everything horrible and shameful flows and where it grows.
>
> Tacitus, Annals xv. 44

This represents the information available to the Roman historian at the beginning of the second century. It is probably based on the police interrogation of Christians and so is not actually independent of the New Testament or Christian tradition.

The second reference is also from a Roman historian, Suetonius, who published his *Lives of the Caesars* around A.D. 121. He says that Claudius, who was emperor A.D. 41–54, "expelled from Rome the Jews who were constantly rioting at the instigation of a certain Chrestus" (Suetonius, *Claudius*, 25). This is the expulsion referred to in Acts 18:2, and the reference is to disturbances in the Jewish community resulting from the preaching of Christian missionaries. Suetonius understood Chrestus to be the individual responsible for the riots.

The Roman sources do not offer us any information beyond that which could be deduced from the New Testament itself. They show that Christian missionaries reached Rome quite early, but that is evident from Paul's letter to the Romans. Only Tacitus says anything about Jesus, and his information probably comes indirectly from Christians. He tells us in effect that Roman historians accepted as factual the Christian tradition that the founder of the Christian movement had been crucified by Pontius Pilate.

There are several possible references to Jesus in the Jewish sources, of which the two most important occur together in the Babylonian Talmud.[8] There we find, first, a *Baraitha* (a tradition ascribed to the first or second centuries A.D.) which reads as follows:

> On the eve of Passover they hanged Yeshu [of Nazareth] and the herald went before him forty days saying, "[Yeshu of Nazareth] is going forth to be stoned

---

[7] A particularly valuable discussion of these is Grant, *A Historical Introduction to the New Testament*, pp. 290–94, to whom we are indebted at a number of points.

[8] The standard discussion of all the possible references to Jesus in the ancient Jewish literature is Klausner, *Jesus of Nazareth*, pp. 18–54. We are indebted to that discussion at a number of points in what follows.

in that he hath practiced sorcery and beguiled and led astray Israel. Let everyone knowing ought in his defense come and plead for him." But they found nought in his defense and hanged him on the eve of Passover.

b Sanhedrin 43a

This is a reference of quite extraordinary interest. Independent of any Christian sources, it offers us three items of information. It tells us that the Jews remembered Jesus as one who "practiced sorcery and beguiled and led astray Israel"; it links the death of Jesus with Passover, as do the Christian gospels; and the reference to pleading in his defense implies that Jesus was executed after a formal trial before Jewish authorities.

The second reference to Jesus in the ancient Jewish literature directly follows the first in the Babylonian Talmud.

Jesus had five disciples, Mattai, Maqai, Metser, Buni and Todah.

b Sanhedrin 43a

The names given here are different from any we find in the New Testament, although Mattai could be a corruption of Matthew and Todah a corruption of Thaddeus. However the important thing is not the names but the testimony to the fact that Jesus "had disciples."

There are several other possible references to Jesus in ancient Jewish literature, but they are either indirect or cryptic or both, and they do not add anything to what we have already learned. In summary, the Jewish sources tell us four things about Jesus. First, he "practiced sorcery and beguiled and led astray Israel." This must mean that Jesus had a reputation as a miracle worker, perhaps particularly as a successful exorcist, and that he had made a strong impression on the Jewish people. This latter point is reinforced by the second thing we are told by these references, namely that Jesus "had disciples." His ministry to the people was successful in that he attracted disciples who carried on his work after him. Then, there is the implication that Jesus was formally tried by the Jewish authorities, and finally, that he was executed on the eve before a Passover.

## Jesus in Christian Sources Other Than the New Testament

### Isolated sayings attributed to Jesus

There are several isolated sayings attributed to Jesus in Christian sources outside the New Testament, and indeed also in non-Christian sources.[9] The two most interesting are the following.

<hr>

[9]On this, see especially Jeremias, *Unknown Sayings of Jesus*, and also Hennecke-Schneemelcher, *New Testament Apocrypha*, vol. 1, pp. 85–90, "Isolated Sayings of the Lord."

When on the same day he saw a man doing work on the Sabbath, he said to him: Man! if you know what you are doing then you are blessed. But if you do not know what you are doing then you are cursed and a transgressor of the law.

This is found in one manuscript of the New Testament (Codex D) after Luke 6:4. Otherwise unattested, it coheres perfectly with something that has multiple attestation in the canonical tradition: the challenge of Jesus to make one's own decisions. It is to be accepted as authentic.

Jesus, on whom be peace, has said: The world is a bridge, go over it, but do not install yourselves on it.

This is found inscribed on the south portal of a mosque in India and is also attested elsewhere in Islamic literature. It is a very beautiful saying, but it does not have the same claim to authenticity as the first one.

## Apocryphal gospels

There are a number of *apocryphal gospels*, gospels which did not achieve recognition in the final formation of the canon of the New Testament. They are known as "apocryphal" ("secret" or "hidden") because they were to be kept from the faithful in the church. Some of them simply develop the tendency of the tradition to create legends about Jesus; others are the vehicles for teaching that came to be regarded as heretical in the church. By and large they offer nothing that can help the historian in his quest for the historical Jesus. There is, however, one exception to this judgment: the gospel of Thomas.

The gospel of Thomas is a document known to us from the discovery in 1945–46 of a whole library of gnostic Christian documents at a place called Nag Hammadi in Egypt.[10] It is written in Coptic and begins, "These are the secret words which the living Jesus spoke and Didymus Judas Thomas wrote." At the end it is identified as the "Gospel According to Thomas." It has no narrative, but is in the form of a series of sayings and parables attributed to Jesus, usually introduced by "Jesus said" or the like. Its form, therefore, is exactly parallel to that attributed by scholars to the hypothetical synoptic gospel source Q. What is particularly important about it in the context of the historical Jesus, however, is that it has versions of sayings and parables of Jesus that in some ways appear to be independent of the versions we find in the New Testament, and which therefore offer us an additional source to use in our attempt to reconstruct the original form of the saying or parable. Further, it offers us new sayings and parables, some of which have claims to authenticity on the basis of the criterion of coherence. A particularly interesting example of this latter type is the parable of the Assassin.

[10]A convenient English translation is by R. McL. Wilson in Hennecke-Schneemelcher, *New Testament Apocrypha*, vol. 1, pp. 511–22.

Jesus said: "The Kingdom of the Father is like a man who wishes to kill a powerful man. He drew the sword in his house, he stuck it into the wall, in order to know whether his hand would carry it through; then he·slew the powerful [man]."                                                                    Thomas 98


On the basis of the fact that this passage coheres with the Tower Builder and the King Going to War in Luke 14:28–32, it has claims to authenticity. The gospel of Thomas does therefore offer us some new material to use in our attempt to reconstruct the teaching of Jesus.[11]

## THE LIFE AND MESSAGE OF JESUS

Our discussion thus far has established that the New Testament itself is our major source for knowledge of the historical Jesus, though it can be supplemented by limited information derived from Jewish sources and some teaching material preserved in various places, especially in the gospel of Thomas. But within the New Testament itself there is a distinction to be made: here, when we refer to the New Testament, we really mean the synoptic gospels.

Outside of the synoptic gospels the New Testament offers little resource for arriving at historical knowledge of Jesus. The gospel of John is so much the end product of intensive meditation and reflection, and so absorbed with the interpretation of Christ as the descending-ascending redeemer, that no way has yet been found of deriving historical information about Jesus from it. The Acts of the Apostles offers us an isolated saying (20:35, "It is more blessed to give than to receive"); Paul betrays no interest in anything about Jesus beyond his death and resurrection; the remainder of the New Testament by its very nature cannot be expected to reveal the historical Jesus. We are limited, therefore, to the synoptic gospels, with some small supplementary help from the Jewish sources, the gospel of Thomas, and some isolated sayings preserved in various places. It is on this basis that we proceed.


### The Situation of the Jews in Palestine at the Time of Jesus

It is impossible to understand the life or the message of Jesus without appreciating the situation of the Jews in Palestine at the time.[12] They were living in a territory under the control of the Romans, whom they regarded as godless Gentiles. Moreover, this territory was sacred to them as the people of God, and it was sacred also to God himself since its center was Jerusalem with its Temple and Holy of Holies, the very special place of God. They were convinced that Roman control of the Holy Land and the Sacred Place of the Temple and the Holy of Holies was an abomination in the sight of God and

---

[11]Both Jeremias, *Parables*, and Perrin, *Rediscovering*, make use of the Thomas material in this way.

[12]For a survey of the history of the Jews in the New Testament period, see Appendix 2.

they were further convinced that God himself was about to remedy the matter. The only questions were how soon would God act and in what ways.

The answers given to these questions were varied and complex. Most Jews held some form of the apocalyptic hope and believed that God was about to irrupt into history to deliver his people. Inspired by this hope some were anxious to start a war against Rome that they believed God would terminate in their favor. The most extreme among this group were the Zealots, who spearheaded the war against Rome when it actually began in A.D. 66. But almost all Jews, except the Sadducees, shared this hope in one form or another and were prepared to take up arms against Rome when the time came. It was also widely accepted that the speed with which God would act to deliver his people depended in some respects on their state of purity in his eyes. The very presence of the godless Gentiles in the Holy City, it was felt, must be due to the sins of the people of God; they must therefore cleanse themselves in God's eyes so that he might find them more worthy, and also so that they might prepare themselves for his coming act of deliverance.

This demand for purity among the people of God had one tragic consequence: it bred a spirit of division within the Jewish community. People who did not measure up to the necessary standards were not only despised by those who felt that they themselves did, they were also hated because they were making the community as a whole unworthy of God's act of deliverance and so delaying it. This spiritual division was to reach a drastic climax during the revolt against Rome, the Jewish War of A.D. 66–70. During that time Jew murdered Jew in the name of God and his Law, and there was a vicious internecine strife in Jerusalem itself which must have aided the Romans in their siege of the city.

During the time of Jesus a group of people especially despised by their fellow Jews were known as "tax collectors and sinners." Tax collectors were hated not only because they were extortioners, which most of them were, but also because, directly or indirectly, they worked for the godless Gentile authorities occupying the land, collecting taxes imposed by the Romans. "Sinners" in this phrase are people whose activities or occupations are an offense to God and his Law. Prostitutes would be an obvious example, especially if their clientele included Roman soldiers. Swineherds would be another, for the care of animals made it impossible to observe the Sabbath, and swine were themselves ritually unclean. It is a crucial point in the parable of the Prodigal Son that the boy becomes a swineherd. That made him an outcast as far as the Jewish community was concerned, and his father should thereafter have rejected him. "Tax collectors and sinners" is, therefore, a general term for Jews who were outcasts in their own community because their activities or occupations were an offense to God, and hence perhaps their very existence was delaying God's act of deliverance of his people.

## The Life of Jesus

We are now in a position to make a general statement about the life of Jesus. He was baptized by John the Baptist, and the beginning of his ministry was in some way linked with that of the Baptist. In his own ministry Jesus was above all the one who proclaimed the Kingdom of God and who challenged his hearers to respond to the reality he was proclaiming. The authority and effectiveness of Jesus as proclaimer of the Kingdom of God was reinforced by an apparently deserved reputation as an exorcist. In a world that believed in gods, in powers of good and evil, and in demons, he was able, in the name of God and his Kingdom, to help those who believed themselves to be possessed by demons.

A fundamental concern of Jesus was to bring together into a unified group those who responded to his proclamation of the Kingdom of God irrespective of their sex, previous background or history. A central feature of the life of this group was eating together, sharing a common meal that celebrated their unity in the new relationship with God, which they enjoyed on the basis of their response to Jesus' proclamation of the Kingdom. In this concern for the unity of the group of those who responded to the proclamation, Jesus challenged the tendency of the Jewish community of his day to fragment itself and in the name of God to reject certain of its own members. This aroused a deep-rooted opposition to him, which reached a climax during a Passover celebration in Jerusalem when he was arrested, tried by the Jewish authorities on a charge of blasphemy and by the Romans on a charge of sedition, and crucified. During his lifetime he had chosen from among his followers a small group of disciples who had exhibited in their work in his name something of his power and authority.

That, or something very like it, is all that we can know; it is enough.

## The Message of Jesus

Intensive work on the material in the synoptic gospels shows that there are four aspects of that material where we can come close to the words of the historical Jesus. These are the proclamation of the Kingdom of God, the proverbial sayings, the parables, and the Lord's Prayer.

### The proclamation of the Kingdom of God

Competent scholars generally agree that four sayings concerning the Kingdom of God have very strong claims to authenticity.

The time is fulfilled, and the kingdom of God is at hand.

MARK 1:15a

(Though the actual formulation of the saying above comes from the evangelist Mark, it echoes the voice of Jesus.)

But if it is by the finger of God that I cast out demons, then the kingdom of God has come upon you.

LUKE 11:20

The kingdom of God is not coming with signs to be observed; nor will they say, "Lo, here it is!" or "There!" for behold, the kingdom of God is in the midst of you.

LUKE 17:20–21

From the days of John the Baptist until now the kingdom of Heaven has suffered violence, and men of violence plunder it.[13]

MATT 11:12

There is no doubt that the proclamation of the Kingdom of God is the central aspect of the message of Jesus. But having said that, one has to ask what it means to say that Jesus proclaimed the Kingdom of God. "Kingdom of God" is an apocalyptic symbol, a way of talking about God's final redemption of the world and of his people in the world; it is a form of the apocalyptic hope. To use the expression "Kingdom of God" is to speak of God acting as King, to speak of him visiting and redeeming his people, and this is the central theme of the message of Jesus.

But did Jesus proclaim this action of God as something to be expected in the immediate future or as something to be experienced already as a consequence of his own ministry? The texts we have quoted show that this is a very difficult question to answer. In Mark 1:15 the Kingdom of God is said to be "at hand," which implies that it is imminent but still something to be expected in the future. The other three texts, however, all use language claiming that the Kingdom is already present. It "has come upon you" (Luke 11:20); it "is in the midst of you" (Luke 17:20–21); it has already "suffered violence" (Matt 11:12). The only conclusion we can draw is that in the message of Jesus there is a very real tension between the Kingdom as present and the Kingdom as future, between the power of God as known in the present and the power of God to be known in the future.

In attempting to understand this tension between present and future it is important to note that Luke 11:20 interprets the exorcisms of Jesus, and that Matt 11:12 refers to the Kingdom's having "suffered violence" in the persons of John the Baptist and Jesus and his followers. In the exorcisms the Kingdom is present in the power to heal; in the violence done to John the Baptist and faced as an ever present possibility by Jesus and his followers the Kingdom is present in the necessity to accept suffering. In both cases the Kingdom is related to the existential reality of the experience of individuals.

Luke 17:20–21, on the other hand, denies the possibility of one particular experience of the Kingdom: the Kingdom is not coming "with signs to be observed"; no one will be able to say "Lo, here it is!" or "There!" To recognize the significance of this saying we have to remember that Jewish apocalyptic, and Christian apocalyptic also, expected the Kingdom to come as an observable historical phenomenon and as the climax to a series of observable historical phenomena. A good example of this kind of thinking is the book of Daniel, where in 11:3–35 we have an account of the history of the eastern

---

[13]This is my own translation. For its exegetical justification, see Perrin, *The Kingdom of God in the Teaching of Jesus*, pp. 171–74, and *Rediscovering*, pp. 74–77.

Mediterranean from the time of Alexander the Great ("a mighty King," 11:3) to the persecution of the Jews by Antiochus Epiphanes ("a contemptible person," 11:21) and the beginning of the Maccabean revolt ("a little help," 11:34—the author has no great opinion of Judas Maccabeus). At that point we reach the time of writing of the book of Daniel, and the author moves from knowledge to expectation. But the tone of his narrative does not change in any way. He describes Antiochus Epiphanes as overweening, as marching toward his doom through all kinds of excesses and aberrations (11:36–39), and then he gives an account of a further war between Ptolemy ("the king of the south," 11:40) and Antiochus ("the king of the north," 11:40) that results in Antiochus' conquering not only Egypt but also Libya to the west and Ethiopia to the south, and then perishing on his way back to Syria along the coastal route (11:40–45). That is the point at which the author expects the Kingdom to come. He expects it in the form of the coming of a catastrophic time of trouble and the appearance of the archangel Michael to deliver the people of God, of a general resurrection and the establishment of the true people of God in a state of eternal blessedness (12:1–3).

The point that concerns us in all of this is that the author is constantly dealing with observable historical phenomena. It is clear that for him the conquests of Alexander the Great, the persecution of the Jews by Antiochus Epiphanes, the expected further war between Syria and Egypt (which incidentally never took place), the appearance of the archangel Michael, and the general resurrection are all historical events of the same order. With this kind of thinking it was possible to give "signs to be observed." The author of Daniel 11 and 12 could have given the Maccabean revolt or the evidences of Antiochus Epiphanes' overweening as such signs. But Jesus categorically refused to give any such sign; instead, he claimed that the Kingdom was of such a nature that no such sign could be given: "nor will they say 'Lo, here it is!' or 'There!' for behold, the kingdom of God is in the midst of you."

Luke 17:20–21 therefore denies that the coming of the Kingdom of God is a historical event in the way that a king's actions, or a war, or the persecution of a people are historical events. But if this is what the saying denies, what does it affirm? What does it mean to say "the kingdom of God is in the midst of you"? The answer is found in the natural antithesis to historical events at the level of kings, wars, and persecutions—namely, historical events at the level of human experience of life in the world. To say "the Kingdom of God is among you" is to say that it is "a matter of human experience,"[14] or a mediated "experience of existential reality."[15] The history with which this saying is concerned is not the history of kings, wars, and persecutions; it is the history of the individual and his experience of reality. This is what it means to move from "signs to be observed" to something that is "in the midst of you."

The message of Jesus concerning the Kingdom of God must, therefore, be held to have a double focus. On the one hand, there is certainly a future aspect to the Kingdom in his message; on the other hand, there is equally certainly a

[14]Perrin, *Rediscovering*, p. 74.

[15]Perrin, "Wisdom and Apocalyptic in the Message of Jesus," *Society of Biblical Literature One Hundred Eight Annual Meeting Proceedings*, vol. 2, pp. 543–72.

reference to present experience of the Kingdom, to the mediation of existential reality in the present. How these things are to be reconciled, or even understood, should become clearer through a discussion of other aspects of the message of Jesus.

## The parables

Modern research on the parables of Jesus has established a number of points about them which may be stated in summary fashion.

(a) Jesus taught in parables, but the early church readily translated them into allegories. The difference is that a parable makes its point as a totality. Moreover, the point is never exhausted by any one apprehension of it, but can be apprehended afresh as the parable is retold in different situations. For that reason the message of the parable can never adequately be expressed except in the metaphorical language of the parable itself; it cannot be translated into a propositional statement.[16] In an allegory on the other hand, the parts count and each individual part bears a one-to-one relationship with what it represents. Once that relationship has been discerned, the message of the allegory becomes clear, and the allegory itself can be abandoned, for its cryptic message can now be—and should be—expressed in noncryptic language.[17] A good example of allegory in the New Testament is the interpretation of the Sower in Mark 4:13–20.

(b) Both the allegorizing of the parables and their present context and application in the gospels are the work of the church and the evangelists. To interpret a parable as a parable of Jesus, therefore, one must first reconstruct the original nonallegorical form of the parable[18] and then interpret it as a parable in the context of the message of Jesus without reference to its context or function in the gospel narratives.[19]

[16]This point has only recently come to be appreciated. It means, for example, that we cannot say that the message of the Sower (Mark 4:3–9) is "Have confidence in God's future!" as I came near to claiming in *Rediscovering*, p. 156. That may be its message to one person in one time and one place, but such a direct statement by no means exhausts the parable's potential meaning.

[17]On this, see especially Crossan, "Parable and Example in the Teaching of Jesus," *New Testament Studies*, vol. 18 (1971/72), pp. 285–307, especially pp. 304–05. Crossan summarizes the distinction as follows: "Allegory is always logically subordinate and functionally secondary with regard to abstract proposition and statement . . . parable is that which is never so subordinate but which essentially says what cannot be said in any other better or clearer fashion. When allegory is seen as fundamentally reducible to abstract proposition, and parable as essentially irreducible to such a statement, the gulf between them is absolute." Crossan's whole article is immensely important and I am indebted to it at a number of points in what follows, as I was in "Wisdom and Apocalyptic."

[18]This insight is the basic contribution of Jeremias, *The Parables of Jesus*, and all subsequent work builds on his in this connection.

[19]Crossan points out, correctly, that despite their recognition of the validity of this point, most modern exegetes (including Perrin) have failed to carry it out in practice. "Parable and Example," pp. 286–87.

(*c*) The fundamental element in a parable is the element of metaphor. *A* is compared to *B* so that meaning may be carried over from *B* to *A*. Normally, *A* is the lesser known and *B* the better known. For example, when the Kingdom of God is the lesser known, aspects of its meaning are illuminated by something better known or more readily envisaged: the story of a man finding a treasure in a field, or of a merchant finding a pearl (Matt 13:44–46).

(*d*) There is, therefore, in the parable a literal point, the meaning of the story or image, and also a metaphorical point, the meaning, the story or image as it is transferred to what it is intended to refer to.

(*e*) The purpose of a parable is normally pedagogical; Jewish rabbis used them extensively to illuminate, illustrate, and instruct. In the case of Jesus, however, this normal use of the literary form "parable" seems to have been subordinated to another and different one. In the hands of Jesus the parable is not only a means of instruction but also a form of proclamation.[20]

Let us take as a concrete example the parable of the Good Samaritan (Luke 10:30–36).

> Jesus replied, "A man was going down from Jerusalem to Jericho, and he fell among robbers, who stripped him and beat him, and departed, leaving him half dead. Now by chance a priest was going down that road; and when he saw him he passed by on the other side. So likewise a Levite, when he came to the place and saw him, passed by on the other side. But a Samaritan, as he journeyed, came to where he was; and when he saw him, he had compassion, and went to him and bound up his wounds, pouring on oil and wine; then he set him on his own beast and brought him to an inn, and took care of him. And the next day he took out two denarii and gave them to the innkeeper, saying, 'Take care of him; and whatever more you spend, I will repay you when I come back.' Which of these three, do you think, proved neighbor to the man who fell among the robbers?"

This is the form of the parable as Jesus taught it. The present context of the discussion with the lawyer (10:25–29, 37) has been supplied by the early church and must be ignored in an attempt to understand the parable as a parable *of Jesus*. In its present context the parable is an exemplary story, illustrating by example the principle of neighborliness. This is absolutely in keeping with the use of parables by Jewish rabbis. However, if we ignore the setting given to the story by the early church, as we must, then it is not an exemplary story. Crossan points out that if it were an exemplary story it would be better to have the Samaritan as the victim and the Israelite as the good "neighbor." No, the story *in itself* focuses attention on the deed of the Samaritan rather than on the need of the injured man. "The focal point must remain, not on the good deed itself, but on the *goodness* of the *Samaritan*. When the story is read as one told to a Jewish audience by the Jewish Jesus, it is impossible to avoid facing the good man not just as good, but as Samaritan."[21] But the Jews of Jesus' day despised the Samaritans on both racial and religious grounds, and relations between the two groups were such that no one could

---

[20]This is Crossan's fundamental point, and on this I am following him closely.
[21]Crossan, "Parable and Example," p. 294.

expect hospitality in a Samaritan village if he were on his way to Jerusalem (Luke 9:52–56). So when the parable confronts the hearer of Jesus at the literai level with the combination *good* and *Samaritan*, it is asking that the hearer conceive the inconceivable. "The whole thrust of the story demands that he say what cannot be said: Good + Samaritan."[22]

What happens when one is confronted by the demand to conceive the inconceivable, to say what cannot be said? Either the demand is rejected, or the person concerned begins to question all that he has taken for granted up to that moment. He is confronted by the necessity suddenly to reexamine the very grounds of his being, by a challenge that is effective at the deepest level of existential reality. The parable has become proclamation.

Crossan speaks of moving from the literal point of the parable to its metaphorical point, and his conclusion is worth quoting in full.

The literal point confronted the hearers with the necessity of saying the impossible and having their world turned upside down and radically questioned in its presuppositions. The metaphorical point is that *just so* does the Kingdom of God break abruptly into a person's consciousness and demand the overturn of prior values, closed options, set judgements, and established conclusions. . . . The hearer struggling with the dualism Good Samaritan is actually experiencing in and through this the inbreaking of the Kingdom upon him. *Not only does it happen like this, it happens in this.*[23]

This conclusion from the Good Samaritan can be supported by a consideration of other parables. An almost exact parallel is the parable of the Unjust Steward (Luke 16:1–9).

He also said to the disciples, "There was a rich man who had a steward, and charges were brought to him that this man was wasting his goods. And he called him and said to him, 'What is this that I hear about you? Turn in the account of your stewardship, for you can no longer be steward.' And the steward said to himself, 'What shall I do, since my master is taking the stewardship away from me? I am not strong enough to dig, and I am ashamed to beg. I have decided what to do, so that people may receive me into their houses when I am put out of the stewardship.' So, summoning his master's debtors one by one, he said to the first, 'How much do you owe my master?' He said, 'A hundred measures of oil.' And he said to him, 'Take your bill, and sit down quickly and write fifty.' Then he said to another, 'And how much do you owe?' He said, 'A hundred measures of wheat.' He said to him, 'Take your bill, and write eighty.' The master commended the dishonest steward for his prudence; for the sons of this world are wiser in their own generation than the sons of light. And I tell you, make friends for yourselves by means of unrighteous mammon, so that when it fails they may receive you into the eternal habitations.

In this case again we must ignore the context, as we must also ignore verses 8 and 9 as early attempts to derive a moral from an amoral story. We are then left

[22]Ibid., p. 295.
[23]Ibid. Italics supplied.

with a story of an absolutely dishonest character who gets away with his dishonesty by compounding it. But the thrust of the story itself suggests that this character is in some way to be admired. The anonymous author of the comment in verse 8 recognized this and struggled to understand it: "The master commended the dishonest steward for his prudence."

Instead of asking how this character can be seen as admirable, as did the author of verse 8, we should rather recognize the dramatic affront to all moral standards that the unjust steward in himself represents. In the case of the Good Samaritan, one needs to be aware of the situation between Jews and Samaritans at the time of Jesus in order to appreciate the impossibility of putting together "Good" and "Samaritan," but with the Unjust Steward, the character's decision and actions are an affront to the common moral standards that make possible any business relationship, any delegation of responsibility in the world. The story itself focuses attention on the steward's dialogue with himself and his decision, and it implies that he was successful in his endeavor to avoid the evil consequences of his first dishonesty by compounding it. In a sense, then, the exegesis that concentrates on his "prudence" or the element of decision is correct in that this is the focal point of the story itself. But we should not remain content with recognizing that the story teases the mind of the hearer into applauding an act of decision in critical circumstances.[24] We must go on to understand that the content of that decision is an affront to the accepted canons of moral behavior that make possible an ongoing world of business relationships. This story is as effective a challenge to the hearer to do what cannot be done, i.e., to applaud a decision of this nature, as the Good Samaritan is a challenge to say what cannot be said. The point of the parable as parable, then, is to admit the presence of an order of reality that at the very moment of the telling of the story is challenging all accepted canons of behavior and forms of human relationships. In a sense, the Unjust Steward is a more radical form of proclamation than is the Good Samaritan, for there is a sense of intrinsic rightness in allowing an act of mercy to challenge religious and racial prejudice. But it is very different to applaud a decision that involves such blatant dishonesty; yet that is what Jesus challenged his hearers to do as this parable became a form of his proclamation.

Having argued the matter in some detail with regard to these two parables, we may now proceed in a more summary fashion with others. A major theme of the proclamation of Jesus was reversal, and Crossan points to a number of examples among the parables. In Luke 16:19–31, the Rich Man and Lazarus: "Jesus was . . . interested in the reversal of human situation in which the Kingdom's disruptive advent could be metaphorically portrayed and linguistically made known." In the case of the Pharisee and the Publican (Luke 18:10–14), "the metaphorical point is . . . the complete and radical reversal of accepted human judgment, even of religious judgment, whereby the Kingdom forces its way into human awareness." The Wedding Guest (Luke 14:7–11) as an example of situational reversal on the literal level "points towards . . . [the way in which] the Kingdom arrives and breaks in on a man

---

[24]This is in effect what I did in my previous treatment of the parable. See *Rediscovering*, p. 115.

so that he experiences God's rule at the moment when his own world is turned upside down and radically reversed."[25]

In the hands of Jesus the parable becomes a form of the proclamation of the Kingdom. As the hearers are challenged to say what cannot be said, to applaud what should not be applauded, to recognize in the reversal of human judgments and human situations the sign of the breaking in of God's Kingdom, so the Kingdom "comes." The power of Jesus to transform the parable into a form of proclamation was at the same time a power to mediate to his hearers the experience of the Kingdom as existential reality.

But Jesus did not always use the parable form in this way. Many of his parables instruct or teach or, to use the word we have been using throughout this book, function as *parenesis*. This must have been so, because the message of Jesus could never have been as effective as its historical consequences demonstrate had it not included instruction in the mode of response to the proclamation. In turning to this aspect of Jesus' use of parables, I am dealing with what is uniformly acknowledged and thoroughly discussed in all the literature on the subject; so I may again proceed in summary fashion.

The Jew of Jesus' day who heard the Hid Treasure and the Pearl (Matt 13:44–46) would certainly have understood the metaphorical point to be the recognition that "a man can suddenly be confronted by the experience of [the Kingdom of] God and find the subsequent joy overwhelming and all-determinative." To the Tower Builder and the King going to War (Luke 14:28–32) we may now add the Assassin from the gospel of Thomas. "Here we have three vivid pictures of men from very different walks of life who have one thing in common: a willingness to prepare themselves realistically for the responsibility they assume. . . The builder calculates his resources, the King estimates his strength against his enemy's, the assassin assures himself that his hand has not lost its skill."[26] The metaphorical point of these parables is recognizing that, as the present writer heard T.W. Manson put it, "Salvation may be free, but it is not cheap." The Importuned Friend (the Friend at Midnight, Luke 11:5–8) and the Importuned Judge (the Unjust Judge, Luke 18:1–8) are rabbinical arguments from the lesser to the greater. The metaphorical position in both is the same. The friend is no real friend at all—otherwise he would be out of bed immediately—and the judge is certainly no true judge; yet both could be importuned into doing what they should. If they can be so importuned, how much more can we not trust God who needs no importuning?

We lack the space here to discuss all the parables of Jesus, but we have said enough to make the point that some of the parables of Jesus functioned as proclamation and others as parenesis. Some mediated the experience of the Kingdom of God as an existential reality to those who heard them, while others instructed the hearer to respond in various concrete ways to the experience mediated by the proclamation. An aspect of the use of the parables by Jesus we have not discussed is that which has apparent reference to the future; we return to this under the rubric "Jesus and the future" below.

---

[25]Crossan, "Parable and Example," pp. 296–303.

[26]I am repeating here my previous exegesis of these parables. See Perrin, *Rediscovering*, pp. 89, 127–28, 128–30.

## The proverbial sayings[27]

The essence of a proverbial saying is that it is based on observation of how things are in the world. It is a flash of insight into the repeatable situations of life in the world, and its aphoristic form not only represents insight but also compels it. "A prophet is not without honor, except in his own country" (Mark 6:4). The proverb readily becomes imperatival, basing instruction on common-sense observation. "Do not throw your pearls before swine, lest they trample them underfoot" (Matt 7:6). The proverb can also be expressed in interrogative form, again compelling insight. "Which of you by being anxious can add one cubit to his span of life?" (Matt 6:27). Naturally, in the context of a firm belief in God, the proverb comes to express insight into the way things are, or should be, in the world ordered by God and a challenge to behavior that God will reward.

> For the Lord honored the father above the children,
> and he confirmed the right of the mother over her sons.
> Whoever honors his father atones for sins,
> and whoever glorifies his mother is like one who lays up treasure.
>
> Sir 3:2–4

In this context the proverb is an affirmation of faith in God's just and orderly rule of the world, as are the Jewish proverbs in collections such as the book of Proverbs in the Old Testament, or the Wisdom of Solomon and the Wisdom of Jesus the Son of Sirach in the Apocrypha.

This, then, is the general background against which we must set Jesus' use of the proverb. We limit ourselves to the proverbial sayings that Bultmann established as authentic on the basis of what later came to be called the criterion of dissimilarity: Luke 9:60a; Matt 5:39b–41; Mark 8:35; 10:23b, 25; 10:31; Luke 14:11; Mark 3:27; 3:24–26; Luke 9:62; Matt 7:13–14; Mark 7:15; 10:15; Matt 5:44–48.[28] we examine these in groups according to our own analysis.

(a)  *The most radical sayings:* Luke 9:60a; Matt 5:39b–41

Luke 9:60a  Leave the dead to bury their own dead.

Matt 5:39b–41  If anyone strikes you on the right cheek, turn to him the other also; and if any one would sue you and take your coat, let him have your cloak as well; and if anyone forces you to go one mile, go with him two miles.

---

[27]In the. following discussion I am consciously indebted to Bultmann, *History of the Synoptic Tradition,* pp. 69–108, especially pp. 104–05, and to Beardslee, *Literary Criticism and the New Testament,* pp. 30–41, "The Proverb," and "Uses of the Proverb in the Synoptic Gospels," *Interpretation,* vol. 24 (1970), pp. 61–73.

[28]Bultmann, *History of the Synoptic Tradition,* p. 105.

These are the most radical of the proverbial sayings of Jesus. Indeed, they are so radical they shatter the form of proverbial saying altogether and become something quite different. Where proverbial sayings normally reflect on life in the world and, as Beardslee puts it, "make a continuous whole out of one's existence,"[29] these sayings overturn the whole idea of orderly existence in the world. To "leave the dead to bury their own dead" is to act so irresponsibly as to deny the kind of personal and communal sense of responsibility that makes possible the act of living in community in the world. Giving the "cloak as well" and going the "second mile" are commandments that are impossible to take literally as moral imperatives. The Palestinian peasant at the time of Jesus wore only those two garments, and so the result would have been indecent exposure. The second command refers to the privilege of Roman soldiers to impress local citizens into service; the result of obeying it would be a lifetime of forced servitude.

The history of the interpretation of these sayings is a mellowing down to the point where they become barely possible of fulfillment and hence extraordinarily radical challenges. In connection with the first the evangelist Luke adds, "but as for you, go and proclaim the kingdom of God" (Luke 9:60b), and so makes the saying a dramatic and radical challenge to Christian discipleship. In connection with the second, T.W. Manson says of the second mile: "The first mile renders to Caesar the things that are Caesar's; the second mile, by meeting opposition with kindness, renders to God the things that are God's."[30] but these ancient or modern interpretations are irrelevant to a historical understanding of the message of Jesus.

As the message of Jesus these are not radical demands but part of the proclamation of the Kingdom of God. They challenge the hearer, not to radical obedience, but to radical questioning. They jolt him out of the effort to make a continuous whole of his existence and into a judgment about that existence. They exactly match the function of the parable as proclamation in the message of Jesus.

*(b)  The eschatological reversal sayings:* Mark 8:35; 10:23b, 25; 10:31; Luke 14:11

| | |
|---|---|
| *Mark 8:35* | For whoever would save his life will lose it; and whoever loses his life for my sake and the gospel's will save it. (The original probably ran something like ". . . for the sake of the kingdom of God.") |
| *Mark 10:23b, 25* | How hard it will be for those who have riches to enter the kingdom of God! . . . it is easier for a camel to go through the eye of a needle than for a rich man to enter the kingdom of God. |
| *Mark 10:31* | But many that are first will be last, and the last first. |
| *Luke 14:11* | Every one who exalts himself will be humbled, and he who humbles himself will be exalted. |

---

[29]Beardslee, "Uses of the Proverb," p. 71.
[30]Manson, *Sayings of Jesus*, p. 160.

These sayings need not delay us. The theme of eschatological reversal is one of the best-attested themes of the message of Jesus. It proclaims the Kingdom as eschatological reversal of the present and so invites, indeed demands, judgment on that present. Again, this use of the proverb exactly parallels a use of the parable in the message of Jesus.

(c)   *The conflict sayings:* Mark 3:27; 3:24–26

Mark 3:27        No one can enter a strong man's house and plunder his goods, unless he first binds the strong man; then indeed he may plunder his house.

Mark 3:24–26   If a kingdom is divided against itself, that kingdom cannot stand. And if a house is divided against itself, that house will not be able to stand. And if Satan has risen up against himself and is divided, he cannot stand, but is coming to an end.

Here we have the same kind of thinking expressed in proverbial sayings as in the Kingdom sayings Luke 11:20 and Matt 11:12. In the latter the Kingdom is proclaimed in terms of the exorcisms of Jesus, the fate of the Baptist, and the potential fate of Jesus and his disciples. The proverbial sayings are an aphoristic expression of an understanding of existence as essentially an arena of conflict in terms of which the Kingdom of God becomes a matter of human experience.

(d)   *The parenetical sayings:* Luke 9:62; Matt 7:13–14; Mark 7:15; 10:15; Matt 5:44–48

Luke 9:62         No one who puts his hand to the plough and looks back is fit for the kingdom of God.

Matt 7:13–14    Enter by the narrow gate; for the gate is wide and the way is easy, that leads to destruction, and those who enter by it are many. For the gate is narrow and the way is hard, that leads to life, and those who find it are few.

Mark 7:15         There is nothing outside a man which by going into him can defile him; but the things which come out of a man are what defile him.

Mark 10:15       Whoever does not receive the kingdom of God like a child shall not enter it.

Matt 5:44–48    Love your enemies and pray for those who persecute you, so that you may be sons of your Father . . . for he makes his sun rise on the evil and on the good, and sends rain on the just and on the unjust. For if you love those who love you, what reward have you? Do not even the tax collectors do the same? And if you salute only your brethren, what more are you doing than others? Do not even the Gentiles do the same? You, therefore, must be perfect, as your heavenly Father is perfect.

In these sayings the normal use of the proverbial saying as parenesis reasserts itself, and Jesus uses the form exactly as his contemporaries among the rabbis would have. There is, of course, one great difference: these sayings are set in the context of the proclamation of the Kingdom of God. Like all the pareneses of Jesus, they are concerned with response to the reality of the Kingdom.

### The Lord's Prayer

We will not discuss the prayer in any detail here[31] but wish to call attention to a comparison between the prayer Jesus taught his disciples and the prayers of his Jewish contemporaries. A made-up parallel to the Lord's Prayer taken from Jewish sources is as follows:

Our Father, who art in Heaven. Hallowed be Thine exalted Name in the world which Thou didst create according to Thy will. May Thy Kingdom and Thy lordship come speedily, and be acknowledged by all the world, that Thy Name may be praised in all eternity. May Thy will be done in Heaven, and also on earth give tranquillity of spirit to those that fear thee, yet in all things do what seemeth good to Thee. Let us enjoy the bread daily apportioned to us. Forgive us, our Father, for we have sinned; forgive also all who have done us injury; even as we also forgive all. And lead us not into temptation, but keep us far from all evil. For thine is the greatness and the power and the dominion, the victory and the majesty, yea all in Heaven and on earth. Thine is the Kingdom, and Thou art Lord of all beings forever. Amen.[32]

The Lukan version of the Lord's Prayer (Luke 11:2–4), generally recognized as being close to the prayer Jesus taught his disciples, reads as follows.

Father,
Hallowed be thy name. Thy Kingdom come.
Give us each day our daily bread;
and forgive us our sins,
   for we ourselves forgive
   everyone who is indebted to [i.e.,
   who has sinned against] us;
and lead us not into temptation.

In sentiment and meaning the two prayers are exactly parallel, and clearly Jesus was echoing his Jewish heritage. Yet verbally the two are worlds apart. The simplicity and brevity of the second express a vastly different understanding of the relationship between the petitioner and his God than do the sonorous phrases of the first. For the person who can pray the prayer of Jesus, in a very real sense the Kingdom has already come.

[31]I offered an exegesis of the prayer in *Kingdom*, pp. 191–98.
[32]Taken from Manson, *Sayings of Jesus*, pp. 167–68.

## Jesus and the future

We come now to an extraordinarily difficult point in the message of Jesus, his expectation and teaching concerning the future. I am convinced that all sayings or teaching ascribed to Jesus in the gospels that give a definite form to a future expectation—for example, a future coming of the Son of Man—fail the test of the criteria for authenticity.[33] But to say this is not to resolve the problem, for the question is not whether Jesus expected a future coming of the Son of Man, but whether he looked toward the future for something different from what was already present in the experience of those confronted by the reality of his ministry and his message.

To bring this question into focus we must call attention to one result of our discussion of the message of Jesus, namely, that Jesus claimed to mediate the reality of the Kingdom of God to his hearers in a way that had not been done before. His proclamation of the Kingdom of God necessarily claims to mediate an experience of existential reality to those of his hearers who responded in the right way to the proclamation. He took the literary form of the parable and pushed it beyond its normal limits, so that it became a medium of proclamation, and the hearers found the Kingdom breaking abruptly into their consciousness as they were forced to say what could not be said and to applaud what should not be applauded. Similarly, on the lips of Jesus the proverbial saying also became a medium of proclamation in its power to jolt the hearer out of the effort to make a continual whole of existence in the world and into a judgment about that existence. In this "jolting" the Kingdom is also "breaking in." Finally, the Lord's Prayer envisages and gives verbal expression to a relationship with God so different from that in the Jewish prayers that for the person who can pray that prayer the Kingdom has, in a real sense, already "come."

But there is another aspect, for within the Lord's Prayer itself we find the petition "Thy Kingdom come." Since we have already recognized it to parallel the petitions of the Jewish prayers in sentiment and meaning, we are forced to recognize that this petition looks toward the future, as the petitions in the Jewish prayers certainly did. Furthermore, there is a group of parables, the Sower (Mark 4:3–9), the Mustard Seed (Mark 4:30–32), the Leaven (Matt 13:33), and the Seed Growing of Itself (Mark 4:26–29), all bearing the stamp of authenticity and all challenging the hearer to look toward the future. At the literal level they move from the present of the sowing, or of the leavening of the dough, to the future of the result of the sowing or the leavening. At the metaphorical level also, therefore, they must be held to challenge the hearer to move from his present to a future.

At this point it becomes important to remind ourselves of several things. First, it is not necessarily the case that a modern conception of time and history can be ascribed to Jesus, a man of the first century. This consideration is reinforced by recalling that at one time, when first-century Jewish apocalyptic came very close to a modern understanding of signs as relating in a

---

[33]I give a detailed discussion of this claim in chapter 4 of *Rediscovering the Teaching of Jesus.*

one-to-one relationship to temporal, historical events and figures, Jesus categorically dissociated himself from such thinking. We are therefore justified in claiming that Jesus looked toward a future, but not necessarily a future conceived in what we would recognize as temporal and historical terms. His message promised his followers a future that would be a consummation of what they already knew in the present of their response to the challenge of his proclamation. In their turn, they interpreted this message immediately in terms of a temporal and historical event, the coming of Jesus as Son of Man. They were not necessarily correct in so doing.

## FROM JESUS TO THE NEW TESTAMENT

The Jesus we can reconstruct historically from the New Testament is, therefore, the proclaimer of the Kingdom of God. More than that, he is one who had the power to mediate to his hearers the existential reality of that which he proclaimed, and who instructed them in ways of responding to that reality so that they might enter ever more deeply into their experience of it. On this basis he taught those who responded to the proclamation to look to the future with confidence.

There are two things conspicuously absent from this picture compared to that given in the gospels. The first is a specific claim by Jesus himself to be the Messiah. It is a striking feature of modern historical research that there is general agreement that the Messianic claims put on the lips of the Jesus of the gospels are exactly that: claims *put on* the lips of the Jesus of the gospels. So far as we can tell, Jesus proclaimed the Kingdom of God but made no explicit claims for himself. Of course, the very fact that he proclaimed the Kingdom of God and challenged his hearers as he did no doubt *implied* claims about himself, but no such claims were ever made explicit. The explicit claims in the gospels reflect the piety and understanding of the early church, not historical data about Jesus of Nazareth.

The second element conspicuously absent from this picture is an interpretation by Jesus of his own death. The fact is that we simply do not know how Jesus thought about his own death. In view of the fate of the Baptist and of the saying Matt 11:12, it is inherently probable that Jesus did recognize the dangers to himself of his last visit to Jerusalem, but the sayings in the gospels and in 1 Corinthians 11 that reflect on his death are also products of the piety and understanding of the early church, and they do not tell us anything about Jesus himself. "The greatest embarassment to the attempt to reconstruct a portrait of Jesus is the fact that we cannot know how Jesus understood his end, his death."[34] That is Bultmann's statement of the case, and it is valid.

We do know, however, that within a short time after his death the followers of Jesus were claiming that God had raised him from the dead. Where he himself had proclaimed the Kingdom of God, they began to proclaim him. The

[34]Bultmann, "The Primitive Christian Kerygma and the Historical Jesus," in *The Historical Jesus and the Kerygmatic Christ*, ed. Braaten and Harrisville, p. 23.

proclaimer became the proclaimed.[35] We have traced the various forms of this proclamation throughout the New Testament; our concern now is simply to note that he who proclaimed the Kingdom of God began himself to be proclaimed as (a) the one who was about to return on the clouds of heaven as Son of Man and agent of God's final judgment and redemption of the world (so apocalyptic Christianity); (b) as the one who "died for our sins and was raised for our justification" (so Paul); and (c) as "the lamb of God, who takes away the sin of the world" (so the Johannine school). The historical details of the movement from the Jesus who proclaimed the Kingdom of God to the New Testament and its various proclamations of Jesus as the Christ, the Son of God, are probably forever lost to us. What we have is the New Testament itself, its proclamation and its parenesis, its myth and its history.


## FURTHER READING

Three of our resource books have a discussion of Jesus.

> Fuller, *Intro.*, pp. 69–103. This is a discussion of gospel criticism and its consequence for life of Jesus research, of criteria for authenticity, and of our fundamental knowledge of Jesus and his message. The reader will find that though Professor Fuller and I share the same general approach, he is much more ready than I am to accept material as authentic. I have made reference to his work at appropriate points in the chapter above.
> *PCB*, pp. 733–47 (J. S. Bowman).
> *IDB*, vol. 2, pp. 869–96 (F. C. Grant). Both Bowman and Grant write from a viewpoint reached before the full force of the impact of the form-critical view of the gospels on life of Jesus research was appreciated.

The literature on Jesus is immense, and the flow shows no sign of diminishing. I gave an annotated bibliography of general work on the [life and] teaching of Jesus in *Rediscovering*, pp. 249–51. I will now give again some of the works listed there, together with a selection from the works published since 1967.

> Bultmann, *Jesus and the Word*. Originally published in German in 1926, this is the starting point for all responsible work on Jesus being carried on today. A careful reading of this book is absolutely indispensable to any study of the subject.
> Bornkamm, *Jesus of Nazareth*. This was published in Germany as scholarship was becoming possible again after the dislocations of the

---

[35]This is Bultmann's famous formulation of the matter. In the essay quoted immediately above, for example, he says: "While the preaching of Jesus is the eschatological message of the coming—more, of the breaking-in of the Kingdom of God—in the kerygma [message of the church] Jesus Christ is proclaimed as the one who died vicariously on the cross for the sins of men and was miraculously raised by God for our salvation" (p. 16).

Hitler period, and of the Second World War and its aftermath. It attempted to present a general picture of the life and teaching of Jesus in accordance with the methods and findings of contemporary New Testament scholarship, and it succeeded magnificently. It is easily the best book on Jesus currently available.

Conzelmann, *Jesus.* An expanded and updated translation of Conzelmann's article "Jesus Christ" in the German encyclopedia *Religion in Geschichte und Gegenwart.*

Vögtle, "Jesus Christ," in *Sacramentum Verbi* (ed. J. B. Bauer), vol. 3, pp. 419–37. A presentation by a leading European Roman Catholic scholar.

McArthur, *In Search of the Historical Jesus.* A selection of articles on various aspects of the subject by representative scholars.

Kee, *Jesus in History.* A valuable discussion of the problems and issues.

A question that has been deliberately omitted from the discussion in this chapter is the "question of the historical Jesus," that is, the question of the significance of historical knowledge of Jesus for Christian faith. This question has been the subject of intensive discussion by scholars since the end of the nineteenth century, when doubts first began to be felt about the position of liberal scholarship that the historical Jesus was the source of Christian faith and hence historical knowledge of him was the foundation of that faith. The debate shows no signs of abating, and any attempt to outline its progress or to indicate the issues currently at stake in it would burst the bounds of this or any introduction to the New Testament. I devoted chapter 5 of *Rediscovering* (pp. 207–48) to it, and gave there an annotated bibliography (pp. 262–65). Two extremely important books on the subject published since the completion of the manuscript of that book in 1967 are the following:

Harvey, *The Historian and the Believer.*
Keck, *A Future for the Historical Jesus.*

# Epilogue
## Ways of Being Religious in the New Testament

No one can read the New Testament without being impressed by its immense variety, and especially by the variety of ways of being religious it exhibits. Although the New Testament is a unity in that all of its books accept the centrality of Jesus Christ, nonetheless it is diverse in that both the understanding of Jesus as the Christ and the understanding of what it means to accept him as the Christ are almost infinitely varied. What is more, the variations are such as almost to run the gamut of ways of being religious in the world. Ascetic and mystic, warrior priest and worker priest, apocalyptic visionary and social revolutionary, ecclesiastical dignitary and street-corner pamphleteer—all these and many more have taken their inspiration from the New Testament or from some part of it. We have constantly been calling attention to this variety within the New Testament; now in this epilogue we briefly summarize some of its major thrusts.

## APOCALYPTICISM

The Christian movement began as an apocalyptic sect and apocalypticism is a major element in the synoptic gospel source Q, in the gospel of Mark and, of course, in the book of Revelation, itself an apocalypse. The apocalyptic visionary is one caught up in the drama of a history hurrying to its close, preparing himself for the imminent future in which all will be different. Christian apocalypticism developed the concept of Jesus as the Son of Man, the powerful redeemer who would descend to the earth on the clouds of heaven to judge and redeem, destroy and remake. But it did more than that, because not only was Jesus the Son of Man; the Son of Man was Jesus. That meant that characteristics of the redeemer figure were always subject to the control of the lineaments of Jesus. (So the evangelist Mark was able to blend together the elements of power and authority and the necessity of suffering.) In many respects, Christian apocalyptic was indistinguishable from Jewish, and

**305**

certainly Christian apocalyptic writers made extensive use of Jewish apocalyptic literature. But the central feature of their visions was always Jesus. Nonetheless, the movement was apocalyptic, with its sense of a world being caught up in the throes of catastrophic change and its belief in the imminence of the final intervention of God that would make all things new and different. Like all apocalypticists, the Christian apocalypticist despaired of the world and its history but had faith in God who was about to change it. As a Christian he believed that Jesus would be the means of that change, and he prepared himself for the imminent coming of Jesus as Son of Man by obeying the teaching that was given in the name of Jesus.

## THE APOSTLE PAUL

"For the good that I would I do not: but the evil that I would not, that I do" (Rom 7:19, KJV). With this cry from the heart of religious humanity we reach one of the classical options of New Testament religion—Paul and his search for justification. Haunted by the sense of stain, of guilt, of defilement, Paul searches for the means of cleansing, of expiation, of redemption, and he finds it in Christ and his cross. That which he could not do for himself, that which the Law could not help him to do, Christ has done for him. He can now stand in the presence of God, from which presence he would before have had to flee, for he now bears not his own righteousness but Christ's. He now lives in the world not the life of guilt and fear but of freedom and power, and this life is Christ's gift to him. Here we recognize a classical form of the Christian experience of religious reality. It is the quest for justification in the sight of God, and the discovery that it can be received only as a gift. Central to this understanding is a concentration on the cross of Christ, interpreting it as a means of reconciling man to God. This understanding of religion is loaded with the symbolism of evil and focuses attention on the means whereby that evil is overcome and a quality of life free from it can be known.

## THE EVANGELIST MATTHEW

With the evangelist Matthew we reach another of the classical options of New Testament religion. Here the central point is the concept of a verbal revelation authoritatively interpreted. The essence of religion is obedience to the revealed truth, and such obedience is possible because the world and life are ordered by the God who has revealed this truth to man. There is order and stability to be experienced; there is the firm basis of a revealed truth on which to build; there are appointed means both to make possible the necessary understanding and also to help attain the necessary level of obedience. These means are present in the church, in the structure and organization of the community of which the individual is a member and in which the risen and glorified Christ is present. In this understanding of what it means to be religious in the world the essential elements are those of revelation and of obedience to revelation, and the conviction that there is a correspondence between the revealed truth and the experienced reality of life in the world such that life in the world can be successfully organized on the basis of obedience to the revelation, and only on that basis.

## THE AUTHOR OF LUKE-ACTS

The author of Luke-Acts is also concerned with revelation but with revelation in the form of a sacred person and a sacred time, and with a structured means of relating to that time. That person is Jesus and his time is that between the descent of the Spirit upon him at his baptism and the return of the Spirit to the Father at the cross. One relates to him and to his time by means of the Spirit, which returned to the church and the believer at the baptism of Pentecost. In his own life Jesus was a paradigm of the possibilities for human existence in the world and the model of what it means to be religious in the world. The presence of the spirit of Jesus in the world, linking the believer with the sacred life and sacred time of Jesus, empowers the believer to exhibit the same quality of life in the world that Jesus did. This is borne out by the heroes of the church whose lives paralleled Jesus' in many respects. To be religious in the world is to imitate Jesus, an imitation made possible by the presence and work of his spirit in the world. To imitate Jesus means to care for the outcast, to concern oneself for the neighbor, to live the life of love in the world and for the world.

## THE EVANGELIST JOHN

In the case of the evangelist John we have a concentration on the cross of Christ almost as strong as that in the case of the apostle Paul. In John, however, the context is not the symbolism of evil but rather the symbolism of glory. The Christ of John's gospel is the descending/ascending redeemer, and the cross is the moment of his glorious return whence he came—having achieved that for which he was sent. While the cross itself is the moment of supreme glorification, there is a series of earlier majestic "signs" by means of which the Christ also manifests his glory. Moreover, a series of solemn discourses explores the glory of this Christ by using primary symbols of life-giving power—water, light, bread—and by claiming explicitly that he gives life and "eternal life" to those who believe in him. Further, he does the Father's work; he is at one with God. Combined with this emphasis on glory and power and on the Christ's oneness with God is an emphasis on the concern of the Christ for the believer—for example, by the use of shepherd and sheep symbolism—and on the believer's oneness with him.

This last point is the key to the Johannine understanding of what it means to be religious in the world. The believer contemplates the glorious majesty of the Christ and of the Christ's oneness with the Father, and then finds himself at one with the Christ in a mystical union by means of which he experiences the life of love in the world. But the emphasis now is on the rapture of love as experienced in the world through knowledge of Christ, whereas in Luke-Acts the emphasis is on the manifestation of love in human relationships. Of course, neither excludes the other (see 1 John 1:9–11), but the emphasis is different.

The gospel and letters of John are the charter of Christian mysticism.

## THE OTHER WAYS

There are other understandings of what it means to be religious in the world in the New Testament, but they are all variations, sometimes very important variations, on the themes we have already established. So, for example, the gospel of Mark reshapes the apocalyptic way of being religious in the world by systematizing the apocalyptic drama, by developing the theme of the Son of Man who "must" suffer, and by showing what these things mean to faith and discipleship. Similarly, the writers of the period of "emergent Catholicism" develop, systematize—and further institutionalize—the "way" of the gospel of Matthew. But we have said enough, we believe, to indicate something of the classical options the New Testament presents.

# Appendix 1
## The Hellenistic World in New Testament Times

The New Testament is a product of the Hellenistic world. Written in its language, Hellenistic or *koinē* Greek, it reflects its concerns, for Hellenistic culture was immersed in religion and philosophy as possible answers to the problem of life in the world.

The Hellenistic world came into being as a consequence of the conquests of Alexander the Great, 356–323 B.C. Alexander was the son of Philip, king of Macedon, and Aristotle was his tutor.[1] He was therefore heir to the classical Greek culture of the Athens of Pericles and Plato, and saw himself as the apostle and emissary of that culture. In a series of extraordinary military feats he gained control of the interminably warring city states of Greece, and then he conquered the Persian empire, establishing a personal dominion extending from Greece in the west to the Punjab of India in the east, and from the Black Sea in the north to the Red Sea in the south. In 333 B.C. Alexander defeated the Persian army at the battle of Issus; within ten years he was dead but the Hellenistic world had been born.

Politically the empire of Alexander did not survive his death; his generals fought among themselves for control of various parts of it and ultimately carved out personal kingdoms. But his conquests "spread Hellenism in a vast colonizing wave throughout the Near East and created, if not politically, at least economically and culturally, a single world stretching from Gibraltar to the Punjab, open to trade and social intercourse and with a considerable overlay of common civilization and the Greek *koinē* as a lingua franca."[2]

These economic and cultural consequences of Alexander's conquests are important to our understanding of the Hellenistic world and the New Testament. Everywhere he went Alexander established cities, including Alexandria in Egypt, as centers of Greek life and culture. His successors in

[1] A brilliant and convincing portrait of the young Alexander has been drawn by the historical novelist Mary Renault in her novel *Fire from Heaven* (1969).
[2] From the article on Alexander in the *Encyclopaedia Britannica* (1968), vol. 1, p. 576.

**309**

their various kingdoms followed his policy, with the result that Greek came to be spoken "from Gibraltar to the Punjab," allowing the dynamic interchange of ideas that was the main feature of the Hellenistic world. Local cultures tended to break down under the impact of Greek culture; but in adapting and responding to that culture they took on new forms and a new dynamism.

A main feature of the Hellenistic world was therefore *movement*. The new cultural and economic unity made it possible for people to leave their homelands and seek their fortunes elsewhere. Not only the Jews but other people as well were spreading out into the wider world. As they took their cultural heritages with them and confronted, and were confronted by, other cultural heritages, an extraordinarily fertile interchange of ideas became possible.

## POLITICAL HISTORY

After Alexander's death in 323 B.C., there ensued a confused period of wars, with fighting among his various generals. Some sought to preserve the empire as a unit and others, as we have said, sought to carve out for themselves personal kingdoms. Known as the period of the wars of the Diadochi (successors of Alexander), this disruption lasted for almost fifty years, until approximately 280 B.C. It ended with an uneasy balance of power between three major kingdoms: that of Antigonus and his successors, the Antigonids, in Macedonia and parts of Greece and Asia Minor; that of Seleucus and his successors, the Seleucids, in Syria; and that of Ptolemy and his successors, the Ptolemies, in Egypt. There was a constant probing of that balance of power, especially in border areas between the kingdoms, and it was the fate of the Jewish people in Palestine to inhabit the border area between the Seleucids in Syria and the Ptolemies in Egypt.

Toward the end of the third century B.C., the relative quiet in Macedon, Syria, and Egypt began to be seriously disturbed. Aggressive kings came to the throne in Syria and Macedon: Antiochus III, known as "the Great," in Syria in 228 B.C. and Philip V in Macedon in 221. They began to consolidate and expand their empires. Then in 205 Ptolemy V, a child, succeeded to the throne of Egypt, and Antiochus and Philip seized their chance and began to attack the Ptolemaic domains. But now there was a new factor in the situation: the rise to power of Rome.

During the previous century Rome had unified Italy and expanded her influence in the western Mediterranean. In 201 B.C. she successfully concluded a war against Carthage—the second of the so-called Punic Wars—and was mistress of the western Mediterranean. Now there were four powers to be considered: the Hellenistic kingdoms of Macedon, Syria, and Egypt—and Rome. The Hellenistic kingdoms appeared strong and flourishing but were no match for Rome's organization and energy. Various appeals for help were made to Rome as the rising power in the West, and she began to intervene more and more in the affairs of the eastern Mediterranean. She seems to have been motivated by a genuine admiration for Greek culture, and a desire to establish stability in the homeland of that culture and a stable eastern frontier to her own domain. But conditions kept pulling that frontier further and further east until Rome found herself the mistress of an empire as broad as Alexander's and destined to last for five hundred years. Gradually, the three major Hellenistic kingdoms were brought under Roman control. Macedon was defeated in a war, 171–168 B.C. Syria became a Roman province in 63 B.C., and Egypt in 30 B.C. The annexation of Syria was part of a settlement in the East by the Roman general Pompey, and it was at this point that the Jewish people passed under Roman control, after a century of independence.[3]

The vast extension of Roman power in the last two centuries before Christ put an immense strain on the Roman system of government, which was republican. There was an ever increasing need for strong leaders and efficient organization, and no short supply of men able and willing to meet those needs. The result was finally the rise to power of Julius Caesar, his murder in 44 B.C., and thirteen years of civil war. But in 31 B.C. Octavian, Caesar's heir, brought the civil war to an end by defeating Anthony at the battle of Actium. In the next year, following the suicides of Anthony and Cleopatra, he annexed Egypt, and the Roman world became an empire with Octavian at its head. He took the title Caesar Augustus, and at this point we reach the New Testament story, for the taxation census with which the birth of Jesus is associated in Luke 2:1 is part of the story of the organization of the Empire carried out by Augustus.

The empire established by Caesar Augustus is the world of the New Testament. The Christian movement began in an obscure province of that empire, and its missionaries traveled under conditions made possible by the establishment of the "peace of Augustus."

## HELLENISTIC CULTURE

The political world of the New Testament is the world of Rome and its empire, but the culture of that world is Hellenism, a culture developed over the three centuries between the conquests of Alexander and the establishment of the Empire by Augustus. Made possible by the spread of Greek as a common language, and by the founding of cities that became centers for the interchange of ideas, Hellenistic culture had an enormous dynamism generated by the world's suddenly being one world with one language. There was no longer the parochialism that sprang from the idea of one city as the center of the civilized world. Rather, a new cosmopolitanism emerged in which any city might become a center for the interchange of ideas from all over the world. In most cities public instruction in the Greek language and Greek rhetoric, literature, and philosophy was available in one form or another, and at centers such as Athens or Alexandria professional scholars were engaged in literary or scientific work at major institutions. Nor was this education available only to the wealthy or the aristocratic; the Hellenistic cities were disseminators of Greek culture and they took their responsibility seriously. An education in

[3]The history of the Jewish people in this period is the subject of Appendix 2.

Greek was available in many places to anyone interested in acquiring it—and there was a real incentive to acquire it, for there was a great demand for people with Greek to fill all kinds of positions in commerce and government. This comparative accessibility of an education in Greek became very important to the Christian movement, because in New Testament times the Christian movement was very much a lower- or, at best, middle-class movement (see 1 Cor 1:26) and yet it could still produce the authors of its literature.

Hellenistic life had its own vicissitudes. Travel was now possible as it had never been possible before, but with it came the spread of diseases to which local populations had no natural resistance. Men were now living in cities in greater numbers than they had ever done before, creating the problem of feeding the new urban populations. The Hellenistic world never did solve this problem satisfactorily and famine was an ever recurring possibility. War too was a constant feature of the Hellenistic world until Augustus established a general peace in 30 B.C., and the practice of enslaving conquered populations was general. So a family could be prosperous in a city one year and sold into slavery the next. In addition, the general breakdown of older, established, local culture meant that the sense of belonging to a natural and continuing community was simply no longer a refuge. These factors all strongly affected the forms of Hellenistic culture, as they affected the growth of New Testament Christianity.

We now briefly review some major aspects of Hellenistic culture, as far as possible by presenting texts from the culture, and calling attention to matters that are important to an understanding of particular parts of the New Testament.

## Philosophy

### Plato's allegory of the cave

Plato's allegory presents a view of the world as a prison in which men experience only the shadow of the real world, the world of ideas. This kind of thinking became characteristic of Hellenism in general, and in the New Testament we find it in such things as the great christological hymns and the role of the tabernacle in the letter to the Hebrews. It became particularly characteristic of Gnosticism.

> And now, I said, let me show in a figure how far our nature is enlightened or unenlightened:—Behold! human beings living in an underground den, which has a mouth open towards the light and reaching all along the den; here they have been from their childhood, and have their legs and necks chained so that they cannot move, and can only see before them, being prevented by the chains from turning round their heads. Above and behind them a fire is blazing at a distance, and between the fire and the prisoners there is a raised way; and you will see, if you look, a low wall built along the way, like the screen which marionette players have in front of them, over which they show the puppets.

I see.

And do you see, I said, men passing all along the wall carrying all sorts of vessels, and statues and figures of animals made of wood and stone and various materials, which appear over the wall? Some of them are talking, others silent.

You have shown me a strange image, and they are strange prisoners.

Like ourselves, I replied; and they see only their own shadows, or the shadows of one another, which the fire throws on the opposite wall of the cave?

True, he said; how could they see anything but the shadows if they were never allowed to move their heads?

And of the objects which are being carried in like manner they would only see the shadows?

Yes, he said.

And if they were able to converse with one another, would they not suppose that they were naming what was actually before them?

Very true.

And suppose further that the prison had an echo which came from the other side, would they not be sure to fancy when one of the passers-by spoke that the voice which they heard came from the passing shadow?

No question, he replied.

To them, I said, the truth would be literally nothing but the shadows of the images.

That is certain.[4]


## Cleanthes, a fragment

Cleanthes was a Greek Stoic philosopher of the third century B.C. The Stoics believed that the world was ordered by a divine reason, the Logos, a spark or seed of which dwelt within man. A man could find his place in the world by obeying the spark or seed of the Logos within himself. The closeness of philosophy and religion can be seen in this fragment:

Thou, O Zeus, art praised above all gods:
many are thy names and thine is all power for ever.
The beginning of the world was from thee:
and with law thou rulest over all things.
Unto thee may all flesh speak: for we are
thy offspring.
Therefore will I raise a hymn unto thee:
and will ever sing of thy power.
The whole order of the heavens obeyeth thy
word: as it moveth around the earth:
With little and great lights mixed together:
how great art thou, King above all for ever![5]


[4]From *The Republic*, Bk. VII, as quoted in Barrett, *The New Testament Background*, pp. 58–59.

[5]As quoted in Barrett, *Background*, p. 63.

*Epictetus,* Discourses

Much of Hellenistic philosophy was an attempt to arm oneself against the unpredictability of life in the Hellenistic world, as this short passage from the *Discourses* of Epictetus shows:

> First then you must make your Governing Principle pure, and hold fast this rule of life, "Henceforth my mind is the material I have to work on, as the carpenter has his timber and the shoemaker his leather: my business is to deal with my impressions aright. My wretched body is nothing to me, its parts are nothing to me. Death? Let it come when it will, whether to my whole body or to a part of it. Exile? Can one be sent into exile beyond the Universe? One cannot. Wherever I go, there is the sun, there is the moon, there are the stars, dreams, auguries, conversation with the gods."[6]

## The Rule of Chance

The vicissitudes of life in the Hellenistic world convinced many people that their lives were controlled by fate or chance. Astrology and all kinds of soothsaying and divination were widely practiced:

> Fate has decreed as a law for each person the unalterable consequences of his horoscope, controlled by many causes of good and evil; and their results are watched over by two self-begotten deities who are her ministers, Hope (Elpis) and Chance (Tyche); these rule over life, and by both deception and compulsion see to it that everyone obeys the law.[7]

## Magic

Magic was widely practiced and we have many records of spells and invocations, oaths, curses, and blessings. Every possible name was invoked, the weirder sounding the better.

> I call upon thee who hast created earth and bone and all flesh and spirit, and hast fixed the bounds of the sea and nailed fast the heaven, who hast separated light from darkness. Thou, great Spirit, who as guardian of law rulest all things; eternal Eye, Daemon of daemons, God of gods, Lord of spirits, unerring Aion, Iao—hearken to my cry! I call upon thee, Lord of the Gods, Zeus who thunderest in the heights, Zeus the Ruler, Adonai, Lord Iao.[8]

---

[6]As quoted in Barrett, *Background,* pp. 75–76.
[7]Vettius Valens (2nd cent. A.D.), as quoted in Grant, *Hellenistic Religions,* pp. 60–61.
[8]As quoted in Grant, *Hellenistic Religions,* p. 47.

## The Hellenistic Religious Cults

As we point out in chapter 3, in many respects Christianity would have appeared to be a typical Hellenistic religious cult. These cults, characteristic manifestations of Hellenistic religiosity, originated in different countries but acquired similar traits as they circulated in the Hellenistic world. They were "mysteries," reserving their rites and their texts only for the initiates, and our knowledge of them is therefore incomplete. But they featured a recital or reenactment of a cult legend of the hero's deeds, an act of initiation, and a sacred meal. They promised the initiate immortality, and they offered membership in a close-knit community and hence a sense of belonging.

One such cult centered around Serapis, an Egyptian deity whose worship spread broadly in the Hellenistic world. The cult center was known as a Serapeum, and some of these in the major cities became famous, especially the one at Alexandria. The initiates apparently went on pilgrimages to such centers and a letter has been found from Egypt testifying to this practice. It is one of the most touching letters from antiquity.

Isias to her brother [i.e., husband] Hephaestion greeting. If you are well and other things are going right, it would accord with the prayer which I make continually to the gods. I myself and the child and all the household are in good health and think of you always. When I received your letter from Horus, in which you announce that you are in detention in the Serapeum at Memphis, for the news that you are well I straightway thanked the gods, but about your not coming home, when all the others who had been secluded there have come, I am ill-pleased, because after having piloted myself and your child through such bad times and been driven to every extremity owing to the price of corn I thought that now at least, with you at home, I should enjoy some respite, whereas you have not even thought of coming home nor given any regard to our circumstances, remembering how I was in want of everything while you were still here, not to mention this long lapse of time and these critical days, during which you have sent us nothing. As, moreover, Horus who delivered the letter has brought news of your having been released from detention, I am thoroughly ill-pleased. Notwithstanding, as your mother also is annoyed, for her sake as well as for mine please return to the city, if nothing more pressing holds you back. You will do me a favour by taking care of your bodily health. Goodbye.[9]

## Gnosticism

Gnosticism was typical in the Hellenistic world. Its point of departure was a sense of two worlds and of man as imprisoned in the lesser world, which in Gnostic thinking became positively evil. Gnosticism took many forms and in several different manifestations it became a major Christian heresy. Insofar as

[9]As quoted in Barrett, *Background*, pp. 27–28.

it directly affects the understanding of the New Testament we describe and discuss it in chapter 6 and Appendix 3.

## The "Divine Man"

At several points we mention the phenomenon of the "divine man," the hero or philosopher who was regarded as embodying the power of a god and who exhibited that power by various miracles, divination, foretelling the future, and so on. One of the most famous of these was Apollonius of Tyana. He lived through most of the first Christian century and shortly after 217 a "Life" of him was written by Philostratus, from which we quote an incident. It is a deliberately literary work and hence rather different from the directness and brevity of the Christian stories, which are only one stage or so removed from oral tradition.

Now while he was discussing the question of libations, there chanced to be present in his audience a young dandy who bore so evil a reputation for licentiousness, that his conduct had once been the subject of coarse street-corner songs. His home was Corcyra, and he traced his pedigree to Alcinous the Phaeacian who entertained Odysseus. Apollonius then was talking about libations, and was urging them not to drink out of a particular cup, but to reserve it for the gods, without ever touching it or drinking out of it. But when he also urged them to have handles on the cup, and to pour the libation over the handle, because that is the part of the cup at which men are least likely to drink, the youth burst out into loud and coarse laughter, and quite drowned his voice. Then Apollonius looked up at him and said: "It is not yourself that perpetrates this insult, but the demon, who drives you on without your knowing it." And in fact the youth was, without knowing it, possessed by a devil; for he would laugh at things that no one else laughed at, and then he would fall to weeping for no reason at all, and he would talk and sing to himself. Now most people thought that it was the boisterous humour of youth which led him into such excesses; but he was really the mouthpiece of a devil, though it only seemed a drunken frolic in which on that occasion he was indulging. Now when Apollonius gazed on him, the ghost in him began to utter cries of fear and rage, such as one hears from people who are being branded or racked; and the ghost swore that he would leave the young man alone and never take possession of any man again. But Apollonius addressed him with anger, as a master might a shifty, rascally, and shameless slave and so on, and he ordered him to quit the young man and show by a visible sign that he had done so. "I will throw down yonder statue," said the devil, and pointed to one of the images which was in the king's portico, for there it was that the scene took place. But when the statue began by moving gently, and then fell down, it would defy anyone to describe the hubbub which arose thereat and the way they clapped their hands with wonder. But the young man rubbed his eyes as though he had just woke up, and he looked towards the rays of the sun, and won the consideration of all who now had turned their attention to him; for he no longer showed himself licentious, nor did he stare madly about, but he had returned to his own self, as thoroughly as if he had been treated with drugs; and he gave up his dainty dress and summery garments and the rest of his sybaritic way of life, and he fell in love with the austerity of philosophers, and donned their cloak, and stripping off his old self modelled his life in future upon that of Apollonius.[10]

## FURTHER READING

PCB, pp. 712–18, "Pagan Religion at the Coming of Christianity" (R. McL. Wilson).

IDB, vol. 2, pp. 479–87, "Greek Language" (E. C. Colwell); pp. 487–500, "Greek Religion and Philosophy" (F. W. Beare); vol. 4, pp. 103–09, "Roman Empire" (R. M. Grant); pp. 109–12, "Roman Religion" (F. C. Grant).

In many respects the best general picture of the Hellenistic world is Tarn and Griffith, *Hellenistic Civilization*, 3rd ed. (1952). Very much briefer, but brilliant and provocative, is Bultmann, *Primitive Christianity in Its Contemporary Setting*, pp. 103–74 ("The Greek Heritage" and "Hellenism").

[10]Philostratus, *Life of Apollonius*, iv. 20, as quoted in Barrett, *Background*, pp. 77–78.

# Appendix 2

## The Historical Situation of the Jewish People
## in the New Testament Period

Christianity began as a Jewish sect and to understand it and the New Testament we need to know something of the history of the Jewish people up to the New Testament period. This segment of the history of the Jewish people begins with their return from the exile in Babylon in 539 B.C. and ends with the collapse of the bar Cochba rising in A.D. 135. It is customary to divide it into three periods: the Persian, 539–333 B.C.; the Greek, 333–63 B.C.; the Roman, 63 B.C.–A.D. 135.

### THE PERSIAN PERIOD, 539–333 B.C.

The religious tolerance of Cyrus, emperor of Persia from 539 to 530 B.C., allowed the Jews to return to their homeland from their captivity in Babylon. Many Jews elected to remain in Babylonia, which remained a center of Jewish life and thought for a thousand years. Those who returned did so in a series of waves, and lived quietly in Jerusalem and its immediate environs in Judea. Details of their life are almost unknown but there was apparently a two-hundred-year period of intense literary activity, for much of the Old Testament as we know it must have taken form at this time. The community was small and it was a theocracy ruled by a High Priest.

During this period a most significant religious development occurred: the Law (Torah) assumed the central role in Judaism that has characterized it ever since. It was the historical figure Ezra, a leader in the affairs of the community shortly after the Return (his actual dates are obscure), who oriented the people toward the Law in such a way as to make them the "People of the Book," which they have remained.

An important aspect of this period was the schism between the Jews and the Samaritans that continued into New Testament times with increasing friction and hostility. The Samaritans were originally Jews who lived in an area immediately north of Judea that had been conquered by the Assyrians in 721

**319**

B.C. At that time the ancient kingdom of Judah, geographically virtually identical with the later Judea, became a vassal of Assyria but was not actually conquered. The Assyrians deported many of the Samaritans in the years following 721 B.C. and settled in their place colonists from other parts of their empire. In due course the colonists intermarried with the remaining Jews, but the resulting population considered itself to be Jewish and heirs to the traditional Jewish faith. The Jews from Judah were deported to Babylonia in the period 597–587, and when they returned to Jerusalem in 539 they brought with them a rather new understanding of their faith and a passionate desire for racial purity. The result was the schism between the two groups that continued into the New Testament period, and indeed into modern times.

## THE GREEK PERIOD, 333–63 B.C.

The Jewish people in Jerusalem and Judea were not immediately affected by the conquests of Alexander the Great and the establishment of the major Hellenistic kingdoms. For the first century or so after Judea came under the control of the Ptolemies, life was calm. But Hellenistic culture spread in Jerusalem and Judea as it did everywhere else. The richer and more aristocratic of the Jews—those who came into closest contact with the Egyptian authorities—tended to accept Hellenism, but the stricter religionists and the ordinary people strenuously resisted it.

Toward the end of the third century the uneasy balance of power between the Hellenistic kingdoms of Syria and Egypt began to be disturbed. Palestine was strategially important; Jerusalem and Judea were a prize to be fought for—and controlled. In 200 B.C., Antiochus III, "the Great," defeated Ptolemy V in battle and the Jewish state became part of his kingdom. Both Antiochus III and his son Antiochus IV were aggressive, intent on keeping what they had won, and to this end it was important to establish firm political and ideological control of Jerusalem and Judea. So they became actively interested in the appointment of High Priests in Jerusalem, and in spreading Greek culture among the Jewish people. Antiochus IV was particularly concerned with this Hellenization: he claimed that the Greek god Zeus had manifested himself to him and called himself Epiphanes, "God manifest" (his enemies punned Epimanes, "madman"). The Jews who were sympathetic to Hellenization— and who were interested in personal political power—were prepared to jockey with one another and with the Seleucids for power and authority, but the anti-Hellenistic Jews resisted, leading Antiochus IV after his accession in 175 to institute a forcible program of Hellenization, which was in effect a persecution of the Jewish religion. An altar to the Greek god Zeus was set up in the Temple at Jerusalem (this is the "abomination of desolation" referred to in Daniel and Mark 13), sacred texts were burned, circumcision and the practice of the Law were forbidden, and sacrifice to Greek gods was demanded of leading citizens as a test of loyalty. The Jewish people resisted and actual revolt broke out in 167, led by a priest named Mattathias and his five sons, the eldest of whom, Judas Maccabeus (said to mean "the hammer [of his enemies]") gave his name to the movement: the Maccabean revolt.

The power of the Syrian and Egyptian kingdoms was on the wane, and neither was able to reestablish hegemony in Palestine. Under Judas (died 160) and his brothers Jonathan (died 143) and Simon (died 134), the Jews achieved religious freedom when they cleansed and rededicated the Temple in 164, establishing the feast of Dedication (Hanukkah) to celebrate this event. They went on to gain political independence, and in recognition of their leadership the sons of Mattathius were allowed to assume the High Priesthood. This office now became hereditary to their family—named Hashmon—and their successors were not only High Priests but also kings of an independent Jewish state—the Hasmonean Priest-Kings. They ruled from the death of Simon in 143 to the coming of Rome in the person of Pompey in 63 B.C.; this was an age of complete independence for the Jews, the first for some centuries and the last for many. The Hasmoneans were able and aggressive rulers, much more like successful Hellenistic kings than Jewish High Priests, and during their rule the Jewish state was extended by conquest and forcible conversion of conquered people until it reached an extent matching the days of David and Solomon. The Jews took great pride in this and there seems to have been a revival of kingship ideology and theology in connection with the Hasmonean kings and their rule. At the same time, the dissolute character and ruthlessness only too often characteristic of the Hasmoneans led to a great deal of dissatisfaction and religious unrest. During this period, for example, the Qumran people felt themselves driven from Jerusalem to establish a purer community in the wilderness.

The simultaneous pride and frustration experienced by religious Jews in the period of the Hasmoneans fed the hope for a king whom God would raise up, who would give them true independence: freedom from all enemies without and from all evil within. This longing for a king anointed by God (a "Messiah") develops very strongly now and becomes a major factor in the next period.


# THE ROMAN PERIOD, 63 B.C.–A.D. 135

## From the Coming of Pompey to the Fall of Jerusalem, 68 B.C.–A.D. 70

In 63 B.C., Rome, unable to tolerate any longer the anarchy on her eastern frontier, sent Pompey to regulate the situation. Roman might was irresistible and the brief period of Jewish independence came to an end. The Jewish territories were absorbed into the Roman province of Syria. The Jews were allowed to keep a Hasmonean as High Priest, the weak Hyrcanus II, but there was a power behind him, the Idumean Antipater, in whom Rome saw a dependable and capable "friend" and whose house gradually became the real center of power. So much was this the case that in 37 B.C. his son Herod, whom history called "the Great," became King of the Jews directly responsible to Rome, not to the legate of the province of Syria. How far he deserves to be called "the Great" is a matter of dispute, but of his immense abilities and determination there can be no doubt. At times he was almost the third man in the Roman Empire, after Caesar Augustus himself and his minister, Agrippa.

The Jews hated him. To them he was a "half-Jew" (the Idumeans had been conquered and forcibly converted to Judaism by the Hasmonean John Hyrcanus I), and his abilities only made resistance the more perilous, as his ambitious building program—which included a new Temple (see Mark 13:1; John 2:20)—only made taxation the more onerous.

The situation went from bad to worse for the Jews. After the death of Herod, his kingdom was divided up among three of his sons: Archelaus had Judea, Samaria, and Idumea; Herod Antipas had Galilee and Perea; Philip had the regions east and north of Galilee. But Archelaus was incompetent and Jerusalem was immensely important as the center of Jewish life and faith. So in A.D. 6 Rome removed him and combined Judea, Idumea, and Samaria into a province under a Roman procurator. This was to the Jews the ultimate indignity: the holy city itself under the direct control of a Roman procurator.

The remaining history of the period is complicated, but a few points are salient. The Romans remained in control, but from A.D. 37 to 44 a grandson of Herod's, Herod Agrippa I, ruled on their sufferance a territory almost equal to his grandfather's. He was a supporter of the Pharisees and is traditionally supposed to have persecuted the early Christian church (Acts 12:1–19). After his death the territory passed into direct Roman control and the Jews seethed in almost constant revolt, certainly always prepared to revolt. In A.D. 66 the decisive rebellion came, the Jewish War began, and in A.D. 70 the Temple was captured and destroyed by the Romans.

## From the Fall of Jerusalem to the bar Cochba Rising, A.D. 70–135

After the catastrophe of the fall of Jerusalem and the destruction of its Temple, there was a general longing for the "restoration of Israel," fed by the memory of the restoration following the first destruction of Jerusalem and its Temple by the Babylonians in 586 B.C. The continuing influence of apocalyptic, with its expectation of the decisive intervention of God into the affairs of his people, contributed to this longing. Matters came to a head in Judea in A.D. 132 when a revolt broke out headed by Simon bar Cochba. He was at first successful in liberating Jerusalem and its immediately surrounding territory and for three years he ruled this territory almost as a personal kingdom, supported by the famous rabbi Aqiba and the priest Eleazor. He was accepted as the Messiah and coins struck in this period speak of the "Liberation of Jerusalem" and the "Restoration of Israel." The name bar Cochba, "son of a star," is said to have been given to him by Rabbi Aqiba because he fulfilled the prophecy of Num 24:17: "a star shall come forth out of Jacob."

But Roman power was irresistible. In 135 Jerusalem fell again, and the fate of the Jewish people was sealed for 1,800 years.

This concludes our brief review of the history of the Jewish people. The various aspects of Judaism that are important to an understanding of the New Testament are discussed at relevant places in the text. Hellenistic Judaism is discussed in connection with the theological history of early Christianity in chapter 3, and again in connection with the canon of the Old Testament in

Appendix 3. Jewish apocalyptic and the Qumran community are discussed in connection with apocalyptic Christianity in chapter 4. Sects and parties in Palestinian Judaism and rabbinic Judaism are discussed in connection with the gospel of Matthew in chapter 8. The Jewish canon of scripture is discussed in Appendix 3.

## FURTHER READING

*PCB*, pp. 126–33, "History of Israel—II. Post-Exilic" (L. E. Browne); pp. 686–92, "The Jewish State in the Hellenistic World" (W. D. Davies); pp. 693–98, "The Development of Judaism in the Greek and Roman Periods" (M. Black); pp. 705–11, "Contemporary Jewish Religion" (W. D. Davies).

*JBC*, pp. 535–60, "Apocrypha: Dead Sea Scrolls; Other Jewish Literature" (R. E. Brown); pp. 686–702, "A History of Israel," the latter part of a longer article (R. E. Murphy and J. A. Fitzmyer). This survey of Jewish history in the relevant period is particularly good.

*IDB*, vol. 1, pp. 790–802, "Dead Sea Scrolls" (O. Betz); vol. 2, pp. 143–49, "Essenes" (W. R. Farmer); pp. 568–70, "Hebrew Religion," the latter part of a longer article (J. Bright); pp. 761–65, "History of Israel," the latter part of a longer article (H. H. Rowley); vol. 3, pp. 774–81, "Pharisees" (M. Black); vol. 4, pp. 160–63, "Sadducees" (A. C. Sundberg); pp. 190–97, "Samaritans" (T. H. Gaster); pp. 476–91, "Synagogue" (I. Sanne).

A good general survey of Jewish history and culture as it relates to the understanding of the New Testament is Foerster, *From the Exile to Christ*. The best survey of the ancient Jewish sects is Simon, *Jewish Sects at the Time of Jesus*. Then, brilliant and provocative as always, there is Bultmann, *Primitive Christianity in Its Contemporary Setting*, pp. 59–100. This is Bultmann's discussion of Judaism and he includes Jesus in this category. The classic study of Hellenistic Judaism is Tcherikover, *Hellenistic Civilization and the Jews*.

# Appendix 3
## The Canon of the Bible

When we speak of the "canon" of the Bible we mean to indicate a *list* of books authoritatively accepted as comprising the Old and New Testaments. The word *canon* is derived from a Greek word (*kanōn*) that means something "made of reeds" or "straight like reeds"—for example, a stave, a rod, or a ruler for drawing or measuring. Metaphorically it can mean a rule, a standard, a model, a paradigm, and so on. The Greek and Latin church fathers used this word, or forms of it, in connection with many things, including lists of church rules (hence "canon law") and lists of clergymen or saints (hence "canonized"). On the occasion of the Easter festival of 367, Athanasius, bishop of Alexandria, used it in a letter to his churches giving a list of books to be accepted as constituting the New Testament. This letter marks the settling of the canon in the West, and it is because of its wording that we use the term *canon* in connection with the Old Testament, the New Testament, or the Bible as a whole.

## THE CANON OF THE OLD TESTAMENT

### The Hebrew Canon

The movement toward a Jewish canon of scripture began in 621 B.C., when a book was found in the collection box of the temple at Jerusalem and accepted by King Josiah and the Jewish people as the authoritative revelation of God to them (2 Kings 22–23; 2 Chronicles 34). This book was in effect the book of Deuteronomy, and King Josiah and the Jews accepted it as the verbal revelation of the will of God to them and as the basis of their relationship with God. It was accepted as "the law [Torah] of the Lord given through Moses" (2 Chron 34:14) to govern their life in the world, and with this the idea of religion as essentially obedience to a verbal revelation was born. But if religion is essentially obedience to a verbal revelation, then the question becomes, what constitutes the verbal revelation? In addition to the book of Deuteronomy, the Jews had historical and legal traditions associated with the figure of Moses, and they also had prophets and prophetic traditions. Further, they developed liturgical literature and literature concerned with moral instruction, and eventually also apocalyptic literature. It therefore became a matter of practical necessity to define the extent of the verbal revelation.

The process toward the definition of a Jewish canon was a gradual one. First to be defined was the Law, the Torah. Gradually, historical and legal traditions associated with the figure of Moses were gathered together around the nucleus of the book of Deuteronomy. This collection of texts eventually became the Torah as it is now known: the five "books of Moses," Genesis, Exodus, Leviticus, Numbers, and Deuteronomy. We do not know the exact date of the acceptance of these five books as God's Law, but it must have been after the return from the Babylonian exile and before the separation of the Samaritans from the Jews (since the Samaritans also accept these five books as scripture). A date about 400 B.C. is therefore probable.

In 400 B.C., however, the Jews had other books that spoke to them of God. Specifically, there were books concerning prophets, either narratives in which they were heavily involved or accounts of their oracles. This class of literature came to be known simply as "the Prophets," and eventually it encompassed eight books: Joshua, Judges, (1 and 2) Samuel, (1 and 2) Kings—the so-called Former Prophets—and Isaiah, Jeremiah, Ezekiel, and the book of the twelve minor prophets—the so-called Latter Prophets. These achieved the form in which we know them and were accepted as authoritative by 180 B.C., at which date Jesus, son of Sirach, speaks of "the law and the prophets," reads the poems of Second Isaiah as part of the book of Isaiah, and knows the twelve minor prophets as one volume (Sir Prologue; 48:24; 49:10).

After "the Law and the Prophets" were accepted as scripture other works were attracted into their orbit. This process was going on in Judaism through the New Testament period and eventually it produced a group of books known as "the Writings." This group consisted of poetry (Psalms, Proverbs, Job); texts read at annual festivals (Song of Solomon, Ruth, Lamentations, Ecclesiastes, Esther); prophecy (Daniel); and history (Ezra, Nehemiah, [1 and 2] Chronicles). This group was achieving authoritative status in the New Testament period. Matthew is conservative in this regard, accepting only "the law and the prophets" (Matt 5:17), whereas Luke accepts "the law . . . the prophets and the psalms" (Luke 24:44), "the psalms" meaning here the Writings designated by their first book. A similar division of opinion existed among Jewish writers of the period.

The final canon of Jewish scripture was fixed by the Pharisees meeting at Jamnia after the destruction of Jerusalem, and a date about A.D. 90 would be appropriate for it. The first known references to the Jewish canon as thus defined are 2 Esdras 14:44–46, which speaks of twenty-four books, and Josephus, Apion I:viii, who speaks of twenty-two. The writer of 2 Esdras is counting five books of the Law (Genesis, Exodus, Leviticus, Numbers, Deuteronomy), eight of the Prophets (Joshua, Judges, [1 and 2] Samuel, [1 and 2]

Kings, Isaiah, Jeremiah, Ezekiel, the twelve minor prophets) and eleven of the Writings (Psalms, Proverbs, Job, Song of Solomon, Ruth, Lamentations, Ecclesiastes, Esther, Daniel, Ezra-Nehemiah [counted as one book], and [1 and 2] Chronicles). Josephus probably unites Ruth with Judges and Lamentations with Jeremiah to get twenty-two books. This canon is called the "Hebrew canon," since the fact that a book was written in Hebrew was a criterion used by the Pharisees at Jamnia in their selection.

## The Greek Canon

Although the Pharisees at Jamnia spoke for the Judaism of the future, in New Testament times the Hellenistic Judaism of the Diaspora was going its own way with regard to the canon as in other matters. Hellenistic Judaism tended to accept as authoritative books that the more conservative Palestinian Judaism represented at Jamnia was beginning to reject. Moreover, the Greek-speaking Judaism of the Diaspora tended to obliterate the Palestinian Jewish division Torah/Prophets/Writings in favor of a division according to literary types. So the "Bible" of the Greek-speaking Jews of the Diaspora was more extensive than that accepted at Jamnia. It is somewhat misleading, however, to speak of it as a "Greek canon," because so far as we know no formal list of books was ever established by Greek-speaking Jews, and the lists we have are those implied by *Christians* as they transmitted texts of the Old Testament in Greek. Here the earlier codices are not in agreement. But it would be fair to say that Hellenistic Judaism produced and used books rejected by the Jews at Jamnia but preserved by Christians. The Jamnia Jewish canon was not followed by Christians until the rise of Protestantism, when a threefold distinction began to be made: Old Testament (according to the Jamnia canon), New Testament, and Apocrypha. The Apocrypha was the collection of Jewish books used by Christians that the Jamnia canon did not include.

The Apocrypha represents, therefore, a Christian collection of the literature of Hellenistic Judaism, but it nonetheless shows characteristic interests and concerns of Hellenistic Judaism. It tends to fall into six classes.

### 1. Historical Books

1 Esdras (concerned with reforms of Jewish worship carried out by Josiah, Zerubbabel and Ezra)

1 Maccabees (an account of the Maccabean revolt and part of the Hasmonean period)

2 Maccabees (an account of the Maccabean period written in the Hellenistic style known as "pathetic history," i.e., history recounted in a way intended to stir the emotions)

### 2. Imaginative History

Tobit
Judith

Susanna
Bel and the Dragon

These are actually moralistic novels.

### 3. Wisdom Books

Wisdom of Solomon
Wisdom of Jesus, Son of Sirach

### 4. Devotional Literature

Prayer of Manasseh
Prayer of Azariah
Song of the Three Young Men

### 5. Apocalyptic Literature

2 Esdras (sometimes called IV Ezra)

### 6. A Letter

The Letter of Jeremiah (a pseudonymous homily and in form, therefore, parallel to some of the "letters" in the New Testament)

## The Christian Canon of the Old Testament

The Christians transmitted the Jewish scriptures in Greek as part of their Bible, for the most part as they were found in the Hellenistic Judaism of the Diaspora. Though in some quarters there was a tendency to accept the decisions made at Jamnia, this tendency did not persist. The Christians in general accepted a canon of the Old Testament that was broader than the canon of Jewish scripture defined at Jamnia, and when Jerome produced his Latin version of the Bible, the Vulgate, he included in the Old Testament the books listed above.

But the knowledge persisted that the Hebrew canon of scripture was different from the Christian Old Testament as defined by the Latin Vulgate. At the Reformation, Martin Luther and his followers were anxious to differentiate themselves from the Catholic church. They also found that some of the doctrines they came to despise had their only scriptural support in books the Hebrew canon had rejected; for example, the doctrine of purgatory had its only possible scriptural support in 2 Macc 12:43–45. At the same time it was absolutely essential for Luther to define the limits of scripture, since he was rejecting the authority of the Papacy and substituting for it that of scripture. In his epoch-making translation of the Bible (1534), Luther published only the books of the Hebrew canon in his Old Testament. He relegated the others to a separate section following the end of the Old Testament, under the heading "Apocrypha: these are books which are not held equal to the sacred Scriptures, and yet are useful and good for reading." The details of what followed do not concern us; it is sufficient to say that this gradually became the practice of Protestantism as a whole. Such authoritative modern English translations as the Revised Standard Version and the New English Bible do not include the books of the Apocrypha in the Old Testament.

In reaction to the practice of the Protestant reformers, the Roman Catholic church reaffirmed the canonicity of all the books of the Vulgate Old Testament (decree dated 8 April 1546). But modern Roman Catholic scholars are sensitive to the problem and tend to distinquish between "protocanonical" books (the Hebrew canon) and the "deutero-canonical" books (the Protestant "Apocrypha"), as do, for example, the writers in the *Jerome Biblical Commentary*.

## THE CANON OF THE NEW TESTAMENT

The process that led to the formation of the New Testament canon, to the recognition of the New Testament as one book, was a gradual one, beginning with the first collection of the letters of Paul and reaching its climax in 367 with Athanasius's letter giving a list of the "books that are canonized and handed down to us and believed to be divine." His list gives the books of the Old Testament and then the twenty-seven books that comprise the New Testament. It became authoritative for the church in the West, although it was resisted in the East, as we shall see below.

### The Collection and Circulation of Pauline Letters

The first collection of letters attributed to Paul probably consisted of nine letters (1, 2 Thessalonians; 1, 2 Corinthians; Romans; Galatians; Philippians; Colossians; and Philemon) with a tenth, Ephesians, added as a covering letter to the whole collection. It is this collection, which must have been in circulation by the end of the first century, that the author of 2 Peter regards as "scripture" (2 Pet 3:15–16).

In the course of time the Pastorals and Hebrews were added to the collection. The Pastorals were added sometime in the second half of the second century; they are in the Muratorian Canon, a list of the books of the New Testament with brief remarks drawn up in Greek in Rome some years before the end of the second century and preserved for us in a Latin translation discovered and published in 1740. The Muratorian Canon does not include Hebrews, but early in the third century, Origen, who succeeded Clement as head of the Christian school in Alexandria in 203, reports that it was accepted everywhere. Although he himself had doubts about Pauline authorship, he justified the acceptance on the grounds that the thought was Pauline.

With the general acceptance of Hebrews as part of the Pauline corpus, this aspect of the New Testament was complete. Other letters circulated in the name of Paul, but these were not accepted. The Muratorian Canon refers to several "which cannot be received into the catholic church, for gold ought not to be mixed with honey."

### The Acceptance of the Four Gospels

There were a comparatively large number of gospels written in the early church, some covering in a more legendary fashion much the same ground as the four that became canonical, others developing the themes of the infancy of

Jesus or the post-resurrection instruction of the disciples by the risen Lord.[1] These competed with the gospels of Matthew, Mark, Luke, and John in the early church, but the latter rapidly gained an ascendancy they never lost.

The earliest testimony to the four gospels as "scripture" comes from the middle of the second century. At that time a homily was written that was ascribed (falsely) to Clement, bishop of Rome, author of the letter to the Corinthians known as 1 Clement. The homily is known as 2 Clement. 2 Clement 2 reads, "And again another scripture says, 'I came not to call the righteous, but sinners,'" and so treats Matt 9:13 as scripture. At about the same time, Justin Martyr, a church father who died as a martyr in Rome somewhere between 163 and 167, in describing an act of Christian worship, speaks of "the memoirs of the Apostles or the writings of the Prophets [which] are read, as long as time permits (Justin, *Apol.* i. 67). Elsewhere he speaks of the "memoirs made by [the apostles], which are called gospels" (*Apol.* ii. 33, 66). From these references we can see that the gospels are gaining scriptural status and that although they originally circulated anonymously they are now being attributed to "apostles." This latter fact is a tribute to the developing dependence on apostolic tradition.

## The Influence of the Heretic Marcion

The next step in the formation of the New Testament canon was taken by a heretic, Marcion, who flourished in the middle of the second century. An altogether remarkable man, he had been raised in the East as an orthodox Christian but was strongly influenced by Gnosticism, so that he came to believe that the creator God of the Old Testament was an inferior deity and that Jesus had revealed the supreme God, the God of love, previously unknown. He further came to believe that the revelation by Jesus had been hopelessly corrupted by the Twelve but preserved by the one true apostle, Paul. In support of his teaching Marcion constructed the first Christian canon, consisting of ten letters of Paul and an edited version of the gospel of Luke. The ten letters of Paul were the extent of the Pauline corpus in his day, and the gospel of Luke was accepted because it was attributed to a companion of Paul. Marcion apparently edited his text of the gospel of Luke, and perhaps also that of the Pauline letters, to bring it into accord with his understanding of the revelation of God by Jesus.

Marcion was extraordinarily successful. Although condemned by the orthodox as a heretic, he attracted a wide following. And in the very course of the struggle against him, his influence was crucial to the development of the New Testament canon.

*The formation of a canon of the New Testament as distinct from the Old Testament*

Before Marcion, the tendency was to add new writings to the Jewish scriptures to make up the Christian scriptures. For example, 2 Pet 3:15–16

[1]The most convenient discussion of this whole literature is Hennecke and Schneemelcher, *New Testament Apocrypha*, vol. 1, *Gospels and Related Writings*.

adds the letters of Paul to the "other scriptures," that is, to the Jewish scriptures. Then Justin Martyr adds the "memoirs of the Apostles" to "the Prophets," the Prophets being a Jewish designation for a part of their scriptures. But with Marcion all this changes, for Marcion flatly repudiated the Jewish scriptures and substituted for them a new Christian scripture, consisting of the "gospel" and the "apostle"—the gospel of Luke and the letters of the apostle Paul. The orthodox churches were ultimately successful in their struggle against Marcion, but in Christianity the Jewish scriptures were henceforward separated from the Christian, a tendency that had not been evident before. The very conception of a New Testament as distinct from the Old may well go back to Marcion's repudiation of the Jewish scriptures.

## The New Testament as the "gospel" and the "apostle"

Marcion's division of Christian scriptures into "gospel" and "apostle" also survived the success of the orthodox Christian struggle against him. The orthodox churches did not repudiate this division but added to it. They fought to add other gospels to that of Luke, and other letters to those of Paul, including the Pastorals, written in the name of Paul and representing the viewpoint of emergent Catholicism rather than that of Marcion. The Pastorals were undoubtedly the more readily accepted because they were effective weapons against Marcion. The division of the Christian canon into "gospel" and "apostle" became as traditional as that of the Jewish canon into "law," "prophets," and "writings."

## The Influence of Gnosticism

Marcion was the first important heretic, and his appearance in the middle of the second century was a foretaste of things to come. As we have said, Marcion was influenced by Gnosticism, and beginning with him Gnosticism became more and more influential in the Christian churches. Late in the second century and in the third, in fact, Gnosticism developed as a specific Christian heresy. At this point there is a problem in terminology, because traditionally the term Gnosticism has designated that specific Christian heresy. However, we now know that Gnosticism was in fact a much broader movement and that the Christian heresy was but one form it took. At various places in this book we have discussed the broader movement, being especially concerned with its earlier phases and its influence on the New Testament. But now we are concerned with the specific Christian heresy.[2]

As a Christian heresy Gnosticism claimed to be an improved or perfected version of the Christian faith. Among other things, it said it possessed secret

[2]A convenient and good account of the specific Christian heresy is given by R. M. Grant, "Gnosticism," *IDB*, vol. 2, pp. 404–06. Grant restricts the term to the Christian heresy, the traditional use.

books of the teaching of Jesus and the apostles above and beyond those used in the orthodox churches. A good example is the Gnostic gospel of Thomas, which begins. "These are the secret words which the living Jesus spake, and Didymus Judas Thomas wrote them down." Marcion is not typical of Gnosticism in his view of scripture, for he limited the Christian canon: Gnosticism normally expanded it. This Gnostic tendency forced the churches to struggle to limit the canon (as compared with the fight against Marcion, where they struggled to expand it) and to emphasize the apostolic authority of their sacred books. Both Gnostic Christian and orthodox Christian churches accepted the idea of apostolic authority as normative.

The combined impact of Marcion and the development of Gnostic Christianity led therefore to (a) the idea of a Christian canon separate from the Jewish, (b) the struggle to expand the Christian canon over against Marcion and limit it over against Gnostic Christianity, and (c) an emphasis on apostolic authority, and ultimately on apostolic authorship for the books of the orthodox Christian canon.

## The Muratorian Canon

The Muratorian Canon, drawn up in Rome toward the end of the second century, is definitely anti-Marcionite in tone. It speaks of a letter "to the Laodiceans, another to the Alexandrians, forged in Paul's name for the sect of Marcion."[3] This canon consists of the four gospels, Matthew, Mark, Luke, John; the Acts of the Apostles; thirteen letters of Paul (including the Pastorals but omitting Hebrews); Jude; 1 and 2 John; the Wisdom of Solomon; and two apocalypses (the book of Revelation and the apocalypse of Peter).

From this point forward the orthodox church maintained the four gospels as canonical, strenuously resisting the inclusion of any others. Acts also had a firm place in the canon, as did the thirteen letters attributed to Paul. But the others mentioned remained in dispute for some time. Some were dropped and others added. However, the tendency was to accept more and more of what we called the literature of emergent Catholicism, an understandable tendency in view of the characteristics of that literature.

## The Canon in the Third Century

In the third century there are two representative figures: Tertullian (about 160–220) who wrote in Latin in the West, mainly in Carthage, and Origen (185–254) who wrote in Greek in the East, mainly in Alexandria.[4] Tertullian is the first writer to speak of the "New Testament" (Novum Testamentum) as

---

[3]We quote the translation conveniently available in Hennecke and Schneemelcher, *New Testament Apocrypha*, vol. 1, pp. 43–45.

[4]In the second century Latin was established as the dominant language in the western Mediterranean, while Greek was maintained in the eastern Mediterranean. By the end of the second century Latin was in general use in the churches of North Africa, Gaul, and Spain, while Greek continued in use in the East. The church at Rome became predominantly Latin-speaking about the middle of the third century.

distinct from the Old, and he accepts the following books as constituting that New Testament: the four gospels, the thirteen letters attributed to Paul, Acts, Revelation, 1 Peter, 1 John, and Jude. Comparing this list with the Muratorian Canon, we see that 2 John, the apocalypse of Peter, and the Wisdom of Solomon are missing, but that 1 Peter has been added. Origen had traveled widely and concerned himself with the acceptance of books by the Christian churches everywhere. He distinguishes between those "acknowledged" and those "disputed." Those generally acknowledged were the four gospels, the fourteen letters attributed to Paul (including Hebrews, as we noted earlier), Acts, 1 John, 1 Peter, and Revelation. Among those disputed in some places he includes James, Jude, 2 Peter, 2 and 3 John. This means that by the time of Origen all the books that finally constituted the canon of the New Testament were known and in circulation, but some were disputed. Origen is the first writer to mention the letter of James.

A feature of the later third century in the East was a dispute about the status of the book of Revelation. In the second half of the century it came to be generally rejected in Alexandria and Antioch, and although it was eventually restored to the canon it never achieved the same status as the other books in Greek-speaking Christianity, and it never achieved canonical status in the Syrian churches.

## The Canon in the Fourth Century

About 325 Eusebius of Caesarea completed his famous *Ecclesiastical History*. In it he reports on the state of the New Testament canon in the Greek-speaking churches of the eastern Mediterranean. He is the first writer to speak of a distinct group of the "seven so-called Catholic epistles" (1, 2, 3 John; 1, 2 Peter; James; Jude) but he notes that James, Jude, 2 Peter and 2, 3 John are all "disputed." He is ambiguous about Revelation. Unambiguously accepted are the four gospels, Acts, the fourteen letters attributed to Paul (with a note that some reject Hebrews because the church at Rome does not accept it as Pauline), 1 John, and 1 Peter.

The great event in the fourth century in the East is, however, the festal letter of Athanasius, bishop of Alexandria, circulated among the churches under his charge in 367. The crucial passage reads as follows.

> Continuing, I must without hesitation mention the Scriptures of the New Testament; they are the following: the four Gospels according to Matthew, Mark, Luke and John, after them the Acts of the Apostles and the seven so-called catholic epistles of the apostles—namely, one of James, two of Peter, then three of John and after these one of Jude. In addition to this there are fourteen epistles of the apostle Paul written in the following order; the first to the Romans, then two to the Corinthians and then after these the one to the Galatians, following it the one to the Ephesians, thereafter the one to the Philippians and the one to the Colossians and two to the Thessalonians and the epistle to the Hebrews and then immediately two to Timothy, one to Titus and lastly the one to Philemon. Yet further the Revelation of John.[5]

[5] As quoted in Hennecke and Schneemelcher, *New Testament Apocrypha*, vol. 1, pp. 59–60.

In the first part of the fourth century the Latin-speaking churches in the western Mediterranean generally accepted a canon consisting of the four gospels, the thirteen letters of the Pauline collection, 1 John, 1 Peter, and Revelation. That is Tertullian's canon minus Jude. In the latter half of the century, however, the influence of Alexandria made itself felt, and when Jerome made the Latin translation of the New Testament that became the standard translation in the West (the so-called Vulgate), he followed the canon as set forth by Athanasius. In a letter to Paulinus written about 385, he defends the canonicity of the seven Catholic epistles, Hebrews, and Revelation, while acknowledging the difficulties some have with them.

## Further History of the New Testament Canon

The festal letter of Athanasius in the East and the work of Jerome in the West mark the formation of the New Testament canon as we know it. This canon gradually became accepted everywhere except in Syria. In Syria until the end of the fourth century the canon was the Diatessaron (a harmony of the four gospels rather than four separate gospels), Acts, and fifteen letters of Paul (including a third letter to Corinth). About 400, a list substitutes the four separate gospels for the Diatessaron and omits 3 Corinthians. In the first quarter of the fifth century Syria moved nearer to the remainder of the church by accepting the four gospels, Acts, fourteen Pauline letters, James, 1 Peter, and 1 John. The accommodation would doubtless have gone further, but in the fifth century fierce christological controversies split the Syrian church and separated it from the rest of the church.

The only other factor that needs mention here is that for some time books were accepted in some places in addition to the twenty-seven-book canon of Athanasius and Jerome; for example, Codex Alexandrinus, a fifth-century Greek manuscript, includes 1 and 2 Clement in the New Testament. Gradually, however, the twenty-seven-book canon gained general acceptance. The acceptance was by common consent rather than by formal pronouncement of a general church council.

## The New Testament Apocrypha

We have seen that several works hovered on the edge of acceptance into the canon of the New Testament, for example, 1 and 2 Clement. Others in this category are the Shepherd of Hermas, the epistle of Barnabas, and the Didache (Teaching of the Twelve Apostles). Although these were not included in the final canon of the New Testament, they continued to exercise considerable influence and came to be known as the "Apostolic Fathers," a designation that also included the letters of Ignatius and some other works. Beyond these, however, a vast quantity of other early Christian literature, some but not all of it Gnostic in character, was definitely rejected by the orthodox churches. This included all gospels except the four, all letters attributed to Paul except the fourteen, acts of various apostles, and many apocalypses. These came to be called New Testament *Apocrypha. Apocrypha* means "hidden," "secret," and these books were to be hidden from the faithful. They are conveniently discussed and in part translated in Hennecke-Schneemelcher, *New Testament Apocrypha*, vols. 1 and 2. An older translation is M. R. James, *The Apocryphal New Testament.*

## FURTHER READING

Kümmel, *Intro.*, pp. 334–58.

Marxsen, *Intro.*, pp. 279–84.

Fuller, *Intro.*, pp. 191–99.

*PCB*, pp. 73–75 (O. T. canon: B. J. Roberts); pp. 676–82 (N. T. canon: J. N. Sanders.

*JBC*, pp. 516–22 (O.T. canon: R. E. Brown and J. C. Turro); pp. 525–31 (N.T. canon: R. E. Brown); pp. 543–46 (Apocrypha: R. E. Brown.)

*IDB*, vol. 1, pp. 498–520 (O.T. canon: R. H. Pfeiffer); pp. 520–32 (N.T. canon: F. W. Beare); pp. 161–69 (Apocrypha: M. S. Enslin.)

Hennecke and Schneemelcher, *New Testament Apocrypha* (vol. 1, *Gospels and Related Writings;* vol. 2, *Writings Relating to the Apostles; Apocalypses and Related Subjects*). A collection and translation of the New Testament apocryphal books, with a general discussion of *canon* and *apocrypha* in volume 1. A most important resource.

# Appendix 4
## The Text of the New Testament

### GREEK MANUSCRIPTS

The various books of the New Testament were originally written in *koinē* ("common") Greek, a later form of classical Greek that was the common language of the Hellenistic world. The church at large continued to use Greek for several centuries, and when in 313 the Christian church became the church of the Empire under Constantine and had the resources to produce fine manuscripts, they were written in Greek. Greek continued to be the official language of a major branch of the Christian church in the East, and manuscripts of the New Testament continued to be produced in Greek until the invention of printing. These manuscripts may be classified as follows.

### Papyrus Codices

These manuscripts are on sheets of papyrus bound together as a book (codex). The use of codices rather than continuous rolls (as in Jewish manuscripts like the Dead Sea Scrolls) is a feature of earliest Christian literary activity. These codices are either of individual books, or of partial collections such as the gospels and Acts or the Pauline corpus. Some seventy-five such codices are now known, all discovered in modern times in Egypt, where the climate preserves papyrus. They date from the second to the eighth centuries and vary in size from fragments of leaves to considerable remnants of a codex. The contents of these codices follow the developing categories of Christian scripture. The collections of books found together are the "gospel" (the four gospels and Acts), the "apostle" (a collection of Pauline letters), and the "catholic epistles" (some of the catholic epistles, often together with books that were not included in the final canon). These papyrus codices are designated by the letter P followed by a number. They include the earliest known texts of books of the New Testament, the earliest of them all being P

52, a small scrap of papyrus containing four verses of John 18. This is dated on paleographical grounds (the age of the form of the letters used) in the first half of the second century, possibly about A.D. 125.

## The Great Uncial Codices

These are manuscripts of the complete New Testament, indeed, of the complete Bible, since they include the Greek Old Testament, known as the "Septuagint." They date from the fourth century onward and some of them include books excluded from the canon of Athanasius (discussed in Appendix 3). They are written on parchment in uncial characters (large or "capital" letters) and are designated by letters, or by numbers prefixed by a zero, since scholars have run out of alphabets! Some of the more important are the following.

*S 01 Codex Sinaiticus (middle fourth century).*   The discovery of this manuscript by Konstantin von Tischendorf in the monastery of Saint Catherine at the foot of Mount Sinai in the period 1844–1859 and its subsequent preservation for the world of scholarship was a dramatic and fitting climax to Tischendorf's life-long devotion to the search for and evaluation of manuscripts of the Greek New Testament. This codex is the greatest of the uncials since it is the only one in which the New Testament is completely preserved. It also includes the epistle of Barnabas and the Shepherd of Hermas. Enamored of his discovery and recognizing its value, Tischendorf designated it Aleph, the first letter of the Hebrew alphabet, since Roman *A* was already used to designate Alexandrinus. Today, since Hebrew characters are often unavailable to printers and are not recognized by most readers, it is often designated *S* (for Sinaiticus).

*A 02 Codex Alexandrinus (early fifth century).*   This manuscript originally contained the Old Testament, the New Testament, 1 and 2 Clement, and the Psalms of Solomon (a collection of noncanonical Jewish psalms composed shortly before the time of Jesus). Originally kept in Alexandria, it was presented to Charles I of England in 1627 and is now in the British Museum.

*B 03 Codex Vaticanus (early fourth century).*   This codex, which originally contained the whole Greek Bible, is the earliest of the great uncials. It has been in the Vatican Library in Rome since before the publication of the first catalogue of that library in 1475; no one knows how it came to be there in the first place.

*D 05 Codex Bezae (fifth or sixth century).*   Another manuscript with a dramatic history, this one, which contains the gospels and Acts, first appears in the hands of the bishop of Clermont at the Council of Trent, where it was used by that worthy in an attempt to lay a biblical foundation for celibacy. (At John 21:22, D reads: "If I wish him to remain *thus* until I come." It is the only Greek manuscript that has "thus" in this passage, although this reading is found in the Latin Vulgate.) After a subsequent checkered history the manuscript finally came into the possession of Theodore Beza, the heir of John Calvin in Geneva, who presented it to Cambridge University in 1581. It is important to scholars in two respects. First, it is the earliest known New Testament manuscript written in both Greek and Latin, having a Greek text and a Latin translation on facing pages. Second, the text of the books it contains is very different from that of other Greek manuscripts. This text—called "Western" because it has much in common with some Latin versions that come from the West—has presented, and continues to present, a major problem to critics attempting to reconstruct the original text of the gospels and Acts.

### The Minuscule Codices

Until the ninth century all biblical manuscripts were written in uncial characters, but then something of a revolution set in and small cursive (run together) characters began to be used. From then on we have minuscule manuscripts, that is, codices written in a cursive script. The use of cursive writing made manuscript production much less laborious, and from the ninth century until 1450 (the invention of printing) we have some 2,500 minuscules, compared with some 250 uncials from the earlier period. The minuscule manuscripts are designated by Arabic numerals (1,2, etc.). No attempt will be made here to describe any of them.

## EARLY "VERSIONS" OF THE NEW TESTAMENT

At the time of the writing of the books of the New Testament and for several centuries thereafter, Greek was the common language of the world in which the New Testament circulated. Gradually, however, the universality of the Greek language broke down and local languages became dominant in various areas: Latin in the West, Syriac in the East, Coptic in Egypt, and so on. Consequently, Christian literature was produced in these languages and books of the New Testament were translated into them. These translations are now known as "versions." The process began well before the establishment of the canon of the New Testament and before the church had the resources to sponsor careful and official translations. A confusing plethora of texts and translations emerged, and in at least two of the linguistic areas of the church, the Latin and the Syrian, this fact, together with the need to either accept the Athanasian canon or establish a variant one, led in turn to the establishment of an "official" text and translation. In the West this task was entrusted to the great scholar Jerome at the end of the fourth century; the result is now known as the Latin Vulgate. Previously existing Latin versions are now designated Old Latin versions. Jerome accepted the canon as promulgated by Athanasius and from his time on there is no dispute about the New Testament canon in the West. Athanasius had spoken for the Greek-speaking church, and in the Latin church the influence of the Vulgate was all determinative.

In the Syriac-speaking church the books of the New Testament were also variously translated, but although the four gospels common in the West were translated as separate entities this version was almost never used. In its place was a harmony of the four gospels, a weaving together of their texts to produce a continuous narrative, prepared in the second half of the second century by the Syrian Tatian, born about 110, who lived for years in Rome and was a disciple of Justin Martyr. It was known as Tatian's Diatessaron ("[one] through four") and was immensely popular. The same multiplicity of texts and translations, and a similar need for a canon, developed in the Syrian church as in the Latin. Early in the fifth century an "official" version was prepared, the Peshitta (from a Syriac word meaning "simple"). It had the four separated gospels. The Diatessaron was subsequently successfully suppressed and unfortunately no copy of it has survived to us. In addition to the gospels, the Peshitta contained Acts, the Pauline corpus (including Hebrews), James, 1 Peter, and 1 John. It did not have 2 Peter, 2 and 3 John, Jude, or Revelation. Syriac versions earlier than the Peshitta are now known as Old Syriac versions.

Other ancient versions of the New Testament in Coptic, Armenian, Ethiopic, and Georgian are less important than the Latin and the Syriac, although the Ethiopic Bible is remarkable in that it preserves complete versions of two Jewish apocalyptic works, the works of Enoch and Jubilees, which would otherwise be known to us only in fragments.

We have now reviewed briefly the manuscripts and versions through which the New Testament has been transmitted to us. The next matter to be considered is that of its text. When we read the New Testament, how near are we to what the original authors actually wrote?

## THE SEARCH FOR THE ORIGINAL TEXT OF THE NEW TESTAMENT

From the very beginning the books that now make up the New Testament were copied and recopied. Possibly Paul himself had his letter to the Romans copied and sent to churches other than Rome. Certainly churches having letters from him circulated them to other churches, and it was not long before there was a Pauline corpus, a collection of his letters, in general circulation. Similarly, the other books now included in the New Testament were copied and circulated. Copies of the gospel of Mark, for example, were available to the authors of Matthew and Luke. Indeed, constant copying and circulation could almost be described as a prerequisite to final inclusion in the New Testament, for books not found generally useful, and hence not copied and circulated, would not have found their way into the canon. But all this was going on in circumstances that made any kind of control over the texts very difficult. For the first three centuries the church rarely had the resources to employ professional scribes or sufficient peace and stability to be able to establish careful control of the texts being copied. Moreover, for a large part of this time the books did not have the status of sacred scripture and its consequent reverential handling. It was not until the epoch of the great uncials that these conditions prevailed, and by this time the damage had been done. Scribal errors of all kinds had crept into the manuscripts, devotional and theological factors had affected them in numerous places, reminiscence of one passage had influenced the text of another, and so on.

The various major church centers undertook revisions of the text of the New Testament in an attempt to bring order out of the chaos, and today we can identify readings characteristic of such revisions, as in the great uncials BSA, which are in part products of a revision or revisions undertaken in Egypt. But by and large the production of manuscripts went on uncritically, and even though more scribal care was now exercised than had been in the past, older corruptions were passed on and newer ones entered the tradition.

The Greek New Testament was first printed, as distinct from being copied by hand, early in the sixteenth century. The initial editions were uncritical printings of late and therefore necessarily defective Greek manuscripts. The first to appear was prepared by the Dutch humanist Desiderius Erasmus (1516), and it was so uncritical that where his few manuscripts were defective Erasmus simply retranslated into Greek the Latin of the Vulgate! Nevertheless, the printing met a real need and the volume went through edition after edition. The second edition of 1519 formed the basis for Luther's German New Testament. In 1522 the Catholic Bishop Ximenes published a Greek New Testament as part of his Complutensian Polyglot (a version of the Bible with Hebrew, Aramaic, Greek, and Latin in parallel columns), and in 1546 the Protestant printer-editor Robert Estienne (Stephanus) began to publish a Greek New Testament that was essentially a reproduction of a later edition of Erasmus' text, but which gave an apparatus of variant readings found in different manuscripts. It too went through edition after edition. The third (1550) became very influential in England and was used in the preparation of the English King James Version translation. The fourth (1557) first introduced the verse divisions we use today.

The Stephanus text became the *Textus Receptus* ("received text") in the English-speaking world and the object of what can only be called veneration. The availability of a printed Greek text had made possible the translation of the New Testament from the original Greek into the vernacular languages, and this had become an essential part of the great religious vitality of the Reformation. The role of the Luther Bible in Germany and of the various English translations culminating in the King James Version in England cannot possibly be exaggerated; and men who were part of this revitalization naturally felt themselves indebted to the printed Greek texts. But despite its religious importance the Erasmus-Stephanus text was in fact somewhat far removed from the earliest Greek manuscripts, and to accept it uncritically was to ignore the immense problems involved in the reconstruction of a reasonably accurate text of the New Testament. Since the Erasmus-Stephanus text achieved real religious significance, we can of course ask, why tamper with it in an attempt to reconstruct an earlier text nearer to that written by the authors of the various books? The answer is comparatively simple. Erasmus was a man of the Renaissance, in fact the greatest of the northern Renaissance, and his concern was, first, to bring the more learned of his contemporaries back from the Latin Vulgate, then dominant in the West, to the original Greek of the New

Testament, and, second, to make a vernacular translation of that Greek available to every man and every woman. In this connection he wrote a passage that became famous:

> I could wish that every woman might read the Gospel and the Epistles of St. Paul. Would that these were translated into each and every language. . . . Would that the farmer might sing snatches of Scripture at his plough, that the weaver might hum phrases of Scripture to the tune of his shuttle, that the traveler might lighten with stories from Scripture the weariness of his journey.

These lines are a memorable expression of the driving force behind the work of Erasmus, of Stephanus, and of the men who translated their texts into the vernacular languages. But this is the Renaissance and the Reformation; it is not yet the Enlightenment. These men were concerned with a text in the original Greek; they were not yet concerned with the text as it was actually written by the original authors. But the Enlightenment came, and with it an intense interest in history "as it actually happened," in things as they actually were. Men of the Enlightenment could not rest content with the Erasmus-Stephanus "received text"; they were driven by the spirit of the age in which they lived to go beyond it to the original text of the Greek New Testament, as far as it could be reconstructed. This has remained a major concern of biblical scholarship.

After the establishment of the Erasmus-Stephanus "received text," at least three factors combined to undermine its authority. In the first place, the growth of the Enlightenment spirit made inevitable the search for a more historically authentic text. Second, the discovery, publication, and study of the great uncials and other ancient Greek manuscripts dramatically called attention to ancient manuscripts with readings very different from those of the "received text." In 1707 an Englishman, John Mill, climaxed thirty years of searching ancient manuscripts by publishing an edition of the Greek New Testament in which he reported having found some thirty thousand variant readings, that is, readings varying from the "received text." This was a serious blow to the authority of that text. Third, great strides were made in the textual criticism of ancient classical texts in Greek and Latin, and the techniques learned in this discipline were then applied to the study of the text of the New Testament. Richard Bentley, one of the great figures in the history of classical scholarship, published in 1720 a set of *Proposals* for the preparation of an edition of the Greek New Testament in which he explained that he would base his text on the oldest manuscripts and restore the text known to Origen, which was the standard of the church fathers at the Council of Nicea. He did not in fact produce his edition of the Greek New Testament, but after his day resources developed in the field of classical scholarship were freely used by scholars of the Greek New Testament.

Three hundred years of scholarship in all nations climaxed in the work of B. J. Westcott and F. J. A. Hort, whose *New Testament in the Original Greek* (1881–82) sounded the death knell for the "received text" and established the critical text that provides the basis for all modern work on the Greek New Testament.

Westcott and Hort recognized that the ancient manuscripts could be sorted into various groups, each representing the text of a given area of the ancient church, and they went on to claim that one of these groups did in fact represent almost the original text of the New Testament transmitted in a comparatively uncorrupted form. This was for them the "Neutral Text," essentially that of the great uncials Vaticanus and Sinaiticus. Their Greek New Testament was built upon the foundation of these two witnesses.

The non-Greek-reading student can readily grasp what was involved in this overthrow of the "received text" by comparing the English Revised Version (or the American Standard Version) with the King James Version, for Westcott-Hort provided the basis for the former as Erasmus-Stephanus had for the latter.[1] A few examples at random follow.

**Mark 1:2**
KJV: As it is written in the prophets,
ERV: Even as it is written in Isaiah the prophet,

The later manuscripts had corrected an error; the quotation being introduced actually is a combination of Malachi and Isaiah.

**Luke 11:2**
KJV: When ye pray, say, Our Father which art in heaven, Hallowed be thy name.
ERV: When ye pray, say, Father, Hallowed be thy name.

The original reading of Luke, "Father," had been conformed to the Matthaean "Our Father which art in heaven." The Lukan reading becomes important in the study of the teaching of Jesus.

**Acts 8:37**
KJV: And Philip said, If thou believest with all thine heart, thou mayest. And he answered and said, I believe that Jesus Christ is the Son of God.

ERV omits the above verse. Some ancient scribe had inserted into the account of the conversion of the Ethiopian eunuch this dialogue he thought fitting and that probably reflected the baptismal practice of the church of his own day.

**1 John 5:7, 8**
KJV: For there are three that bear record in heaven, the Father, the Word, and the Holy Ghost: and these three are one. And there are three that

---

[1]The ERV was published in 1881 at the same time as the publication of the Westcott-Hort text. Both Westcott and Hort were active members of the committee that prepared the text for the translators. That committee originally had two other members, but one of them, S. P. Tregelles, was prevented by ill health from taking any part in the work of the committee. The fourth member, F. H. A. Scrivener, was of a conservative persuasion, leaning toward the Byzantine text (virtually the same as the "received text"). It is said that the decisions of the committee were regularly reached on the basis of a vote of two to one.

> bear witness in earth, the Spirit, and the water, and the blood; and these three agree in one.
>
> ERV: For there are three who bear witness, the Spirit, and the water, and the blood: and the three agree in one.

An ancient scribe, in the West, had added a reference to the Trinity.

**1 John 4:19**
KJV: We love him because he first loved us.
ERV: We love, because he first loved us.

The omission of the pronoun makes a considerable difference to the teaching in this passage.

Since the work of Westcott and Hort it has been shown that their Neutral Text, although ancient, had in fact been subjected to considerable editing. It could not be, therefore, as near to the original as Westcott and Hort claimed. Today, thanks to renewed study of the texts represented by the various groups of manuscripts, to extensive investigation of the texts represented by the ancient versions, and above all to the discovery of the papyrus codices, we know that there was a period of such significant disturbance of the text in the earliest times that it may well be that the original text of the New Testament will lie forever beyond our grasp. But we are constantly making new discoveries and textual critics are constantly refining their tools, and the various revisions of the Greek New Testament text published by the Bible societies do represent better and better texts.

## FURTHER READING

Kümmel, *Intro.*, pp. 360–86.
*PCB*, pp. 663–70 (Text: K. W. Clark), pp. 671–75 (Versions: B. M. Metzger).
*JBC*, pp. 561–89 (P. W. Skehan, G. W. MacRae, R. E. Brown).
*IDB*, vol. 4, pp. 594–614 (M. M. Parvis).

The most comprehensive discussion of this material is Metzger, *The Text of the New Testament*, 2nd ed. (1968).

# Appendix 5
## English Translations of the Greek New Testament

### THE TRADITION OF THE KING JAMES VERSION

#### The Path to the King James Version

The translation of the New Testament from the original Greek into the vernacular languages of Europe was an aim of Renaissance humanism, and it gathered impetus in the Reformation, becoming indeed a main goal of the Reformers. Luther's translation of the New Testament into German, published in 1522, was an example followed in other lands. In England William Tyndale (1494?–1536) undertook the task, but he had great difficulties because of English hostility to Luther, led by King Henry VIII. He carried out his work in Reformed Europe, therefore, and finally got his translation printed in Worms in Germany in 1526.

Tyndale's translation aroused great controversy in England when it appeared, but the political climate changed, King Henry quarreled with the Pope, and although Tyndale continued to be considered a dangerous heretic and was never able to return to England, the demand for copies of the New Testament in English was allowed to grow. Tyndale's translation was often printed in pirated editions and with unauthorized revisions. Motivated in part by a desire to counteract changes in his work of which he disapproved, Tyndale in 1534 published his own revised version of his translation. This 1534 translation is an altogether magnificent one so far as its language is concerned, and much of the force and power of the King James Version is Tyndale's. "Nine tenths of the Authorized New Testament is still Tyndale, and the best is still his."[1]

The following is the opening paragraph of Hebrews in Tyndale's 1534 edition.

[1]H. W. Robinson, quoted in Bruce, *The English Bible* (rev. ed., 1970), p. 44.

God in tyme past diversly and many wayes, spake vnto the fathers by
Prophetes: but in these last dayes he hath spoken vnto vs by his sonne,
whom he hath made heyre of all thinges: by whom also he made the worlde.
Which sonne beynge the brightnes of his glory, and very ymage of his
substance, bearinge vp all thinges with the worde of his power, hath in his
awne person pourged oure synnes, and is sitten on the right honde of the
maiestie an hye, and is more excellent then the angels, in as moche as he
hath by inheritaunce obteyned an excellenter name then have they.

In the Greek text this is all one long sentence with its clauses carefully
organized according to the principles of Hellenistic Greek rhetoric.

Tyndale died for his work. He spent his last years in the free city of Antwerp
but was kidnapped in 1536 and taken into Catholic Europe, where he was tried
and executed for heresy. He is said to have died with the prayer on his lips.
"Lord, open the King of England's eyes."

The next major English translator is Myles Coverdale (1488–1569), who, like
most of the translators of this period, did his work in the safety of Reformed
Europe. In 1535 he published the first complete printed Bible in English. It was
printed in continental Europe, probably in Cologne, but copies imported into
England carried a dedication to Henry VIII. It was hoped that the king would
authorize the translation to be read in English churches; he did not do so
formally but neither did he forbid its circulation. A second edition in 1537 was
authorized and appeared with the words, "Set forth with the kinge's most
gracyous license" on the title page. In the same year another English Bible was
authorized by the king—"Matthew's Bible," translated by one Thomas
Matthew. But "Thomas Matthew" was a pseudonym. Matthew's Bible was in
fact Tyndale's translation of the New Testament and, as far as it had been
completed, the Old Testament also. Gaps in the Old Testament were filled by
using Coverdale's translation. It is ironic but fitting that within a year of his
death Tyndale's New Testament was circulating in England with the king's
authorization.

Coverdale was not proficient in Hebrew and Greek, so he did not translate
from the original text. What he did was to prepare a version using five existing
translations: Tyndale's, the Latin Vulgate, a more recent Latin translation
published in 1528, Luther's German translation, and a version of Luther's
German translation adapted to the Swiss dialect of German. His New
Testament was basically Tyndale's revised, not always very happily, in the
light of the German translations.

There is no need for us to follow the vicissitudes of the English translations
of the Bible through the closing years of Henry's reign (died 1547), the brief
reigns of Edward VI (1547–53) and Mary (1553–58), or the long years of
Elizabeth I (1558–1603). The English Bible came to achieve an influence over
the English people that was not to be shaken, despite the various efforts to
contain or nullify the effects of the Reformation. But the various versions of
the new Testament published during these years were all basically revisions of
Tyndale, not new translations.

## The King James Version

At the death of Elizabeth in 1603 the crown passed to James I, who was already ruling in Scotland as James VI. To regulate the affairs of the English church he called a conference of churchmen and theologians at Hampton Court in 1604, which agreed on only one thing, that a new translation should be made of the whole Bible and that it should be authorized for use in the churches of England. King James liked the suggestion and took a leading part in organizing the work of translation. The result appeared in 1611: the Authorized Version (AV), as it is known in England, the King James Version (KJV), as it is known in America.

This translation of the Bible became a landmark in the religious history of English-speaking people, and indeed in their general cultural history. Its phrases and its images are deeply embedded in English-speaking piety and culture. For many it is still *the* Bible, and one who has grown up with it finds himself forever returning to it. Its translation of the opening paragraph of Hebrews is as follows.

> God, who at sundry times and in diverse manners spake in time past unto the fathers by the prophets, hath in these last times spoken unto us by his Son, whom he hath appointed heir of all things, by whom also he made the worlds; who being the brightness of his glory, and the express image of his person, and upholding all things by the word of his power, when he had by himself purged our sins, sat down on the right hand of the Majesty on high; being made so much better than the angels, as he hath by inheritance obtained a more excellent name than they.

The sonorous phrases of what is in effect Elizabethan English, the language of Shakespeare, match the rhetorical flourishes of the long Greek sentence.

## The Revision of the King James Version

That the KJV established itself at the heart of English-language piety and culture does not change the fact that it was a translation from a late and comparatively poor Greek text, and with the passage of time better texts came to be established. English-language usage also changed, so that while some of the phrases of the KJV proved unforgettable, others became unintelligible. The result was that in England in 1870, after more than two and a half centuries, a revision of the KJV was undertaken.

The terms under which this revision was undertaken testify to the hold of the KJV, for the revisers were instructed to introduce as few changes as possible and, where possible, to take the language for those changes either from the language of the KJV or earlier English versions. Almost the only freedom the scholars were permitted was to work from a better Greek text. The result was the English Revised Version (RV or ERV) of the New Testament, published in 1881. The American scholars involved in the project had been rather unhappy about the very conservative conditions imposed upon the revisers, but they agreed to give the new version twenty years before publishing a further revision. In 1901, therefore, they published their own version of this revision, the American Standard Version (SV or ASV). The changes over against the RV were, however, only minor. Here is the RV translation of the opening paragraph of Hebrews.

> God, having of old time spoken unto the fathers in the prophets by divers portions and in divers manners, hath at the end of these days spoken unto us in his Son, whom he appointed heir of all things, through whom also he made the worlds; who being the effulgence of his glory, and the very image of his substance, and upholding all things by the word of his power, when he had made purification of sins, sat down on the right hand of the Majesty on high; having become by so much better than the angels, as he hath inherited a more exellent name than they.

In one respect the ERV was a success: it translated a good Greek text. But in other respects the terms laid down for the revision made an effective new translation impossible, and the ASV could make only minor changes. As translations, therefore, these versions were never a success. In 1937 in America a decision was made to undertake a further revision of the KJV or, more accurately, a revision of the ASV. The result was the Revised Standard Version. The New Testament appeared in 1946 and the whole Bible in 1952. In the 1952 edition there were further minor changes in the New Testament. In the RSV the opening paragraph of Hebrews reads as follows.

> In many and various ways God spoke of old to our fathers by the prophets; but in these last days he has spoken to us by a Son, whom he appointed the heir of all things, through whom also he created the world. He reflects the glory of God and bears the very stamp of his nature, upholding the universe by his word of power. When he had made purification for sins, he sat down at the right hand of the Majesty on high, having become as much superior to angels as the name he has obtained is more excellent than theirs.

For the first time in this tradition the long sentence has been broken up to correspond more readily to English diction, and the archaic English usages are gone ("hath" has become "has," etc.). The result is a good translation, which succeeds in blending the twin responsibilities of remaining as true as possible to the original Greek text and at the same time representing the meaning of that text effectively in English.

# BREAKING WITH THE TRADITION OF THE KING JAMES VERSION

## The New English Bible

In 1946 the Church of Scotland suggested that a completely new translation of the Bible be made, translating the Greek text afresh and not simply revising further the tradition of the KJV. The suggestion was eagerly adopted by the Church of England and the major denominational churches, and the translation of the New Testament was entrusted to a committee under the conv enership of C. H. Dodd (General Director of the whole project after 1949). The result was the New English Bible (NEB), of which the New Testament was published in 1961 and the whole Bible, with a slightly revised New Testament, in 1970. This is the opening paragraph of Hebrews in the NEB.

> When in former times God spoke to our forefathers, he spoke in fragmentary and varied fashion through the prophets. But in this the final age he has spoken to us in the Son whom he has made heir to the whole universe, and through whom he created all orders of existence: the Son who is the effulgence of God's splendour and the stamp of God's very being, and sustains the universe by his word of power. When he had brought about the purgation of sins, he took his seat at the right hand of Majesty on high, raised as far above the angels, as the title he has inherited is superior to theirs.

The NEB is a very effective translation, and any choice between it and the RSV would have to be made on personal grounds.

## Today's English Version

The break with the tradition of the KJV in America came from the American Bible Society, which in 1966 published *Good News for Modern Man: The New Testament in Today's English*, a translation of the New Testament by Robert G. Bratcher. This is usually known as Today's English Version (TEV). It is a good translation, published in paperback and considerably enhanced by some very effective line drawings (by Annie Vallotton). Here is the opening paragraph of Hebrews in today's English.

> In the past God spoke to our ancestors many times and in many ways through the prophets, but in these last days he has spoken to us through his Son. He is the one through whom God created the universe, the one whom God has chosen to possess all things at the end. He shines with the brightness of God's glory; he is the exact likeness of God's own being. and sustains the universe with his powerful word. After he had made men clean from their sins, he sat down in heaven at the right hand of God, the Supreme Power.

# PRIVATE TRANSLATIONS

The translations reviewed above are all "official" in that they have been produced by committees or societies representing major churches or associations of churches. Moreover, they are the best-known and most widely circulated translations. But anyone is free at any time to publish a translation of the New Testament, and many such "private" translations have in fact been published. The three most important are probably those by James Moffat,

Edgar J. Goodspeed, and J. B. Phillips. Moffat, a Scottish New Testament scholar, published a translation of the New Testament in 1913 as *The New Testament: A New Translation* and of the Old Testament in 1924. His translation of the whole Bible appeared in one volume in 1928 as *The Bible: A New Translation*. Moffatt's translation is fresh and vigorous and he does not hesitate to trust his own scholarly judgment in such matters as the rearrangement of the text of the gospel of John. Goodspeed, an American New Testament scholar, published a translation of the New Testament in 1923. A parallel version of the Old Testament appeared in 1927, translated by several scholars, and the two were published together by the University of Chicago Press in 1931 as *The Bible: An American Translation*, often called the Chicago Bible. Goodspeed's translation of the New Testament ranks with the best ever achieved. Phillips, a vicar of the Church of England, published between 1947 and 1957 a translation of the New Testament in four volumes. In 1958 they were brought together and published in one volume as *The New Testament in Modern English*. It is a lively and readable translation, but Phillips exercises great freedom in his handling of the original Greek text so that his translation frequently approaches paraphrase. He is sometimes very successful, as in his translation of the Pauline letters ("Letters to Young Churches"), which makes them sound "as if they had just come through the mail."[2]

## ROMAN CATHOLIC TRANSLATIONS

Until recently Roman Catholic translations of the New Testament have not been translations of the Greek New Testament but of a Latin version, usually the Vulgate. A change came, however, beginning in 1935 with the publication of the Westminster Version in England and continuing in America in 1954 with the publication of the Kleist-Lilly New Testament, "an attempt to do for Catholic circles what Goodspeed had done for non-Catholic circles."[3] Neither of these translations was particularly successful but they were important pioneering efforts. Then from 1948 to 1954 a translation of the whole Bible with introductions and footnotes appeared in French under the editorship of the Jerusalem Dominicans. A one-volume abridgment of the French work has been translated as the Jerusalem Bible (1966). Though it is an important achievement of contemporary Roman Catholic biblical scholarship, the translation is essentially a translation of a translation: the Greek reaches English via French.

The first major Roman Catholic translation of the Greek New Testament directly into English is the New American Bible, published in 1970. Both in title and in style it resembles the NEB, for the translators deliberately abandoned the tradition of revising former translations, in this case translations of a Latin text, in favor of a completely new translation from the Greek into modern English. Protestant scholars were invited to assist in the

---

[2]R. E. Brown in *JBC*, p. 587.
[3]Brown, *JBC*, p. 588.

final stages of the project. The NAB renders the opening paragraph of Hebrews as follows.

> In times past, God spoke in fragmentary and varied ways to our fathers through the prophets; in this, the final age, he has spoken to us through his Son, whom he has made heir of all things and through whom he first created the universe. This Son is the reflection of the Father's glory, the exact representation of the Father's being, and he sustains all things by his powerful word. When he had cleansed us from our sins, he took his seat at the right hand of the Majesty in heaven, as far superior to the angels as the name he has inherited is superior to theirs.

It can be seen that responsible modern translations are drawing very close together, and that a choice between them will now almost always be made on grounds other than the validity of the translation itself. Each translation has its own virtues.

## FURTHER READING

PCB, pp. 24–28 (A. Wikgren).
JBC, pp. 586–89 (R. E. Brown).

The most complete survey of the subject is F. F. Bruce, *The English Bible: A History of Translations*, rev. ed. (1970).

# Bibliography

Adams, H. *The Interests of Criticism: An Introduction to Literary Theory.* New York: Harcourt Brace Jovanovich, 1969.

Althaus, P. *The So-called Kerygma and the Historical Jesus.* Edinburgh: Oliver and Boyd, 1959.

Auerbach, E. *Mimesis.* Garden City, N.Y.: Doubleday, Anchor Books, 1957.

Barrett, C. K. *The Gospel According to St. John.* London: S.P.C.K., 1955.

――――. *The New Testament Background: Selected Documents.* Harper Torchbook No. 86. New York: Harper & Row, 1961.

――――. "Paul's Opponents in II Corinthians." *New Testament Studies,* vol. 17 (1970–71), pp. 233–54.

Bartsch, H. W., ed. *Kerygma and Myth.* Harper Torchbook No. 80. New York: Harper & Row, 1961.

Beardslee, W. A. *Literary Criticism of the New Testament.* In *Guides to Biblical Scholarship.* New Testament Series. Edited by Dan O. Via, Jr. Philadelphia: Fortress Press, 1970.

――――. "The Uses of the Proverb in the Synoptic Tradition." *Interpretation,* vol. 24 (1970), pp. 61–76.

Berger, K. "Zu den sogennanten Sätzen Heiligen Rechts." *New Testament Studies,* vol. 17 (1970–71), pp. 10–40.

Boobyer, G. H. "Galilee and Galileans in St. Mark's Gospel." *Bulletin of the John Rylands Library,* vol. 35 (1952–53), pp. 334–48.

Bornkamm, G. *Jesus of Nazareth.* New York: Harper & Row, 1960.

――――. *Paul.* New York: Harper & Row, 1971.

――――. "The Risen Lord and the Earthly Jesus: Mt. 28:16–20." In *The Future of Our Religious Past.* Edited by J. M. Robinson, pp. 203–09. New York: Harper & Row, 1971.

Bornkamm, G., Barth, G., and Held, H. J. *Tradition and Interpretation in Matthew.* Philadelphia: Westminster Press, 1963.

Bousset, Wilhelm. *Kyrios Christos.* Nashville and New York: Abingdon Press, 1970. German original 1913.

Brandon, S. G. F. *The Fall of Jerusalem and the Christian Church.* London: S.P.C.K., 1951.

Brown, R. E. *The Gospel According to John.* 2 volumes. The Anchor Bible. Garden City, N.Y.: Doubleday, 1966.

――――. *New Testament Essays.* Milwaukee: The Bruce Publishing Company, 1965.

Bruce, F. F. *The English Bible: A History of Translations.* Revised edition. New York: Oxford University Press, 1970.

――――. *New Testament History.* Garden City, N.Y.: Doubleday, Anchor Books, 1972.

Bultmann, R. *The Gospel of John: A Commentary.* Oxford, B. Blackwell, 1971.

**353**

_____. *The History of the Synoptic Tradition.* New York: Harper & Row, 1968.

_____. *Jesus and the Word.* New York: Charles Scribner's Sons, 1934, 1958. German original 1926.

_____. *Jesus Christ and Mythology.* New York: Charles Scribner's Sons, 1958, and London: SCM Press, 1960.

_____. *Primitive Christianity in Its Contemporary Setting.* New York: Meridian, 1956.

_____. "The Primitive Christian Kerygma and the Historical Jesus." In *The Historical Jesus and the Kerygmatic Christ.* Edited by Carl A. Braaten and Roy A. Harrisville. New York and Nashville: Abingdon Press, 1964.

_____. *Theology of the New Testament.* 2 volumes. New York: Charles Scribner's Sons, 1951 and 1955.

Caird, G. B. *The Gospel of St. Luke.* Pelican Gospel Commentaries. Baltimore: Penguin Books, 1963.

Cairns, D. *A Gospel Without Myth? Bultmann's Challenge to the Preacher.* London: SCM Press, 1960.

*Cambridge History of the Bible II. The West from the Reformation to the Present Day.* New York: Cambridge University Press, 1963.

Campbell, Joseph. *Myths to Live By.* New York: Viking Press, 1972.

Conzelmann, Hans. *History of Primitive Christianity.* New York: Abingdon Press, 1973.

_____. *Jesus.* Philadelphia: Fortress Press, 1973.

_____. *The Theology of St. Luke.* New York: Harper & Row, 1960.

Crane, R. S., ed. *Critics and Criticism, Essays in Method.* Abridged edition. Chicago: University of Chicago Press, 1957.

_____. *The Languages of Criticism and the Structure of Poetry.* Toronto: University of Toronto Press, 1953.

Cross, F. M. *The Ancient Library of Qumran and Modern Biblical Studies.* Revised edition. Garden City, N.Y.: Doubleday, 1961.

Crossan, J. D. "Parable and Example in the Teaching of Jesus." *New Testament Studies,* vol. 18 (1971–72), pp. 285–307.

Davies, W. D. *The Setting of the Sermon on the Mount.* Cambridge, England: Cambridge University Press, 1964.

Dibelius, Martin. *From Tradition to Gospel.* New York: Charles Scribner's Sons, 1935.

_____. *Studies in the Acts of the Apostles.* London: SCM Press, 1956.

Dodd, C. H. *The Interpretation of the Fourth Gospel.* Cambridge, England: Cambridge University Press, 1953.

_____. *The Johannine Epistles.* Moffatt New Testament Commentary. London: Hodder and Stoughton, 1946.

Donahue, John R. *Are You the Christ? The Trial Narrative in the Gospel of Mark.* SBL Dissertation Series 10, 1973.

_____. "Tax Collectors and Sinners." *Catholic Biblical Quarterly,* vol. 33 (1971), pp. 39–61.

Edwards, R. A. "An Approach to the Theology of Q." *Journal of Religion,* vol. 51 (1971), pp. 247–69.

_____. *The Sign of Jonah in the Theology of the Evangelists and Q.* Studies in Biblical Theology. London: SCM Press, and Naperville, Ill.: Allenson, 1971.

Eliade, Mircea. *Cosmos and History: The Myth of the Eternal Return.* Harper Torchbook No. 2050. New York: Harper & Row, 1959.

_____. "Myth." *Encyclopaedia Britannica,* vol. 15, pp. 1132–42, 1968.

_____. *Myth and Reality.* Harper Torchbook No. 1369. New York: Harper & Row, 1963.

_____. *The Quest: History and Meaning in Religion.* Chicago: University of Chicago

Press, 1969.

Evans, C. F. "I will go before you into Galilee." *Journal of Theological Studies*, n.s. 5 (1954), pp. 3–18.

Feine, P., Behm, J., and Kümmel, W. G. *Introduction to the New Testament*. New York and Nashville: Abingdon Press, 1966.

Fenton, J. C. *The Gospel of St. Matthew*. Pelican Gospel Commentaries. Baltimore: Penguin Books, 1963.

Fitzmyer, J. A. "The Languages of Palestine in the First Century A.D." *Catholic Biblical Quarterly*, vol. 32 (1970), pp. 501–31.

Foerster, W. *From the Exile to Christ*. Philadelphia: Fortress Press, 1964.

Fortna, R. T. *The Gospel of Signs: A Reconstruction of the Narrative Source Underlying the Fourth Gospel*. London: Cambridge University Press, 1970.

Fuller, R. H. *A Critical Introduction to the New Testament*. London: Duckworth, 1966.

―――. *The Foundations of New Testament Christology*. New York: Charles Scribner's Sons, 1965.

―――. "The 'Thou Art Peter' Pericope and the Easter Appearances." *McCormick Quarterly*, vol. 20 (1966–67), pp. 309–15.

Funk, R. W. *Language, Hermeneutic and Word of God*. New York: Harper & Row, 1966.

Funk, R. W. ed. *Journal for Theology and the Church VI: Apocalypticism*. New York: Herder and Herder, 1969.

Gaston, L. *No Stone on Another. Studies in the Significance of the Fall of Jerusalem in the Synoptic Gospels*. Leiden, The Netherlands: Brill, 1970.

Gennep, A. Van. *Rites of Passage*. Chicago: University of Chicago Press, 1960.

Georgi, D. "Forms of Religious Propaganda." In *Jesus in His Time*. Edited by H. J. Schultz. Philadelphia: Fortress Press, 1971.

―――. *Die Gegner des Paulus im 2. Korintherbrief: Studien zur religiosen Propaganda in der Spätantike*. WMANT II. Neukirchen-Vluyn: Neukirchener Verlag, 1964.

Gogarten, F. *Demythologizing and History*. London: SCM Press, 1953.

Grant, F. C. *Hellenistic Religions*. Indianapolis and New York: Bobbs-Merrill, 1953.

―――. *Hellenistic Religions*. New York: Liberal Arts Press, 1953.

Grant, R. M. *The Bible in the Church: A Short History of Interpretation*. New York: Macmillan, 1948.

―――. *A Historical Introduction to the New Testament*. London: Collins, 1963.

―――. "The Origin of the Fourth Gospel." *Journal of Biblical Literature*, vol. 69 (1950), pp. 305–22.

Grant, R. M., ed. *Gnosticism: An Anthology*. London: Collins, 1961.

Haenchen, E. *The Acts of the Apostles*. Philadelphia: Westminster Press, 1971.

Harnack, Adolf. *What is Christianity*. New York, Harper & Row, 1957.

Harris, R., and Mingana A. *The Odes and Psalms of Solomon, II. The Translation*. New York: Longmans, Green, 1916–20.

Hartman, Lars. *Prophecy Interpreted*. Coniectanea Biblica New Testament Series No. 1. Lund, Sweden: G. W. K. Gleerup, 1966.

Harvey, Van A. *The Historian and the Believer*. New York: Macmillan, 1966.

Henderson, I. *Myth in the New Testament*. Chicago: H. Regner, 1952.

Hennecke, E., and Schneemelcher, W. *New Testament Apocrypha*. 2 volumes. Philadelphia: Fortress Press, 1965.

Hoskyns, E. *The Fourth Gospel*. Edited by F. N. Davey. London: Faber and Faber, 1940.

Hoskyns, Edwyn, and Davey, Noel. *The Riddle of the New Testament*. London: Faber and Faber, 1948.

Howard, W. F. *The Fourth Gospel in Recent Criticism and Interpretation*. Revised by C. K. Barrett. London: Epworth Press, 1955.

*The Interpreter's Dictionary of the Bible*. 4 volumes. New York and Nashville:

Abingdon Press, 1962.

Jaspers, K. and Bultmann, R. *Myth and Christianity: An Inquiry into the Possibility of Religion Without Myth.* Translated by N. Guterman. New York: Noonday Press, 1958.

Jeremias, Joachim. *Jesus' Promise to the Nations.* Naperville, Ill.: Allenson, 1958.

_____. *The Parables of Jesus.* Revised edition. New York: Charles Scribner's Sons, 1963.

_____. *The Problem of the Historical Jesus.* Philadelphia: Fortress Press, 1964.

_____. *Rediscovering the Parables.* London: SCM Press, 1966.

*The Jerome Biblical Commentary.* 2 volumes bound together. Englewood Cliffs, N.J.: Prentice-Hall, 1968.

Jonas, H. *The Gnostic Religion.* Boston: Beacon Paperback, 1963.

Jones, G. V. *Christology and Myth in the New Testament.* London: Allen and Unwin, 1956.

Kähler, Martin. *The So-called Historical Jesus and the Historic Biblical Christ.* Philadelphia: Fortress Press, 1964.

Käsemann, Ernst. "Epheserbrief." In *Die Religion in Geschichte und Gegenwart.* Third edition. Vol. II, pp. 518–19. Tübingen: J. C. B. Mohr, 1958.

_____. *Essays on New Testament Themes.* Studies in Biblical Theology, 41. London: SCM Press, 1964.

_____. *New Testament Questions of Today.* Philadelphia: Fortress Press, 1969.

_____. *The Testament of Jesus: A Study of the Gospel of John in the Light of Chapter 17.* London: SCM Press, 1968.

Keck, L. E. *A Future for the Historical Jesus.* New York and Nashville: Abingdon Press, 1971.

Keck, L. E., and Martyn, J. L., eds. *Studies in Luke-Acts.* Nashville: Abingdon Press, 1966.

Kee, Howard Clark. *Jesus in History.* New York: Harcourt Brace Jovanovich, 1970.

Kelber, Werner H. *Kingdom and Parousia in the Gospel of Mark.* Unpublished Ph.D. dissertation, University of Chicago Divinity School, 1970.

Kelber, W., Kalenkow, A., and Scroggs, R. "Reflections of the Question: Was There a Pre-Markan Passion Narrative?" In *The Society of Biblical Literature One Hundred Seventh Annual Meeting Seminar Papers* (1971), pp. 503–85.

Kingsbury, J. D. "The Jesus of History and Christ of Faith in Relation to Matthew's View of Time—Reactions to a New Approach." *Concordia Theological Monthly*, vol. 37 (1966), pp. 500–10.

_____. *The Parables of Jesus in Matthew 13.* London: S.P.C.K., 1969.

Klausner, J. *Jesus of Nazareth.* New York: Macmillan, 1925, and Boston: Beacon Press, 1964.

Knigge, H. D. "The Meaning of Mark." *Interpretation*, vol. 22 (1968), pp. 53–76.

Kümmel, W. G. *The New Testament: The History of the Investigation of Its Problems.* New York and Nashville: Abingdon Press, 1972.

Kümmel, W. G., ed. *See* Feine, P.

Lightfoot, R. H. *The Gospel Message of St. Mark.* Oxford Paperbacks 41. New York: Oxford University Press, 1962.

_____. *History and Interpretation in the Gospels.* The Bampton Lectures. New York: Harper and Bros., 1934.

_____. *Locality and Doctrine in the Gospels.* New York: Harper and Bros., 1936.

_____. *St. John's Gospel.* Oxford: Clarendon Press, 1956.

Lindars, B. *New Testament Apologetic.* London: SCM Press, 1961.

Macquarrie, J. *The Scope of Demythologizing; Bultmann and his Critics.* London: SCM Press, 1960.

Manson, T.W. *The Sayings of Jesus.* London: SCM Press, 1949.

_____. *The Teaching of Jesus.* Cambridge, England: Cambridge University Press, 1931.

Martyn, J. L. *History and Theology in the Fourth Gospel.* New York: Harper & Row, 1968.

Marxsen, Willi. *Introduction to the New Testament.* Translated by G. Buswell. Philadelphia: Fortress Press, 1968.

_____. *Mark the Evangelist.* Translated by R. Harrisville. New York and Nashville: Abingdon Press, 1969.

McArthur, Harvey A. *In Search of the Historical Jesus.* New York: Charles Scribner's Sons, 1969.

McKnight, E. V. *What is Form Criticism?* In *Guides to Biblical Scholarship: New Testament Series.* Edited by Dan O. Via, Jr. Philadelphia: Fortress Press, 1969.

McNeill, W. *The Rise of the West.* Chicago: University of Chicago Press, 1963.

Meeks, Wayne A. *The Writings of St. Paul.* Norton Critical Editions. New York: W. W. Norton, 1972.

Metzger, B. M. *The Text of the New Testament.* Second edition. New York: Oxford, University Press, 1968.

Moule, C. F. D. *The Birth of the New Testament.* London: A. & C. Black, 1962.

Neihardt, G. *Black Elk Speaks.* Lincoln: University of Nebraska, 1960.

Neill, S. *The Interpretation of the New Testament, 1861–1961.* London: Oxford University Press, 1964.

Nineham, D. E. *The Gospel of St. Mark.* Middlesex: Penguin Books, 1963.

Nock, A. D. *Early Gentile Christianity and Its Gentile Background.* Harper Torchbook No. 111. New York: Harper & Row, 1964.

Ogden, S. M. *Christ Without Myth.* New York: Harper & Row, 1961.

*Peake's Commentary on the Bible.* Revised edition. London and New York: Thomas Nelson and Sons, 1962.

Perrin, Norman. "The Christology of Mark: A Study in Methodology." *Journal of Religion,* vol. 51 (1971), pp. 173–87.

_____. "The Composition of Mark IX.1." *Novum Testamentum,* vol. 11 (1969), pp. 67–70.

_____. *The Kingdom of God in the Teaching of Jesus.* London: SCM Press, and Philadelphia: Westminster Press, 1963.

_____. "The Literary Gattung 'Gospel'—Some Observations." *Expository Times,* vol. 82 (1970), pp. 4–7.

_____. "The Modern Interpretation of the Parables of Jesus and the Problem of Hermeneutics." *Interpretation,* vol. 25 (1971), pp. 131–48.

_____. "The Parables of Jesus as Parables, as Metaphors and as Aesthetic Objects." *Journal of Religion,* vol. 50 (1970), pp. 340–46.

_____. *The Promise of Bultmann.* In the series *The Promise of Theology.* Edited by M. Marty. Philadelphia and New York: J. B. Lippincott, 1969.

_____. *Rediscovering the Teaching of Jesus.* London: SCM Press, and New York: Harper & Row, 1967.

_____. "The Son of Man in the Synoptic Tradition." *Biblical Research,* vol. 13 (1968), pp. 1–23.

_____. "Towards the Interpretation of the Gospel of Mark." In *Christology and a Modern Pilgrimage: A Discussion with Norman Perrin.* Edited by H. D. Betz, pp. 1–78. Claremont, Calif.: New Testament Colloquium, 1971.

_____. "The Use of (para)didonai in Connection with the Passion of Jesus in the New Testament." In *Der Ruf Jesu und die Anwort Der Gemeinde: Festscrift für Joachim Jeremias.* Edited by E. Lohse. Göttingen: Vandenhoeck & Ruprecht, 1970.

_____. *What is Redaction Criticism?* Revised edition. In *Guides to Biblical Scholarship.* New Testament Series. Edited by Dan O. Via, Jr. Philadelphia: Fortress Press, 1971.

_____. "Wisdom and Apocalyptic in the Message of Jesus." *Society of Biblical Literature One Hundred Eighth Annual Meeting (1972) Proceedings*, vol. 2, pp. 543–70.

Reumann, J. *Jesus in the Church's Gospels*. Philadelphia: Fortress Press, 1968.

Ricoeur, Paul. *Le Conflit des Interpretations: Essais d'hermeneutique*. Paris: Editions du Seuil, 1969.

_____. *Freud and Philosophy: An Essay in Interpretation*. New Haven: Yale University Press, 1970.

_____. *The Symbolism of Evil*. Boston: Beacon Press, 1969.

Robbins, V. *The Christology of Mark*. Unpublished Ph.D. dissertation, University of Chicago Divinity School, 1969.

Robinson, J. M. "Hermeneutics since Barth." In *The New Hermeneutic*. Edited by J. M. Robinson and J. B. Cobb. New York: Harper & Row, 1964.

Robinson, J. M., and Cobb, J. B., eds. *The New Hermeneutic*. New York: Harper & Row, 1964.

Robinson, J. M., and Korester, H. *Trajectories through Early Christianity*. Philadelphia: Fortress Press, 1971.

Rohde, Joachim. *Rediscovering the Teaching of the Evangelists*. Philadelphia: Westminster Press, 1968.

Rowley, H. H. *The Relevance of Apocalyptic*. Revised edition. New York: Association Press, 1964.

Russell, D. S. *The Method and Message of Jewish Apocalyptic*. Philadelphia: Fortress Press, 1964.

Sanders, J. T. *The New Testament Christological Hymns: Their Historical Religious Background*. SNTS Monograph Series. New York: Cambridge University Press, 1971.

Schmidt, Karl L. *Die Rahmen der Geschichte Jesu*. Berlin: Trowitzsch & Sohn, 1919.

Scholes, R., and Kellog, R. *The Nature of Narrative*. New York: Oxford University Press, 1966.

Schweitzer, Albert. *The Quest of the Historical Jesus*. New York: Macmillan, 1964.

Simon, M. *Jewish Sects at the Time of Jesus*. Philadelphia: Fortress Press, 1967.

Strauss, David Friedrich. *The Life of Jesus Critically Examined*. Philadelphia: Fortress Press, 1972.

Strecker, G. "The Concept of History in Matthew." *Journal of the American Academy of Religion*, vol. 35 (1967), pp. 219–30.

Suggs, M. Jack. *Wisdom, Christology and Law in Matthew's Gospel*. Cambridge, Mass.: Harvard University Press, 1970.

Tannehille, R. C. "The 'Focal Instance' as a Form of New Testament Speech: A Study of Matthew 5:39b–42." *Journal of Religion*, vol. 50 (1970), pp. 372–85.

Tarn, W., and Griffith, C. T. *Hellenistic Civilization*. Third edition. London: Arnold, 1952.

Taylor, V. *The Gospel According to St. Mark*. London: Macmillan, 1952.

Tcherikover, V. A. *Hellenistic Civilization and the Jews*. New York: Atheneum, 1970.

Thompson, W. G. *Matthew's Advice to a Divided Community*. Analecta Biblica 44. Rome: Pontifical Biblical Institute, 1970.

Tödt, H. E. *The Son of Man in the Synoptic Tradition*. Philadelphia: Westminster Press, 1965.

Vermes, G. *The Dead Sea Scrolls in English*. Baltimore: Penguin Books, 1962.

Via, Dan O., Jr. *The Parables: Their Literary and Existential Dimension*. Philadelphia: Fortress Press, 1967.

Vögtle, A. "Jesus Christ." *Sacramentum Verbi II*. Edited by J. B. Bauer, pp. 419–37. New York: Herder and Herder, 1970.

Weeden, T. J. *Mark—Traditions in Conflict*. Philadelphia: Fortress Press, 1971.

Weiss, J. *The Preaching of Jesus Concerning the Kingdom of God*. Philadelphia: Fortress

Press, 1971.

Wheelwright, Philip. *The Burning Fountain*. Revised edition. Bloomington: Indiana University Press, 1968.

_____. *Metaphor and Reality*. Bloomington: Indiana University Press, 1962. Paperback 1968.

Wilder, A. N. *Early Christian Rhetoric: The Language of the Gospel*. New York: Harper & Row, 1964. Revised edition, Cambridge, Mass.: Harvard University Press, 1971.

_____. "Eschatological Imagery and Earthly Circumstance." *New Testament Studies*, vol. 5 (1958–59), pp. 229–45.

_____. "The Rhetoric of Ancient and Modern Apocalyptic." *Interpretation*, vol. 25 (1971), pp. 436–53.

Wood, James D. *The Interpretation of the Bible*. Studies in Theology. London: Duckworth, 1958.

# Glossary

**APOCALYPSE.** An apocalyptic writing.

**APOCALYPTIC.** From the Greek *apokalypsis*, "an uncovering." The word is used to describe a movement in Judaism and Christianity in which the writers characteristically claimed that God had "uncovered" for them (revealed to them) the secrets of the imminent end of the world. The movement is described in detail in chapter 4. Apocalyptic is a feature of religions in the Hellenistic world other than Judaism and Christianity, but we are concerned only with its Jewish and Christian forms.

**APOCRYPHA.** From the Greek *apocryphos*, "hidden." The word is used of books that were not accepted into the final canon of Jewish or Christian scripture. Such books were to be "hidden" from the faithful in the church. When used alone *Apocrypha* refers to the Apocrypha of the Old Testament, that is, to the books rejected from the final Jewish canon of scripture but transmitted by Christians as part of the Old Testament. After the Reformation, the Protestant churches accepted the Jewish canon of scripture as defining the Old Testament. The Roman Catholic church continued to accept the broader canon of the ancient church.

**CANON.** From the Greek *kanōn*, which means something made of reeds or something straight like reeds. It came to be used of an authoritative list. In the Christian church it was used of a list of regulations, hence "canon law"; of a list of clergy or saints, hence "canonize"; and of a list of books to be read in the churches, hence "canon of the New Testament," and "canon of the Old Testament."

**CATHOLIC.** From the Latin *catholicus*, "universal" or "general." It is used in connection with the later letters in the New Testament, the "Catholic Epistles," because they are addressed to the church at large rather than to individuals or separate churches. It is then used of the church as a whole as distinct from one particular part of the church, e.g., the "catholic church" as distinct from the "Syrian church." In discussing the period after the Reformation it distinguishes the Roman Catholic church from the Protestant churches. In that last context it is always capitalized, "Catholic."

**CHRISTOLOGY.** From the Greek *Christos* (=Hebrew *Messiah*) and *logos*, "word" or "teaching." Hence, teaching concerning the person of Christ.

**CHURCH ORDER.** A text setting out the polity and discipline of a church with regard to its officers and members.

**CORPUS.** The Latin word for "body." It is used of a complete or comprehensive body of writings. The "Pauline corpus" is the body of writings attributed to the apostle Paul.

**DEMYTHOLOGIZING PROGRAM.** A proposal by Rudolf Bultmann to understand the myths in the New Testament as essentially expressions of ideas about the existential reality of human existence in the world and to interpret them in that way.

**DIASPORA** (or **DISPERSION**). From the Greek *diaspora*, "a dispersion." The community of Jews living outside their homeland, Palestine.

**DOXOLOGY.** From the Greek *doxologia*, "a praising." The act of praising God. In New Testament studies specifically used in connection with formal praises of God to be found in prayers, letters, and the liturgy of the church.

**ESCHATOLOGY.** From the Greek *eschatos*, "furthest," and *logos*, "word" or "teaching." Teaching concerning the last things, the end of the world or the end of history. It is related to apocalyptic in that apocalyptic features a particular kind of eschatology.

**EVANGELIST.** From the Greek *euangelion*, "good news." A preacher of the gospel or, more especially in New Testament studies, the author of one of the gospels.

**FORM CRITICISM.** A translation of the German *Formgeschichte*, literally "form history." A description of this movement in New Testament scholarship is given in chapter 1.

**GOSPEL.** From the Middle English *godspell*, "good spell," i.e., "good news." It translated the Greek *euangelion* "good news." Originally it referred to the good news of what God had done in Christ, then to the literary form created to narrate and proclaim the event.

**HELLENISM** (Adjective: **HELLENISTIC**). From the Greek *Hellenismos*, "imitation of the Greeks." The culture that developed in the world conquered by Alexander the Great as that world adopted the Greek language and imitated Greek ways.

**HERMENEUTICS.** From the Greek *hermēneutēs*, "an interpreter." The science of interpretation, especially the interpretation of written texts. It is becoming usual to use *hermeneutic* of a particular method of interpretation and *hermeneutics* of the science as a whole.

**HISTORY OF RELIGION.** A translation of the German *Religionsgeschichte*. It denotes the comparative study and analysis of religions, e.g., the study and analysis of early Christianity in comparison with the religions and philosophies of the Hellenistic world.

**KERYGMA.** The Greek word for proclamation. It is used to denote the preaching, proclamation, or central message of the New Testament as a whole or of any part of it, and similarly of the church as a whole or of any part of it.

**KOINE.** The Greek word for "common." It describes the form of Greek which became the lingua franca, the common language, of the Hellenistic world.

**LIFE OF JESUS RESEARCH.** A comprehensive term designating every possible kind of historical research in connection with the life and teaching of Jesus.

**LIFE OF JESUS THEOLOGY.** The theology based on the conviction that the results of Life of Jesus research are normative for Christian faith.

**MIMESIS** (Adjective: **MIMETIC**). The Greek word for "imitation." It is used as a technical term for literature that is deliberately realistic, i.e., imitative of life.

**PARENESIS.** From the Greek *parainesis*, "exhortation," "advice." A technical term used to denote exhortation, advice, instruction, encouragement, etc.

**PAROUSIA.** The Greek word for "presence." In Hellenistic Greek it became a technical term for the visit of a high official, especially a king or emperor, to a province or place. In the New Testament it came to be used of the expected coming of Christ in glory to judge the world and redeem his people, and in this sense it has become a technical term of theological and Biblical scholarship.

**PASSION.** When used alone ("Passion" or "the passion") this term always refers to the suffering and death of Jesus. The "passion narrative" is the narrative account of that suffering and death.

**PASTORALS (PASTORAL EPISTLES** or **LETTERS).** The letters written in the name of Paul and addressed to Timothy or Titus. They give advice to a "pastor" of a church with regard to his responsibilities to his "flock," hence their designation.

**PERICOPE.** From the Greek *peri*, "about," and *"koptein,"* to cut. An extract from a larger work, a unit of narrative or discourse.

**PSEUDONYMITY.** From the Greek *pseudos*, "false," and *onyma*, "name." The practice of writing under a false name.

**REDACTION CRITICISM.** The usual translation of the German *Redaktions-geschichte* (literally "redaction history"). The study of the redaction or editing of traditional material as it is transmitted or used. A description of this aspect of New Testament scholarship is given in chapter 1.

**SEPTUAGINT.** From the Latin *septuaginta* ("seventy"). The Greek translation of the Jewish scriptures, transmitted to the Old Testament by Christians. It received its name from the legend that it was translated in seventy days by seventy-two translators, six from each of the twelve Jewish tribes.

**SITZ IM LEBEN.** A German term meaning "setting in life." It is used as a technical term for the context in which a given oral or literary form functions (e.g., sermon, ethical instruction, etc.) and for the purposes for which it was developed. It is discussed in the section on form criticism in chapter 1.

**SOTERIOLOGY.** From the Greek *sōtēr*, "savior," and *logos*, "word" or "teaching." Teaching about the death of Jesus as the means of man's salvation.

**SYNOPTIC GOSPELS.** From the Greek *synoptikos*, "seeing the whole together." The gospels of Matthew, Mark, and Luke are called the "synoptic gospels" because they tell the same general story in the same kind of way. A contrast is intended to the gospel of John.

**SYNOPTIC TRADITION.** The traditional material that has been used in the synoptic gospels.

**WITNESS.** One who bears testimony to his or her faith, or the act of bearing testimony. The Greek word is *martyr*, and later it came to be used specifically of those who "witnessed" to their faith to the point of dying for it.

# Index of Names
# and Subjects

# Index of Passages in the Synoptic Gospels

# Index of Biblical References, by Chapter and Verse

Note: Only those references are indexed in which there is a discussion of the text involved.

7
8
G 9
H 0
I 1
J